आ नो भद्राः क्रतवो यन्तु विश्वतः

aa no bhadraah kratavo yantu visvatah

Let noble thoughts come to us from every side

Rig Veda I - 89-i

VAALMEEKI RAAMAAYANA
A Revelation

न अस्ति गङ्गा समं तीर्थम्, न अस्ति मातृ समः गुरु
न अस्ति विष्णु समः देवा, न अस्ति रामायणात् परम्।।
(No waters like Ganges, No teacher like one's own mother,
No lord like Vishnu, and nothing excels Raamaayana.)

BECAUSE

Vaalmeeki's Raamaayana is No Story Book
Vaalmeeki's Epic is No History
Vaalmeeki's 24,000 Slokas are Not Just Poetry or Literature

INDEED

वेद सम्मतम् न अत्र संशयः
न अनृतं अत्र भविष्यति काव्ये।

(Vaalmeeki's Raamaayana is वेद (Veda),
Truth, Nothing but Truth Sustains This Epic.)

THUS God Brahma Proclaims to Sage Naaradha.

VAALMEEKI RAAMAAYANA

A Study and Translation by
LOKNATH SWAMINATHAN

1. Vaalmeeki Raamaayana – A Revelation

2. Vaalmeeki Raamaayana – A Treasury (3 Parts)
   (Collection of Slokas from Raamaayana
   with Commentary in English)
   Baala Kaanda, Ayodhya Kaanda, Aranya Kaanda — (Part 1)
   Kishkindha Kaanda, Sundara Kaanda — (Part 2)
   and Lanka Kaanda — (Part 3)

3. Vaalmeeki Ramayana – Full Text with
   English Rendering in 14 Vols.

श्रीमद्वाल्मीकीय रामायणम्

VAALMEEKI RAAMAAYANA

A Revelation

L. SWAMINATHAN

First MLBD Edition: Delhi, ***2018***
First Published in Chennai, 2005

ISBN: 978-81-208-4216-8

Also available at
MOTILAL BANARSIDASS
41 U.A. Bungalow Road, Jawahar Nagar, Delhi 110 007
1-B, Jyoti Studio Compound, Kennedy Bridge, Nana Chowk, Mumbai-400 007
203 Royapettah High Road, Mylapore, Chennai 600 004
236, 9th Main III Block, Jayanagar, Bengaluru 560 011
8 Camac Street, Kolkata 700 017
Ashok Rajpath, Patna 800 004
Chowk, Varanasi 221 001

MLBD Cataloging-in-Publication Data
Vaalmeeki Raamaayana : A Revelation
by L. Swaminathan
Includes Addenda with
important information and details
ISBN: 978-81-208-4216-8
I. Grand Epic, II. Raamaayana
III. Vaalmeeki, IV. Swaminathan, L.

Published by
Motilal Banarsidass Publishers Private Limited
www.mlbd.com • mlbd@mlbd.com
Printed by Replika Press (P) Limited

BENEDICTION

I BOW TO HIS HOLINESS SWARGIYA SRI SRI ABHINAVA VIDYA THEERTHA MAHAASANNIDHAANAM, WHO STIMULATED MY INTEREST IN VAALMEEKI RAAMAAYANA, BY ENLIGHTENING ME ABOUT USAGE OF ONE WORD SHARANAM शरणं (REFUGE) THAT HAD SOMEWHAT DISTURBED ME EARLIER IN IGNORANCE.

I BOW TO MY KULA GURU, HIS HOLINESS SRI SRI BHARATHI THEERTHA, SANNIDHAANAM, THE JAGADGURU SHANKARAACHAARYA OF SRI SHARADA PEETAM, SRINGERI.

I BOW TO MY LORD SUBRAHMANYA THE SKANDHA, THE DHEVA SENAAPATHI, THE SHANMUKHA

I BOW TO SAGE VAALMEEKI.

LOKANATHA SWAMINATHAN

C.V.Sundaram
(Former Director,
Indira Gandhi Centre for Atomic
Research, Kalpakkam)

Chennai 20
August 2004

FOREWORD
to
Vaalmeeki Raamaayana - A Revelation

Whether the story of- the Raamaayana had really happened or it is a creation of the human imagination is difficult to argue. But the story is unusually (and at the same time, beautifully) structured—original in content, and with remarkable characters and stunning events—that it is more likely that it is all happened fact and not fabricated fiction. Mixed with divine and human elements, the story has had an irresistible appeal from time immemorial.

The oldest and the most complete version of The Raamaayana is by Sage Vaalmeeki. Legend has it God Brahma Himself had ordained that Vaalmeeki should write the Raamaayana and the gist of the story was narrated to Vaalmeeki by sage Naarada. It is amazing how from a brief narration, Vaalmeeki could fill in all the details to compose a monumental epic of about 22,000 verses. It shows the power of Vaalmeeki's vision.

Over the years, there had been other versions of the story in other Indian languages, two of the more famous ones being Ramacharita Manas by Saint Tulsi Das in Hindi and Kamba Raamaayana by Poet Kamban in Tamil. It has been a popular theme for musical compositions (by St. Thyagaraja in Telugu and Arunachala Kavi in Tamil) and also for Dance-Drama presentations in the medium of Yakshagaana and Kathakali. The story has also migrated to countries in South East Asia, where it appeared with the 1ocal colour. In the modern period, scholars like Sri C.Rajagopalachari (Rajaji) and Rt. Hon'ble V.S Srinivasa Sastry, have responded to the literary, intellectual and spiritual appeal of the story to present their own studies of the epic. Most recently the serialised television production of the Raamaayana by Ramananda Sagar, had demonstrated the strong hold that the story had on the Indian psyche irrespective of religion, caste or creed.

Amidst all these, the Raamaayana of Vaalmeeki stands out as the fountain head of original inspiration.

As the saying "Age has not withered, Nor custom staled its infinite variety"

And as the Lord said

यावत् स्थास्यन्ति गिरय: सरित: चमहीतळे

तावत रामायण कथा ळोकेषु प्रचरिष्यति

(As long as mountains stand and rivers flow on earth, the story of Raarnaayana will ever remain current in the world)

The present work by Sri.L.Swaminathan, is an analytical study to bring out the beauty and the power of the Vaalmeeki epic. Swaminathan belongs to a family of scholars and teachers. Son of renowned economist, Professor Dr.P.S.Lokanathan (who was Professor of Economics, Madras University) and nephew of Professor P.S. Subrahmania Iyer (who was head of Dept. of Physics, Presidency college) he took Industrial Chemistry as his profession and served in various factories in India and abroad as a production chemist. The Factory schedule and the pre-occupation with production allowed him little time for any other activity. When he retired in around 1986/88, he turned to the study of Vaalmeeki Raamaayana. At school he had the good fortune to be taught Sanskrit and English by dedicated and excellent teachers. With the large Sanskrit-English Dictionary by Sir Monier Williams (Oxford University publication) as his sole guide and companion, Swaminathan carried out an exploratory study of the classic for sometime and then took on the ambitious task of translating the entire Raamaayana -all the 22,000 slokas , stanza by stanza - almost word for word. With systematic discipline and determination he could render the English version of Vaalmeeki Raamaayana in 8 or 9 years. It was a work of quality and fidelity, regarding which the late Sri. S.Ramakrishnan, General Editor, Bhavan's Book University had this to say. "It is an inspired devoted and incredible labour of love. It is a Bagiratha Prayathna, a monumental effort, reflecting an enormous, dedicated and unremitting labour by Sri.L.Swaminathan over a long period". That Bharatiya Vidya Bhavan came forward to publish the book in an attractive set of 8 volumes was thus no surprise.

Swaminathan does not want to stop. The propagation of the message of Vaalmeeki has become a passion with him. He felt that the 22,000 stanza epic will be too much for a general reader to start with. That is why he has worked on a condensed version which is the present work Vaalmeeki Raamaayana - A Revelation.

This book, a Revelatory Digest, is made up of Four Parts.

Part I: An introductory section giving a gist of the story in the same sequence as presented in the 6 cantos by Vaalmeeki.

Pat II: This part forms the core of the book. It is devoted to the portrayal of the major characters in the story, namely Raama, Seetha, Lakshmana, Bharatha, Hanumaan and Raavana and also quite a few of the minor characters like Guha and Vibheeshana who have played important roles. The portrayal is based on the words and deeds of the characters themselves, in the language of Vaalmeeki. In the course of such a distributed treatment the story is traversed many times over so that important messages get well registered in our minds.

Part III: In the structuring of part II, there were still a few aspects and episodes that could not be incorporated like for example (a) the argument between Vaali and Raama when Vaali is mortally wounded (b) the meeting between Raama and Seetha when Seetha returns from Ashoka Vana. These are collected as 'Panorama" in Part III.

Part IV: This last section as Addendum illustrates the general knowledge and poetic gifts of Vaalmeeki.

When Swaminathan was writing this Revelatory digest, he had sent me the first 15 pages of introduction as a preview sample. It so happened that I started reading it late one night and I immediately fell under the spell of both the high quality of the subject matter and the simple grandeur of the language. I read the article through, enjoying it thoroughly, and I felt compelled to read it again. I was reminded of the poem by the famous English poet, John Keats, where he had described his experience on first looking into Chapman's Homer: I quote...

"Oft of one wide expanse had I been told
That deep-browed Homer ruled as his demesne;
Yet did I never breathe its pure serene
Till I heard Chapman speak out loud and bold:
Then felt I like some watcher of the skies
When a new planet swims into his ken;
Or like stout. Cortez when with eagle eyes
He stared at the Pacific - and all his men
Looked at each other with a wild surmise-
Silent, upon a peak in Darien.

Swaminathan's new book is now completed. It is packed with drama. It is a "distillate" of the essence of Vaalmeeki. It a delight to read, and experience.

I am happy to note that my friend Sri. R.Ramachandran (RRC, formerly of The Hindu editorial board) has done the editing of the book.

In the course of writing the book, Swaminathan used to call me off and on and say "I do not think I am writing this book. Some superior force, some power is actuating me to do it" This is a mark of true humility. It has been said that when one is on a Quest after Truth, one has to reduce oneself to a Zero, for the Truth to unravel itself. In the constant company of Vaalmeeki, Swaminathan has become a Vaalmeeki Bhaktha, and his Daasa. He is quite advanced in age, but remarkably youthful in spirit.

May Lord Brahma, Sage Naarada, Sage Vaalmeeki, and the divine couple Seetha and Raama, bless him with peace and joy as he travels the road ahead.

C V Sundaram

(C.V. SUNDARAM)

S. ARJUNA RAJA
Director
RAMCO INDUSTRIES LIMITED
Executive Director
MADRAS CEMENTS LTD.

11th June 2004

PREFACE

When my friend Swaminathan requested me to write a Preface to his new book on Rama, "Vaalmeeki Raamaayana - A Revelation" I could not refuse him for more reasons than one. I used to know his father, Dr.P.S.Lokanathan, an eminent Economist. His uncles, particularly P.S.Ananthanarayana, were close to members of Rajapalayam family.

But the personal relationship was not the only reason for my acceptance of his wish. Even as a very young student of Ramakrishna Mission Students' Home at Chennai, I was drawn to Lord Rama and Raama Naama Taraka Manthra became part of my very existence. So Swaminathan's request became a command when he presented me the unedited, trial copy of his new book "Revelation".

The RAMCO Group with which I have the privilege of being closely associated for the last five decades has always "lived by Lord Rama's Virtues" since the days of its founder Sri P.A.A.C Ramasamy Raja. When Swaminathan completed his mammoth work of rendering a stanza by stanza version in English of Vaalmeeki, no wonder our institution came out with support and grant to his commendable work. This 8 volume (3,000 page work) was formally released by Sri R.Venkataraman, former President of India, on behalf of Bharatiya Vidya Bhavan at a simple but well attended function on Rama Navami day in 2002.

But quite a number of us like our Chairman Sri Ramasubrahmaneya Rajha and Sri Ramakrishnanji of The Bhavan (who, alas, is no more) felt that Swaminathan should bring out another edition of Vaalmeeki - A Sanskrit - English Edition - which will satisfy the need of all. I am happy to hear that this work which is in 14 volumes (in 6,000 pages) is nearing completion and will be ready early next year.

In modern world, because of pressure of work, we fail to appreciate our values and culture. Every one of us is pressed for time. But we cannot ignore Lord Rama or Raama Naama. In bringing out this book "Vaalmeeki Raamaayana - A Revelation", the essence of Vaalmeeki Raamaayana is brought out. Rama is the embodiment of Dharma, the 'Maryada' Purusha. And Sanathana Dharma verily is The Religion of India that is Bharath.

In the first 100 pages of his 600 page book, he has condensed Vaalmeeki, to give an idea of the epic. Even those who are not familiar with Vaalmeeki Raamayana can get a fairly good idea.

Raamaayana is a book of Character. In about 275 pages, Swaminathan has analysed various principal characters in Vaalmeeki Raamaayana. As he has given reference to the original Text at every place in his book, when we have time, we can read in detail the original text or its translation later.

Under ''Panorama' he has taken up for study various events. I am happy to say, he has never lost sight of projecting the values, the Dharma of Vaalmeeki in his write up.

In the last section of the book, he has given lots of information. He has even written about Metric System of numbering of vary large numbers! He has written about trees listed by Vaalmeeki.

Swaminathan made a request to me that I should allow him to publish some relevant portions of my writings. I could nor refuse him. The last page of his book carries a Benediction by Vaalmeeki. I am happy that just before this, the Efficacy of Raama Naama, The Dharma of Raama Raajya and finally the 'worship' of the divine lady SITA are carried in Swaminathan's book "Vaalmeeki Raamaayana – A Revelation".

The prophetic pronouncement of the Sage Vaalmeeki has so far not been belied;

> As long as mountain ranges stand,
> And rivers flow upon the earth,
> So long will the Ramayana survive
> upon the lips of men.

This Book is a handy book, worthy of any library. This will stimulate interest in study of the Vedha, that is Raamaayana. As I am a staunch devotee of Lord Rama and Bhagawan Sri Sri Sri Sathya Sai Baba - Sai Ram - I always welcome studies on Rama.

(SANJEEVI ARJUNA RAJA)

HOMAGE

1. My father Dr.P.S.Lokanathan, a teacher, renowned Economist who served India well.

2. My mother Smt Janaki Lokanathan, a deeply religious person, a woman of charitable disposition.

3. My father-in-law, Sri T.V.Rajagopalan, an embodiment of patience and composure.

4. My uncle, P.S.Ananthnarayana, a typical village farmer, full with earthy wisdom, from whom I learnt some of our classics as a boy.

5. Shri Arcot Shamanna, my teacher in P.S.High School, an authority on English grammer, a very endearing man.

6. Shri R.Subrahmanya Sastrigal, my Sanskrit teacher in P.S.High School who stimulated my interest.

7. Shri S.Ramakrishnan, CEO & Director General of Bharatiya Vidya Bhavan, who inspired me to continue my study of Raama and Vaalmeeki.

L.SWAMINATHAN
Tel.24490377

Chennai 600 041,
June 2004.

WRITER's PAGE

After 40 years of service in Industry as an Industrial Chemist and Plastic Technologist, this writer took to the study of our ancient works For the past 10 years, stimulated by blessings of His Hiliness Swargiya Sri Sri Jagadguru Abhinava Vidya Theertha Maha Sannidhanam of Sringeri, study of Vaalmeeki Raamaayana was undertaken.

To popularise Vaalmeeki Raamaayana which is a Vedha, (that is when Raamaayana became a Vedha at the hands of Vaalmeeki) a stanza by stanza of the 22,000 slokas of Vaalmeeki's Text was rendered in English. This 8 volume set (3,000 pages) was released by Hon'ble Sri R.Venkataraman former President of India on behalf of Bharatiya Vidya Bhavan at Chennai, appropriately on Rama navami day in 2202, at a simple but well attended function at Bhavan's premises.

Friends and well wishers like Sri Ramasubrahmaneya Rajha, Vice President Bharatiya Vidya Bhavan, and Ramakrishnanji of The Bhavan (who alas is no more) felt that a Sanskrit - English version of Vaalmeeki must be brought out in a presentable form. Thus, work is now going on for a 14 Volume (6000 page) set, and is expected to be completed by early next year. Left hand pages carry Sanskrit Text - Sloka by Sloka of Vaalmeeki, every sloka numbered. The right hand pages carry corresponding rendering in English.

After 10 years of study of Vaalmeeki, your writer felt that a readable book should be brought out which will give the Gist and Essence of Vaalmeeki Raamaayana. Thus a 600 page book "Vaalmeeki Raamaayana - A Revelation" is now offered to the public with the hope that when time permits, readers will study Vaalmeeki in original or in stanza by stanza translation in English.

"The Revelation", this 600 page book, covers four sections. In the first section, your writer has merely condensed Vaalmeeki's work, giving gist of Kandams-Sargams (chapter by chapter). In the second section he has covered various characters in Vaalmeeki Raamaayana, including Sage Vaalmeeki, the author of this epic. In the third section, under "Panorama" various events have been covered and the last section gives additional information contained in The EPIC.

This writer is indebted to Smt.Shantha Srinivasan, a scholar and Indologist for contributing an article on the Poetry-the Sloka format of Vaalmeeki.

Three articles are contributed to this book by SRI.Sanjivi Arjuna Raja, a highly cultivated man, as these writings bring out the importance of the study of Raama and Seetha. This book ends with a Benediction by Sage Vaalmeeki Himself after he had completed his mammoth work-the Epic.

After studying Vaalmeeki in depth for over a decade, this writer is convinced that there is room for more dissertation on Raamaayana. We have "story" of Rama by very great and noble men like Kamban in Tamizh and by Tulsi Das in Hindi. There are some studies but a serious comparative study is called for, which would be very useful. There are references in Vaalmeeki about Herbals in Himalayan range. Vaalmeeki talks about 'Elements' found in mountains. And there is no research on the Musical format adopted by Lava and Kusha who set Vaalmeeki Raamaayana to Music. As a man of science, this writer is even interested in chemistry of Wines and Liquors of ancient Bharath. As for Musical instruments like Veena, we should study the type of strings that was used in Vedhic times. If they had used steel wire, where did they lean technology!

This writer, when he took to the study of Vaalmeeki Raamaayana, had no idea of publishing his studies. But friends, well wishers and even a scholar, pressed him to make available his studies in book form for general public. Under "Acknowledgement" this writer expresses his gratitude to all those who supported him in many ways. But for the diverse support, encouragement and assistance, it would have been impossible for your writer not only spend hours daily on study of Vaalmeeki during the decade but also could never have brought out in book form, his study and effort. When completed and printed, your author's work on Raamaayana will comprise 24 volumes (about 10,000 pages in all) including this book "Raamayana - A Revelation" If the list under Acknowledgement is long, Vaalmeeki's Epic is such! This writer's fear is that he may miss out some, when he expresses his gratitude to all those who made this possible.

ACKNOWLEDGEMENT

I acknowledge with gratitude the support rendered to me in diverse ways, by many, for my work on Vaalmeeki and Lord Raama, over a decade. I cannot but remember my friend the late Sri Ramakrishnanji, the Director General and CEO of Bharatiya Vidya Bhavan who was very keen that all my work on Lord Raama should be published through Bhavan. On this occasion, I thank the following.

Sri Ramasubrahmaneya Rajha, Vice President Bharatiya Vidya Bhavan, and Chairman Ramco Group Companies. Rajapalaiyan Rajas are known for their munificence. He was keen that I should do Sanskrit-English version of Raamaayana. This 14 volume (6,000 pages) work is expected to be ready in 10 months.

Sri Arjuna Raja, Executive Director, Madras Cements Ltd. Who not only favoured me with a Preface to this book but contributed three articles that I have carried in my book at the end, along with Vaalmeeki's Benediction.

C.V. Sundaram, former Director, Indira Gandhi Center for Atomic Research, Kalpakkam, with whom I share my thoughts regularly and who wrote a Foreword for this book.

R.Ramachandran (RRC formerly of the Editorial Board of The Hindu and founder of Hamsadhwani), with whom I share a 70 year endearing friendship and who, incidentally, edited this book.

Smt.Shantha Srinivasan a scholar and Indologist, who clears my doubts. This book carries a 'Write up' by her on Vaalmeeki's Sloka format.

Sri.B.Ramani, Managing Director of M/s.Officecare Systems Pvt. Ltd., who formatted all my writings on Raama and printed the books.

Sri M.R. Hariharan, a business man who looks beyond business when it comes to serving society.

Krishnamachari Srikkanth, former Captain of India, a deeply religious man who does service quietly.

Arun Sarathy, a business man, son of my friend (late) RP.Sarathy, a cultivated man who values our culture and tradition highly.

(Cleveland) V.V. Sundaram, who has been doing yeoman service to foster our art and culture in USA for over 3 decades.

Dr. Nalli Kuppuswamy Chetty of House of famous NALLIS, whose service to education, art and sport is well known.

Shri M. Gopalakrishnan, President of Hamsadhwani and my colleague in this cultural organisation, who has been serving society in diverse ways.

I cannot but write about some members of my family on this occasion. My daughter Rita and my son in law PN Mohan pamper me. Not only my mundane needs are taken care of by them during my hours of study of Vaalmeeki, I have been living a life of 'luxury' under their care. During earlier years of my study of Vaalmeeki, my son Gautham and his wife Padma took care of me. Quite a few members of my family supported my work. I must mention Smt.Akila Ramajayam who was ever enthusiastic about my study of Raamayana, my co-brother R.N.Ratnam (former Director EID Parry Ltd.) N.S.Sivaramakrishnan, a deeply religious man who was certain that my study and work has 'divine' sanction and command! My brother-in-law R.Srivatsan insisted that I should publish all my work on Raama. He was very happy to see my 8 volume (3000 pages) work released by The Bhavan. But alas he is no more. I am denied the privilege of sharing his joy when this book is released.

My grand children Priya, Sandhya, Dhruva and Drishya have grown up since I started study of Raamaayana some 10 to 12 years ago. I write this because they do not taunt me now "Oh! Thatha is at it! When is he going to study something else for a change!" Yes, they now know I am a devotee of Raama.

Lastly, I am indebted to my wife Smt.Sukanya Swaminathan, who has been part of my life for almost 60 years.

(Sarvay Janaah Sukhino Bhavanthu)

May The Entire World Be Happy & Content Ever.

L. SWAMINATHAN

VAALMEEKI RAAMAAYANA

Introduction

The object of presenting this is to stimulate interest in study of Vaalmeeki Raamaayana. There can never be substitute for a study of this Epic than by reading through the Sanskrit Text. If we have no knowledge of Sanskrit, even reading a translation in a language we are conversant with, will do us good. After all, this Epic by Vaalmeeki is a Vedha. At the hands of Sage Vaalmeeki it became a Vedha. (Knowledge- 'Vid' to know)

Vaalmeeki Raamaayana consists of about 21,700 slokas (Stanzas) in 6 Kaandams (Books) covering 537 Sargams (chapters). In the world we are living now, most of us are not blessed with leisure and time away from our mundane activities. And as no Indian can afford to ignore this Vedha, a Guide to this great Epic is offered bringing out some of the "Wisdom, Truths, and Dharma' contained in this Vedha of Vaalmeeki, in the hope, that later in one's life, Raamaayana Text by Vaalmeeki or in stanza by stanza translation of Sanskrit Text will be read. Time and again noble sons of India have maintained that Vaalmeeki Raamaayana is not just mythology or a history of Raama. Dheergadharshi, (The 'Seer') C.Rajagopalachari (Rajaji) after completing his condensed version of Raamaayana in English, for Bharatiya Vidya Bhavan, said that nothing in his life gave him such satisfaction and solace as this 'effort'. We may read also what that great teacher, scholar, orator and statesman, who was a mentor to Mahatma Gandhi, Rt.Hon'ble VS Srinivasa Sastry said "One immortal product of human mind I have kept to the end, The Raamaayana I hold to be almost without rival in the world's literature....whether we judge by the grandeur of the theme, by the variety of characters portrayed, the tone of idealism, or the appeal that it makes to the devoted heart, it ranks among the noblest of poetic genius..all parts of the book reward the reverential reader....I open the "Book" at all times....It never fails me" And this great, noble man, by way of sympathising with those who have no knowledge of Sanskrit, exhorts them to read Vaalmeeki through stanza by stanza rendering in translation. He says "To those who cannot read it in the original, I would unhesitatingly recommend resort to translation. Because, the wise say, that if you cannot scale The Himalayas, you would do well to get to the base of The Mountain and take in the infinite variety that meets the Eye" Yes Vaalmeeki Raamaayana Is Himalaya.

Now what is so great about this Epic. A book that we read today is soon out of date. When a "Book' survives century after century, there must be something in it. Well. For a child this is a mighty story book. So many stories are contained in it. For the youth and young ones, this is poetry, romance. For the Grihastha, the average citizen, it is <u>practical</u> wisdom. For the old and the aged, it is religion and philosophy. It deals with character, nature, human relationships, war and peace.............No wonder the Epic has survived post atomic era and will survive post Computer - IT era as well. Infact, as The Creator God Brahma, says "Till mountains stand and till rivers flow,this 'tale' of Raama will live in all the three worlds". (Bala – Chapter 2 - Slokas 37 &38)

Dharma is the basis of religion in India. Infact, there is no such thing as Hinduism. Even word India is a misnomer. What constitutes religion in India that is Bhaaratha Varsh, it is <u>Sanaathana Dharma</u>. (Eternal Dharma). And Dharma is found in our scriptures, Vedha-s and Upanishads. And Raamaayana is a Vedha as well.

Scholars and Indologists have taken some exception to calling Vaalmeeki Raamaayana, a Vedha. Their main argument is that unlike Rig, Yajur, Saama and Atharvana Vedha and the Shruthis and Smrithis, which were never written by mortals but came into being by the experience and wisdom over the ages of sages and noble men of lore, Raamaayana was written by a human being, Vaalmeeki. Thus they reject the claim that Raamaayana is a Vedha. But in as much as Lord Naradha who could move freely in all the Three Worlds for the welfare of all, has affirmed as such, we need not be apologetic. Vaalmeeki Raamaayana is a Vedha. (Bala – Chapter 1- Sloka 98). And let us not forget that God Brahma ordains Vaalmeeki and it is HIS wish and the poetry that comes out of Vaalmeeki is only at HIS will and pleasure.(Bala – Chapter 2 – Sloka 32) and so the history of Raama, The Raamaayana, cannot but be a Vedha in Vaalmeeki's hands. God Brahma is Vedha.

A handicap is understanding the terms "Vedha" and "Dharma". With no equivalent in English, these words are very significant and difficult to comprehend. As Vedhas are based on Sanaathana Dharma, and as Raamaayana is a Vedha, it is Dharma that clothes this great Epic. Now what is Dharma. (From 'root' 'Dhar' - sustaining, preserving, bearing). Dharma covers a large ground-gamut. (Firm, Established, Decree, Law & Justice, Usage, Norms & Practices, Moral Code, Conduct, Virtue, Religion). If a citizen of this great land, Bhaarath, is liberal, we can affirm without contradiction, that it is born out of his very birth in this Karma Bhoomi and by his own understanding of Dharma which he practises. In Raamaayana, the noble, wise and aged cabinet minister to King Dhasharatha, Jaabaali, is avowed agnostic-(even atheist). Yet he is venerated even by a man of Religion, Sage Vasishta, spiritual adviser & family priest of Ikshwaaku kings. (Ayodhya II-110-1&2). As Jaabaali is a man of Dharma, it is of no consequence even if he rejects conventional religion. Because he practises other values of Dharma. As we read Vaalmeeki, this aspect will become more embedded in our hearts. We will learn to be more considerate to our fellow human being.

For the religious, Raamaayana is a Book of Prayer. And Raamaayana is a book on Character. Ecology is close to Vaalmeeki. Human relationships, Father-son relationship, brother-brother relationship, Nature & Seasons and The Water Cycle, Administration, Qualities of Ministers, even qualities of a good ambassador are touched upon in the Epic. The four way approach (Saama-conciliation: Dhaana-offer of gifts, money territory as settlement: Bhedha-threats and divisions -and the last resort, Dhanda, the stick-use of force). At random, some of them have been listed.

This Book will begin with The Format of Vaalmeeki. The Six Books (Kaandams)- I Baala Kaanda, II Ayodhya Kaanda, III Aaranya Kaanda, IV Kishkindha Kaanda, V Sundhara Kaanda, VI Yudhdha Kaanda. There is a short synopsis of each Kaanda. And details of every chapter (sargam) are given so that the reader may follow this book easily, when the 'Body' of this work- the Guide, is presented. The relevant Sanskrit portion is given. by reference, to Vaalmeeki's Text.

It is the prayer of the author, that we should not treat Raamaayana as just mythology. This is a treasure that will enhance our lives only when we read Vaalmeeki without any ill will or contempt. Vaalmeeki himself begs us (Bala - Chapter 5 – Sloka 4). Ofcourse it is rather hard on us all when Vaalmeeki talks about gifts of gold offerings in billions, elephants by 100,000 and so on. The monkey army of Sugreeva is in billions and trillions! Ah!. There is that Pushpak Air craft. You will not be on waiting list at the Airport when Pushpak is around. It just expands sideways and top ways to suit passenger traffic. Ah! Ah! But we can take recourse to what that great noble son of India, Rajaji said about quite a few of things found in Vaalmeeki that are rather hard to 'digest'.

"You have to peel off the Banana skin, before you enjoy the banana. When it comes to coconut juice, it is even a harder exercise. But once we get through the shell of coconut, who can regret the effort........"

Vaalmeeki Raamaayana is such!

Koojantham Raama Raama Ithi: Madhuram Madhura Aksharam: Aaruhya Kavithaa Shaakhaam, Vandhey Vaalmeeki Kokilam

कूजन्तं राम राम इति मधुरं
मधुराक्षरं आरुह्य कविता
शरवां वन्दे वाल्मीकि कोकिलम्

I bow to poet Vaalmeeki whose poetry is sweet like the cooing of the kokila bird, perched on the branches of the ever growing tree of poetry, cooing Raama, Raama.....

L. SWAMINATHAN

VAALMEEKI RAAMAAYANA

A REVELATION

CONTENTS OF THE BOOK

PUBLISHER'S NOTE

About a year ago Shree Loknath Swaminathan approached Motilal Banarsidass to hand over entire rights in perpetuity related with his English renderings of Vaalmeeki Raamaayana along with Sanskrit Text in 14 Volumes. Perusing the contents of his translation as well as his devotion towards the sacred text like Vedas, we accepted his offer in good faith. The English translation of entire Vaalmeeki Raamaayana for the benefit of devotee of Lord Shree Raama as well as laymen will be published in due course.

Apart from English translation Shree Swaminathan also handed over to us his studies on Raamaayana in the form of A Revelation and three-Volume set of A Treasure. All of them are quite useful for a first time reader as well as for research scholars, as they not only introduce the subject matter but also explain several technical nuggets of information.

Finally, we're extremely thankful to Shree Swmaminathan for the trust reposited in our publication house. To begin with we've taken up the publication of A Revelation first, so that the esteemed author in his advanced age (he is already 94) gets to see his devotion in print at the earliest and also have the satisfaction to note that his decision to hand over his life-long academic treasure to us was absolutely right.

VAALMEEKI RAAMAAYANA

REVELATION

PART I

(GUIDE TO VAALMEEKI'S TEXT)

Vaalmeeki's Format

Synopsis: Chapter by Chapter

PART I - VAALMEEKI'S FORMAT

Contents

FORMAT OF VAALMEEKI RAAMAAYANA

Kanda	Contents	Sargam	Sloka
1: BAALA:			
	Raama's birth Training under Vishwaamithra His Marriage to Seetha	77	2354
2: AYODHYA:			
	Momentous events at Ayodhya. Raama's exile Death of king Dhasharatha Bharatha taking over as regent during Raama's 14 year exile	119	4357
3: AARANYA:			
	Raama's life in forest Seetha's abduction by Raavana	75	2539
4: KISHKINDA:			
	Search for Seetha Meeting of the great Hanumaan. Sugreeva's friendship. Killing of Vaali by Raama	67	2539
5: SUNDHARA:			
	Seetha found in Lanka Hanumaan's Great achievement	68	2884
6: YUDHDHA:			
	War: Killing of demons & Raavana by Raama who takes over as king of Ayodhya	131	6049

VAALMEEKI'S RAAMAAYANA

A short summary of the story

The classic was presented by Sage Vaalmeeki. After being enlightened by the celestial sage Naaradha, and ordained by God Brahma, The Creator, Vaalmeeki gave this epic to the world in the sloka format (poetry). This divine work is in six Kaandams (Books): Nearly 21,500 slokas (stanzas) in 537 Sargams (chapters) adorn this monumental work which depicts the life of Raama. This master piece is rendered in lucid, simple but effective style in Sanskrit, the classical language of ancient Bhaarath (India) by Vaalmeeki, who was not a literary man, but by grace of God, turned out to be first among the poets.

The epic was sung by Lava and Kusha, sons of Raama, and thus it was first introduced to the public as a Musical.

It is Indian tradition that classical works are 'inspired' In this case, Vaalmeeki was inspired as a result of being enlightened by the celestial Naaradha, who moved freely in all the three worlds for welfare of all. And with blessings of God Brahma, no wonder Vaalmeeki wrote this which is considered the Fifth Vedha, after Rig, Yajur, Saama and Athaarvana Vedhas. At the hands of Vaalmeeki, this story book became a Vedha!

Story: The story appears simple. The world was tormented by evil forces, particularly by the demon king Raavana. The celestials beg God Vishnu to 'save' the worlds. God Vishnu decides to be born on earth as Raama, son of king Dhasharatha of Ayodhya, who was doing Yaaga to beget a son! And Raama, born as son of Dhasharatha was banished from the kingdom for 14 years, to make room for his younger brother Bharatha, who was born to his stepmother Kaikeyi. King Dhasharatha, unable to bear separation from his beloved eldest son Raama, dies. Much against his wishes, Bharatha reluctantly agrees to rule the kingdom of Ayodhya, as regent, during the 14 years of exile of his elder brother Raama.

Raama, accompanied by his wife Seetha and another brother Lakshmana, leaves Ayodhya to serve his exile in forest, to serve his banishment and keep up his commitment to his step mother Kaikeyi. During exile, his wife Seetha, renowned for her beauty and chastity was kidnapped by demon king Raavana and taken away to Lanka 1,000 miles away from the Southern 'tip' of India where she is kept prisoner. During her captivity Seetha does not give any encouragement to Raavana and totally rejects Raavana when he presses her to be his wife.

In the mean time Raama, along with his brother Lakshmana is making a search for Seetha. He establishes contact with Sugreeva, makes him king of monkeys after killing Sugreeva's brother Vaali. and forms a treaty of friendship. Sugreeva's minister Hanumaan who is on a search of Seetha finds Seetha in Lanka.

With Sugreeva's assistance and with the huge army of monkeys, Raama invades Lanka and wages a mighty war with Raavana and his demons. Raavana is killed. The Demons subdued. 14 years of exile being over, Raama returns to Ayodhya and takes over the kingdom from his brother Bharatha. Raama then ruled the kingdom perfectly with the norms of Dharma. Raama's rule -Raama-Raajya- became synonymous with good governance.

1: THE BAALA KAANDA

Synopsis of the first book of Raamaayana

This first book of Vaalmeeki Raamaayana contains 2,354 stanzas in 77 chapters. Details are given later in the Guide.

Vaalmeeki's Raamaayana may be said to begin from the 5th. chapter. But Baala Kaanda begins with the meeting of Sage Vaalmeeki with the divine celestial sage Naaradha who narrates the gist of the story of Raama. And later, God Brahma Himself appears before him. He blessesVaalmeeki and ordains him to render the epic to the world.:

An incident happens which causes great anguish to Vaalmeeki. The killing of a bird by a heartless hunter while it was making love to its beloved. Vaalmeeki curses the hunter. And this curse comes out of his mouth in the form of poetry. So by the grace of God Brahma, Valmeeki who becomes the first among poets, begins this great history. AlthoughVaalmeeki got only the gist of Raama's story from Naaradha, as he begins his work, all events present themselves before him as clear as picture. There was no stopping and Vaalmeeki finished the epic. Raama's sons, Lava and Kusha whom Raama had not seen before as these two boys were born to his pregnant wife when she had been bansihed by Raama due to a misunderstanding, sang Vaalmeeki's Raamaayana, before vast audiences. Vaalmeeki's epic was popularised as a Musical.

Raamaayana begins from the 5th chapter, with the description of Ayodhya, the noble qualities of its king Dhasharatha, his great council of ministers. And how, as this king had no sons, he decided to perform Ashwamedha Sacrifice=Yaaga= His minister and friend Sumanthra advises his king, that, for the success of the Yaaga, and for progeny, he should bring the very old sage Rishyashringa to Ayodhya and perform the Yaaga under his patronage. Sumanthra narrates the story about this saint, his greatness. The Yaaga is then successfully completed. Rishyashringa then performs the yaaga for the progeny for Dhasharatha. A holy ghost appears, bringing with him, divine holy milk. The three queens of Dhasharatha partake this milk and they conceive.

And for quite some time, the worlds were terribly agitated because evil forces were tormenting them. The celestials beg God Brahma to put an end to this suffering., particularly to destroy demon king Raavana. And God Vishnu, goaded by God Brahma, decides to be born on earth and He chooses to come down as an Incarnation. The occasion is appropriate! The Lord becomes the son of Dhasharatha who had no sons and who had just completed the Yaga for begetting sons. As Raama, The lord is 'born' to Dhasharatha's first wife Kowsalya. Likewise, Lakshmana and Shathrugna are born to Dhasharatha's second wife Sumithra. And Bharatha as son to Kaikeyi. And ofcourse Dhasharatha did not know that his sons are Vishnu's incarnation. Infact, very few knew that Raama was none other than Vishnu in human form. Even Raama was not aware!

The old king Dhasharatha is a happy and contented man. His four sons were growing up nicely at Ayodhya. At about this time, the great sage Vishwaamithra seeks an audience with king Dhasharatha. He wants the service of prince

Raama, the warrior, to offer protection to the yaaga he is performing in his hermitage. He wants to scare away evil demons who are causing havoc in the hermitage during such ceremonies. Dhasharatha does not like this. He feels his son is too immature to fight demons But under advice of his chief priest and mentor Vasishta, he finally agrees to send Raama along with Vishwaamithra.

This event of Raama going along with Vishwaamithra even as a very young man, is of great sigificance. Raama is taught chants of Bala-Athibala, use of all weapons, both conventional and divine, by Vishwaamithra. Raama thus becomes a mighty warrior, with experience. He kills demoness Thaataka, drives away the terrible demons Maareecha and Subaahu who were 'playing' havoc in this region.

Having successfully completed his yaaga with Raama guarding his hermitage against evil forces. Vishwaaamithra starts back to Ayodhya. with Raama and his brother Lakshmana who had also accompanied him during his visit to Vishwaamithra's hermitage. But hearing of a great divine bow that was with King Janaka at Mithila, he decides that Raama should take a 'look' at this mighty bow which could not be even 'touched' by mighty warriors before. And King Janaka had offered Seetha as prize for valour to any one who could lift the Bow and string it up.

The return journey is full of anecdotes and stories. Vishwaamithra, who long long ago, was a mighty king and who later became a Brahma Rishi, narrates numerous stories, to these princes. He enlightens them with the history and geography of these places. He is also a great historian and knows history and geography of these places.

As examples, a description of the Kaama hermitage, the history of demon Sundha, Maarecha, The Sidhdha hermitage, the Story of Ganges, the birth of Skandha, the Origin of Maruth-s, Himaalayas and elements, and so on.

On the way to Mithila, Vishwaamithra takes them through Vishaala region. There Raama 'liberates', resurrects, Ahalya, the wife of sage Gauthama, who had been cursed to become a stone for years for her transgression and 'affair' with Indra.

At Mithila, Vishwaamithra is well received by King Janaka. Shathanandh, Janaka's minister tells Raama how fortunate he is that he has the patronage of such a great sage like Vishwaamithra. And how blessed he is. Then he narrates story after story about Vishwaamithra. From chapters 51 to 65, it is all about Vishwaamithra, who was once a mighty king. About his enmity to Vasishta, about his various penance and how he finally became a man of peace and a Brahma Rishi.

At MithilaVishwaamithra informs King Janaka the purpose of his visit. He has brought Raama, the son of Dhasharatha to Mithila so that he may take a 'look' at the mighty Bow with him. Raama, not only lifts the Bow, but under the pressure of his arm, it breaks. King Janaka is very happy. Because he now has a warrior to whom he can bestow his daughter Seetha in marriage as per his commitment. King Janaka sends emissaries to kingDhasharatha informing him about his son Raama's valour and how he has won Seetha as a prize and if Dhasharatha is pleased, he should give assent to his son's marriage with Seetha. Dhasharatha is only too pleased and so with a huge entourage starts from Ayodhya for Mithila. There is great rejoicing at Mithila as Raama weds Seetha, Lakshmana weds Oormila, and

Bharatha weds Maandvi and Shathrugna, Shruthakeerthi. Vasishta performs the marriage rituals. As per custom the Lineage of Dhasharatha & Janaka are announced. during marriage

After rejoicing and feasting are over, the mariage party of Dhasharatha starts back to Ayodhya. from Mithila. But on their way, Dhasharatha is horrified to see before him the terrible Brahmin, the Brahmin Raama, Parashu-Raama who seeks confrontation with Dhasharatha's son Raama. Raama humbles this Parashu Raama.

Finally, when they return to Ayodhya, the sons with their newly wed wives, are, well received by their mothers happily.

And none is happier than the old king Dhasharatha

But 'The Drama' is reserved for the next Book, The Ayodhya kaanda!

2: AYODHYA KAANDA

Synopsis of the second book of Raamaayana

This book of Vaalmeeki Raamaayana covers 4357 stanzas in 119 chapters Details given later in the Guide.

King Dhasharatha is a happy man. His four sons Raama, Lakshmana, Bharatha, Shathrugna are happily married. and settled down. As he is very old, a thought strikes him that he should crown his eldest son Raama as Crown prince to take up the responsibility of taking over the rule of his vast kingdom even as he was alive. Being a democratic king, he seeks the opinion of citizens and VIPs before a large assembly. They are all so happy that with one voice they affirm and gladly accept Raama to become their 'ruler'. Dhasharatha feels that his son should be crowned forthwith although his other two sons Bharatha and Shathrugna are away on a holiday at Bharatha's maternal grandfather's capital. Chief priest, sage Vasishta is requested to make the arrangements for the coronation ceremony. The capital city Ayodhya is in great joy.

Manthara, the hunch back who is confidante and mentor to Kaikeyi the last of the three queens of Dhasharatha and mother of Bharatha, 'works' upon Kaikeyi, poisons her mind, tells her that if Raama is crowned, she would be reduced to 'slavery' along with her son Bharatha. She must see to it that Bharatha is crowned instead. And Raama must be banished from Ayodhya. And this evil genius has a strategy to achieve this. She reminds Kaikeyi of the two open boons she had received from her husband Dhasharatha long ago when she had saved his life in the battlefield during a war with Asuras. And she had not utilised the boons ever since. Manthara tells Kaikeyi that the time to ask for and utilise the boons is 'here and now' She should press her husband thus: By the first boon Raama must go on exile for 14 years. By the second boon, her son Bharatha should be crowned instead.

King Dhasharatha is shocked Kaikeyi is firm and adamant. Inspite of advice and admonishment from seniors and elders like Sumanthra, Sidhaartha and even Vasishta, Kaikeyi must have her way. She must have the two boons now and only this way. Raama must go. Bharatha must be the ruler! Being an Ikshwaaku king, he could not break a promise, even after any number of years, even if it is detrimental to his interest. So he banishes Raama on 14 year exile. But after sending Raama away who was accompanied by his wife Seetha and his other brother Lakshmana, unable to bear separation from Raama, king Dhasharatha dies.

Urgent summons are sent to Bharatha to return to Ayodhya cutting short his holiday. Ayodhya is without a ruler. Raama and Lakshmana are away on exile. Bharatha and Shathrugna at Kekeya on holiday. Bharatha returns. He is shocked to hear that his father had passed away. And another shock strikes him. His brother Raama driven away on exile. Bharatha cannot tolerate this 'crime' committed by his mother Kaikeyi, ostensibly for his welfare. He will not be king. He rebukes her. Only his brother Raama is and is fit to be king. After performing last Rites for his father, he draws a large army with him, and goes to the forest to crown Raama there itself along with VIP-s, citizens from all walks of life, his mothers and all.

As the vast army reaches the banks of the Ganges, he is met by Raama's friend Guha. And after staying at the Bhardhwaja hermitage for the night where his entourage was treated to a grand hospitality, he gets news about Raama's abode at Chithrakoot from sage Bhardhwaja.

Bharatha meets Raama. Presses him to return forthwith to Ayodhya as king. But Raama is firm. He has to abide by his father's and his step mother Kaikeyi's command. He will return only after14 years exile as stipulated. And he warns Bharatha that he should also obey his father's command to rule Ayodhya during his exile. Bharatha realises that nothing can change Raama, as he is a man of Dharma and wedded to Truth.

As a compromise, Bharatha takes Raama's Sandals and returns to Ayodhya. He establishes a temporary caretaker government at a village called Nandigram, not far from Ayodhya. As far as he is concerned, only Raama can be king at Ayodhya. Placing Raama's Sandals on the 'throne' at Nandigram, Bharatha rules the kingdom for 14 years from this place. But only as Raama's representative. He worships the ''throne' daily, which is adorned with Raama's sandals, as though Raama is giving all the commands as 'king'!

Raama continues his exile, goes away deep into the forest, of Dhandaka.

From now on it is all about Raama. Vaalmeeki takes leave of Ayodhya here. It is all about Raama's 14 years of exile.

3: AARANYA KAANDA

Synopsis of the third book of Raamaayana

This book of Vaalmeeki covers 2539 stanzas in 75 chapters. Details given later in the Guide

Aaranya Kaanda is about Raama's exile in forest. Readers may remember, Raama's exile is for 14 years. Almost 13 years of his life is covered in Aaranya kaanda.

Raama, accompanied by Seetha and Lakshmana, enter Dhandaka forest. He gives the assurance that he will offer protection to the residents of forest against evil demons. He will protect Rishi-s and sages living there. There is an interesting dialogue between Seetha and Raama. Seetha does not want Raama to take up arms, as he is no longer a Kshathriya prince but is 'supposed' to be a mendicant leading the life of a simple forest man, a man of peace. But Raama cannot bear to remain a silent spectator to the suffering of residents of the forest. He cannot absolve himself of his responsibility of protecting these innocent men, even though he has chosen a life of a mendicant in the forest. He is still a Kshathriya warrior although not a prince! And he had given his word to them.

Raama kills demon Viraadha. And during his life there he meets sages like Sutheekshana, Sharabanga. And he meets the great Agasthya, who advises him that he should settle down for sometime in Panchavati, near river Godhavari in the south. Agasthya blesses him with the offer of a divine Bow and Sword for his protection. Raama meets Jataayu, the king of birds.

At Panchavati, one day they have a visitor, in the form of a demoness. Shoorpanaka, a cousin of demon king Raavana. She makes love to Raama first and then to Lakshmana. When she is rejected by them, she gets mad and tries to kill Seetha, Lakshmana cuts her nose. He could have killed her but a warrior like Lakshmana cannot kill a woman as per norms. Shoorpanaka rushes to her brother demon chief Khara and wails before him. Khara sends a few demons to kill Raama. But they are slain. Then 14,000 demons of terrible deeds. They are also slain by Raama. And when Khara along with Dhooshana and Thrishiras go after him, Raama kills all of them. News reaches Raavana at his island kingdom of Lanka. A demon spy Akampana informs Raavana about the killing of his chiefs at Dhandaka. He suggests to his king that Raavana should kidnap Seetha because Raama would then give up life as he cannot live even for a moment without his beloved wife. Raavana in wrath flies to India but his demon friend Maareecha advises him to restrain his anger and not go anywhere near Raama as it would be disastrous to him.

But Shoorpanka who takes her own complaint to Raavana, works upon him. She gives him The Bait - Seetha. She tells him that Seetha is such a gem of a woman, that only Raavana must have this Gem!

Raavana makes up his mind. He goes to his demon friend Maareecha again, but this time he commands him. Maareecha should take on the form of a golden deer, entice Seetha who is fond of deer and when Raama tries to capture the golden'deer' he should run away and take him far away from Raama's hermitage. And when Raama is drawn away thus, he should utter a magical sound, a wail, as though

Raama is in distress. And Lakshmana hearing 'Raama's' voice, will also rush out of the hermitage to help his brother. When the two brothers are thus drawn away from their hermitage, when Seetha is alone, Raavana will easily kidnap her and take her to Lanka, 1,000 miles away. Maareecha is horrified by this strategy. Refuses to help Raavana. But when Raavana threatens to kill him, he succumbs. This scheme, the strategy, works. Maareecha (in the form of the golden deer) is of course killed by Raama after a long chase. But harm is already done. Lakshmana leaves the hermitage. Seetha is alone. Raavana at first enters the hermitage as a Brahmin mendicant. Soon he discloses who he is and kidnaps Seetha.

As Raavana flies along with Seetha, the loud wail and cry for help of Seetha is heard by the old Jataayu, the king of birds. It puts up a brave fight, but is mortally wounded by Raavana. And when Raavana reaches Lanka, he tries to induce Sita to accept him as his wife. But Seetha being so pure does not give him any encouragement. She is kept in isolation at the Ashoka forest nearby Raavana gives her one year to become his wife.

In the meantime, Raama and Lakshmana find to their horror, Seetha missing from their hermitage. When no one tells Raama about Seetha's whereabouts he is in such a wrath that he threatens to burn up even animals and trees and all. But Lakshmana advises Raama to calm down and like a true warrior make every effort and search for Seetha.

On their search for Seetha, they see the old bird Jataayu mortally wounded by Raavana when he tried to stop him from carrying away Seetha. Raama performs the Last Rites for Jataayu who although just a bird, had done service for him.

They continue the search for Seetha. By good fortune, they are confronted by a gruesome demon Kabandha. This demon was not born a demon but by curse was turned into a demon. He was called Dhanu, a handsome youth. As Kabandha he tells Raama that if he is killed by Raama, the curse on him would disappear and he will get back his normal form and stature in life. Raama and Lakshman a then cut his hands off and when he is thus 'killed', Dhanu, while going up the sky, advises Raama to seek Sugreeva and make a treaty of friendship with him because it is he who will assist him in finding Seetha. Raama should therefore go towards Pampa region and meet Sugreeva, the lord of monkeys. And Dhanu also advises that on their way they should meet Shabari, the old woman, a monk who did yeoman service to rishis and sages there.

Raama is happy. At last they have some hope to find Seetha. They go towards Pampa. They meet Shabari who extends hospitality to them. By her divine power, Raama and Lakshmana 'see' (like in TV) the entire oceans and regions.

Raama and Lakshmana see this old monk Shabari, who was only waiting to extend hospitality to them. She gives up her form of an old woman but ascend to heaven as a young lady fully decorated.

Raama and Lakshmana reach Pampa.

4: KISHKINDA KAANDA

Synopsis of the fourth book of Raamayana

This book of Vaalmeeki covers 2539 stanzas in 67 chapters. Details are given later in the guide.

On the advice of Kabandha, Raama and Lakshmana go to the Pampa region, to meet Sugreeva and seek his assistance to find Seetha. The monkey chief Sugreeva who is a refugee, having been driven out of the kingdom of Kishkindha by his wrathful brother Vaali owing to a misunderstanding, is living in mountain of Rishyamukh. When Sugreeva, from a distance watches Raama and Lakshmana walking along towards them, he becomes very apprehensive. Is terribly scared. He thinks Vaali has sent them to kill him! He sends his wise minister monkey chief Hanumaan to meet them to find out about them as to who really they are and what their purpose is to wander in this region.

A pleasant surprise awaits Raama and Lakshmana as they are met by the great Hanumaan, the very person Raama wants to meet.

A great friendship between monkey Sugreeva and prince Raama develops. Sugreeva narrates his tale of woes. How his brother Vaali not only kicked him out of his kingdom but also snatched away his wife Ruma. Raama vows to kill Vaali and make Sugreeva, the king at Kishkindha. And Sugreeva vows before Raama that he will find Seetha and help him to retrieve her.

And keeping up his promise, with just one arrow, Raama kills Vaali from behind his back and crowns Sugreeva as the king of monkeys. The killing of Vaali is a never ending debate in Vaalmeeki Raamaayana!

As it is the rainy season, Raama gives Sugreeva three months lay off before he begins the search for Seetha. And Sugreeva sends four mighty army of monkeys in four different directions of the world for the search of Seetha. The Armies sent to North, East and West return, without finding Seetha. Before sending his armies out, Sugreeva had stipulated a time limit of one month for search and then get back to report to him. But the army sent out to the South, under Angadha and Hanumaan fail to return within one month as they were so devoted that they lost track of time. Infact when they realise that they had overstayed the time limit, they even contemplate suicide. By good fortune, as they were about to decide on a fast unto death, they meet a very old bird Sampaathi, the brother of Jataayu. Sampaathi tells them that Seetha may be found only in Lanka,1,000 miles away from the southern tip of India. Sampaathi's son had seen Raavana carrying off Seetha towards Lanka.

The task before this Southern army of Search for Seetha is quite clear. They reach the shores of the southern ocean. But who can fly 1,000 miles to the island of Lanka and get back? Ofcourse it is Hanuman who can do this. Hanumaan is excited, gets ready for The Take off from the cliffs of Mahendra mountain range in far south of India.

5: SUNDHARA KAANDA

Synopsis of the fifth book of Vaalmeeki

This book of Vaalm. eki covers 2884 stanzas in 68 chapters. Details are given later in this Guide.

It is said that if one does not have time to read Vaalmeeki Raamaayana, but reads this book Sundhara kaanda, even a few chapters of it, he will be most blessed in the world! Such is the beauty and content of this book.

Hanumaan who is chosen to fly over to Lanka, crossing over1,000 miles of the ocean of Mahodhadhi, gets ready for the take-off. From the top of Mahendra mountain in the Southern most part of India, he prepares his 'jump' Applying pressure, he leaps and flies over the mighty ocean. His mission- Find Seetha-

As he flies, he overcomes many obstacles. The obstacle of mountain Hiranyanaabha that rises from the bottom of the ocean,. the obstacle by Lady Sarasa of the reptiles, the obstacle by Simhika. Hanumaan after surmounting all the difficulties en-route lands at Lanka late in the evening.

Landing at Lanka `his entry to Lanka is checked by the Spirit-guardian of Lanka, a demoness, whom Hanumaan easily overpowers. As he enters Lanka, he moves around, unseen, taking the form of a tiny ordinary monkey. He begins his search for Seetha. Visits various mansions, palaces. He sees Raavana's divine Aircraft-Air station Pushpak. He is awed by the sheer beauty and splendour of Lanka. He even enters the inner apartments of palaces at night. When he sees Mandodhari, the queen of Raavana, sleeping in a golden cot, for a moment he thought it was

Seetha. But quickly changed his mind. He searches pleasure gardens, Banquet hall, places of worship and every building there But not finding Seetha Hanumaan becomes depressed. At one point he even contemplates ending his life!

But the wise Hanumaan ponders. And he decides to search Ashoka forest. Hiding himself between the branches of a large tree, he finally finds Seetha under a tree, presenting a most pitiable sight to him. Hanumaan grieves.

It is now early morning. Raavana makes a visit to Ashoka forest, to make another attempt to persuade Seetha to accept him as his wife voluntarily. But Seetha treats him with utter contempt. Raavana is in wrath. He threatens her. If within two months she does not accept him, he will make a meal of her for his morning breakfast! The guards, the demonesses watching her, use the carrot-stick technique upon her after Raavana departs. They threaten her, cajole her with some sweet talk. But, for Seetha there can never be another man than Raama in her life. Seetha even contemplates suicide by choking herself with her long bunch of hair. And like a needle in haystack, there is a good demoness called Thrijata, among the guards, who confides in her about a dream she saw at night which indicated that Raama will come soon to retrieve her and will annihilate Lanka and Raavana.

Hanumaan is watching all this, unseen, from the branches of the tree. He feels the time was ripe for him to draw Seetha's attention. But how to go about it? Demonesses are watching Seetha all the time. And Seetha might think that he is a spy of Raavana. When demonesses are somewhat sleepy, Hanumaan in a language only she can understand, starts 'singing' Raama's story in a feeble voice. Seetha looks up. Wonders who is talking about Raama in a demon land. Who is talking about my husband, the mighty Raama?

Finally, Hanumaan convinces her that he is Hanumaan, not a spy of Raavana, but is there as an emissary of Raama. And as a token of remembrance, hands over a ring with Raama's Insignia, that was given to him by Raama when he left Kishkindha on the search mission.

Hanumaan assures Seetha that Raama, along with Sugreeva and his huge army of monkeys, will soon invade Lanka and destroy Raavana and his evil demons. Before taking leave of her, Seetha gives Hanumaan a token of remembrance, an ornament-Choodaamani- to be handed over to Raama when he returns to India. At one point Hanumaan suggests that she could save herself from further agony by riding back with him. Fly back He could take her to Raama in just under a day! But Seetha refuses. When she taunts him, Hanumaan shows his true form to her. Seetha is convinced Hanumaan is no ordinary monkey, but a divine being.

As Hanumaan leaves, he ponders. Feels he has some unfinished business yet at lanka, which he should take care of before going back. He feels that he should take a good look at the defenses of Lanka He should also meet Raavana and convey Raama's message. He destroys Ravana's wonderful pleasure garden. Raavana is terribly angry. Sends a few demons to arrest or kill the monkey. And Hanumaan kills them. And finally when he is 'bound by Brahma asthra from Inderjith, son of Raavana, he accepts his seizure as he is sure he will be presented before Raavana.

Raavana orders death penalty. But his brother warns Raavana that it is against all norms to kill an 'ambassador' So Raavana offers Hanumaan a milder punishment. His tail is set fire to. But by the grace of his foster father Lord of Wind, Hanumaan does not feel the heat as a cool wind cools off his tail. With the flames on his tail, Hanumaan sets fire to various mansions and plays havoc on Lanka

His mission totally successful, Hanumaan flies back to the southern tip of India where his search army under Angadha is eagerly looking forward to Hanumaan's safe return, carrying with him the good news about Seetha.

After 'victory' celebrations at the famous Wine = Madhu forest, they return to the headquarters where they are cheered. by Sugreeva and others.

Hanumaan hands over the ornament = choodaamani = to Raama. He narrates the conversation he had with Seetha. at Lanka. Everyone is extremely delighted that Seetha was found at last.

6: THE YUDHDHA KAANDA

Synopsis of the sixth book of Vaalmeeki

This book of Vaalmeeki covers 6049 stanzas in 131 chapters. The details will follow later in this Guide

This is the last of the six books of Vaalmeeki's Raamaayana It deals with war between Raama & Raavana.

When Hanumaan returns after finding Seetha at Lanka, he is extolled by Raama. Sugreeva gets ready with his huge army of monkeys. Hanumaan describes the defences of Lanka. Accompanied by Sugreeva's huge army of monkeys, Raama leaves Kishkindha and reach the southern 'tip' of India. They face the mighty ocean.

In the meantime, spies convey to Raavana that a mighty army is standing in the southern tip of India, ready to cross the ocean and invade Lanka. Raavana is naturally worried. Calls a meeting with his chiefs and ministers. They all flatter him. Only Vibheeshana, his youngest brother, advises him to give up Seetha and thus avoid war with Raama. Raavana is so enraged that he threatens him. Under no circumstances will he restore Seetha to Raama. Vibheeshana, feeling that no useful purpose will be served by remaining in Lanka and realising that his life may be in peril at the hands of his wrathful brother, deserts Raavana. Along with five of his closest demon chiefs, he seeks asylum under Raama. One may say that this is the first casualty of war for Raavana. There is s strong view that in as much as Vibheeshana is the brother of the enemy, he should not be acepted nor asylum given to him. Hanumaan is the only person who justifies the action of Vibheeshana.

And Raama accepts Vibheeshana.. Infact Raama seeks his advice from time to time during the war.

As the monkey army face the ocean, Vibheeshana advises Raama that unless the entire army is able to cross over the ocean and reach Lanka which is 1,000 miles, they cannot win a war with Raavana. When under his advice, Raama offers prayer to the Lord of Ocean for safe passage of his army to Lanka and when his prayer is not answered by the Lord of the Ocean, Raama decides he will use force against the ocean itself. He will even dry up the ocean, in such a wrath is he! When finally the Lord of the Ocean appears before Raama, he assures him that when a bridge is constructed over the ocean, he will allow some space and the ocean will be tranquil.. Under the supervision of monkey chief Nala, a bridge is constructed in just under 5 days and the monkey army moves into Lanka comfortably.

Inspite of spies telling Raavana that Raama's army of monkeys are at the door of Lanka, Raavana cannot believe it. His Lanka has been in isolation for such a long time that none can trespass the island. Even at this time, with war being imminent, Raavana refuses good advice but will never give up Seetha and seek peace with Raama.From the Tower he surveys Raama's army. When Raama officially sends an ultimatum to Ravana through Angadha,. Raavana not only rejects the ultimatum but threatens to kill the emissary. So it is war. Between Sugreeva's army of monkeys and Raavana's army of demons. A very gruesome war.

Like in the modern war, like in World War II, we see a lot of strange happenings. The strategy of deceit is employed.

Like the head of 'Raama' being exhibited before Seetha, the 'Head' being produced through magic. And to make Raama give up fight, Seetha's 'head' was produced and shown to Raama, during the battle, by magic! The demons are master magicians and can fight even at night.

The war casualties are very high on both sides. When Raavana's other brother Kumbakarna takes the field, it is disaster for monkeys. Kumbakarna had advised Raavana but he had not heeded his advice. But unlike Vibheeshana, his other brother, Kumbakarna does not desert Raavana but fights for him ultimately. He swallows the monkeys up like fire flies on lamp. Finally he is killed by Raama. One after the other, demon chiefs are killed by Sugreeva's army. The list is long. Chapters 42 to 111 it is all war.

When Indrajith, Raavana's brilliant son is killed Raavana knows that he has no hope. Yet being a warrior decides to continue the war. But killing demons is one thing. Killing Raavana is a different matter. It is at this time; Lord Indra sends his chariot with charioteer Maathali for Raama to fight Raavana riding on a chariot. It was an uneven fight till then, as Raavana was on chariot and Raama was fighting as a foot soldier.

And Sage Agasthya knowing the importance of victory for Raama and realising Raama's victory over Raavana alone will bring prosperity to all comes down and offers blessings by expounding the Chant of Chants, The Aadithya Hridhaya.

And Raama finally kills Raavana: War Ends

When Raavana is killed, Raama advises Vibheeshana to perform his Last Rites. But Vibheeshana declines. The noble Raama tells him that after death enmity ceases and we should do our duty. Vibheeshana cremates his brother with due honours. Then Vibheeshana is crowned king of lanka.

A great tragic episode follows. After all, war was fought by Raama with the help of Sugreeva and his army, to retrieve his wife Seetha. When Raama asks Vibeeshaṇa to fetch Seetha and present her fully decorated with jewels one would have expected that he would be excited to see his beloved wife Seetha and would be looking forward to a life with her. But nothing like this happened, at least immediately. Because, when Vibheeshana presents Seetha, Raama addresses her sharply that it would be a mistake if she thought that war was fought because he wanted to take her back. He had fought this war only to save his honour, and to offer punishment to the thief who stole his wife. Nothing more. He had thus fulfilled his duty as a prince of Ikshwaakus. And as for Seetha, she may choose to lead her life elsewhere, anywhere, with whom so ever she chooses. Seetha is no timid girl. To prove that she is pure and devoted, she enters fire. But Fire does not burn her. The Lord of Fire comes up from Fire mound lifting her up, even as she is dressed up in silken robes and wearing all jewels. Raama accepts her happily.

The 'Gods' and celestials who were watching this scene could not believe their eyes. God Brahma descends on Lanka along with Indra. Even Raama's father Dhasharatha comes from heaven. They tell Raama who he really is when Raama says = I am but a man. I know myself only as a man

= Brahma enlightens Raama that he is none other than God Vishnu on earth, having come down for the welfare of all. When LordIndra offers a boon, Raama wants only this- that all the monkeys who lost their lives in war for him should come back alive. A tall order, this, but Indra, with God Brahma looking on accepts Raama's request and all the dead monkeys are resurrected.

Raama, along with Seetha and Lakshmana want to get back to Ayodhya where his brother Bharatha would be anxiously waiting for him. After all 14 years are about to be over. Vibheeshana offers his divine Air-station Pushpaka for flight back to India. No need for crossing the ocean now. This Pushpaka Air-station is such a unique spaceship it can accomodate any number of passengers, even millions! They all fly back. On their flight, Raama who is now happy wih Seetha describes all that had happened after she was kidnapped. He indicates where he met Sugreeva. Seetha makes a request. She has no company.of women .So Aircraft makes a landing and Sugreeva's women folk also get into it.

When they reach Bhardhwaja's hermitage, Raama sends Hanumaan in advance to Ayodhya, Bharatha is thrilled. When they all reach Ayodhya, Bharatha hands over the rule of kingdom, and Raama is finally crowned.

Vaalmeeki ends his Raamaayana by telling us all that Raama ruled the earth for 11,000 years and his rule was synonymous with the best Government. Raama-Raajya.

Concluding his great epic, which is Vedha, Vaalmeeki offers a Benediction.Whoever reads, or sings, or writes the story of Raama as expounded by him, will obtain tranquility and material prosperity.

CONTENTS OF FIRST BOOK
BAALA KAANDA

Chapter and Contents (slokas in bracket)

1: Vaalmeki seeks enlightenment from sage Naaradha. With four stanzas, wishes to know about a good, noble man in the world, if any! Naaradha enlightens him about Raama with 90 slokas. Narrates his story (100)

2: Vaalmeeki's interest in Raama is kindled. The Krauncha bird incident when a heartless hunter kills a bird while it was making love. Vaalmeeki curses the hunter. The curse comes out of his mouth as poetry. God Brahma appears before him. Ordains him to do Raaama's story in poetry.(44)

3: By the grace of God Brahma, Vaalmeeki perceives the entire story of Raama as clear as a picture. (40)

4: Vaalmeeki expounds The Raamaayana. Teaches Lava and Kusha, the sons of Raama his epic. They set it to a musical format and sing before rishi-s and sages and also before their father. (36)

ENTIRE STORY PRESENTED AS A MUSICAL

Story begins

5: Description of Ayodhya (24)

6: King Dhasharatha's Rule (28)

7: Dhasharatha's council of ministers (23)

8: Dhasharatha decides to perform Ashwamedha yaaga for begetting sons (24)

9: Minister Sumanthra narrates the story of saint Rishyashringa as unfolded by Sanathkumaara (19)

10: Sumanthra advises his king to invite Rishyashshringa and request him to preside over his yaaga (32)

11: Rishyashringa brought to Ayodhya with his wife Shantha from the Anga kingdom (30)

12: Preparation for Ashwamedha yaaga. A well groomed horse ready. Materials for yaaga procured. (21)

13: A ceremonial centre near Ayodhya established around banks of river Sarayu. Vasishta extends an invitation to all VIP-s citizens and other rulers. (37)

14: Dhasharatha performs Yaaga with Rishyashringa as patron.in.chief.. Great hospitality. Feasting. Rituals. Deities invoked. King's wives take part. (60)

15: Rishyashringa performs rituals for progeny for Dhasharatha. At about this time, the celestials under Lord Indra beg of God Vishnu to be born on earth to save the world from evil demons. God Vishnu accedes to be born as a human being Vow to kill Raavana (35)

16: God Vishnu decides to be born as son of Dhasharatha (as Raama). after his completion of the Yaaga. At the Yaaga hall, a Holy Ghost appears, bringing holy milk for Dhasharatha. The three queens Kowsalya, Sumithra and Kaikeyi partake of this milk. They conceive (34)

17: The creation of monkeys and bears to assist Vishnu when HE is born Raama, to fight demons. Earth full with brave monkeys (37)

18: Vishnu incarnates as son Raama to Kowsalya and Dhasharatha. Likewise Bharatha is born to Dhasharatha's other queen Kaikeyi. And Lakshmana and Shathrugna to queen Sumithra. Great rejoicing at Ayodhya. They are growing up nicely. The King is even contemplating their marriage, when Vishwaamithra arrives at Ayodhya and seeks audience with Dhasharatha (58)

19: The purpose of the sudden visit of Vishwaamithra. He wants the assistance of Raama to protect a Yaaga he is performing at his hermitage (23)

20: Dhasharatha is aghast at this request. Refuses to send Raama with him….. Wrath seizes Vishwaamithra (22)

21: But under the assurance of Vasishta, Dhasharatha agrees to send Raama with Vishwaamithra (23)

From this chapter-to-chapter 73, it is all Vishwaamithra

22: Vishwaamithra leaves Ayodhya with Raama and Lakshmana to his hermitage. On their way, Vishwaamithra teaches Raama, the chant of chants, =Bala and Athi Bala= by which these two princes will never get fatigued, hungry or thirsty (23)

23: Continuing their journey they reach the Kaama hermitage. The story of the Lord of love being burnt by Shiva (23)

24: They go to Thataka forest. The history and geography of Sarayu river described by Vishwaaamithra: also about the demoness Thataka and the territory of Maladha and Karusha. (32)

25: Vishwaamithra wants Raama to kill Thataka at once. Raama being a man of chivalry hesitates. But Vishwaaamithra quotes precedents when evil women had been killed. (24)

26: Raama still hesitates to kill Thaataka. But Vishwaamithra presses him. Raama kills Thaataka (41)

27: Vishwaamithra teaches Raama divine mystic weapons. A long list of weapons. (27)

28: Vishwaamithra teaches the control of these weapons (24).

29: They reach the Sidhdha hermitage of Vishwaamithra. He narrates the story of the incarnation of Vishnu as Vaamana. How Vishnu humbled king Bhali. (54)

30: As Vishwaamithra starts his yaaga at his hermitage, he takes on total Dheeksha (vow of silence, meditation and non violence) and when demons Subaahu and Maareecha start 'playing' their mischief, Raama kills Subaahu and hurls Maareecha miles away (26)

31: After the successful completion of his Yaaga, thanks to Raama, Vishwaamithra decides to take Rama with him to Mithila where king Janaka is performing a yaaga. (24)

32: On the way, as usual, Vishwaamithra narrates many stories. He begins to tell him about the origin of his own family. The family of Kowshiks. Narrates an incident how Lord of Air, misbehaved with 100 daughters of King Kushanaabha. (27)

33: The marriage of these 100 daughters with Brahmadatta, the son of spiritual lady Somadha. He was born to her through the grace of Sage Chooli.(26)

34: Vishwaamithra narrates about his birth to Raama (23)

35: Vishwaamithra continues his narration. Introductory story about Ganges- Uma Parvathy (23)

36: The glory of Uma-Paarvathy. Prelude to the birth of Skandha, son of Shiva (28)

37: Vishwaamithra narrates the birth of Skandha. Ganga bears this divine conception (creation). This 'power' in her womb. Premature birth. Celestial ladies, the Krithikas, breast feed Skandha, thus becomes Kaarthikeya. (34)

38: Vishwaamithra tells Raama about his ancestor Sagara. King Sagara's Ashwamedha yaaga.

39: Sagara's sacred horse stolen by Indra. Obstacle to his Yaga. Sagara sends his 100 sons on search of the horse. These sons, while searching for the horse, molest the earth and innocent inhabitants who complain to Brahma (29)

40: Vishwaamithra continues. Sagara's sons search more thoroughly. They rip open the earth, go up to the under worlds. Molest every one on mere suspicion. By Vishnu's power and grace, through Kapila, these 100 sons are reduced to ashes. (30)

41: Sagara sends his grandson Amshumaan on a search of the horse and his 100 sons. Sagara sees his uncles reduced to ashes at Paathaala. Returns with the stolen horse. Sagara's Yaga is then completed (28)

42: Vishwaamithra continues narration. As only the Ganges can purify and resurrect the 100 sons reduced to ashes, Amshumaan tries to bring the Ganges from heaven. Fails. His son Dhileepa also fails after penance (25)

43: The Descent of Ganges. How Bhageeratha brings the Ganges down from heaven, on to earth and then to underworld. where his ancestors were burnt to ashes.

44: Bhageeratha performs rituals over the ashes of his ancestors with the waters of Ganges. They go to heaven. (20)

45: Vishwaamithra narrates yet another story when they reach Vishaala territory. The churning of the milky ocean for Nectar, using Vasooki as rope and Mandara Mountain as churning rod. During churning, the mountain- rod sinks and .God Vishnu incarnating as a Tortoise, lifts this up and churning is continued. Description of all that came forth of this churning. Finally Nectar. (57)

46: Yet another story. The creation of Maruth-s. Lord Indra's criminal and cruel act (23)

47: The story, the history of Vishaala region.(22)

48: Story of Ahalya, how her husband sage Guathama cured her to become stone for 1000 years, because of her affair with Indra (38)

49: Vishwamithra leads Raama through this territory with a purpose. He knows that Raama's very presence will resuurrect Ahalya. Ahalya rises from stone and rejoins her husband sage Gauthama (24).

50: Vishwaamithra accompanied by Raama and Lakshmana reaches Mithila. They are welcomed by King Janaka and his minister Shathaanandh. As Shathaanandh is the son of Ahalya and Gauthama, he is very eager to know about his father and mother from Vishwaamithra. Vishwaamithra tells him that his parents are happily re-united. (28)

From chapters 51 to 65 Shathaanandh narrates about Vishwaamithra, about his greatness as a man of penance and tells Raama that he is indeed most fortunate and blessed that he has Vishwaamithra as his Guru.

51: Shathanandh begins story of Vishwaamithra, of his being a mighty king once, his meeting with Vasishta (28)

52: Vasishta extends hospitality to Vishwaamithra when he visied his hermitage as a king with his army. Vasishta's holy cow Kaamadhenu prepares a great feast! (23)

53: When Vishwaamithra was astounded by the hospitality extended byVasishta in the forest, and coming to know that the divine cow Kaamadhenu-shabala- had arranged all this, Vishwaamithra abusing his hospitality, 'requests' sage Vasishta to barter away this 'cow' to him for a price! And sage Vasishta refuses (25)

54: Beginning of enmity between 'king' Vishwaamithra & sage Vasishta. Vishwamithra tries to seize the cow (23)

55: When Vishwaamithra tries to abduct, the divine cow Kaamadhenu, with the permission of SageVasishta, 'creates' an army. 'King' Vishwaamithra's army is routed! (28)

56: The infuriated, Vishwaamithra does rigorous penance to obtain boons- knowledge of Dhanur-Vedha- weapons. His sole aim is to attack Vasishta. And with the knowledge of these weapons, when he again attacks Vasishta, he is totally humiliated. (24)

57: 58: 59: Convinced that real power is not in conventional but divine weapons, he again does rigorous penance. It goes to waste because of Thrishanku. This man was a forefather of Raama who wanted to go to heaven with his human body. He approached Vasishta who told him that none could go to heaven in human form. Then he approached Vasishta's sons to do a yaaga for him so that his 'passion' would be fulfilled. They not only ridiculed him but cursed him to be an Untouchable. In this state, he approached Vishwaamithra to do yaaga for him as he knew that Vishwaamithra would take this as a challenge against his enemy Vasishta. Vishwaamithra is only too happy to settle scores with his enemy. He agrees to use the power of his penance to send Thrishanku to heaven as he wished. He curses Vasishta's sons (23,24,22)

60: By the power of his penance Vishwaamithra tries to send Thrishanku to heaven He creates a 'world' for him in the ethereal region when Indra kicked Thrishanku from heaven. He had 'created' a new heaven! But the point is Vishwaamithra, had wasted his penance. (35)

61:62: Vishwaamithra does penance again. But again he wastes this when he tries to save one Shunashepa who was offered as a sacrifice by king Ambareesha for the yaaga he was doing. Vishwaamithra saves him by the power of his penance. Again his objective is lost. (23,28)

63: And more rigorous penance for Vishwaamithra. Again he wastes it by his affair with damsel Menaka (26)

64: Again more rigorous penance. When Indra sends Ramba to put obstacles to his penance, he simply curses her. Again penance wasted (20)

65: Finally, Vishwaamithra does a penance unparalleled in history of penance. Without food, taking very few breaths of air he does such a penance, that even the celestial world is dismayed. Vishwaamithra by now had given up wrath and enmity not only towards Vasishta but to all. Brahma appears before him and blesses him with Brahma Rishi title, the highest honour. Vasishta, also a Brahma Rishi, honours Vishwaamithra by accepting him as a great sage and Brahma rishi (39)

Janaka's minister Shathaanandh thus described Vishwaamithra's greatness, from a king, to the highest state of Brahmam. Narrated story after story about Vishwaamithra to Raama.

66: Vishwaamithra had brought Raama to Mithila specifically for Raama to take a look at The Bow with king Janaka. Janaka describes the history of the Bow. How mighty warriors could not even 'touch'! And he had offered Seetha as a prize for valour to anyone who could lift it and string it up (27)

67: Vishwaamithra asks Raama to take a 'look' when Janaka brought this to the Council hall. Raama not only lifted the Bow but under the pressure of his arm, breaks this. Janaka who is very happy, offers his daughter Seetha in marriage. Janaka sends news to Raama's father Dhasharatha at Ayodhya through his emissaries. (26)

68: Dhasharatha is happy. Leaves at once with a huge entourage to attend Raama's marriage (22)

69: Dhasharatha arrives at Mithila. Janaka receives him (20)

70: Vasishta describes the lineage of Dhasharatha (45)

71: And Janaka describes his lineage. He affirms to marry Seetha to Raama. (24)

72: Pre- marriage rituals, like Godhaana, performed (25)

73: Marriage at Mithila Raama weds Seetha, Lakshmana weds Oormila. Bharatha weds Maandvi and Shathrugna weds Shruthakeerthi Vasishta performs rituals for the ceremony. (45)

74: After marriage, Dhasharatha along with his newly wed sons leaves Mithila for Ayodhya. But on the way the terrible Brahmin ParashuRaama confronts him (17)

75: ParashuRaama wants a combat with Dhasharatha's Raama He has brought another Bow with him and wants Raama to exhibit his power by wielding this Bow and stringing it up(33)

76: Dhasharatha's Raama not only lifts this Bow but fixes an arrow. A death arrow, ready to be discharged. Parashu Raama accepts defeat and goes away to Himaalyas. (26)

77: Dhasharatha enters Ayodhya. with his marriage party All are happy. The mothers are happy to receive their sons and their wives.(38)

CONTENTS OF SECOND BOOK: AYODHYA KAANDA

Chapter and Contents (slokas in bracket)

1: Dhasharatha describes the qualities of Raaama before his citizens at the Council hall in Ayodhya. Bharatha and Shathrugna are away on holiday (51)

2: Dhasharatha seeks counsel before a large assembly at the council hall. He wants to crown Raama as crown prince and take over from him. They all acclaim this decision and praise Raama (55)

3: Preparation at Ayodhya for Royal coronation. Dhasharatha informs Raama about his decision (50)

4: Fixing the date and time for Raama's coronation. Dhasharatha again talks to Raama and gives him advice on the responsibility he is about to shoulder. Raama's mother Kowsalya is happy (45)

5: Sage Vasishta advises Raama about the observance of vows before coronation. City is cleaned up. Citizens look forward to this great event with joy (26)

6: Raama takes to vows as part of pre-coronation rituals. Citizens pour in at Ayodhya from the kingdom (28)

SETBACK TO RAAMA'S CORONATION

7: Hunch back Manthara, the evil-minded confidante of queen Kaikeyi enters the scene. Wants to stop Raama's coronation and make Kaikeyi's son Bharatha the successor instead. (36)

8: Manthara disturbs Kaikeyi's mind. Although Kaikeyi loved her 'step' son Raama, Manthara poisons her mind, 'works' on her. She tells Kaikeyi that if Raama is crowned she and her son Bharatha will be reduced to 'slavery'

9: Kaikeyi succumbs. Manthara has a strategy by which Kaikeyi's son Bharatha can become 'king' and Raama sent out. She reminds Kaikeyi of the two unused boons she had received from Dhasharatha long ago. Time for asking for the fulfillment of these two boons is 'here and now'. By the first boon, Kaikeyi must press her husband to banish Raama from the kingdom for 14 years. By the second boon, Bharatha must be crowned immediately. And Manthara advises Kaikeyi that she should leave her palace apartments and enter the house of Sorrow instead to receive Dhasharatha (66)

10: Dhasharatha enters. Is terribly agitated to see Kaikeyi lying down in the House of Sorrow. Not realising what is in store for him, he assures Kaikeyi he will do anything for her, as he cannot tolerate to see her like this (40).

11:Having got such an assurance, Kaikeyi demands these two boons. Raama to go & Bharatha crowned (29)

12: A long chapter. Dhasharatha is aghast. He curses his beloved wife Kaikeyi. He will never send away Raama. Tries hard to persuade her not to press with these cruel demands. Uses Carrot-Stick technique But Kaikeyi threatens to commit suicide if refused (115)

13: Dhasharatha again tries to persuade her. (27)

14:Dhasharatha curses Kaikeyi again. His effort to change her mind in vain. This night had been one of horror for Dhasharatha. And .Kaikeyi is firm. And all arrangements for Raama's coronation in the morning completed. Minister Sumanthra makes an early morning call on king Dhasharatha.He is unaware of the 'drama' at night.Kaikeyi asks Sumanthra to fetch Raama at once. (69)

15: Sumanthra enters Raama's palace. Early morning. and everything ready for the coronation of Raama. (50)

16: Raama leaves at once to meet his father and Kaikeyi As Raama goes along the royal boulevard, every where vast crowds have already gathered to witness his coronation. (48)

17: As Raama enters his father's palace, all extoll him and offer him blessings (22)

18: As Raama enters the inner apartment, he is horrified to see his father in such a state, particularly as his coronation is to take place in a few hours. Worrying about his father's health, he asks his stepmother Kaikeyi. It is then Kaikeyi tells Raama about the midnight 'drama' and her boons by which Raama must go and Bharatha must take over (41)

19: Without a second thought Raama agrees to go on exile to make way for his brother Bharatha. He assures her that he will leave Ayodhya at once after taking leave of his mother and Seetha. (40)

20: Raama informs his mother Kowsalya. There is no coronation for him but only 14 years of exile. Kowsalya is terribly upset. Without Raama she cant live! Even her husband may not care for her without him. (55)

21: Lakshmana, who was with Raama will not take this lightly. Will use force against his father if need be to restrain him from sending Raama on exile. Will see to it Raama's coronation takes place! But Raama is firm. He will abide by his father and 'mother' Kaikeyi and fulfill their wishes. An important chapter Raama expounds Dharma of Truth. When his mother Kowsalya threatens to accompany him to the forest, Raama advises her that as a good wife, her place is with her husband at Ayodhya. (65)

22: Important chapter. Raama expounds a Truth: The ways of fate and destiny. (30)

23: But Lakshmana is angry. Can't accept Raama's decision to go one exile. Has scant regard for the so-called fate! But Raama affirms. Swears by Truth. Will obey father's command. Will go on exile (42)

24: Raama enlightens his mother Kowsalya. Consoles his mother crying. When Kowsalya realises that nothing will stop his son Raama who is bound by his Dharma, she accepts reality (36)

25: Kowsalya, being a deeply religious woman, then invokes all the deities and blesses Raama. (47)

26: Trying to take leave of Seetha after informing her about the midnight drama, and about his resolve to go on exile immediately, Raama gives Seetha advice as to how she should be at Ayodhya during his exile. (38)

27: But Seetha is determined to go along with Raama. She begs of him to take her also. (23)

28: Raama does not want a young girl to suffer forest life. He talks about difficulties of life in forest (26)

29: But Seetha is no timid girl. She must go with her husband. Treats these difficulties enumerated by Raama as of no consequence to her. (26)

30: Raama has no choice. Seetha is determined to go with him. And she had presented her case strongly! She is a strong personality. She even taunts Raama (47)

31: And like Seetha. Lakshmana cannot be denied. He also must go with Raama because for Lakshmana Raama is everything in life. (35)

32: Raama's total detachment to royal life is revealed. He gives up his private possessions and wealth as he is going to live as a mendicant in forest for 14 years. There is a very interesting episode- The Thrijata episode. Raama indulges in jest to bring home a Truth. (45)

33: Raama, accompanied by Seetha and Lakshmana go to bid farewell to his father and other mothers. Citizens wail. They all curse Kaikeyi. But Raama is firm (31)

34: Dhasharatha swoons on seeing Raama. Dhasharatha wants all his wives to be present when Raama leaves. He even begs Raama to countermand his order and refuse to go on exile. But Raama will never make his father a man of untruth. Even if it is hard on Dhasharatha, he must stand by his commitment to Kaikeyi through the two boons. A long chapter, this. (61)

35: Dhasharatha's friend and minister Sumanthra could not stand it! He censures Kaikeyi. He even talks about her mother who was driven away by her father when she became wicked. But Kaikeyi is adamant (37)

36: Now it is the turn of another wise minister, Sidhdhaartha. He tries hard to dissuade Kaikeyi from using her boons this way. But she is unmoved. (31)

37; Raama's acceptance of forest life is total. He discards Royal dress. When Seetha is also forced to wear a forest dress before leaving, the entire assembly shivers. Vasishta insists that Seetha will go with Raama fully dressed like a princess. (37)

38: Before leaving, Raama particularly prays for his mother Kowsalya. He begs of his father to be considerate to her during his exile. (38)

39: Finally Raama leaves. Dhasharatha orders Sumanthra to take Raama, Seetha and Lakshmana on a chariot and leave them in forest. Kowsalya enlightens Seetha about the duty of a faithful wife. Ofcourse Seetha needs no such enlightenment, as she is the purest of womanhood. Seetha's rejoinder (41)

40: Noble lady Sumithra gives advice to her son Lakshmana. And as chariot moves along the crowded streets, citizens in terrible anguish, try to follow Raama. Raama wants a quick 'get away' to avoid prolongued agony. But the citizens, who are following, are keeping close to the chariot. They shout at Sumanthra.to go slow and control the horses. Sumanthra is baffled! (51)

41: As Raama leaves with Seetha and Lakshmana, the city of Ayodhya is in turmoil. Every activity stops (20)

42: As he sees his son going away, Dhasharatha wails. And like a common man, goes out into the street to get a glimpse of Raama. Finally he sees only dust engulfing the area caused by the movement of chariot and the vast crowd. He curses Kaikeyi. He renounces her and surprisingly, his son Bharatha as well (35)

43: Raama's mother Kowsalya wails. She thinks she is suffering because of sin in her previous birth. (21)

44: Queen Sumithra is a very wise and noble lady. Her son Lakshmana also is going to be away for 14 years. Yet she consoles Kowsalya.And she extols Raama. (31)

Scenes shifts from Ayodhya

45: The Chariot is moving away from Ayodhya. They are on their way to the forest to begin 14 years exile. Some adventurous citizens follow the chariot. They won't remain in Ayodhya without Raama. They shout at Raama to return. Try to stop the chariot. They reach Thamasa river (33)

46: Raama is distressed to see his citizens like this, leaving their homes. When they are sleepy, resting on banks of Thamasa, .the clever Raama 'tricks' them by driving away deep into the forest fast by a strategy. (34)

47: When the citizens wake up, not finding Raama or his chariot, they reluctantly get back to Ayodhya. (19)

48: At Ayodhya the women folk wail. They curse Kaikeyi and Dhasharatha.They lose interest-their household duties. (37)

49: Raama crosses river Gomathi (18)

50: And on the banks of the Ganges, Raama is greeted by his friend Guha, the chief of hunters. Guha wants to entertain Raama with a small feast. But Raama declines. He is no longer a prince, but an ordinary mendicant. But he wants Guha to take care of the horses. (51)

51: Lakshmana also declines Guha's hospitality like food and the comfort of a nice bed for the night's stay there. He keeps vigil as Raama rests. They converse (27)

52: With the boat provided by Guha, Raama, Seetha and Lakshmana cross the Ganges. Before crossing, Raama requests Sumanthra to get back to Ayodhya with his chariot and convey news about them to Dhasharatha. Sumanthra is upset. He wants to remain with Raama and act as his charioteer. There is a dialogue between these two. But no more chariot or luxuries for Raama. (102)

53: After crossing the river, Raama tells Lakshmana, that as this is their first day without chariot and all and as they begin their exile, they should have no regrets at all. They talk about their folks back home. (35)

54: Raama goes to Bhardhwaja hermitage. He introduces himself and Seetha and Lakshmana as well.to the great sage. He recommends Chithrakoot for their stay.(44)

55: As advised by the sage, they walk up towards Chithrakoot after crossing riverYamuna (35)

56: On their way they meet Vaalmeeki. At Chithrakoot Lakshmana constructs a beautiful cottage. House warming ceremony done (41)

Scene shifts to Ayodhya

57: The minister and charioteer Sumanthra who was 'discharged' and asked to return to Ayodhya by Raama, gets back to Ayodhya and enters the palace. (34)

58: Sumanthra conveys the message from Raama to king Dhasharatha. He tells the king what all Lakshmana had told him and what Seetha spoke to him. (38)

59: Dhasharatha wails as he hears news about Raama from his friend and minister Sumanthra (38)

60: Sumanthra consoles Kowsalya. He assures her that Raama, Seetha and Lakshmana are cheerful. (24)

61: Kowsalya blames her husband Dhasharatha for all this suffering for her and for Raama, Seetha and Lakshmana., little realising how hard it is on him as well (27)

62: Dhasharatha tries to pacify his wife Kowsalya. (20)

Dhasharatha recalls an incident in his early life: A curse

63: Dhasharatha narrates an incident when he was a young prince. On hunt he had accidentally killed a young sage who was taking bath in the river in the darkness of the early morning, thinking it was an animal coming for water. How he was cursed by the father of this sage that he will die due to separation from his own son. (54)

64: Dhasharatha continues the narration of that incident to Kowsalya. The curse comes true. Unable to bear separation from Raama, he passes away at midnight in sleep (80)

65: All the ladies wail as Dhasharatha dies in sleep. (30)

66: As all the four sons are away (Raama and Lakshmana on exile; Bharatha and Shathrugna on holiday) the ministers preserve the body in herbal oil, waiting for a son to return to Ayodhya to do the last rites. (29)

67: What happens when there is no king or a ruler in a kingdom? Vaalmeeki describes. (38)

68: Messengers are sent to fetch Bharatha. Vasishta. Commands Bharatha to return to Ayodhya at once (22)

Scene shifts to city of Rajgriha, his maternal grand father's place, where Bharatha is on holiday

69: Bharatha has no sleep. Something is worrying him, although he does no know his father is dead nor his brother is on exile. He sees a bad dream & is disturbed (21)

70: When messengers arrive at Rajgriha from Ayodhya they merely tell Bharatha that by the command of Vasishta he should return at once. Bharatha takes leave of his uncle and grandfather who present him gifts, plenty. (30)

71: Bharatha enters the city of Ayodhya after a long journey. Is shocked by its 'appearance' (46)

72: Bharatha is in for a shock as he meets his mother Kaikeyi who tells him that his father is dead. And the second shock. Raama driven away from Ayodhya.Kaikeyi advises him not to grieve but take over the kingdom Bharatha swoons (55)

73 &74:: Bharatha censures his mother Kaikeyi Curses her to 'perish' More abuses. Regrets that he was born to her. After performing the last rites for father will bring back Raama. He will never satisfy Kaikeyi's dream (39 &36)

75: Bharatha vows to bring back Raama from the forest cutting short his exile. When Kowsalya 'censures' Bharatha unwittingly, as though he had a hand in her son Raama's exile, Bharatha unable to bear this, showers curses on himself, with a long list of sins (66)

76: Bharatha performs Last rites for his father (24)

77: Bharatha and Shathrugna lament (26)

78: Unable to tolerate all this Shathrugna, when he sees Manthara, the hunch back, who had done all this mischief, attacks her. Bharatha restrains him. A warrior should never do harm to a woman, evil though she may be (26)

79: After 13 days of Rituals for his father was over, Bharatha, decides to take a huge army- VIP-s, citizens, to go to forest to bring back Raama. (17)

80: For smooth journey to forest from Ayodhya, the route is 'cleared up' by advance party (26)

81: Bharatha goes to the Royal assembly (16)

82: Army gets ready to go to forest Bharatha rejects advice of Vasishta to take over as king (32)

83: Bharatha starts with Army, entourage, for forest (26)

84: Near Shringabaerapura, Bharatha meets Guha, who at first, is suspicious of Bharatha.as he sees a vast army (18)

85: Guha extols Bharatha when he told him the purpose of his visit to the forest with such a huge army (22)

86: Guha talks about Lakshmana, who was so devoted he kept vigil for Raama. (25)

87: Guha talks about Raama who had refused hospitality as he was no longer a prince but a mendicant (23)

88: Bharatha again vows to bring back Raama. If he does not come back he will remain with him in forest (30)

89: Enroute to Bhardhwaaja's hermitage Bharatha crosses the Ganges (23)

90: Bharatha meets sage Bhardhwaaja. The sage makes it known to the world what a noble man Bharatha is (24)

Now comes an interesting event: Bhardhwaaja's feast

91: Realising that Bharatha has come with a huge army and entourage, by his divine power, Bhardhwaaja extends great hospitality to them in his hermitage. Matching the hospitality one obtains in the capital city of Ayodhya. A sage does not cease to be a sage! (84)

92: After the night's stay when his army was entertained to 'wine, women and song' so to speak, Bharatha leaves for Chithrakoot to meet Raama as directed by Sage. (40)

93: Bharatha's search for Raama's hermitage (27)

Scene at Chithrakoot: Raama's hermitage

94&95: Raama is enjoying his stay at Chithrakoot as though he is in Ayodhya. Describes the beauty of Chithrakoot to his wife Seetha. Describes the lovely river Mandakini (27 &20)

96: While Raama was enjoying the scenery, Lakshmana observes the huge army at a distance. He is agitated. Thinks that Bharatha has come with such an army to do harm to Raama and to make sure the kingdom is his! (31)

97: But Raama knows his brother Bharatha. He is certain that Bharatha has come to take him back. (32)

98: Bharatha's search for Raama continues (18)

99: Bharatha sights the hermitage. After stationing his army at a distance, accompanied by Sumanthra and Vasishta, he walks up to the hermitage to meet Raama.A poignant scene as Bharatha sees Raama in the garb of a mendicant. He falls at his feet. So does Shathrugna (42)

100: Raama asks about the welfare of all at Ayodhya. Before Bharatha tells him anything at all, Raama being concerned with the administration of Ayodhya, enlightens Bharatha how he should rule. This is a long and important chapter. Poet Vaalmeeki lists the qualities of good administration (76)

101: Bharatha wails as he listens to Raama's dissertation. Informs him about the death of their father (09)

102: Raama wails, so does Seetha and Lakshmana. They perform WaterRituals for their father. He consoles citizens who had come with Bharatha. (50)

103: Raama and Lakshmana meet the mothers (32)

Chapters 104 to 107 - Dialogue between Raama and Bharatha. Bharatha is determined to get Raama back. And Raama is firm to go through with 14 years exile

104: Raama asks the purpose of Bharatha's visit leaving kingdom 'empty'.Bharatha presses Raama to return And Raama is firm to abide by his father's order (27)

105: An important chapter. Raama will go through 14 years exile to honour his father's commitment to his 'mother'Kaikeyi. Raama backs this up with a dissertation on Dharma and quotes precedents. (46)

106: Bharatha again begs Raama to return and take over the kingdom. Bharatha gives his own reasons (36)

107: But Raama commands Bharatha to get back and rule the kingdom for 14 years as per the command of his mother Kaikeyi. and his father.

Now there is an interesting dialogue between the old and wise Jaabaali, an atheist & Raama (108 & 109 important)

108: To press Raama to return cutting short his exile, Jaabaali, enunciates the ATHEISTIC philosophy (18)

109: Raama condemns Jaabali for such blasphemy. He will obey Dharma, which means that he will obey his father and mother. (40)

110:Vasishta is aghast at Raama's tirade against the wise, old Jaabaali, the atheist. Raama should not treat him with such contempt. Jaabaali knows the origin of species.!To calm down Raama, he narrates Raama's lineage (36)

111: Bharatha is not convinced. He appeals now directly to the citizens who have come along with him and force Raama to get back. He threatens Sathyagraha, made famous by Mahathma Gandhi. (32)

112: Finally he gives up and accepts to rule Ayodhya, as a caretaker, with Raama's Sandals on the throne for inspiration and guidance (31)

113: His mission partially successful Bharatha returns. And he bears 'Raama's sandals as though Raama is before him. When he passes through Bharadwaaja's hermitage the sage blesses him (25)

114:Bharatha returns to Ayodhya.Nothing is the same (31)

115: Bharatha establishes a temporary capital at Nandigram. Crowns Raamaa's Sandals Rules the kingdom only as Raamaa's agent. (27)

Scene shifts back to Raama and his forest life

116: In the forest, the sages there narrate to Rama about their suffering at the hands of demons like Khara (26)

117: Raama leaves Chithrakoot to stay far away in the deep forest. On their way they meet Saptha Rishi- Athri and his wife Anasooya, a woman of penance, (30)

118: Anasooya is curious to know about Seetha. She offers her lovely ornaments and blesses her (54)

119: This is the last chapter in Ayodhya Kaanda. Raama goes to Dhandaka forest to live out his exile. (22)

CONTENTS OF THIRD BOOK: AARANYA KAANDA

Chapter and Contents (slokas in bracket)

1: Sages living in Dhandaka forest seek refuge under Raama. They beg him to offer protection (23)

2: Demon Viradha confronts Raama.He seizes Seetha (26)

3: Viradha is so strong he carries away Raama and Lakshmana. He is beaten up. (26)

4: On hearing that they are Raaama and Lakshmana, Viradha narrates his life. Viradha is buried in a big trench. Viradha attains salvation (32)

5: And a very great sage is awaiting Raama, so to speak. Infact. Lord Indra wants to take him to heaven. This is sage Sharabanga. After meeting Raama, Sharabanga immolates himself and goes up to heaven (40)

6: Raama gives assurance to sages living there that he will offer protection to them, although he is not a prince but a mendicant. It is and will be his purpose (26)

7: Raama then meets sage Sutheekshana. By his spiritual power, he offers Raama heaven and all. Raama will not want all this for the 'taking' He will earn all this by his own Dharma and by service to people. (24)

8: Raama leaves and goes deep into Dhandaka forest under the advice of Sutheekshana (20)

9: Seetha feels that as Raama is no longer a prince but a mendicant

, he should live like one and forget about bow, arrow and sword! Lead a life of non-violence. She even narrates a story to justify her request (33)

10: Raama tells Seetha why he has to bear arms (23)

11: Raama wants to meet the great sage Agasthya, He narrates stories about Agasthya to Lakshmana, How he had destroyed mighty demons like Vaathaaapi and Subaahu. Raama stays with various sages by rotation as their guest. Altogether 10 years pass away. From Agasthya's brother, he gets to know Agasthya's place. (95)

12: Finally Raama meets Agasthya. Agasthya presents Raama a divine bow with endless number of arrows. A sword. and an Armour. He also tells him that when he needs, Lord Indra will send a chariot along with his charioteer Mathaali, to assist him when he fights cruel demons. (40)

13: While Raama was taking leave, Agasthya tells him how fortunate his father is. But Raama says he is fortunate that he has a father like Dhasharatha. Agasthya gives advice to Raama. He must offer protection to these sages. He leaves for Panchavati A long chapter (65)

14: Raama meets celestial bird Jataayu, a friend of his father. Jataayu describes various creations (37)

15: Raama establishes residence in Panchavati. He has high praise for Lakshmana when he constructed a nice abode for them (32)

16: Description of the winter season at Panchavati (44)

An event that changes Raama's life in forest

17: Demoness Shoorpanaka, a cousin sister of Raavana visits Raama's hermitage. She is astounded to see two charming young men. She is captivated by Raama and Lakshmana and makes amorous overtures. She threatens to cut Seetha into bits, first (32)

18: Raama plays a jest. Suggests Lakshmana as ideal husband for Shoorpanaka. Lakshmana refuses. She gets terribly angry. Lakshmana cuts off her nose (26)

19: Shoorpanaka takes her complaint to demon chief Khara. He sends 14 demons to kill Raama. (28)

20: These 14 demons are easily killed by Raama. (27)

21: Shoorpanaka informs Khara about the killing of his 14 demons. She is in rage. Tells him that Raama is no ordinary human being (22)

22: Now Khara along with chiefs Thrisharas and Dhooshana leaves for battle with Raama. (26)

23: On the way Khara sees bad omens (35)

24: After giving instructions to Lakshmana to protect Seetha, Raama goes to fight Khara and his army single handedly. (36)

25: Entire army of 14,000 was annihilated by Raama (49)

26: Raama kills demon chief Dhooshana (39)

27:28: Raama kills Thrishiras (21) and

Raama takes on Khara himself. (33)

29: Raama threatens and fights him (30)

30: Lot of boasting by Khara. But Raama kills him (42)

31: When Khara and the entire army at Dhandaka forest in India was annihilated by Raama single handedly, demon spy Akamapana, rushes to Raavana at Lanka to inform him. He even suggests to his king Raavana that the only way to stop Raama is by a strategem. Raavana should kidnap Seetha. As Raama is passionately in love with her, he will give up his life if he is not able to find Seetha. Raavana flies to India. Meets his demon friend Maareecha who advises him not to go near Raama. Raavana gets back. (50)

32: 33: But Shoorpanaka who is in wrath takes her own complaint to Raavana. She taunts him She reviles him. Tells him that he has no business to remain a king as he is not aware of the calamity at Dhandaka. (25,24)

34: Shoorpanak tells lies about Raama. Goads Raavana to kidnap Seetha and make her his wife. (28)

35: Raavana flies to India and again goes to his friend Maareecha (42)

36: Raavana presses Maareecha for assistance n kidnapping Seetha. He tells him about his strategem to kidnap her. Maareecha taking the magical form of a golden deer should wander near Raama's hermitage and captivate Seetha. Raama will try to capture the 'deer'. Lakshmana also will follow to help Raama. When Seetha is alone, Raavana will kidnap her (24)

37: Mareecha advises Raavana not to go near Raama. Vaalmeeki's famous stanza (26)

38: Maareecha describes Raama's greatness. How Raama had hurled him 1,000 miles away. Warns Raavana that if he faces Raama in hostility, that will be his end (33)

39: Maareecha refuses to help Raavana in his scheme of kidnapping Seetha. So scared is he of Raama! (25)

40: Ravana presses Mareecha to help him by taking on the form of a golden deer and wander around Raama's hermitage to captivate Seetha. Raama will then go after the 'deer'. And Lakshmana also will go out when "deer" Maareecha shouts in a voice resembling Raama's as though Raama is in trouble Then Ravana will kidnap Seetha. And Raavana does not give any choice for Maareecha. If he disobeys him he will kill him rightaway. (40)

41: Maareecha advises Raavana again. But Raavana is firm. So he 'succumbs' to this scheme (20)

42: Maareecha takes on the form of a golden deer. Raavana is delighted. (35)

43: As Maareecha in the form of a golden deer wanders, Seetha is captivated begs Raama to capture this 'deer' as a pet for her. Lakshmana being wise tells Raama that this is no deer but the magic form of a demon. But Raama goes after the deer. Lakshmana stays to protect Seetha (50)

44: Raama goes after this 'deer' (Maareecha the) 'deer draws him away far. Finally Raama kills this deer and skins it. But before 'deer' (Maareecha) is killed, he utters a sound as though Raama is calling for help (28)

A very painful chapter follows Seetha for once loses her composure. Questions integrity, character of Lakshmana

45: Hearing the false alarm, the 'false' call for help as though from Raama, Seetha asks Lakshmana to leave at once to help Raama. But Lakshmana knows that this is only a false voice of Raama. And Raama never needs help.So refuses to leave the hermitage. It is then Seetha starts abusing Lakshmana and this chapter makes painful reading. Lakshmana leaves the hermitage (41)

46: Situation ideal for Raavana at Raama's hermitage. Raavana enters as though he is some brahmin. Posing as Sanyaasi, he talks to Seetha who extends him hospitality. But not for long. He reveals himself (38)

47: Raavana is treated with contempt by Seetha when she comes to know him as abductor. Raavana is stunned by her beauty. Praises her for her beauty! (52)

48: Raavana boasts before Seetha thinking that she will submit to him voluntarily as his wife. (24)

49: Seetha refuses his advances. Raavana uses force to kidnap her. And carrying her off, he flies off in his aerial car to Lanka On way she cries aloud. Sees Jataayu (42)

50: Jataayu watches this gruesome scene. At once goes to rescue Seetha. He attacks Raavana (28)

51: Combat between Jataayu and Raavana. An uneven fight.

Raavana cuts off his wings. Jataayu falls down (47)

52: Seetha wails, Oh Raama, Oh Lakshmana!.Calls for help, invokes deities, (46)

53: As Seetha was being carried away by Raavana; she curses him, calls him a coward Scene described (27)

54: ***Scene shifts to Lanka*** But while they were flying over, Seetha drops her upper garments in the hope some one might find them and carry them to Raama for information.

They reach Lanka. Raavana commissions demon spies to watch over Raama in India (29)

55: Raavana tries to allure Seetha. Takes her through city and apartments to exhibit his glory. But Seetha has heart only for Raama. Raavana deludes himself! (38)

56: As Seetha is adamant and will not submit to him, Raavana gives her 1 year to change her mind. She is taken to nearby Ashoka forest, demonesses guarding her (37)

57: Scene shifts back to India and Raama Raama, after killing deer returns, but sees ill omens on the way to his hermitage. Perhaps Lakshmana also might be out of his hermitage hearing his 'false' call for help, leaving Seetha alone. As feared, he sees Lakshmana on the way. (25)

58: It has happened, as Raama had feared. Seetha was left alone, alas! And he describes Seetha's qualities (20)

59: For once Raama censures his brother Lakshmana.for disobeying his order, coming out of the hermitage, leaving Seetha, alone. Lakshmana told him he had no choice as Seetha had questioned his morality (27)

60: When Raama and Lakshmana reach their hermitage, they find Seetha missing. Raama talks about Seetha.They search for her nearby (40)

61: Search for Seetha begins. They search places where she is likely to go to. Lakshmana suggests they should search Dhandaka forest thoroughly (32)

62: Raama wails unable to find Seetha. So depressed is he that he asks Lakshmana to get back to Ayodhya, as no life is possible for him without Seetha (21)

63: Lakshmana consoles Raama. He instils confidence in Raama. (20)

64: Now Raama is in wrath. He wants to destroy everything around because Seetha is not found and none informs him about her. Long chapter (76)

65: Lakshmana begs Raama to give up wrath. How can Raama destroy everything because of one single painful incident to one individual. It is against Dharma. (19)

66: Lakshman pacifies Raama. As a warrior, Raama should punish the evil doer and retrieve Seetha (20)

67: While on search they see the mortally wounded Jataayu. At first they suspect the noble bird. Jataayu tells them that Raavana had carried away Seetha (29)

68: Raama wails. Performs Last Rites for this bird. Before dying Jataayu assures Raaama that he is sure to retrieve Seetha as the time of kidnapping is bad forRaavana (42)

69: After performing Last rites, they continue their search. They go towards Ayomukh Demoness of Ayomukhi is also killed. Then they see a horrible looking demon Kabandha, confronting them.

70: Demon Kabandha is a horrible figure. He was not a demon by birth but by a curse he became one. As his salvation is at the hands of Raama, he requests him to cut off his hands first (20)

71: When Raama had cut his hands off, Kabandha narrates his story. How he who was handsome looking Dhanu by name, was cursed by rishi Sthoolashiras. But his salvation was when Raama cremated him. (33)

72: They prepare a huge pyre and cremate him. As he goes up, released by curse, Dhanu reveals to Raama that it is Sugreeva who is going to find Seetha for him In revealing the means to find Seetha Dhanu speaks some words of wisdom. (31)

73: And Dhanu (Kabandha) directs the route to Rishymukh where Sugreeva is. And he narrates the story about Sugreeva. While 'going up' he says = Make friendship with Sugreeva = He also advises them to meet Shabari (46)

74: Under advice from Dhanu, Raama visits Shabari. They are treated to hospitality by this tribal woman of penance. By her spiritual power she 'exhibits' even oceans to Raama like in TV. Then she goes to heaven (37)

75: Raama and Lakshmana on their way to meet Sugreeva reach Pampa. (31)

CONTENTS OF THE FOURTH BOOK : KISHKINDHA KAANDA

Chapter and Contents (slokas in bracket)

1: Raama wails on seeing Pampa, as he cannot enjoy the scenery without Seetha. Vaalmeeki's poetry! Lakshmana comforts Raama. Only sustained effort can yield results. Lakshmana is sure they will retrieve Seetha (150)

2: Even as Raama and Lakshmana are wandering over the area, Sugreeva, observing them from the mountaintop at Rishyamukh, gets agitated. Suspects these two are there, sent by his wrathful brother Vaali to do harm to him. So he sends his minister Hanumaan to find about them (29)

3: Taking the form of a Brahmin, monkey Hanumaan meets Raama and Lakshmana even as they are wandering to meet Sugreeva. In a short crisp speech, Hanumaan tells them who he is and for whom he has come to meet them. He narrates how his king Sugreeva is suffering at Rishyamukh being driven away by his brother Vaali from Kishkindha. (40)

4: Raama is happy that the person whom he wanted to meet, that person has sent an emissary to him. What a fortune. Hanumaan now takes them to Rishyamukh (35)

5: Hanumaan introduces them to Sugreeva. Lakshmana tells Sugreeva that his brother seeks refuge under Sugreeva to find his wife Seetha. And Sugreeva is happy that he has a friend in Raama. With Fire as witness Raama and Sugreeva form a treaty of friendship (33)

6: When Raama tells Sugreeva about his wife who was abducted, Sugreeva then exhibits some of the ornaments his monkey chiefs had picked up when these were thrown away during flight by Seetha, not knowing at that time these jewels were those of Raama's wife's. Raama confirms that these are Seetha's. And he wails (27)

7: Sugreeva consoles Raama. Raama requests that he should do everything in his power to search and find out Seetha. Sugreeva tells Raama that although he has also 'lost' his wife, he does not give way to despondency like him. And he is after all a monkey (25)

8: On hearing Sugreeva's tale of woes how he was kicked out of his kingdom by his wrathful brother Vaali who had seized his wife Ruma, Raama resolves to kill Vaali Friendship means helping friend in need (46)

9: Raama is curious to know about the enmity between brothers. Vaali and Sugreeva. Sugreeva narrates all. how he was treated badly by Vaali. (23)

10: For no fault of Sugreeva, Vaali drove him from the kingdom. He even kept his wife Ruma. (36)

11: When Sugreeva tells Raama that unless Vaali is killed he will have no peace. And although Raama had vowed to kill Vaali, it was not such an easy task. Sugreeva narrates stories about Vaali's valour. (95)

12: Ofcourse Sugreeva does not know Raama's power. Raama instills confidence in Sugreeva by the exhibition of his power. Fully satisfied, Sugreeva invites his brother Vaali for a fight. hoping that Raama will come to his aid and kill Vaali.But instead he is thrashed by Vaali. Sugreeva is very bitter that Raama had let him down. But Raama tells him that when the two brothers were fighting he could not fix his arrow on Vaali as they were like twins. So Raama suggests that next time when he goes to fight Vaali, he should wear a garland, which will distinguish him from his brother (44)

13: Raama sees Sapthajana hermitage. Sugreeva narrates about this place, residence of 7 great sages (30)

14: Sugreeva again invites his brother Vaali for a combat This time he is wearing a garland to distinguish him from Vaali. (23)

15: Vali's wife Thaara is a wise woman. She does not want her husband to rush out in haste because she fears that Sugreeva has called him for combat with some support. She has heard that Raama is around. She suggests that Vaali make friendship with Raama and avoid fighting Sugreeva who after all is his own brother (31)

16: But Vaali rejects her advice. He is in wrath. Goes out. When the two brothers are fighting, Raama who was hiding himself behind a tree fixes an arrow and shoots at Vaali. Vaali fall down, mortally wounded (40)

Chapters 17 and 18: A never-ending debate

17:18: Vaali who is about to die censures Raama because he had killed him from behind his back when he was in combat with his brother. Vaali's charges against Raama and Raama's reasons for killing Vaali. These two chapters are to be read together. Even the best legal brain cannot beat the arguments by both Vaali and Raama, one condemning the other for killing and the other justifying the killing, (54 & 69)

19: Hearing of her husband's death, Thaara rushes to the battlefield. Afterall Vaali had ignored her advice (29)

20: Thaara wails on seeing her husband mortally wounded, dying. Vaali was a loving husband (27)

21: Hanumaan consoles Thaara. A very important chapter as Hanumaan expounds philosophy 16)

22: Vaali gives up life. Before he dies, he advises his brother Sugreeva. Infact he presents him the divine golden chain he is wearing. Blood is thicker than water! (33)

23: Again Thaara wails. She asks her son Angadha to take a last look at his father. (31)

24: This time it is Rama who consoles Thaara. Sugreeva is also terribly upset; he thinks only of the good in Vaali Raama expounds the laws of fate (45)

25: Sugreeva performs the Last Rites for his brother Vaali. Vaali cremated with full royal honours. (54)

26: Sugreeva is crowned king of monkeys at Kishkindha. Under advice from Raama, Vaali's son Angadha is crowned crown prince. Raama advises Sugreeva that as it is rainy season he may start the search for Seetha after the season is over. (42)

27: It is now the rainy season. Not conducive for any action.Raama rests in Prasravana hills not far from Kishkindha. Raama expects Sugreeva to honour his commitment in the matter of search (48)

28:Vaalmeeki's poetry as he describes the rainy season (67)

29: After becoming the King of monkeys, Sugreeva gives himself up to 'wine, women and song'. He forgets he has a commitment to Raama in the matter of search for Seetha after the rainy season is over. Hanumaan reminds him that he should not be seen by Raama as a man of ingratitude (35)

30: It is autumn. Poet Vaalmeeki goes poetic (85)

31: Raama is upset that Sugreeva is not doing anything about the search for Seetha. Lakshmana is angry as well. Raama sends him to meet Sugreeva, to remind him and warn him. Angadha informs his uncle Sugreeva (57)

32: Lakshmana is angry. Hanumaan begs Sugreeva to pacify him. If not, the consequences will be disastrous (22)

33: Sugreeva is a clever monkey. He sends Thaara to pacify Lakshmana. Lakshmana tells her why he is angry. Sugreeva has forgotten about his commitment to send an army on search but is indulging in cheap pleasures. Thara is a wise woman. She pacifies him somewhat (66)

34: Lakshmana meets Sugreeva. He warns him of the consequences of ignoring Raama. (19)

35: Thara again tries to pacify Lakshmana, but is taken aback at the vehemence of Lakshmana. (24)

36: Now Sugreeva himself pacifies Lakshmana. assures him about his sincere friendship for Raama. (20)

37: Sugreeva gives order for the assembly of monkeys with their chiefs at Kishkindha from all over They are to be ready for the search for Seetha (37)

38: Sugreeva presents himself before Raama, having made preparations for the search of Seetha. Sugreeva assures Raama. Afterall it is Raama who made him king. Raama is happy when he sees the huge army of search (34)

39: Size and formation of the army announced. This is Sugreeva's army of search for Seetha. (44)

Sugreeva sends armies to four directions on search of Seetha. He also directs them to look out for Seetha, by enlightening them with details of the region.

40: Under Vinatha, an army is sent to search for Seetha in the East. (71)

41: Under the command of Angadha and Hanumaan he sends an army on search for Seetha to South (52)

42: And Sushena with an army is sent to the West (59)

43: Shathbali is sent to the North with a huge army (65)

44: Raama is watching all this. Man of wisdom, he is almost certain that it is Hanumaan who is going to find Seetha. So he gives him his Signet Ring to be handed over to Seetha when Hanumaan finds her. (17)

45: All the armies leave to search for Seetha. (17)

46: Raama expresses his surprise that Sugreeva knows the history and geography of the globe so thoroughly. Sugreeva gives the reason how he came to know (26)

47: After a search of one month, armies from the North, the East and the West return without finding Seetha (15)

48: The Southern army on search. In the caves of Vindhyas (25)

49: Angadha orders a search in the Rajatha mountain (22)

50: The Southern army on search, enter Riksha cave. They see the lady monk Swayamprabha. (41)

51: Swayamprabha extends hospitality in the cave. (19)

52: Hanumaan tells her why they entered the cave. (20)

53: Unable to find Seetha and one month of search having gone by, the monkeys decide to fast unto death, fearing for their lives if they return to Sugreeva without finding the whereabouts of Seetha (40)

54: Hanumaan threatens Angadha that this is no solution. They must continue the search (22)

55: Yet monkeys want to fast unto death. (24)

56: While they were fasting, an old bird Sampaathi which is watching all this is happy that when these monkeys die, he will have a good meal of them all. But hearing his brother Jataayu's name being mentioned by the monkeys, Sampaathi talks to Angadha (25)

57: Angadha narrates all to Sampaathi. Tells him about their mission of finding Seetha for Raama. (20)

58: Sampaathi indicates that Seetha is in Lanka, carried away by Raavana. (37)

59: Narrates how his son Supaarswa saw Raavana carrying Seetha off to Lanka (30)

60: Sampaathi narrates his own story (21)

61: How his feathers were burnt up when he and his brother Jataayu, when they were young, flew to reach the Sun. How he has no mobility now (17)

62&63: Sampaathi continues. How sage Nishaakara told him that he will get back his wings when he did service for Raama by informing about Seetha And Sampaathi gets new wings. (16 and 16)

64: Armed with information, the monkey army goes to far south and face the ocean at the 'tip' of India How to cross over the ocean, 1000 miles into Lanka (25)

65: Who has the capability to fly 1,000 miles and return. Monkey chiefs talk about their capability in flying (35)

66: The old wise Jaambavaan knows. If there is one person who can do this, it is Hanumaan for certain. He goads Hanumaan. The entire army requests him so to speak (40)

67: Hanumaan is happy and exhilarated. He climbs over the peak of Mahendra mountain in the southern tip of India.

He is ready for the Take off. Ready to fly 1,000 miles to Lanka. Not only that.He roars that he will uproot Lanka if need be to find Seetha (53)

CONTENTS OF THE FIFTH BOOK: SUNDHARA KAANDA

Chapter and contents (with slokas in bracket)

1: If Vaalmeeki has devoted 228 slokas for this chapter it is understandable. He describes the remarkable solo flight of Hanumaan over the ocean. Hanumaan meets with a lot of obstacles during the flight, but he overcomes them (228)

2: Reaching Lanka late in the evening, Hanumaan takes a full view of Lanka from the Lamba mountaintop. He is astounded by the beauty of Lanka.Hanumaan ponders (58)

3: The city is guarded by a Spirit--This lady protector is of immense strength. Hanumaan overcomes her who tells him that Hanumaan will succeed in his mission (52)

4: Search for Seetha begins. Hanumaan, in the form of a tiny monkey wanders around. He is surprised that in the demon land Vedha recitations are heard (31)

5: Hanumaan takes a good look at the demons and all (27)

6: Hanumaaan enters Raavana's abode. And 'sees' the mansions of other demon chiefs (46)

7:8: Hanumaan sees the divine Aircraft-Airstation Pushpak.which Raavana snatched away from Kubhera.He takes a good look (17 and 8)

9: Pushpak! Hanumaan is wonderstruck. He sees lovely ladies fast alseep after a night of pleasure. Vaalmeeki devotes a long chapter describing all this. Raavana's harem is very large! (75)

10: Searching for Seetha, he sees queen Mandodhari. For a moment thinks that she may be Seetha. Sees Raavana asleep. And many more ladies around him. (55)

11: Hanumaan realises that Mandodhri cannot be Seetha and he searches the Banqueting Hall for Seetha. He is sad that at the dead of the night, he intrudes into the privacy of womenfolk. But consoles himself that he is seeing women for the sake of a pure woman Seetha.(48)

12: Not finding Seetha, Hanmaan is depressed. (25)

13: Hanumaan is crestfallen. He had combed most parts of the city but Seetha is not found. He even thinks of 'suicide' or a life of a vagabond. But Hanumaan is no ordinary monkey. Resolves to search thoroughly (73)

14: Hanumaan searches the Ashoka forest nearby. Reasons that she may be there. Looks around from the tree top, hoping to find Seetha. (52)

15: At last Hanumaan finds Seetha.. Hanumaan is distressed as he sees Seetha surrounded by demonesses acting as guards, sitting under a tree. He is sure it is Seetha because she was in a pitiable state, thinking only about Raama, wearing a single garment to protect her body. Her other garments were hung up on the branches of a tree which Hanumaan could identify as hers (55)

16: Hanuman grieves over Seetha. Fate can never be overcome, even a divine lady has to undergo suffering Wonders how Raama can live without her (32)

17: Hanumaan takes a look at all these demonesses guarding her. Demonesses of all description (33)

18: While Hanumaan was watching Seetha, unseen, from a tree, Raavana makes a visit to the Askoka forest to press Seetha to accept him as her husband. (33)

19: It was a terrible sight as Hanumaan sees Seetha before Raavana. Vaalmeeki brings out the contrast between Seetha the pious good lady and Raavana (23)

20: Raavana tries to allure Seetha. Promises her all the luxury, almost everything she may desire. (36)

21: But Seetha rejects him totally. Treats him with contempt. Advises him to turn away his mind from her. Only Raama is her husband. Raavana can never be (35)

22: Raavana uses the carrot and stick technique. Any other woman, he would have killed her at once. Raavana fails. He gives her two months time to change her mind. If she is adamant he will make a meal of her for breakfast before leaving he asks demonesses to change her mind (47)

23: Demonesses 'work' upon Seetha by threats and sweet words to change her mind (22)

24: The demonesses threaten to kill Seetha if she does not obey Raavana. Seetha cries (48)

25: Seetha wails. Feels that she must have committed a lot of sins in her previous birth to suffer all this (20)

26: Seetha remembers service of Jataayu. She is wondering whether Lakshmana will know about her place now. She feels she must somehow end her life. She goes philosophical. (51)

27: When Seetha was wailing before her guards, these demonesses again began to harass her. But one good demoness Thrijata began to describe a dream she had seen that indicated good for Seetha and ruin for Raavana (67)

28: As no other means are available for Seetha to escape from this suffering Seetha contemplates choking herself to death with her long hair. (20)

29: Suddenly Seetha sees some good omens (8)

30: Hanumaan was watching all this from behind the branches of a tree, unseen. He ponders. Feels time is ripe for him to draw Seetha's attention. But how to do it without gruesome guards noticing it. Strategy. By singing about Raama in low voice, Seetha's attention will be drawn (45)

31: In a low voice Hanumaan 'sings' Rama's story. When the guards are somewhat sleepy. Seetha looks up (21)

32: When Seetha hears the story of Raama being sung, she wonders. Perhaps this monkey is a spy sent by Raavana. Or perhaps this is a dream. (14)

33: Hanumaan begins to talk gently. Making sure she is really Seetha, although he tells her that by her appearance she must be Seetha. Seetha tells him who she is (32)

34: Seetha is amazed. Feels that her patience is rewarded. But warns Hanumaan that if he is really a spy of Raavana she will not talk to him. Hanumaan to build confidence in her, talks about Raama, Lakshman, Sugreeva (41)

35: To make sure that Seetha will accept him as an emissary of Raama, Hanumaan describes the personality of Raama, his physical attributes. Interesting chapter (90)

36: When Hanumaan had left Kishkindha, Raama had given his signet ring as a token of remembrance for Seetha.Now

Hanumaan hands over this to Seetha. Seetha's joy is indescribable. Tells him that he is no monkey. She talks to him freely (47)

37: Hanumaan suggests that Seetha, to save herself from further agony, should accept his offer of carrying her back on his shoulders to India and Raama. Seetha rejects this but with a rather cruel remark. Hanumaan is terribly hurt. He exhibits a mighty =Vishwa roopa= form. Seetha realises her mistake. But she wants only Raama to come and get her and exhibit his valour (66)

38: Hanumaan wants to get back to India and report to Raama. Seetha narrates various incidents in her life with Raama that Raama should recall when Hanumaan gets back to him. And she hands over a jewel= Choodaamani= to be handed over to Raama by Hanumaan. (73)

39: Seetha is still crying now and then. Hanumaan consoles her that Raama will soon come over to Lanka along with Sugreeva and a huge army and retrieve her. But she wonders how Raama and Lakshmana will cross over 1,000 miles. How will a monkey army cross this distance? Hanumaan assures her. They will come, all of them (54)

40: Seetha gives leave for Hanumaan to go back. (25)

41: Hanumaan feels he has still some 'unfinished' business in Lanka.He wants to draw attention of Raavana and to give him a sort of ultimatum. Destroys Ashoka forest (21)

42: When news reaches Raavana, he is in wrath. He sends terrible demons, the Kimkaras to capture Hanumaan, dead or alive. Hanumaan destroys all of them (43)

43: Hanumaan roars. Victory roars for his king Sugreeva! The roar is heard. (27)

44: Raavana sends Jambumaali. Hanumaan kills him (24)

45: Raavana is terribly disturbed. Sends sons of some ministers. Hanumaan kills them all (17)

46: Raavana now sends five of his army chiefs. Hanumaan after a fierce combat kills them all as well (39)

47: Now Raavana sends his son Aksha, a very brave warrior and a highly 'cultivated' person. Even he is killed by Hanumaan who had to put in all his 'strategy'. Even the celestials watching this from heaven are wonderstruck (39)

48: Raavana has no alternative but to send his most brilliant son, Inderjith. He advises him that he should not treat Hanumaan with contempt as though he is an ordinary monkey. Inderjith uses The Weapon = Brahma Asthra=

Hanumaan, although blessed by Brahma Himself, voluntarily submits himself for seizure (62)

49: Hanumaan is bound by ropes and dragged to Ravana's palace In broad daylight he sees the opulence of Raavana.He is wonderstruck (20)

50: When Hanumaan was 'presented' before Raavana who was very angry, he is questioned by Prahastha. (20)

51: Hanumaan addresses Raavana. He had come to Lanka to find about Seetha whom he had kidnapped. He has come from Sugreeva and his purpose is for Raama. He gives advice to Raavana. To return Seetha back to Raama and surrender to him. He would have crushed Lanka himself, but has no mandate from Sugreeva or Raama. And Raama surely will destroy Lanka soon!.(45)

52: Raavana not only rejects his advice but in great wrath orders his punishment with death. But his brother Vibheeshana advises him not to do so as it is against norms to kill an emissary or ambassador (33)

53: For once Raavana accepts advice. But he must offer Hanumaan some punishment as he had humiliated him. So orders setting fire to his tail and thus maim him. His tail is set fire to. (43)

54: With fire on his tail, Hanumaan goes on the rampage. But Hanumaan sets fire to the mansions of various chiefs and destroys gardens, forests, around. There is total chaos in Lanka. Every one is crying (52)

55: Suddenly a thought seizes him. In his indiscriminate arson, perhaps Seetha might also have been burnt. up. But soon stops worrying and gives up this fear. After all-even fire on his tail has not burnt him up because the Lord of wind, his foster father, had blown icy wind over it. Fire cannot prevail over Fire (Seetha) (34)

56: After meeting Seetha and bowing to her Hanumaan flies back to India, having fulfilled his mission (34)

57: Hanumaan reaches the southern 'tip' of India, where his army is waiting for his return on the shores of the mighty ocean. He is warmly greeted by them. Angadha extols him. (52)

58: Naturally the entire army is eager to know all about Hanumaan's mission to Lanka. Hanumaan in this long chapter describes in detail all his exploits (166)

59: Hanumaan concludes his narration by describing about Seetha's pitiable condition as prisoner at lanka (16)

60: Angadha, Jaambavaan deliberate about further action. Jaambavaan advises Angadha they should get back to Sugreeva at once and convey news about Seetha (23)

61: On their way this Southern army of search for Seetha under Angadha passes through a Wine-Madhu forest owned by Sugreeva. The monkeys are on a drinking spree, as part of the Victory celebration. They beat up guards (23)

62: The guards protecting this forest are beaten up as the monkeys are on the rampage. Even the wise Hanumaan gives his monkeys a free hand to drink as much as they like. The guards dont like this (40)

63: The chief guard of Sugreeva's Madhu forest takes his complaint to Sugreeva, how his army is ravaging his favourite garden. (29)

64: Instead of getting angry, Sugreeva is extremely happy as he knows Hanumaan has found Seetha by this army's victory celebration. His army is entitled to such an orgy after completing his mission successfully. The army is asked to return by message sent through the chief of guards And Sugreeva is happy to announce that it is Hanumaan who has found Seetha The army returns to headquarters. (41)

65: Hanumaan hands over the ornament Choodamani that was given to him at Lanka by Seetha. His narration.to

Raama about what all Seetha said to him before he left Lanka. Raama wails (27)

66: Raama listens further, what all Seetha told Hanumaan finally (15)

67: And Hanumaan tells what finally Seetha told him and how he consoled her before he left (37)

68: Hanumaan concludes his narration about his visit to Lanka. He describes the plight of Seetha. And what all he had told her finally to console her and assure her that she will be retrieved by Raama with the help of Sugreeva and his army of monkeys (29)

CONTENTS OF THE SIXTH BOOK: YUDHDHA KAANDA

Chapter and Contents (with slokas in bracket)

1: Raama while extolling Hanumaan, differentiates between three types of men. (19)

2: Hearing about the plight of Seetha from Hanumaan, Raama wails. Sugreeva comforts him (26)

3: Raama asks about the defences of Lanka. Hanumaan describes Lanka (35)

4: Accompanied by Sugreeva and his army, Raama reaches the southern 'tip' of India and face the mighty ocean. The entire army is on the move. Raama and Lakshmana are carried on their shoulders by Hanumaan and Angadha. Vaalmeeki describes the army on move A long chapter (125)

5: Again Raama wails, seeing the ocean confronting him. It is Lakshmana who consoles Raama (23)

6: Scene shifts to Lanka As the huge army under Sugreeva and Raama reach the Southern tip of India, Raavana gets news at Lanka. He is worried and he seeks ministerial counsel. (20)

7: All his chiefs who should know the reality of the situation merely flatter Raavana, as though there can never be danger to him from any one (26)

8: Raavana's chief, demon Prahastha speaks. Then Dhurmukha and Vajradhamshtra. They assure him that Raama is no match for Raavana (24)

9: But Raavana's youngest brother Vibheeshana alone tenders advice that would be good for Raavana and Lanka.

War should be avoided. Seetha must be given back (24)

10: Vibheeshana again goes to Raavana to advise him privately. Tells Raavana to give up Seetha and make peace with Raama. Raavana is unmoved (30)

11: Raavana is worried though. He again seeks counsel. All important demon chiefs deliberate in the Council hall (32)

12: Raavana's other brother Kumbhakarna gives him some advice, although he is angry with Raavana who had abducted Seetha without realising the consequences of his action. But, if there is war, he will fight for Raavana (42)

13: Demon chief Mahaapaarswa flatters Raavana. Raavana discloses a curse on him by which if he rapes a woman, his head will be split up at once (21)

14: Again Vibheeshana advises Raavana to seek peace by returning Seetha to Raama (22)

15: When Vibheeshana presses Raavana to seek peace by returning Seetha to Raama, Inderjit, the brilliant son of Raavana abuses his uncle (14)

16: Now, having been flattered by one and all excepting Vibheeshana, Raavana is angry with him. So angry, that he would have even killed his brother Vibheeshana for such 'wrong' advice. Vibheeshana feels no useful purpose will be served by his remaining with Raavana.. Along with five of his chiefs, he defects to Raama. They surrender to Raama who has stationed himself on the shores of the ocean with a huge army ready to invade Lanka (69)

17: First war casualty for Raavana! Vibheshana along with his five chiefs goes over to Raama.and seeks refuge under him. He introduces himself. But Sugreeva and others consider him a spy from the enemy camp. (69)

18: As Raama hears Vibheeshana and also the views of Sugreeva and others, Hanumaan and he alone feel that Vibheeshana should be given asylum. Raama goes against the views of Sugreeva and others, accepts Vibeeshana (40)

19: Almost the first action of 'enemy' Vibheeshana after his 'surrender' is to give sound advice to Raama. When they wonder how the army is going to cross the ocean to invade Lanka, Vibheeshana asks Raama to seek the favour of the Lord of Ocean through prayer, for safe passage. Raama accepting his advice lies on a bed of grass to pray (44)

20: Scene shifts back to Lanka Hearing through his spies that Raama is ready for invasion, clever Raavana thinks he can create dissension in Raama's army. So sends message to Sugreeva, telling him that unlike Raama he is his friend, and should not fight for Raama. Spies inform Raavana that Sugreeva treated him with contempt (36)

21: Scene shifts back to India When Raama's prayers are not answered by the Lord of Ocean, Raama takes on wrath. Raama's wrath is not like others. The Lord of Ocean appears before him. Gives passage to build a bridge (37)

22: Building of the bridge under Nala's supervision. Long chapter. Description of the 1,000 mile long bridge (91)

23: On this wonderful bridge the army easily crosses over 1,000 miles into Lanka (16)

24: Raavana does not see the 'writing on the wall. He only flatters himself Raama and his army no match for him! (46)

25: Spies Shuka and Sharana advise Raavana to seek peace with Raama even at this time. They were caught by Vibheeshana and handed over to Raama when they were spying Sugreeva's army for the sake of Raavana. But the noble soul Raama had released them. (35)

26: From the mountain top, Raavana takes an 'aerial view' of the vast Army of Sugreeva that is on the outskirts of Lanka. Ready for war. Asks his spy Shuka about them (53)

27: And spy Sharana points out to Raavana about the various chiefs in Sugreeva's army, their valour (49)

28: The army of monkeys of Sugreeva is so vast that Vaalmeeki estimates it in a systematic way using the metric system and using the power of ten. Interesting reading (45)

29: And Raavana being worried sends spy Shardoola to find out about the enemy, the happenings there (33)

30: Spy Shardoola returns without finding much. Tells his king that this army cannot be spied upon (36)

31: Raavana being a coward, a warrior only before some, feels that by stupefying Seetha, he can get her! And once Seetha becomes his, Raama will give up the fight and run away! Prouduces a "head" of Raama by magic. With magic Bow resembling Raama's. Seetha is stupefied (49)

32:Seetha wails thinking Raama is dead. Raavana presses her to become his mistress. But Raama is very much alive Raavana rushes to his council hall. (44)

33: Even in demon land you find some good women. One such is demoness Sarama who sees Seetha as her friend! She consoles her saying that Raavana was trying to dupe her through this magical 'head' of Raama. Raama is certainly not killed (41)

34: And Sarama tells her about Raavana's intentions. She informs Seetha about happenings in Raavana's camp (29)

35: Maalyavaan, uncle to Raavana's mother, gives him sound advice. Even as war is at the door step, it is not too late. Seetha may be given back to Raama. Make peace, he says. But Raavana will have none of this (43)

36: Raavana rejects advice. Discusses the Defence of Lanka.against invasion (23)

37: At Raama's camp The Army formation. All monkeys, although they can take on any form they pleased must fight as monkeys. Only Raama, Lakshmana, Sugreeva and Angadha will fight as men. (41)

38: Now Raama takes a look at Lanka from the top of Suvela mountain. Along with Vibeeshana, Sugreeva and monkey chiefs, he takes a look (21)

39: The sight of Lanka from a distance stuns Raama Its opulence. (31)

40: A strange occurrence! Without informing Raama or taking his permission, Sugreeva jumps from the mountain cliff and goes to Raavana and fights a combat. And returns.

Raama chides him for this reckless act. Wars are not won by skirmishes (34)

41: Raama being a man of Dharma officially sends an ultimatum to Raavana through prince Angadha. If Raavana does not restore Seetha to him, he and his Lanka will be destroyed by him and his army. Long chapter. Raavana not only disregards the ultimatum, he tries to seize this ambassador Angadha (104)

42: War begins. Between monkeys and bears on Raama's side and demons on Raavana's side. (48)

43: Various combats described. Monkey chiefs with demon chiefs. Monkeys with demons and so on. (48)

44: Even at night war continues. This is against Geneva, sorry, war conventions prevailing at that time. But demons are very brave at night. Celestials watch the war from the sky, unseen (46)

45: The brilliant Inderjith, son of Raavana binds Raama and Lakshmana with Reptile-=Naaga= Asthra -weapon. They are immobilised and are down on earth (29)

46: Grief seizes Sugreeva and others as they see Raama and Lakshman down..Monkey army is in disarray. Vibheeshana consoles Sugreeva. Raama and Lakshmana are not dead but inactive for time being. But Inderjith rushes to inform his father about this 'victory' (51)

47: Raavana is excited. His first reaction is that Seetha must take a look at her husband's plight. Seetha is taken on Pushpak aerial car and exhibited. (26)

48: Seetha wails as she sees Raama down, from the aerial car. But her friend demoness Thrijata consoles her saying Raama is just immobilised, not dead (41)

49: Raama wakes up. But he is aghast to see Lakshmana down and in pain due to Naaga weapons=asthra. Infact tells Sugreeva that no useful purpose is served for him any more as Lakshmana is in a state of dying. Raama thanks Sugreeva for services he had rendered and asks him to go back without continuing the war (35)

50: Even Vibheeshana is disheartened to see Raama and Lakshmana in that state. Lot of confusion. But the King of birds, Celestial Garuda, comes there and releases them from the effects of the =Naaga=Repitile=weapon. Before leaving Garuda gives advice to Raama (60)

51: Raavana is surprised that Raama and Lakshmana are alive! He sends chief Dhoomraaksha to battle (40)

52: After a fierce fight Hanumaan kills Dhoomraaksha (41)

53:54: Battle with demon chief Vajrdhamshtra. He is killed by prince Angadha after a terrific fight ((35,40)

55:56: Now the great demon warrior enters the battlefield He is Akampana. Hanumaan kills him (33,39)

57:58 Demon chief Prahastha enters fight. A terrible combat ensues between Neela and the demon. Ultimately the demon is killed by Neela ((48,67)

59: Raavana makes a visit to the battlefield when he finds some of his brave chiefs are killed. He is in wrath as he leaves for battlefield. Vows to kill Raama. Vibeeshana points out Raavana to Raama. Hanumaan has a duel with

Raavana. Lakshmana fights him. Finally Raama confronts his enemy Ravana. And Raama humiliates Raavana in combat asking him to return in better health! (157)

60: When Raavana was humiliated by Raama thus who as a man of chivalry had allowed him to retreat, he is in real fear. Feels the time had come to wake up his brother Kumbhakarna and ask him to take on Raama. It is not so easy to wake up Kumbakarna. Raavana commissions tough demons to wake him up and bring him. Scene described. Finally Kumbakarna wakes up, refreshes himself with wine and food. (106)

61: As Kumbakarna goes upto meet his brother king Raavana, Vibheeshana describes him to Raama. Raama is stunned by Kumbakarna's stature and form. (43)

62: Raavana tells Kumbakarna the calamity that had struck Lanka while he was sleeping. He alone can save Lanka (28)

63: Kumbakarna chides Raavana, for not giving thought to his action of abducting Seetha.He is now 'enjoying' the fruits of his thoughtless action. He should have paid heed to Vibeeshana's advice. Raavana rebukes him, what he wants from Kumbakarana is action not advice! (59)

64: And demon chief Mahodhara rebukes Kumbakarna because he had the temerity to talk to king Raavana thus. Mahodhara boasts he can take on Raama. (36)

65: Kumbakarna taunts Mahodhara. The situation in Lanka is in this plight all because men like Mahodhara had given wrong advice to their king. Yet, as a brother, Kumbakarna will go to war and fight to save them all (60)

66: Kumbakarna enters. Monkeys are destroyed in thousands by the minute Monkeys think that this Kumbakarna is no demon but a war machine (36)

67: Killing of Kumbakarna. This is a very long chapter indicating how difficult it was to kill him. Even Sugreeva is seized once by Kumbakarna. All take part in the fight. Hanumaan fights him. Lakshmana fights him. But finally Raama kills him (187)

68: Naturally Raavana wails. He was dependant on this mighty brother to save Lanka. (24)

69: It is demon Naraanthaka's turn Angadha kills him after a long fight (104)

70:Demon chiefs like Dhevaanthaka, Mahaapaarswa Mahodhara, Thrishiras, Matha & Unmatha killed (68)

71: Demon Athikaaya is next only to Kumbakarna in stature.Vibeeshana describes this learned son of Raavana as he enters battle.All monkeys are wonderstruck and fear him.Lakshmana kills him (115)

72: Now Raavana is really in great distress. (20)

73: Raavana has no alternative than to send the crown prince Inderjit who is 'thirsting' to go to war..Kills monkeys in thousands. And he uses the weapon of weapons The Brahma Asthra, on Raama and Lakshmana They are immobilised (74)

74: The entire army of monkeys totally depressed even monkey chiefs think Raama and Lakshmana are dead. The wise old Jaambavaan, realising that they still have some life in them,asks Hanumaan, to fly out to India and Himaalyas, and bring life saving Herbals from the Oushadhi range there. Hanumaan flies and brings these They are revived. (80)

75: Monkeys are exhilarated Raama and Lakshmana are back. It is again a terrific war. Monkeys roam about and set fire to Lanka at night (73)

76 One after other, demon chiefs are killed. Kumbha and Nikumba enter the arena. Kumba killed by Sugreeva (98)

77: And Hanumaan kills Nikumba (25)

78:79: Son of Khara, Makarraksha, leaves for war. He is killed by Raama (21,43)

80: With almost all his chiefs gone, Raavana is in great trouble. He has no choice but to send Inderjith (44)

81: Inderjith is master of magic apart from being a very great warrior. To create confusion, he produces a Seetha by magic and kills her in front of Hanumaan. Kills illusory Seetha! Even Hanuman is fooled! He is in wrath (38)

82: Inderjith is a deeply religious man. Has obtained boons. He always prays at Nikumbila temple for victory. (29)

83: When Raama comes to know that 'Seetha' was slain by Inderjith he cries and falls down unconscious. Lakshmana consoles Raama. A very important chapter. Lakshmana's dissertation on his view of Dharma (44)

84: Vibeeshana knows that Seetha is not killed but Inderjith had tried to dupe them all. by his magic. However he warns that if Inderjith is allowed to complete his prayers at temple Nikumbila, it is almost impossible to kill him (23)

85:Lakshmana leaves to kill Inderjith. Paying heed to Vibeeshana's advice, and commissioned by Raama he prevents Indrajith to complete rituals at Nikumbila. They now know Seetha is not killed (39)

86: Battle with Inderjith begins. Hanumaan at first fights him Vibeeshana wants Lakshmana to kill him (36)

87: Indrajith abuses his uncle Vibeeshana and taunts him as he had joined the enemy camp. Vibeeshana tells him that his conduct and character was such he could not be with Raavana but only with Raama, a man of Dharma. (35)

88: Battle between Inderjith and Lakshmana begins. These two are almost evenly matched (41)

89: Fierce combat between these two even as Vibeeshana is standing by. (44)

90: At first Inderjith's chariot is destroyed. Vibeeshana suggests that he should not be spared but attacked forthwith. He would himself have killed this evil genius, but afterall Inderjith happens to be his brother's son! Celestials are watching this fight from sky, unseen (56)

91: A terrific battle ensues. Lakshmana invokes deities for blessings, for his victory over Inderjith. He discharges a great weapon that finally takes away his life (101)

92: Lakshmana is extolled. He had killed a very great warrior. Inderjith was next only to Raavana (32)

93: Raavana wails. He realises that war is almost lost. Yet he must fight on. He wants to kill Seetha, but a warrior never kills a woman. Prepares for last battle (70)

94: Fierce battle in full strength. Tumultuous war. Raavana in council hall, very much dejected. War continues. Everywhere destruction. (39)

95: As every woman has lost some one dear to her at Lanka, these demonesses wail. They curse Shoorpanaka who 'started' all this for Raavana. (44)

96: Now Raavana starts for the final assault. with the remaining chiefs, like Mahodhara and Viroopaaksha. (52)

97: Viroopaaksha is killed by Sugreeva (35)

98: Mahodhara also is killed by Sugreeva (46)

99: Mahaapaarswa is killed by Angadha (26)

100: Battle between Raama and Raavana again. No demon chief is left with Raavana. Very fierce battle with exhibition of celestial weapons (50)

101: But Lakshmana falls down by a Shakthi weapon hurled on him.by Raavana when he had killed Raavana's charioteer. Some life is still left in Lakshmana. (65)

102: When Raama sees his brother Lakshmana down, he is so shattered that he had no desire for life. Vaalmeeki describes Raama's grief. Chief of medical core Sushena calls Hanumaan and asks him to fly to India and Himalayas to get life saving herbals. With these brought by Hanuman, Lakshmana is revived. Battle continues (54)

103: It is even fight between Raama and Raavana. Lord Indra sends his chariot with charioteer Mathali. Now both fight from chariots. (36)

104: This is the combat of combats. Two mighty warriors, demon Raavana and prince Raama are fighting it out for their lives. Celestials are watching from sky, unseen. Raavana's famous spear is destroyed by Raama (37)

105: As Raavana is shaken up, and as he seemed to be tired, his charioteer makes a retreat from the war front. Raavana feels humiliated and rebukes his charioteer. But the charioteer being a very devoted soldier tells Raavana he had to do this to protect him (33)

106&107: When they resume fight, Sage Agasthya realising that Raama cannot so easily kill Raavana, 'teaches' him the Holy Prayer for his victory. The Aadhithya Hridhaya. As Raamayana is also a book of prayers, we read this chapter with devotion (29 & 31)

108: Bad omens are seen for Raavana as he resumes the fight But Raama is happy that Raavana is afflicted (39)

109: Now slowly Raama gets upper hand. With the blessings of Agasthya and riding on Indra's chariot. (31)

110: Vaalmeeki compares the fight between Raama and Raavana poetically. Even cutting off Raavana's head does not kill him and he has 10 heads! (40)

111: Finally,it is Maathali, Indra's charioteer who now is serving Raama as his charioteer, who suggests to Raama that he should now use The asthra of asthra, the Brahma asthra as he has been blessed by Agasthya with Aadhithya Hridhaya Raavana falls. War ends (34)

112: Blood is thicker than water. Vibeeshana cries over his brother. Raama's advice (26)

113: Wives of Ravana wail. Entire harem is in sorrow (28)

114: Raavana's queen Mandodhari wails. Last Rites for Raavana to be performed. But surprisingly Vibeeshana refuses to do this as he feels Raavana does not deserve this from him. Raama advises him. Long chapter. At last Vibeeshana performs Last Rites with royal honours for his brother Raavana (127)

115: Vibeeshana is crowned king of Lanka. Investiture ceremony conducted by Lakshmana. (25)

116: Raama sends Hanumaan to Seetha to inform her about his victory over Raavana and that Vibeeshana is now king of Lanka. When Hanumaan meets Seetha, she is so happy that she tells him that no gifts from her will be adequate for services rendered by him When Hanumaan threatens to kill demonesses who had made her suffer, Seetha stops Hanumaan (56)

117: Now Raama asks Vibeeshana to fetch and present Seetha before him fully decorated. Vibeeshana along with his wife, goes to Seetha and conveys Raama's message. She is happy but refuses to wear ornaments or take bath. She wants Raama to see her in the condition she had been all the year. But Vibeeshana presses her (37)

118: This is rather a painful (even disgusting) chapter. Seetha has suffered so much. But this beats them all. Raama speaks the most cruel horrible words to her. Tells her that war was not for her but to save his honour! (35)

119: Seetha is shocked. Tells her husband that she had never sinned as to receive such a harsh treatment from her husband. Unable to bear all this, and as there was no remorse in her husband, she decides to immolate herself. Lakshmana, who was in terrible wrath and agony over his brother, prepares a Fire. She enters the fire exclaiming = May Lord of fire protect me who am sinless=

The entire assembly is aghast at this scene. (35)

120: All the deities and important celestials like Kubhera, Varuna, Yama, and Gods Shiva and Brahma, come down to Lanka. They extol him God Brahma tells Raama that Seetha is goddess Lakshmi, Raama is Vishnu. And Brahma describes the all pervasive God Vishnu.. But Raama merely says =I know myself, consider myself, a man. (36)

121: And from the Fire mound Lord of Fire personally brings up Seetha, untouched by fire. Lord fire who is considered the 'witness' of the world tells Raama that Seetha is blemishless. Fire cannot touch fire! Raama accepts Seetha happily, but says he had asked for the test because he wanted the world to know Seetha (23)

122: God Shiva appears. And even Dhasharatha descends on Lanka.and talks to Raama, Seetha and Lakshmana. (37)

123: Indra who was also there, was so pleased that he offers boons to Raama. And Raama accepting the offer asks that the dead monkeys who had fought for him get back their life. All the dead monkeys are resurrected (25)

124: King Vibeeshana wants Raama to stay on and enjoy hospitality at Lanka. But Raama wants to get back to Ayodhya. (29)

125: But king Vibeeshana cannot be denied. He extends lavish hospitality to monkey chiefs and the army. And he offers Pushpaka the divine Air-craft -station for all of them to fly back to India. (28)

126: Raama, accompanied by Seetha, Lakshmana, Sugreeva and all the monkeys fly out to India.on Pushpaka. While flying, Raama points out various places they had visited while on search for her. While they were flying over Kishkinda Seetha requests that wives of monkey chiefs also accompany her to Ayodhya. Pushpaka makes a landing. Women like Thaara and Ruma also get into Pushpaka. (58)

127: They all reach Bharadhwaaja's hermitage. The sage is very happy to see Raama back. Tells him that he knew about the happenings, like Seetha's kidnapping (24)

128: From Bharadhwaja's hermitage Raama sends Hanumaan to inform Bharatha about his arrival, in advance. Raama wants to make sure that Bharatha really wants Rama to take over kingdom of Ayodhya (46)

129: Hanumaan meets Bharatha and narrates Raama's story. Bharatha is excited. Is looking forward to see Raama and hand over the kingdom (57)

130: As Raama lands the Pushpaka Aircraft, Bharatha meets Raama.Joyous scenes. Bharatha while asking Raama to take over tells him that, by his grace, he has made Ayodhya ten times prosperous during his absence (63)

131: Coronation of Raama. Long and very important concluding chapter as Poet Vaalmeeki completes his Vedha of 22,000 stanzas with a Benediction (120)

VAALMEEKI RAAMAAYANA

REVELATION

PART II

CHARACTER

REVELATION

PART II

CHARACTER

CONTENTS

A: THE AUTHOR

There is every reason to believe that the author of this Epic, the History of Raama, was Sage Vaalmeeki. Yet we should recognise some studies and research by scholars and Indologists who have questioned the authorship. Some have maintained that quite a few slokas and even chapters do not conform to the regular style of Vaalmeeki.. At best they accept that bulk of the work was done by Vaalmeeki. We know that poetry came out of Vaalmeeki, when in anguish, he cursed the hunter who killed a bird while it was makinglove to another. Thus (Grief) Soka (शोक) became (poetry) sloka (श्लोक) at his hands. (Bala - Chapter 2 – Sloka 15)

In a special dissertation on the Sloka format, Smt.Shantha Srinivasan, a scholar and teacher writes later, about Vaalmeeki's style = The Structure and Meter =. Vaalmeeki is considered the author of the Sloka format in poetry. But even here, there are some scholars who maintain that Sloka format existed even before Vaalmeeki and Vaalmeeki used it while writing the epic. You can say that Vaalmeeki is the first among poets who used the Sloka format with great effect. All this is a never ending debate.

There have been any number of authors who wrote the history of Raama subsequently. Kamban wrote Raamaayana in Tamizh. There was ofcourse Saint Tulsi Das in Hindi. Many more in various languages. Each is distinct. There is enough room for a comparative study of the various authors of Raamaayana. But Vaalmeeki's Raamaayana is indeed the first! Let us not forget. God Brahma had ordained Vaalmeeki.

The origin of Vaalmeeki is wrapped in mystery. One may say it is obscure. Quite a few believe Vaalmeeki was a hunter by birth who turned out to be a sage by constant prayer. But we feel strongly that Vaalmeeki was a man of good birth who took to Sanyaasa (Renunciation-Thapas) later in life. He lived around Dhasharatha's time and lived through Raama's life. Vaalmeeki was a noble person, a sage. No wonder even the divine sage Naaradha who moved freely in all the Three Worlds for the welfare of all, visits him in his hermitage. And when Vaalmeeki seeks enlightenment from Naaradha, the celestial lord enlightens him. Vaalmeeki is such a noble and good person, he was disheartened by evil men around. So he asks Naaradha whether there is any one at all left in the world who possesses some noble qualities. Five questions (slokas) he puts before Naaradha. And Naarada answers him with 95 slokas-. (Bala – Chapter –1 Sloka 100) Thus Vaalmeeki's interest in Raama is kindled. Only Raama is such!

And God Brahma Himself appears before Vaalmeeki and blesses him to do the history of Raama. Although Vaalmeeki had only a glimpse of the history of Raama from Naaradha, as he began to contemplate, out of his utter devotion,, all events began to appear before him like "Action replay" in TV. And God Brahma had blessed him, ordained him to undertake this work. Thus, at his hands, this epic became a Vedha. After all he was expounding all this only at the "command" of God Brahma who is Vedha personified….. (Ref: Bala – Chapter 2 – Slokas 31 & 32)

After blessing him, God Brahma tells Vaalmeeki= When you do this work, "...your work will reach all parts of the

Globe...will survive ages and ages... Your words will never be but true (to history)...... (Ref: Bala – Chapter 2 - Slokas 32 to 38)

We all know that Vaalmeeki sees (queen) Seetha in forest when she is banished from (capital) Ayodhya by her husband (King) Raama due to some misunderstanding. Infact the pregnant Seetha gives birth to two divine sons Lava and Kusha who grow up around his hermitage. And when Vaalmeeki completed his Epic- this history of Raama- the first persons who are 'taught' Raamaayana by Vaalmeeki are Raama's two sons. And they, in turn, set Vaalmeeki's master piece of 22,000 sloka-s to Musical format. As a Musical, Vaalmeeki Raamaayana came to be introduced to the world. We may thus observe that The Text we read today is The Musical Rendering of the Entire Epic (of about 22,000 slokas) by Lava and Kusha.

(Ref: Bala – Chapter 1 – Slokas 4 to 12) That Vaalmeeki's Raamaayana rendered itself to Music Score to be easily adapted by Lava and Kusha for various Raaga-s (of Indian music system) is because of the genius (rather, the divinity) of Vaalmeeki. One form of art (poetry) could turn out into another form of art (music) so easily...so flexible... It is rather a shame not much research has gone into this aspect. For the last 100 years we hear so much about Saint Thyagaraja. (Carnatic Music) But alas, nothing about the Music Score of Lava and Kusha of Vaalmeeki Raamaayana. (Ref: Bala – Chapter 4 – Slokas 8 to 19)

Reading through the epic, one cannot fail to appreciate certain features of Vaalmeeki's rendering. His style of exposition is lucid. The words are expressive, very effective. There is nothing false (No अनृत) in Vaalmeeki. We should never forget what God Brahma told him.(Your words will ever be true)

Vaalmeeki never tried to shy away from the "unpleasant" He accepted reality. He wrote without fear or favour. But he wrote with devotion. To give an example. Quite a few of us were exercised by the use of the word "Surrender-Refuge" (शरणम्) in Kishkinda Kaanda. Lakshmana tells Sugreeva/Hanumaan that he and Raama seek Refuge under Sugreeva. (Kishkindha – Chapter 4 – Slokas 4-17). Even making allowances for the fact that Sugreeva's assistance is needed for the two princes Raama and Lakshmana to trace the whereabouts of Raama's wife Seetha who had been kidnapped by Raavana, it is rather difficult for us to accept this word. After all they are Ikshwaaku princes. And Sugreeva is just a monkey prince. Vaalmeeki could have used the word Sahaayyam - Sakhyam - friendship (सहाय्यं – सख्यं) instead of Sharanam (शरणं). Kings dont seek "refuge" under monkeys. Yet Vaalmeeki uses this word in Kishkinda kaanda, chapter 4 (in 10 or 11 slokas). Jagadguru Shankarachaarya Sri.Sri Abhinava.Vidya Theertha Maha Swaamin, enlightened us when in ignorance we questioned the use of the word 'Sharanam' by Vaalmeeki. "When the chips are down, even lords have to bend and surrender for seeking help..... Raama was no exception..Vaalmeeki can never be wrong...." Vaalmeeki is such an author!

How effective Vaalmeeki's choice of words is, can be seen clearly as one reads along Vaalmeeki Raamaayana. We have an example here. (रामस्य रामत्वं) Raamasya -

Raamathwam. Raama is the delighter of all. Rare to see an angry faced Raama. But when Raama gets angry, what is Raama's wrath like! The world cannot bear his wrath. Raama's wrath is never wasted. In one word Vaalmeeki has said it all. (Raamasya Raamathvam Pashyanthu). (Ref: Yudha – Chapter 101 - Slokas 58)." Let the world see the prowess of Raama, being Raama".

Being the first among poets, Vaalmeeki takes liberty and indulges in the luxury of poetry from time to time. He cannot be restrained. Vaalmeeki goes "poetic" in describing scenery or even certain incidents. But he never loses sight of the realities. His story of Raama is true, true to history, ever.....Vaalmeeki never compromises. His poetry merely enhances the beauty of The Epic.

Even Vaalmeeki fails! He is lost for words in describing the grim, gruesome war between Raama and Raavana. How can any one describe this war. How can any one describe the vastness & depth of the Ocean. How can any one describe the limitless sky. The poet of modern times Shakespeare says "A rose, is a rose, is a rose" This great English poet is lost for words to describe the beauty of rose. Vaalmeeki could not describe effectively this war between Raama and Raavana. He resorts to this technique. The sky can be compared only with sky. And Ocean only with ocean. Raama-Raavana war can be compared with only Raama - Raavana war. No other comparison is adequate (Ref: Yudha – Chapter 110 – Slokas 24 to 25).

As Vaalmeeki can never be restrained. The poet in him reveals. For instance in Kishkindha Kaanda when Raama wails without Seetha.who had been kidnapped by Raavana.

"Sight is denied, grief overpowers me: And there is this sight- yet grief overpowers me all the same!."....Seetha's sight is denied, so Raama suffers. And there is this beautiful sight of the spring season before him. This does not bring him joy either." (Kishkindha – Chapter 1 – Sloka 36) The beauty of Vaalmeeki can never be fully brought out in translation when he goes 'poetic'.

In a mammoth writing of this sort, it is difficult for an author to maintain continuity. He may even suffer from a lack of sense of proportion. Vaalmeeki has no problem. He has put all the stories, events, in proper place. Further, he does not waste words. In the six books of his Raamaayana, covering almost 21,700 slokas- in 536 chapters, you will find him devoting just a few sloka-s in a chapter while he devotes more than 200 sloka-s in some chapters. (Ayodhya-Kaanda chapter 81- 16 slokas) (Sundhara Kaanda Chapter I-228 slokas.): 16 slokas- are just enough to make Prince Bharatha reach his Council Hall at Ayodhya! And Hanumaan's unbelievable solo flight across the Indian ocean (Mahodhadhi) to reach Lanka 1,000 miles away on search of abducted Seetha, necessarily calls for 227 slokas!

Modern writers should study Vaalmeeki if for nothing else: for his sense of proportion. There is no need to edit Vaalmeeki.

In the succeeding pages, as we take readers through Vaalmeeki's description of the Seasons (Spring-Summer & Rainy season- Winter) they will be introduced to the beauty of Vaalmeeki's poetry. Yet Vaalmeki was never over whelmed by his incomparable art. He never lost sight of

The Goal of presenting Sanaathana Dharma to the world through the History of Raama.

Yet, Vaalmeeki has come in for some criticism. Rt.Hon'ble VS Srinivasa Sastry could not appreciate Vaalmeeki's brevity ir Baala Kaanda when Vishwaamithra leaves Mithila after his protégé Raama gets married to Seetha. (I-74-1). Vaalmeeki 'dismisses' Vishwaamithra in just one line of a sloka in chapter 74 of Baala Kaanda. Readers know what all Vishwaamithra did for Raama. (Baala Kaanda chapters-22 to 74). Infact one may say Baala Kaanda is Vishwaamithra-Kaanda. He moulds Raama. Teaches him Manthra of Manthra-s, Bala and AthiBala. Makes him a warrior of experience. Teaches him divine weapons. Teaches him history and geography. And he gets Raama and Lakshmana married. Sastry could not reconcile or appreciate how there was no formal leave taking of this great sage Vishwaamithra at Mithila by Raama's father, King Dhasharatha, There is not even a word of thanks from Dhasharatha when Vishwaamithra leaves Raama at Mithila after he had done so much for his son Raama. We should read Sastry's Lectures on Raamaayana- a Classic. He was rather severe on Vaalmeeki. Perhaps there was really no leave taking for Vishwaamithra at Mithila. So Vaalmeeki had to rest content with just one line sloka and bids Vishwaamithra "Good Bye". We dont hear about this mighty man of penance, during the entire history after his departure at Mithila (Baala Kaanda chapter 74- stanza 1)

Vaalmeeki's love of nature is obvious. He should have been a bird watcher as well. His heart bled when he watched a lovebird killed by a hunter while it was making love to its mate. His grief over this 'unnecessary' killing came out of his mouth as curse on the hunter and this curse turned out to be poetry-sloka. No wonder when Vaalmeeki describes forest scenery, he is in his elements. As example, in Kishkinda Kaanda, while describing Rainy season, he describes the migration of Chakravaka birds to Himalayas-Manasarovar. (Kishkindha – Chapter 28 - Sloka 16). And he goes poetic. When bees start humming in forest amidst thunder of clouds, with monkeys making noise, Vaalmeeki the lover of Nature remarks that a Music Concert is going on! Bees providing string music accompaniment, thunder of clouds providing rhythm with Vocal support from monkeys! (Kishkindha – Chapter – Slokas 28-39). And Vaalmeeki cannot be restrained. In the very next sloka, as he observes peacocks, it appears to him that a dance recital is going on. with cooing from birds perched on trees providing music support for 'dancing' peacocks!

Ecology is always close to Vaalmeeki. Trees are listed and described. Later in this guide, we will try to list all the trees that Vaalmeeki lists in his epic. His knowledge of trees is remarkable. When, after Seetha was abducted, Raama wails before an Ashoka tree, (Ashoka tree- Jonesia-Asoka-Roxb) Literal meaning - the tree that removes grief. Vaalmeeki is in his elements. As Raama wails, unable to find his beloved wife Seetha, he says "Oh! Ashoka that removes sorrow. Grief stricken as I am (please) make me (renamed) with your name, by showing me my beloved Seetha). "Here is poetry for you. (Aaranya – Chapter 60 - Sloka - 17).

Vaalmeki always expresses himself strongly, clearly and poetically when situations demand such treatment. Readers of Raamaayana know how the mighty demon Maareecha who was a friend of Raavana tried to dissuade Raavana to abduct Seetha. "Raavana! Dont go anywhere near Raama or have anything to do with him and his folks if you know what is good for you" Raavana does not follow his advice and abducts Seetha and the rest is history. (Raavana and his Lanka are destroyed by Raama.) How to put fear into Raavana. Maareecha who had a taste of Raama's wrath (Baala Kaanda – Chapter 30 – Sloka 16 to 18) advises Raavana to stay away from Raama. Valmeeki puts this beautifully, poetically to convey what fear is when Raama is in wrath; In Aaranya kaanda chapter 39 slokas14,15,16,17 Maareecha describes what Fear is like! Fear that seizes a person when Raama is transgressed.: "Oh Raavana! In every tree I see only Raama, nay 1,000s of Raama with bow in hand: Infact as I roam about, the entire forest seems to be full of Raama-s. In my dream I see Raama and am scared." Finally, Vaalmeeki's masterpiece. "Why! Ever since I had a taste of Raama's wrath, I lost interest in Rathna- (Gems, precious stones) because they begin with letter "R"....." This is poetry for you from Vaalmeeki! Before we leave Maareecha and his advice to Raavana, a "Gem" from Vaalmeeki expounding a truth, must be presented now. When Maareecha's advice is ultimately rejected and Raavana decides to go through with his obnoxious, cowardly act of stealing Raama's wife through the assistance of demon Mareacha, Maareecha succumbs to help Raavana, but not before he expounds a universal eternal truth. Mythology cannot 'rub' off this truth. (Aaranya – Chapter – 37 – Sloka 2) "Oh King Raavana! "(says Maareecha).." It is always easy to find flatterers, men who speak sweetly. But rare (indeed)to find one who speaks 'unpleasantly' but (speaks) what is good and salutary. (and rarer still) to find one who will listen to him (and accept advice although unpleasant to hear)" This is in response to Raavana's boast, that he is the greatest and mightiest of demons in the world and none to equal him. His "friends" and ministers all flatter him, only to deceive him.. But Maareecha was the only true friend of Raavana by advising him what was good for him. Alas, Raavana failed to realise this truth. Vaalmeeki's artistry is obvious. And truth expounded by Vaalmeeki is eternal. A true friend is one who offers sound advice even though harsh on his friend's ear. If that friend respects friendship, he should listen and abide by his advice. However unpalatable it may be. Alas!

Vaalmeeki after completing his mammoth work, The Raamaayana, was somewhat worried. "Who is going to read all this" (Baala Kaanda – Chapter 4 – Sloka 2&3) We all know that an author's greatest satisfaction is in finding a good publisher who will present the work to the reading public. Books are to be read and not become an ornament in book shelf. As this work is not just History but a Vedha, by divine grace, Lava and Kusha appear before him and we all know that Vaalmeeki Raamaayana became known to the public as a Musical. Sage Vaalmeeki was content. His work was in safe hands.- the two sons of Raama who add beauty to this epic by formatting into Music and singing before vast audiences. His worry and concern that his epic may become obscure is unbecoming of a genius. Even in his lifetime Raamaayana became known to the public. Even Vaalmeeki is human! But what a beauty he produced. Whether read or sung, the epic of Vaalmeeki was sweet (musical) like the strains from Veena. which has 7 strings, each representing the seven qualities of Shringaara-romance, Karuna-compassion, Veera-valor, Roudhra-wrath, Bhaayaanaka-fear; Haasya-laughter, Bhhebatsa-revulsion, disgust. (Bala – Chapter 4 - Sloka 8 & 9).

After completing his work, after he writes about the Coronation of Raama at Ayodhya and his rule (Raama-Raajya) Vaalmeeki offers benediction. (Yudhdha kaanda – Chapter 131 – Slokas 105 to 130).

Lastly, there is no doubt Raama is the principal character of Raamaayana. But as we read through Raamaayana, Vaalmeeki steals our heart. Raama is the greatest human being and a total personality, this Bharatha Varsh (India) has seen and will ever see. To write about such a Raama and his momentous life, it takes a Vaalmeeki. When Kaali offered her blessings to an obscure shepherd, he became Kaalidasa, The Poet... Enlightened by celestial sage Naaradha and blessed and ordained by God Brahma Himself, is it any wonder that Sage Vaalmeeki became The Author. Yes. Vaalmeeki is author, Unaparalleled. Let us begin our journey ....

B: THE SLOKA FORMAT OF VAALMEEKI

We are indebted to Smt. Shantha Srinivasan for enlightening us about the poetry of Vaalmeeki. She writes, later in this book.

C: LAVA & KUSHA

Earlier we had indicated how Vaalmeeki's Epic was first introduced to the public. So we should write about this. Lava and Kusha were born to their mother Seetha when she had left her husband King Raama during her pregnancy due to a misunderstanding. The young princes were never told that Raama was their father. Raama did not know them either as they were growing up in isolation in the forest in a hermitage not far from Vaalmeeki's. They grew up as young sages in forest. But blood tells. After all they are of Royal birth. So they are also masters of Gandharva art (like music, sculpture, painting). When Vaalmeeki had completed his mammoth work and was showing some concern and was worrying about making his work known to the public, by divine will & grace, Lava and Kusha meet him, prostrate before him, seek his blessings. Vaalmeeki knew that there was divine sanction for this meeting. And he knew that the boys should be the first to be taught his Raamaayana, which he knew was a Vedha. They are taught under Guru-Kula-vaasa (Students living and studying in a teacher's home. The Guru becomes the 'father' under this system) So, befittingly, it is the sons of Raama who are taught by Vaalmeeki (Baala kaanda - chapter 4-). The princes set this to music. They sing the entire Raamaayana of Vaalmeeki before Rishi-s and sages in the forest and around. The Rishi-s and sages are thrilled. They knew that this was no music but exposition of Vedha through Music. These Rishi-s were masters of Saama Vedha... so they knew. They extol the boys. They offer him presents. All this is listed in chapter 4 of Bala kanda. They sang melodiously, in three octaves in various Raaga-s suited to the text of Vaalmeeki. They sang in the Maarga Format. And it was not long after, when King Raama of Ayodhya hears about these boys and their extraordinary music, which narrated his own past history. He invites the boys to his court. And they all listen with awe. Thus Raamaayana became well known. Vaalmeeki's Raamaayana is blessed in many ways. The Gandharva celestial sage Naaradha, God Brahma, Vedha personified, and the many Rishi-s of great rigorous penance, have all blessed THIS...Indeed, Vaalmeeki Raamaayana is eternal.

D: IKSHWAAKU KINGS

In India that is Bharath there were many kingdoms. Rulers of merit adorned the throne at Kaashi, Mithila, and Kosala during the Vedhic period. But the rulers at Ayodhya were like emperors. They belonged to the Solar lineage. Raama, the principal character, is an Ikshwaaku. Vaalmeeki describes Raama's ancestors through the lips of Brahma Rishi, Sage Vasishta, who was the family priest of Dhasharatha. At two places there is this reference. In Baala Kaanda, before the marriage ceremony of Raama and Seetha at Mithila. King Dhasharatha requests his family priest to narrate his lineage to King Janaka, the father of his daughter-in-law Seetha. (Bala–Chapter 70– Sloka 20 to 43).

Again, in Ayodhya kanda, when angry Raama goes on a tirade against the atheist Jaabaali, his father's cabinet minister of renown, Vasishta who was aghast at Raama's wrath on such a renowned, noble man Jaabaali, simply because Jaabaali was not a man of conventional religion, reminds Raama of his lineage. telling him that Jaabaali was no ordinary man. "He knows the "Origin of Species"/(Ayodhya kaanda- Chapter 110). Vasishta, the man of Religion and Rituals, talks so highly of Jaabaali, the atheist and non believer. India was Bharath those days. Sanaathana Dharma was the constitution of Bharath Varsh.and it was not a paper constitution, of India that is Bharath Very liberal. So an example, if you need one! On both occasions it is Vasishta who gives the description of Raama's lineage.... From God Brahma.....we have Mareechi. His son was Kaashyapa. Then Vivaswaan (thus solar lineage). And Manu, the first law giver (thus general term-man). Manu's son was Ikshwaaku. The first king of Ayodhya. Kukski, Vikukshi, Bhaana, Anaranya, Prithu, Thrishanku (who went to heaven in his own body, thanks to Vishwaamithra – Ref – Bala Kanda – Chapter 60), Dhundhumara, Yuvasha, Mandhatha, Susandhi, Dhruvasandhi, Prasenajith, Bharatha (not to be confused with Rama's brother later on). Then Asitha. During Asitha's regime, a temporary set back to Ayodhya. Enemies de-throne him and he seeks refuge in the Himalayas with his two queens who were pregnant there. One of them wanted to kill the foetus of the other co-wife. Out of jealousy So offers poison - Gara (गर) But thanks to the blessing of sage Chyavana, the son of sage Bhrigu, everything is set right when a son is born and appropriately he is named Sagara (Sa-Gara- born with poison). Sagara's 100 sons by his first wife perish. Then sadistic Asamanja who was driven out of the kingdom because of the citizens' request. But his son Amshumaan was a noble man. He was followed by Dhileepa. And his son the famous, Bhageeratha who brought the Ganges and made her flow in Three ways. And Kaakuthsa was his son followed by Raghu. (Thus Raama is often called Kaakuthsa or a Raghu).Then Sowdhasa, Purushasadhaka, Kalmashapadha, Pravridha. Shankana, Sudharshana, Agnivarna, Sheegraga, Maru, Prashushruka, Ambareesha, Nahusha, Naabhaaga, Aja & Suvratha. Aja/s son is Dhasharatha. And King Dhasharatha has four sons. Raama, Lakshmana, Bharatha, and Shathrugna.

CHARACTER

1. RAAMA

Raamaayana is a book on character. Raama is the principal figure. We shall talk about Raama's character. Incidentally, it is interesting to observe that those days, the very names indicated the basic character of a person. For instance, we have Raama, which means "one who delights' (रमते)

Raama is The Delighter.

His younger brother Lakshmana is Lakshmi-vaan. Lakshmi-vardhana (लक्ष्मी वर्धनः)

Prosperity is his name! Association with him, brings and fosters prosperity. He never leaves Raama. Raama never leaves him either.

And Bharatha is one who "bears' (Bru-Bar to bear,to sustain = भृ – भर).Remember, he bears Raama's Royal Sandals on his head Paaduka- Pattabhishekam - Takes on the mantle of rule of Ayodhya under trying circumstances for 14 years. Infact he "bears" Dharma itself. As for Shathrugna, which means 'destroyer of enemies' Vaalmeeki in Ayodhya Kaanda first sloka of first chapter brings out his true. greatness. (Shathrugna - The Nithya Shathrugna = नित्य शत्रुघ्नः

When we recognise our enemies, we can take care of them. Enemies are seen. But Vaalmeeki talks about Nithya-Shathru. the unseen enemies, the enemies within us, the enemies that are always with us and follow us, like wrath, passion, greed, and jealousy ...... It is difficult to "conquer" these enemies. But Shathrugna, the conqueror of enemies is also the conqueror of these 'daily' enemies that are within, that are difficult to overcome. No wonder in 22,000 slokas, we hear a lot about Raama, Lakshmana and Bharatha. But Vaalmeeki devotes only a few sloka-s to Shathrugna. What is there to write about him.. This prince is a sage and like a rishi has overcome Nithya Shathru-s. and Vaalmeeki has said it all. in one word, in brevity: Shathrugna, The Nithya-Shathrugna! Now back to Raama......

Naaradha on Raama:

When Vaalmeeki sought enlightenment from Naaradha, Naaradha describes Raama. (Bala – Chapter 1 – Sloka 7 to 18) Naaradha begins by telling Vaalmeeki.. "Rare indeed is a person endowed with so many qualities enumerated by you." And he can think of only one man who has such qualifications listed by Vaalmeeki. Naaradha begins...

He is called Raama by people. Born in the Ikshwaaku family. Resolute; man of immense strength. Man of composure. Brave, brilliant. People dote on him & willingly surrender to him. A wise man; man of justice; has command over speech; endowed with 'riches'. A destroyer of enemies. Physically, he has broad shoulders; has long hands, hands reaching out to his knees; neck conch shaped. Broad chest; robust cheeks; collar bones well concealed-not bony; nice forehead and lovely head; master of archery; has nice gait; He is of medium heights. well proportioned body; glossy complexion (Here the expression used is Snigd-varna)- endearing complexion; handsome with bright features; wide eyes;

He knows Dharma; Ever an upholder of truth.Virtaous; A man of wisdom who is highly venerated by citizens. Ever concerned with their welfare. Infact he is like God Brahma on earth. He is ever "The Giver" A great conciliator. Dutiful. So people 'surrender' to him. willingly. Protector of ecology; Dharma; of his own Dharma (He is not above the laws of Dharma) And thus he is the protector of the people. Knows Vedha-s and ancillaries. Expert in Dhanur Vedha (Science of war). Knows Shaasthra-s, compendium of codes. And he has tremendous memory endowed with clarity of thought always. Loved by all, strong in spirit, a good man, far sighted, good folks flock to him like rivers heading towards the ocean. He bestows a pleasing eye on one and all (never discriminates). Many diverse rich qualities. And to his mother Kowsalya, he "radiates" happiness. In generosity he is like Ocean. Like the Himaalayas in patience and forbearance. In valour, like God Vishnu. But in appearance pleasing like the moon. In composure, like mother earth. In charity like Kubhaera, the lord of wealth. But when he is in wrath, he is like Pralaya-at the annihilation of the universe. But in Truth, he is Dharma personified.

Dhasharatha on his son Raama: Character of Raama.

When King Dhasharatha decides to retire and wants his eldest son Raama to take over, like a true democrat (Yes.those days, good monarchs, despite having the divine right to appoint their own children, used to abide by the wishes of their subjects). Dhasharatha calls an assembly of citizens and VIP-s. at the Council Hall at Ayodhya. (Ayodhya kaanda, chapter 2). But before he expresses his wish, he ponders over Raama's qualities. He feels justified in making Raama his successor to the throne ultimately. This is what crosses his mind about Raama's qualities. (Ayodhya kaanda - Chapter 1- 8 to 43) Raama is like Lokpalas (mystic protectors of the world). Rama is even more beloved of the world than himself in as much he ever desires the prosperity of all. In valour, he is equal to the Lord of celestials Indhra. & Lord of death Yama. In intellect, another Brihaspathi.

Thus having decided to retire and make his son take over, he addresses the vast assembly thus:(Ayodhya kaanda-chapter 2-)

Dhasharatha's address before the assembly:

"Having lived a life of many 1,000 years, my body is worn out. I wish to give rest. Having served you all to the best of my ability, my body is decaying. I wish to retire. I wish to appoint my son Raama as my successor- crown prince-yuva raaja. In bravery he is like lord Indhra and he is the destroyer of enemies' fortresses. In qualities, he takes after me. (He is thus worthy enough). He is a man of splendour. If the three worlds can 'shine' under one lord, verily it is my son Raama. When I hand over the responsibilities to my son, I can enjoy spiritual bliss (through meditation of the supreme)" Having spoken thus, the democrat that he is, king Dhasharatha adds "This desire has been well deliberated by me. But if you have any alternative to my request, please be free to tell me".

And Vaalmeeki expounds a Truth: (Ayodhya – Chapter 2 - Sloka 16) "Only when a matter is deliberated and examined by others, prosperity results" Dhasharatha should not be accused of having vested interest. Therefore Vaalmeeki expounds this Truth. Only outsiders can deliberate any issue dispassionately for the well being of all. The concept of Democracy was different those days. Democracy is a tool to satisfy the wishes of the people but today owing to the political party system, the party's interest comes first and the objectivity is forsaken. We have another example before us in Vaalmeeki Raamaayana. Dhasharatha's forefather King Sagara exiles his son crown prince Asamanja when the people could not stand his sadism. It is his grandson Amshuman who takes over the kingdom of Ayodhya after Sagara passes away..... (Bala – Chapter 42 – Sloka 1&2). Now back to Character:

When Dhashartha stops his address before his assembly after presenting his son's case and after he enumerates a few qualities of his son Raama, there was such an ovation from the vast assembly hailing Dhasharatha's wish, that for a moment, Dhasharatha was stunned. He had not expected such a quick response and affirmation from the multitude. So the old fox (Dhasharatha) having "goaded" his subjects to accept Raama, pretends and says (Ayodhya - chapter 2- slokas 24 & 25). "How is it that moment you heard me, you all desire to make my son Raama the crown prince. This raises some doubt in me.... how come, even when I am alive, you want Raama to take over" Two things bothered Dhasharatha at such an overwhelming endorsement. Perhaps the people were tired of his rule and wanted change. And secondly, he expected his assembly to deliberate like true democrats and then only give their opinion. But "the people" had made up their mind. They know "Their Raama". Nothing could give them greater joy than seeing their Delighter Raama on the throne. So they tell Dhasharatha.

Rama's character as seen by the people. Here it goes: Rama's character described again.

(Ayodhya kaanda - chapter 2 - slokas 26 to 55) (Gist)

Oh King! Your son is endowed with many auspicious qualities. Infact he is more like a celestial. His qualities bring joy to all. He is brave, like Indhra. He is the embodiment of goodness. Resolute in following Truth & Dharma. It appears that Dharma itself has taken form on earth as Raama. He is free from jealousy. Like the moon he is pleasant and brings joy. Very indulgent. (even to sinners). Gentle, conciliatory, tender, and soft-spoken. He is a man of gratitude. Has conquered passions like wrath. Righteous ever, he is a man of composure, free from envy. He speaks sweetly to one and all but his words are always truthful. And he is well versed in Vedha-s and so respects learned Brahmins. Master of weapons...even Dheva-s, Asura-s and of course men cannot equal him. And he is a cultivated man in as much as he has mastered the Ghandharva vedha- arts. He is never depressed (keeps his problems to himself). Royal and majestic. And going out of Ayodhya along with his brother Lakshmana, he never returns without "conquest" after a fight. Mounted on a chariot or elephant, when he returns after an encounter with the 'enemy' he meets us to inquire about our welfare during his absence.. about our sons .... Raama speaks like this = Do your disciples perform their duties by you = And when grief afflicts us, he is in sorrow. And during festivities he shares joy with us. Although a great wielder of the bow, he serves the aged and elders. Has the unique capacity to 'radiate' prosperity all around. Will never indulge in cheap conversation. But (an excellent conversationalist) who gives proper rejoinders. He is a man of Letters - a Vaachaspathi. (In Physical appearance) has endearing eyes, with a streak of red and with lovely eye brows. He is as though God Vishnu has descended on the earth!! (Readers know that Raama is Vishnu- but even Raama did not know). ......"

After describing Raama, they all say, "By our good fortune, he is born to you.... In every household they offer prayers for Raama"... Ofcourse Dhasharatha is mightily pleased with such response to his wish of making Raama, an excellent his successor.

Ideal son, prince, man and husband.

Raama ever followed his father's orders. Performed the duties of the kingdom. Was ever duty bound. Time and again he did the duty by his mothers (mother Kowsalya and step mothers) as the devoted son. He showed great consideration and respect to teachers like a student. And with his young newly wed wife Seetha, Vaalmeeki has this to say: Seetha shone doubly when she was with him. Entwined in love, their feelings were mutual: (their hearts were one, although in different body).

(Baala kaanda - chapter 77- Slokas 29 to 38)

Raama the ideal student:

Even as a teen-ager Raama had developed such profound and noble qualities, that as we read Vaalmeeki we will know Raama's diverse qualities. In this Revelation, we will refer to this as situations arise. But we ought to mention now Rama's devotion to his mentor and 'Guru' Vishwaamithra. Readers know that the great and mighty man of penance, Sage Vishwaamithra had sought Raama's assistance for the protection of a "yaga' he was performing in his hermitage. Vishwaamithra is such a powerful Rishi he could, by the power of his "Thapas" ward off any interruption to his spiritual exercise. No demon or evil can dare to spoil his yaga. But the yaga he was performing in his hermitage was such that calls for total restraint from him. And only Rama can stand by him in his hermitage when he is in total "Deeksha'. Vaalmeeki thus reveals Raama's character; his valour & prowess. It is Raama and Raama alone Vishwaamithra wants. (Baala kaanda - chapter 19 - slokas 9 to 16). When Dhasharatha in exasperation offers Vishwaamithra protection for his Yaaga in his hermitage through his mighty Foursome army - Akshowhini- Vishwaamithra treats this offer with contempt. "Raama alone can fight evil, the evil minded demons Maareecha and Subahu who are spoiling Vishwaamithra"s penance can be destroyed only by Raama" (Bala kaanda - chapter 19 - sloka 12) When Raama along with Lakshmana leaves Ayodhya with Vishwaamithra to his hermitage, the sage realises that in Raama he has an ideal student. And so, for the welfare of the world, he teaches Raama all the divine weapons of which Vishwaamithra is a master. Raama's "education" in arms is total and complete. Vishwaamithra begins his 'education' by teaching Raama the two Manthra-s Bhala & Athibhala. Even a great warrior suffers from tiresomeness after prolonged fighting. Vishwaamithra says while teaching these Manthra-s "There will be no weariness in you. None is equal to you. when you master these two chants, none will be ever equal to you" (Bala Kaanda = chapter 22- slokas 12 to 19). Vishwaaamithra would not have taught these mystical Manthra-s if Raama was not qualified to receive them. Later (chapters 27 & 28) Vishwaamithra completes Rama's education by teaching him divine weapons as we had said earlier.

Raama's interest in History & Geography:

Raama being a prince, Vishwaamithra teaches him geography and history of various places they visit. Here again Rama's character is revealed. It is Rama's curiosity that forces Vishwaamithra to reveal history and geography. Raama is such a 'student' And ofcourse Vishwaamithra is such a "teacher' (Time and again Vaalmeeki uses the expression = Kowthuhalam - Curiosity)

Endearing to all Raama charms even a great sage

Raama is such a sweet person, Vishwaamithra loves him like his own son. This character is revealed when Raama entering a hermitage in forest asks "whose hermitage is this" Vishwaamithra replies. "It is mine and as this is mine, it is yours as well" (Bala-chapter 29 - sloka 46). A great rishi is supposed to have no attachment! Ah!

Raama's sense of duty

It is well known that even on holiday, a doctor, if he is true to his noble profession, will have to attend on patients in need. Stethoscope is always an ornament across his neck! Prince Raama is on a 14 year exile. He even wears forest dress of bark and sports a mendicant's hairstyle, but he does not absolve himself of his responsibility as a prince of Ikshwaaku family. So when the sages and folks living in the forest seek his assistance to protect them from evil minded Rakshasas, Raama is quick to assure them that he will stand by them to offer them protection. Vaalmeeki puts this beautifully. This is what Raama says when they beseech him (Aaranya kaanda - Chapter 6- slokas 22 to 25) "What a shame that you should talk to me like this, request me. You should not talk to me like this. Because I am at the command of men of penance. It is my business. I have entered the forest for this purpose. I came accidentally to fulfill my father's command, it appears to me. ...May men of penance see my prowess and my brother's prowess while we are in forest. I desire to destroy these evil demons".

But his wife Seetha will have none of this. She begs him to give up 'arms': Aaranya kaanda- chapter 9 is a telling write up: Seetha even narrates a parable. Raama, as long as he is undergoing 14 years of exile in the forest to fulfill his father's (and Kaikeyi's) command, should behave like a man of penance and not as a Kshathriya (soldier- Ikshwaaku prince). "You must abandon royal duties here" she begs him. But Raama, is a refuge for all good folks. So he will not give up arms, as he must protect the good folks here. Duty comes first before Raama. And he is a Kshathriya warrior, always. Will not take cover under the garb of a mendicant and fail to do his Dharma.

Raama's sense of humour:

Raama's personality was total. A warrior, master of Vedhas, lover of art and master of Gandharva Vedha, a good conversationalist, friendly and easily accessible to all his citizens..... We can add to the long list his sense of humour. (Aaranya Kaanda - chapters 17 & 18) When demoness Shoorpanaka, a cousin of demon king Raavana accidentally meets Raama and Lakshmana in the forest, she is struck by passion over these two. This stupid wicked woman wants to have Raama! (Slokas-26 to 29). "You are indeed (fit to be) my husband. Consider me as your wife. I will eat up this Seetha...." Raama's sense of humour reveals itself when he suggests that Lakshmana will be the ideal husband for her in as much as he has no woman with him at the moment unlike himself. A woman like her cannot tolerate a co-wife if she married him. (chapter 18 slokas 2 to 5). Shoorpanaka being fooled thus approaches Lakshmana who in turn, taking after his brother Raama in jest, tells her (slokas 9 to to 12) "Why do you desire to be my wife. Afterall I am a servant of Raama! Raama it is who will be ideal for you because after marrying you, he will give up this "ugly, dreadful woman (Seetha) and he will all be yours" When this 'rally' goes on, Shoorpanaka is enraged and she attacks them. Lakshmana maims her and the rest is history.

And there was this jest Raama played. But this served a great purpose and brought out a great Truth. (Ayodhya kaanda - chapter 32 - slokas 29 to 43). The Thrijata incident. When Raama was getting ready to leave Ayodhya on exile of 14 years to fulfill his father's command (under obligation to Kaikeyi) a poor man by name of Thrijata, of from him as he had heard that Raama was distributing his personal wealth to all and sundry, before Rama left Ayodhya on exile. Ofcourse Rama could have straightaway offered some moneys/gifts to this man but he thought he should play a jest with him. Rama tells this Thrijata, who appeared as a man of ridicule. "Alas! cows in thousands have already been given by me. (I have nothing to give now) But in as much as you have received not even one from me, look, this is what I will do for you. You can receive as much as would cover when you throw your walking stick" Thrijata, although abjectly poor, is a Thapaswi. He tightens his garment. And throws. Like a javelin this travels high and far and falls far away near a Cow pen. "Raama hugged Thrijata and tells him why he played such a jest. People around him should know the power of penance. Thrijata was a man of penance. A thapaswi. In playing a jest on him, he wanted the public to know the efficacy of Thapas. And ofcourse Thrijata receives a bounty of gifts from Raama. And before leaving, he "offers" (and repays) Raama, with blessings, for his safety during his life in forest of exile. Blessings from this poor man of Thapas is more than all the wealth any one can offer.

When we go along, as Raama is the principal character of Raamaayana, his various qualities are revealed. We shall write about these as we proceed along. But it is but proper to write about Raama's physical attributes. His form and figure. In Sundhara Kaanda (Chapter 35) Hanumaan describes Rama's personality to his wife Seetha who is kept prisoner at Lanka by demon king Raavana. Seetha has a lurking doubt that Hanumaan may be a spy of Raavana or perhaps a monkey in disguise. She does not trust Hanumaan who has come from Raama on search of Seetha. Hanumaan describes Raama's personality in detail. Seetha is thus convinced Hanumaan is Raama's envoy.

Raama's Physical attributes:

Raama has just about a perfect personality (physical). Vaalmeeki through the mouth of the great and wise Hanumaan describes Raama's physical features. But Hanumaan also describes Raama's greatness.

(Oh Seetha! You may please listen to me.... as I speak about the qualities and personality of Raama and the Lakshmana as observed by me = chapter 35 sloka 8)

"Raama will capture the hearts of all who meet him. Born with beauty. His eyes like lotus petals. Very compassionate. In brilliance, equal to the Sun. In forbearance like mother Earth. In wisdom, a Brihaspathi. In fame, an Indhra (on earth). Protector of all living beings. Protector of his folks. Protector of his own (noble) conduct. Protector of Dharma. Destroyer of enemies. He is protector of all - of all the four castes (without discriminatin). Protector of Norms and codes. He is The Instrument of action. He is bright, luminous. Always 'worshipped'. Steadfast in observing vows, celibacy. Ever helps the good. In action, knows the proper course (always). Well versed in political science (State craft). Has sound knowledge of scriptures. Very modest, yet tormentor & conqueror of enemies. Well versed in Yajur Vedha. He is honoured for his erudition by even those foremost in Vedha-s. And ofcourse master of Dhanur-

Vedha (Science of arms and war.)" After saying thus, Hanumaan proceeds to describe his physical attributes......

"He has broad shoulders. mighty long hands, neck Conch shaped, Very pleasant face, Not bony, covered by muscles (appropriately). His eyes tinged red. And he is (verily) called Raama by citizens. His voice like Dhundhubi (drum). Magnetic complexion. (Very attractive, endearing-Snigda varna). Majestic in appearance. Well proportioned body. Every part of his body well formed. He is of medium height. Royal blue coloured body. ..." Now Hanumaan describes part by part. Vaalmeeki's master piece.

Three parts - firm (chest, knee, biceps)

Three parts -long (eye brows, hands, legs)

Three parts-Equal-medium (hair forelegs, knees)

Three parts-Elevated (abdomen, navel, chest)

Three parts -Red (nails, corner of eyes, palm)

Three parts -Glossy (heel, hair on head, vital organ)

Three parts-Impressive / majestic (voice, gait, stance)

There are three lines (folds) in his neck and abdomen. deep set lines in sole. His breast and nipples rigid, well set. His neck, back of organ, knees are short. He has three 'spirals' on his head. Four lines on his toes and forehead. He is of four cubits in height (about 6 ft) Well proportioned arms, knees, thighs, cheeks.

Pairs that are Equal = (eye brows, nostrils, eyes, lips, ears, eye brows, wrists, knees, loin, legs, arms. His teeth well set, last four (end) sharp, pointed teeth.

*Four (different) gaits - (Like lion, leopard, elephant, bull) (*all four characteristics of his mobility).

Parts (Lovely)	(Lips, Jaw, nose)
Five Parts –smooth / shining	(Hair, eyes, teeth, skin, feet)
The Eight parts – Long	(Backbone, trunk, limbs, fingers toes, nose, eyes and eye lashes)
Ten Parts- Lotus like	(Face, mouth, eyes, tongue, lips, nails, hands, legs, forehead)
Ten parts -broad/big	(chest, head, forehead, neck, arms shoulder, navel, flanks)
Three attributes –renowned	(valour, fame & wealth)
Six parts – elevated	(armpits-abdomen, chest, nose, arms and forehead)
White -	(teeth and eyes)
Nine Parts – charecteristic	(Locks of hair, hair on chest, moustache, nails, fingers, skin eyes, organ and his 'brain')
And the three (parts of day,evening, night)	devoted to righteous duties wealth and pleasures(in order)

He is a man of Dharma. Man of good judgement, knows the proper time and place for action, steadfast in truth. An accumulator of wealth but fond of distributing wealth. He ever speaks sweetly (kindly) to all.

Thus Hanumaan describes Raama before his wife Seetha in Lanka in the Ashoka forest where she was kept prisoner by the demon king Raavana. (Sundara Kaanda- chapter 35). And Hanumaan describes Lakshmana also to Seetha to make sure that Seetha would believe that he is an emissary of Raama who had come to Lanka to find about her whereabouts and not a spy of Raavana nor Raavana himself in disguise.

Raama is a strong personality. Where truth and Dharma are concerned he will be firm. When Agashthya extolls him and goes to the extent of saying that his father King Dhasharatha went to heaven because of having a son like him and so on Raama is quick to stop him We ought to remember that Agasthya was no ordinary sage. He had restrained the Vindhya range of mountains which had threatened ecology, even life in the Southern hemisphere, by the power of his penance. Agasthya's observation and Raama's rejoinder (Aaranya-chapter 13slokas 13 &16) "Oh Raama! ...your father is indeed blessed by having you as the eldest son, as he, like (your forefather) king Yayathi, was "saved".... "To which Raama replies thus, without showing any disrespect to the great Rishi. "Oh sage Agasthya! The king (my father Dhasharatha) was not 'saved' by me.... (helped to cross over to the other shore of the ocean of sin) By his own virtues, he crossed the ocean of sin (& went to heaven)" Strong words, but true. Dhasharatha had performed so many yaagas and offered munificent gifts and charities, heaven was his for the taking.

Raama is such a great, noble & rare character that we cannot do full justice to him. Without reference to his behaviour under various situations and trying circumstances.. We shall take leave of Raama for the time being. His character will reveal itself as we go along.

2: KING DHASHARATHA

Dhasharatha of the Ikshwaaku lineage is a renowned king of Ayodhya; father of Raama, the principal character of Vaalmeeki Raamaayana. As his name suggests, he is a mighty warrior (Dhasa- Ratha= having ten-chariots: He could, at a time, take control of fast moving horses yoked to ten chariots). He was a very liberal king. His council of ministers and advisers included deeply religious persons and sages like Vasishta, and also a person who was an atheist-agnostic (Jaabaali). So liberal was he. A strong person, yet he always sought counsel from wise people around him. His minister and charioteer Sumanthra was his friend as well.. Sumanthra had free access to his inner apartments at all times. (Ayodhya kaanda-chapter 14-sloka 44) So close was he to his king. You may say he was minister in waiting, using modern parlance. We will be reading about Dhasharatha's ministers later. But we should make a reference to the special relationship of Dhasharatha with his minister Sumantra.

When Dhasharatha had no sons from his three queens Kowsalya, Sumithra and Kaikeyi, he decides to perform Ashwamedha Yaaga and also Yaaga for begetting sons. It is the old trusted friend and minister Sumanthra who advises Dhasharatha, that for successful completion of Yaaga and for begetting sons, he should invite the old Sage Rishyashringa to be The Patron of the Ceremonies. (Bala kaanda-chapter 9 sloka 18) After hearing about the greatness of Rishyashringa from the lips of his friend and minister Sumanthra, Dhasharatha invites Rishyashringa along with his wife Shantha (Bala Kaanda-chapter 11-slokas-26, 27) and as predicted by Sumanthra, Dhasharatha's three wives conceive and in due course give birth to fours sons, Rama, Lakshmana, Bharatha and Shathrugna. However powerful a king may be, unless he is well served by his ministers who offer proper advice, a king cannot rule over the kingdom for long. If Dhasharatha was a mighty ruler (infact a sort of emperor) it was because he was served by ministers who were great and noble men. And Sumanthra was a confidante of Dhasharatha. He was also his charioteer. In those days, a charioteer was more than a charioteer (He was not like a modern car driver for his boss). On many occasions, it is Sumanthra who is commissioned by Dhasharatha.

Dhasharatha's very dexterity became the cause of his ruin. Dhasharatha was such a "Marksman" that even at night, by mere sound, he could hit a target with precision. He could hunt animals even at night, even when it was cloudy and rainy, without seeing the "Kill".the very breath of a animal was enough for him. So dexterous was he. (Ayodhya-Chapter 63- 21 to 26). We all know how Dhasharatha when he was a young prince, on a hunt early morning, killed an innocent Brahmin sage when he was taking bath, thinking that this was an elephant drinking waters of the river. This young sage dies and his old father curses Dhasharatha. Years and years later, when Raama is exiled at the instance of Dhasharatha's third wife Kaikeyi, the curse takes effect and Dhasharatha dies unable to bear separation from his beloved son Raama. (Chapters 63-64 of Ayodhya kaanda). Vaalmeeki expounds a truth. A killing of an innocent person, even unwittingly constitutes a sin and one has necessarily to pay for it. The noble Dhasharatha was a victim, although he did not deserve this curse and eventual death through the curse. We will get back to Dhasharatha when we write about the "Midnight Drama" before Raama's coronation that did not take place.

3: DHASHARATHA'S CAPITAL AYODHYA

Before we describe the character of the ministers and advisers of king Dhasharatha, we may describe the capital city of Ayodhya from where King Dhasharatha extended his rule over the powerful kingdom of Kosala., along with his ministers. So powerful and prosperous, dukes and chieftains used to visit Ayodhya to pay tribute. Merchants used to flock. (Bala Kaanda - chapter 5). It was a trading centre. lovely Sarayu river flowed around the city. The city itself was constructed in the Ashtapada style of architecture. (Like Checquer Board). The city was 12 yojanas by 3 yojanas (About 100 miles by 25 miles). Constructed on flat surface. Mansions and palaces like mountains. With fine stone & gem work. Broad Boulevards. Fine roads. Rows of houses well constructed but close. The city was so joyous, that musical strains were always heard. Vedhic recitations from learned scholars and Brahmins always reverberating the city. The city was well guarded with defences all around, with forts, moats ... by warriors who never stretched their bows against good folks but who were a terror to enemies. It is interesting to find Vaalmeeki talking about the city water supply. Can any city survive without water. Vaalmeeki says that the water was sweet, like sugar cane juice! And Vaalmeeki gets so carried away that he says "Even the celestials in heaven like, Indhra, Varuna and Kubhera had no such beautiful city". Dhasharatha had made the city beautiful, joyous, clean with clean supply of water and free from any enemy attack. (A-YUDH)

Such a city Dhasharatha had as capital, to rule over his kingdom of Kosala, along with his ministers.

4: DHASHARATHA's MINISTERS

A King, however mighty unless well served by a council of ministers who have character, cannot rule over for long nor bring prosperity to his subjects. King Janaka of Mithila had Shathanandh, a great sage and son of Rishi Gauthama and Ahalya, as his Adviser/Minister.Dhasharatha had a council of ministers of such renown, that every one of them was a noble man of distinction. (Bala - chapter 7) Dhrishti, Jayantha, Vijaya, Sidhdhartha, Ashoka, Manthrapaul, Ardhasadhaka. Sumanthra, the eighth, was also his charioteer. And Dhasharatha had two other rishis, Vasishta and Vaamadheva.. Vasishta was family priest. Besides he had men of distinction like Jaabali and Suyagnya to advise him. All were clean men devoted to serve kingdom well. Men of scholarship. Men of honour. Modest. Men with self control & discipline eminent masters of Vedhic studies. Resolute. Renowned. Ever kept their word and commitment. But men of enormous patience. Never uttered untruth either out of passion, or anger or for pecuniary benefits. There was nothing that was not known to them through their ambassadors or spies: What happened, what was happening or even what was to happen, either in their own kingdom or elsewhere. Very skilled in settling disputes. Tested men in matters of heart and friendship. And Vaalmeeki adds (Sloka 9) " If such a moment arose, they will not hesitate to punish even their own sons" society's interest was never jeopardised because of their personal feelings and attachment. The affairs of the state was their concern. (And Vaalmeeki adds) (sloka 10) "they protected The Treasury, The Army, ''As for treasury and protection of State's finance, only tested men were appointed controllers of finance. They never harmed the poor. Vaalmeeki says (sloka 13) "they (the Ministers) all moved as equals: had the same objective of welfare of state And they never spoke a lie" All of them had the "eye of Prudence" (ever vigilant) It was character they imbibed from their teachers. Men of vision.and noble qualities. They were never arrogant of their qualities (or status). So they were renowned even in other kingdoms. They were cleanly dressed, even wore jewelleries. They knew the art of making treaties. And also the art of breaking treaties. They kept oath of Secrecy. clear headed in intricate matters pertaining to the state. After enumerating such qualities, Vaalmeeki concludes (slokas 22-23) Dhasaratha ruled 'the earth' like Lord Indhra. ruling the celestial world. Surrounded by such ministers who were able, clever, devoted and who ever bestowed sound ministerial advice that was always salutary, Dhasharatha became endowed with brilliancy, like the rising Sun with its rays.

The concept of democracy was different in our ancient land. While kings had a divine right to rule, you will find many kings were men whose sole concern was the welfare of their citizens. To assist them, they had ministers who were 'tested' men who were learned, noble and wise. Dhasharatha always consulted his citizens before taking important decisions. His forefather king Sagara, drives away his own son Asamanja from the kingdom, on exile, bowing to the wishes of his people. In Aaranya Kaanda (chapter 1-slokas 18,19,20) Vaalmeeki states "It is the king who is the bearer of the 'Rod' of justice. A king protects with a fourth (of the duties) of Lord Indhra.. As we are residents of your domain we should be protected, whether you live in city or forest" It is the Dharma of Kshathriya a king followed. So Vaaalmeeki brings this out through rishi's living in forest.

5: SEETHA

Introduction:

It is rather strange that many believe that Seetha, the daughter of King Janaka of Mithila and the wife of Raama is a weak woman. Women always had a high place in society in Vedhic times. Purda was unknown. The most powerful person in mythology is Goddess Paarvathy, the consort of God Shiva as Ardhanaari. She is also Durga and Kaali, the terrible. In no other "religion" you find a Goddess of such power and grace. Allah, or Jesus Christ, or Buddha, remember, are all men! But under Sanathana Dharma, a woman had her place in society which was different in concept from what prevails in modern India. For the garb of equality and democracy, we should not condemn the status of woman in Vedhic India. Let not our ignorance of the distant past, cloud our thinking. If women today 'suffer', Seetha is not to be blamed. The suffering is certainly not the legacy of Vedhic India.

Mythologically, Seetha became 'daughter' of King Janaka when (as part of the ceremony) he was ploughing and preparing land for a Yaaga ceremony he was about to begin. The child came out of earth and Janaka was so the happy that he considered her as his daughter from the moment he took the babe in his arms. (Bala - chapter 66 - slokas 14/15). In the entire Raamaayana, it is only Seetha who had no natural birth, whose birth was not known (obscure). Even God Vishnu who descends on earth as

Raama had to spend 10 months in the womb of Kowsalya. Seetha, the 'woman' has her pride of place in Vaalmeeki. That is why her father, Janaka decides that she should wed a man of trusted valour. Janaka knew that Seetha was a divine gift to him as a daughter.

In Ayodhya Kanda (chapter 118 & 119) The great sage Athri, who is one of The seven rishi-s (Saptha-Rishi's), talks about his wife, Anasooya after welcoming Raama, Seetha and Lakshmana in his hermitage. The point is that in those days women were equals, although their duties were different. (slokas 9 to 14) Athri talks about his wife Anasooya, the lady of mighty penance. Anasooya was his equal. He says "when the world was continuously without the rain for 10 years, Anasooya - by her thapas- created fruits -tubers. She made the Ganges swell. For 10,000 years she performed penance, (Penance was not the monopoly of men). She is 'bathed' in vows. She is sinless. She is like a mother to you (all) " .... Indians today should read history, not read just the history written about but the history of our ancients, of Vedhic era. Our history does not begin with Alexander or Chengiz Khan or the Mughal- Muslim domination or freedom from British imperialism.

Seetha is affectionately received by Anasooya. She praises Seetha for her qualities = an ideal woman- and wife. = When this old lady of Thapas, Anasooya enlightens Seetha about the virtue of being an ideal wife, Seetha is quick with her rejoinder. Seetha is no timid lady. She says". For a woman, husband is her Guru. This is well known to me " (as though telling Anasooya, that her advice to her is wasted as she knows as much about Dharma as she) But Seetha is also a polite, cultivated woman. She says "that you a noble lady spoke thus to me, should not cause me surprise "(I will take it in good spirit)".

And this is not the first time Seetha sets the record straight. She knows all the Dharma of the land. She need not be enlightened about the duties of a woman and wife. When her mother-in-law, Kowsalya, at the time of her departure to the forest on 14 years exile from Ayodhya, starts giving her advice,, she is quick with her rejoinder. Today, in 21st century, with all the freedom, there is a never-ending feud between the mother.in.law and the daughter.in.law. But our modern girls should read (Ayodhya-chapter 39- slokas 20 to 31). Seetha is no timid woman. But she is always composed and speaks sweetly, though. She tells her mother.in. law (remembering old adage = Sathyam the Brooyaath, Priyam Brooyaath =) : "How a wife should behave towards her husband (when her husband passes through bad times) is well known to me. (I have been well advised by my own mother and father). Yet as I am now being enlightened by my noble mother-in-law, I will do all that. And when Kowsalya had quoted precedents, Seetha, tells her firmly " You should not compare me with ordinary vulgar women" Seetha assures her that she will follow Dharma. The point is that Seetha followed the Dictum of the old: = Tell the Truth: Tell firmly but sweetly without hurting the listener = But Seetha would not stand any "nonsense'. Raama is a good man, a noble man. So Seetha will ever follow him as his beloved wife, even giving up the luxury of a royal life in Ayodhya for 14 years. She needs no advice or enlightenment, not even from her legal husband's mother.

Seetha is a noble woman. Although she becomes the wife of a great warrior (a Kshathriya prince), she cannot accept her husband Raama wielding bow in the forest during the 14 year exile. "In Rome do as the Romans do" According to her, Raama should eschew violence and live a life of a simple mendicant and follow the "Dharma" of the forest. Raama is no longer a prince: So he need not take the responsibility of protecting the folks here. He has ceased to be a Kshathriya. Every one is expected to perform Dharma according to his vocation. - according to his varna-caste. So she presses Raama thus (Aaranya kaanda - chapter 9 - slokas 2-15). We give the gist: "Oh Raama! Dharma (and fruit of Dharma) is obtained in the world by practising subtle laws.by desisting from actions caused by passion. Basically there are three sins arising out of passion. The first sin is the one that leads us to speak untruth. Coveting another's wealth and woman is the second sin. These two sins never afflict you. And never will. But I am talking about even a greater sin. The sin of violence. The cruelty of harming another without provocation. The moment you go out in forest when you see a demon, your hand takes grip on your Bow. Your going to Dhandaka forest (to kill demons there) does not please me. It is a sort of target practice for you, is it not? Oh Raama! Where is weapon? Where is a peaceful forest life? ..... and so on" Having said this Seetha narrates a parable. In those days, in any tight situation, the people went by norms, experience, stories and precedents by way of convincing Raama and to press her point of view she narrates a parable. (Aaranya kaanda - Chapter 9 - Slokas 16 to 22). Here it goes ..."Oh Raama! Once upon a time there was a pure noble man of penance in forest. Lord Indhra (being jealous of this man of penance) with a view to putting obstacles to his penance, brought with him a lovely shining sword, appearing before him as a soldier. He offered this sword to the great man of penance as a sort of protection for him in the animal infested forest. From then on this sage never went out without this sword. It became an obsession with him. Then he began to do cruel deeds, armed as he was with this divine sword. That was the end of his penance. By his cruel deeds he went to hell." Association with weapon brought his downfall. And Seetha pleads with Raama. "Oh Raama! Abandoning royal duties here in forest if you devote yourself to peaceful activities as a Muni, great Dharma will come by you "Seetha is upset because Raama even dons the dress of a muni, wearing dress of Bark materials and deer skin. He sports Munis hair style. (hair permanent!) Yet he does not give up bow and arrow. Ofcourse Raama rejects Seetha's advice but for entirely different reasons. Vaalmeeki brings home a truth through the lips of Seetha. Almost all statesmen in the world are of the opinion that possession of arms will not be conducive to world peace. Mere possession of weapons like nuclear bombs will lead to destruction. Any number of treaties cannot be effective. Nations may profess restraint. But the possession of weapons is a disease that has to be treated totally. Mahatma Gandhi, who was a Bhaktha of Raama, and a Vaishnavite, devoted his entire life for propagating Non Violence and rejection of arms.

Vaalmeeki through Seetha expounded this universal truth. long, long ago.

Seetha's strength of character reveals itself fully when Raama refuses to take her along with him to forest on his 14 year exile. (Ayodhya Kaanda - chapters 26 to 30). By way of taking leave of Seetha before going on exile, Raama, tells her that Seetha should remain in Ayodhya during his

14 year sojourn in forest and take care of his old father and mother Kowsalya during his absence from Ayodhya.. Not only that, she should attend on his stepmothers Kaikeyi and Sumithra as well. And Raama says (chapter 26-sloka 33) that as Bharatha and Shathrugna are dearer to him than his own life, she should consider them as her 'son' and 'brother'. And Raama warns Seetha that in as much as Bharatha was going to be Yuva Raja taking on the burden of rule over the kingdom, Seetha should not treat him like before (taking liberty with him as a 'brother') (sloka-34,35,36). "Seetha! You should never displease Bharatha, because he is now lord of our kingdom and lord of our family as well. Kings are pleased only when they are served with diligence. Treating Bharatha with respect due to a king, you remain here itself ....." (***Incidentally***, ***Vaalmeeki expresses a Universal Truth***.) When one becomes a minister or a judge, his sons and relatives and friends should not take liberty with them like before, because society's interest will be jeopardised).

Seetha's immediate reaction to Raama's refusal to take her along to the forest, was one of anger. (Ayodhya chapter 27) Seetha says "It is indeed mockery that you should speak in a light hearted way and command me (to remain here without you). A son, brother, father, mother, daughter.in.law enjoy (the fruits of) their own (deeds and) merit- the punya. But a woman alone obtains (and shares) her husband's fortunes. For this reason, I should share forest life with you"...Seetha thus is clear about the Indian concept of Dharma of a wife. The duty of a wife may be to obey her husband. But Seetha is no timid person. She reminds Raama about the duties of a wife. Serving a husband at the 'shadow of his feet' is better than living in a luxurious palace. To remind us that Seetha is no timid girl, she says (sloka 9) "I have been taught in many ways by my father and mother about my duties. I need not be told- (reminded - by you)." Strong language from a "timid" girl! The point is that where Dharma is concerned Seetha is no timid person. ***Vaalmeeki brings* home this point.** Modern girls should understand Seetha through the eyes of Sanathana Dharma. Seetha knows Dharma. Did she not observe before Raama (Aaranya-chapter 9-sloka 30) "(Only) From Dharma, Artha (activity, wealth, substance) follows. Only through Dharma (real) happiness results. Infact one can obtain everything through Dharma. The world has Dharma as its Root."

And more to follow from Seetha (sloka11) " Not caring for comfort of all the worlds, I will live in forest as though I am living in your father's palace, when I am with you.".... And Seetha's relationship with Raama is not just physical. She says in sloka 12.." Oh brave Raama! With great restraint, leading a life of celibacy, in the sweet smelling forest, serving you, I will enjoy myself in forest" The young girl Seetha will be a Brahmachaarini - celibate woman - even in passionate lovely gardens of the green forest. And to press her demand of going to forest with Raama on a 14 year exile, she says in sloka 20 "Even if a stay is offered in heaven and comes by me, I desire not" Seetha says in effect "why do you tempt me with the luxury of stay in your father's palace in Ayodhya."

Raama ofcourse was unmoved. He wanted Seetha to stay on at Ayodhya during his 14 year exile. Raama is also a clever man. To justify his stand, he talks about forest life. Forest life is not meant for a sweet young girl! Ayodhya- Chapter 28 is all about Raama's arguments Seetha should not follow him to the 'terrible' forest. Raama says (sloka 3) "remaining here you follow Dharma, giving me thus satisfaction". And he is firm: "Give up this idea, of life in forest"."A forest is always spoken of as full of danger" Then Raama narrates the difficulties encountered in forest. (There is no bathroom with hot water supply) One has to take bath three times a day and perform rituals in forest (life). (No Royal maids to fetch flowers). ".....Flowers to be procured by oneself...." And Raama describes the vagaries of weather, the fear of terrible animals and, the path strewn with thorns. But Seetha is no timid girl. She is firm. She is not scared of forest life. She must accompany her husband. Seetha replies firmly. "All these difficulties spoken by you, Raama, I consider them infact as beneficial to me. But I know you spoke (of these difficulties) because of your (excessive) attachment to me and consideration for me" And talking about animals, she tells Raama that moment the animals see him and face him, they will all run away. There is this sloka from Seetha about women (sloka 18) ":A woman is always protected, father protects her, then her husband and in the last years her son". As now Raama is her husband she has to be protected, protected in forest as well "...And Seetha taunts Raama: (Ayodhya - Chapter 30 - sloka 3) "Oh Raama! Did my father the Vidheha king, consider you, a son.in.law, as a woman in the garb of a man when I obtained you (as my beloved husband) "....Seetha's character is revealed here. Nothing would stop her. She even takes the liberty of taunting her husband and questioning his valour- valour in protecting a lady in forest. And Seetha cannot be stopped. She is clever and she knows where to 'hurt' her husband = Chivalry - Valour =. In the next sloka, she says "What a shame, this world, out of ignorance, would speak falsely of you (as one) lacking (in bravery and) brilliance like those in the burning sun." (That is how the world will view it if you are 'afraid' to take me along with you to forest)..

Raama could not resist Seetha's arguments. Although he had told her that she should remain in Ayodhya and serve his parents who are "Gods" to him. (Ayodhya - chapter 30 - sloka 33) Raama goes to this extent when he affirms "Why is it a deity which is not close -invisible-is being propitiated in many ways, transgressing one's mother, father and teacher (who are 'Gods' at hand!) But finally he decides to take her with him to forest. Seetha is such a lady. She wins!

It may not be out of place to mention, that Raama never forgot "the Taunt" of Seetha. So at the first opportunity that presents itself in forest, he exhibits his valour. When (in Aarańya Kaanda) Khara and his 14,000 demons attack him, he remembered Seetha's taunt, and took them on, single handily, although the brave and mightily strong, Lakshmana was with him, but only as a silent spectator. He destroyed the terrible demon chief Khara and his 14,000 warriors. Of-course, it is well known Seetha used this taunt only to press her case. Seetha is a wise woman & she knew her Raama well. She 'hit' him where it will 'register' most. No wonder ***Vaalmeeki uses expressions*** like the "...burning Sun..." while comparing Raama's brilliance. Seetha knows that Raama can be compared only with Sun.

And Raama never forgets, has tremendous memory. So when the three (Raama, Seetha, Lakshmana) set out of Ayodhya on the 14 year exile, on their first night in forest, alone without charioteer Sumanthra who had dropped them in the deep forest, Raama takes a dig at Seetha. He tells his brother, Lakshmana (Ayodha-chapter 52-sloka 97) "....Seetha the Vaidhehi will now appreciate what life in forest is ..." But Raama's remark is wasted on Seetha. Seetha knows well the hardship of forest life. But Dharma is foremost to her. And being and sharing with her husband, is the foremost Dharma for her.

Vaalmeeki's treatment of characters:

A feature, a distinct feature is that Vaalmeeki never shied away from reality. There never was and never will be a nobler man in India that is Bharath, than Raama. We also know the character of Seetha. The ideal woman. Raamaayana has many other personalities whose character was distinct, remarkable, praiseworthy. But Vaalmeeki never hero worshipped them to such an extent to hide their failings. He wrote facts. He wrote without fear on favour. Vaalmeeki's treatment of even Rama, Seetha, Lakshmana, Shathrugna and Bharatha was factual. Although a great Rishi, he was also human. We should read the various events in Raamaayana without forgetting Vaalmeeki, his realism and his acceptance of human weaknesses. We may mention Vaalmeeki's treatment of even great sages like Vishwaamithra, his treatment of the criminal deeds of Lord Indra, particularly his debauchery in his affair with Ahalya. We have to take note of this before we proceed to write about the characters. in Raamaayana. But let us continue the character of Seetha.......

Seetha is indeed a pure woman Yet during her entire exile in forest with Raama she never forgave her step mother.in.law, Kaikeyi. As readers know, under pressure from his third wife-queen Kaikeyi, Dhasharatha had sent Raama on exile to forest to make Kaikeyi's son. Bharatha, his successor-Yuva raja. While she never spoke ill of her father.in.law Dhasharatha, at every opportunity she spoke ill of Kaikeyi. The truth is she is also a girl, and very human. She could never reconcile herself to her husband Raama who was a noble and good man to be sent away from the capital for good for no fault at all. This, in spite of the fact that Kaikeyi later had realised her folly particularly after her son refused the throne after Dhasharatha's death and had severely reprimanded his mother. Yet Seetha never forgave Kaikeyi. In Aaranya kaanda - chapter 49-sloka 32- she says as she is being kidnapped by Raavana "Only now has Kaikeyi, along with her own folks, would be a woman whose wishes are totally accomplished..." meaning that Raama and Seetha would perish. Contrast this with her husband Raama's character. When Lakshmana talks ill of his brother Bharatha or Kaikeyi for preventing Raama's accession and his exile, he will have none of it. Raama is firm- (Aaranya-chapter 16 - slokas 36,37 38) when Lakshmana had talked like this "Raama! How could a lady Kaikeyi, to whom Dhasharatha was a husband, to whom Bharatha is a son, be so cruel and wicked" And Raama tells Lakshmana "Oh dear lad, Lakshmana! Your lovely (step) mother Kaikeyi, should not be reviled whatsoever. But you may talk about your (brother) Bharatha , the lord of Ikshwaakus (and praise him as much as you like) ..."

Seetha was fond of deer, trees, plants She loved 'Nature'. She loved the forest and the life it offered. Not deeply religious like her mother.in.law, she worshipped Nature. When they cross Yamuna river (near the modern

Allahabad) she prays to Goddess Yamuna. For her, nature was deity. (Ayodhya - chapter 55-slokas 20,21,22) And she prays for Raama thus:" Oh Kaalindhi-Yamuna! I am crossing you. May my (husband) Raama fulfill his Vow (of exile)" And follows this by praying and affirming " ... when we return, (after 14 years exile) I will worship you with an offering of 1,000 cows "Ofcourse Seetha has nothing to offer at the moment, her husband having given away his personal wealth when he had left Ayodhya. The point is that Seetha worships Nature. (Here the sacred Yamuna) Elsewhere she worships the Holy Ganges. And approaching a mighty Banyan tree she prays -sloka 25 and 26. "....Oh great tree! I am bowing to you. May my lord (Raama) fulfill his vow ..... I should see again Kowsalya and Sumithra ..." A few points may be noted. Our 'religion' (if you can call it religion at all in a conventional sense) recognises ecology as a source of inspiration, an instrument for prayer, As rivers follow Dharma by providing the water cycle, and as "Hinduism" is Sanaathana Dharma, no wonder our ancients worshipped rivers. A Banyan tree, in its own way follows Dharma- the Dharma of giving shade and protection to the homeless and needy. The second point, Seetha makes no reference to Kaikeyi, the other (step) mother of her husband Raama. Throughout, Seetha never forgave her step mother.in.law Kaikeyi. Seetha was ever curious about plants, trees. And Raama had knowledge of botany. Raama patiently enlightens his wife about trees. (Sloka 31) "The docile (Seetha) who had not seen such creepers laden with flowers, such trees and croutons, asked about them as she saw them (with amazement) ..." And the devoted Lakshmana, brought her exotic flowers of forest . (Ayodhya - chapter 55 - sloka 32) "And Lakshmana, thrilled by

Seetha's words (of inquiry to Raama) brought various beautiful stalks (branches of) trees laden with flowers. ..." In the next sloka, we find ".... (Seetha) daughter of Janaka saw the river full of waters, with lovely sand embankments..... sounds from swans and sarasa birds.... she rejoiced ..." It is obvious Seetha was enjoying the forest. Raama was wrong!

It is an irony that Seetha's love of animals like deer, caused calamity to her, Raama, and Lakshmana. We refer to the kidnapping of Seetha by the demon king Raavana, who used his friend demon Mareecha to dupe her, to raise passion in her, to entice her.. We will refer to the story of the kidnapping later. Maareecha who was a master of magical arts, appears before Seetha as a "Golden Deer". Seetha was captivated at once. Asks Raama to capture this "Deer" alive for her. Raama goes out of the hermitage. Lakshmana follows Raama. When the hermitage is deserted, Raavana comes and snatches away Seetha who was alone, and takes her to Lanka. This is the tragedy. Vaalmeeki should be read in original. (Aaranya Kaanda chapter 43-sloka 1 &2) Seetha was captivated as she saw this "Golden Deer" (demon Maareecha in disguise). One would have expected that Seetha who was ever in the company of pets like deer, should have known that this was an illusory deer. Lakshmana ofcourse, being a very wise man, was quick to recognise this as a demon in disguise. (Aaranya-chapter 43-sloka 4 to 8). "Oh Raama! I consider this deer as demon Maarecha in disguise. Kings who were thrilled in forest while on hunt, have been killed by this sinner who can take on any form ....There is no such deer that is studded with gems in all the world ... this is the work of magic (magical prowess) of demon Maareecha"

Still, Seetha presses her husband to bring this 'deer' to her, catch this alive. (slokas 9 to 21) We will give the gist of what all Seetha said "This will be for my amusement in our hermitage. Nothing comparable seen before. Oh Raama! If this is captured alive, it will be most wonderful ... It will cause wonderment to your brother Bharatha (back home at Ayodhya, when we take this along with us)" And she adds. "If this is not captured alive, its skin will please me (as bed spread). I desire to sit by your side, sitting on this, over a bed of Dharba grass" But Seetha realises that a lady leading a forest life should not get so passionate over such a deer. She says (sloka 20) "It is (popular) belief that it is improper for a woman (of forest) to be overcome by desire (and passion), as this will cause misfortune" How true.

Poet Vaalmeeki expresses the Truth, through Seetha. Passion blinds a person.

Even the divine lady Seetha who had given up the luxury of Ayodhya, succumbs to passion and "Fate".

There is even a greater tragedy that confronts us. It is not just that Seetha was kidnapped by Raavana which of-course was one of the most cruel, most painful, hard to bear events in Seetha's (and Rama and Lakshmana's) life. Let us narrate the background leading to the tragic event of the kidnapping of Seetha by Raavana. Seetha's passion over the "Golden" deer forced Raama to go out of the hermitage to capture this 'magical deer' dead or alive, although he was sufficiently warned by the wise Lakshmana that this was no deer but demon Maareecha in the form of a deer to bring calamity to them all. Raama ofcourse had his reason. He wanted to please Seetha. But before he leaves his hermitage on hunt he gives a reason (Aaranya-chapter 43-sloka 37) "Oh Lakshmana! you are telling me that this is the magic of a demon. Even if it is so (as you conjecture), the destruction (of this cruel demon in form of a deer) must be done by me" And before he leaves on chase of this'deer', Raama 'commands' his brother Lakshmana thus (sloka 45 and sloka 50) " You stay here, armed with bow. Protect Seetha.... You must be vigilant. (looking) all around. always apprehensive and suspicious...every moment ...standing close by Seetha...along with the big bird Jataayu.." Raama, in no uncertain terms commands his brother, not to leave Seetha alone. Yet, when Maareecha the 'deer' was killed by Raama after a long chase, he cries "Oh! lakshmana" taking the voice of Raama by magic, and as though Raama is in dire trouble. When this 'wail' is heard Seetha shivers in her hermitage and presses Lakshmana to go out at once to assist Raama and render help. But Lakshmana is firm. He knows that Raama would never call for help. He is such a warrior. (chapter 45- slokas 10 to 19). We give the gist. "Your husband, Oh Seetha, cannot be conquered by Pannagas, Gandharvas, Dhevas, demons, human beings, no doubt about it .In battle, Raama can never be slain (by any one) .... I will not abandon and (leave you here alone particularly) as you are without Raama.....Your husband will come back soon after killing this demon (deer)....The voice you heard was magic...You have been entrusted as my ward by the great soul Raama. I will not agree to abandon you (and leave you alone)...". This was the situation in Raama's hermitage. Now comes the tragedy we talked about. It is a tragedy because Seetha's noble character takes a beating. We had said earlier that Vaalmeeki wrote facts. He did not spare any one. He wrote without favour or fear.. He was never overwhelmed by personalities. He was human. Thus a most painful reading is this from Vaalmeeki. Seetha loses her composure; understandably so because she heard "Raama's" wail. She was in total fear of her husband's life.

Yet, what all she said to the most noble Lakshmana who had only one goal in life, to serve his brother Raama and his sister.in.law Seetha, is unpardonable, to say the least.. Vaalmeeki did not 'edit' Seetha. He wrote what all she said. She was most cruel, uses obnoxious words, questions morality and character of a great, virtous, noble Ikshwaku prince. Totally unbecoming of her noble character. (slokas 21 to 27) "Oh Lakshmana! seeing (hearing) Raama's plight you are talking all this ...It is not a surprise that harm will befall at the hands of men like you who are enemies in secrecy, who are mischievous....Wicked as you are, concealing your real intentions, you followed Raama who is alone in forest, either at the bidding of Bharatha or ***on my account***. (to have me) ....Yours nor Bharatha's (plan) will ever be fulfilled...How can I desire an ordinary man like you, when I have obtained a husband (like Raama...) Before your very eyes I am going to give up my life...Without Raama, I will not live even a moment in this earth..." Thus Seetha spoke. Lakshmana unable to bear such character assassination from Seetha leaves the hermitage, leaves Seetha alone, ostensibly to 'help' his brother Raama, although Lakshmana knows that Raama does not need any help and that the wail of Raama was only the magic of demon Maareecha.. All Lakshmana can say before he leaves the hermitage (in sheer disgust, unable to hear such obnoxious words from Seetha) is this (Slokas 29,31) "Oh

Seetha! You are like a Goddess to me. I cannot talk back against you..... I cannot tolerate to hear such words that are like burning Naaracha weapons on my two ears...)

The rest is history. Raaavana visits the hermitage when Seetha had none to protect her and it was child's play for him to kidnap her.

This is not the Seetha we know. We can't believe Seetha to talk like this. Yet Vaalmeeki has portrayed her this way. Some commentators take a charitable view. Seetha was in such a pitiable state when she heard 'Raama's' voice for help, she wanted Lakshmana to go immediately to help her beloved husband. The only way she could drive away Lakshmana was to use such a character assasination. Otherwise Lakshmana would never have disobeyed his brother's command that he should never stir out of the hermitage during his absence to hunt the 'deer'. But we are of the opinion that Seetha's threat of suicide was sufficient to drive away Lakshmana to go out to help her husband,.to force Lakshmana to go out of hermitage.. The second view is the traditional view. Seetha succumbed to fate. Fate can blind a person's character. Seetha succumbed to Fate. Her noble character was the casualty. ***But Vaalmeeki wrote all this, leaving us all to ponder over Seetha's behavior under trying circumstances.***

Vaalmeeki narrates the events leading to the kidnapping of Seetha by Raaavana when she was alone, with Raama chasing the golden 'deer' and Lakshmana driven away by Seetha to help her husband who, she thought, was in dire distress. Aaranya Kanda- Chapters 46 to 49. It is rather surprising that Seetha could not recognise Raavana as a demon when he took on the form of a pious mendicant even at first sight, because Raavana, while talking to Seetha, gave himself away by his conversation that was never befitting a pious mendicant. (aaranya-chapter 46- slokas 15 to 32). This is how the "pious mendicant" addresses Seetha. The gist. "Oh Lady with complexion of gold! ...Who may you be... Oh lady with lovely eyes!.. with lovely hips! Are you a Goddess, or wife Keerthi of Indra, or Goddess of wealth, or an apsara....Your teeth are well set, white, polished....your eyes are red at the sides...the pupil of your eyes are dark...spotless eyes...wide eyes...your buttocks fleshy...broad....your thighs are like the trunk of an elephant...your breasts are alluring...big, round and firm...nipples pointed..contiguous breasts.....like the fruits of thala tree..Oh Lady with winsome smile!..you have carried away my heart just as the river carries away banks of a river...your waist is small...you have lovely hair..." These are not the words of a pious mendicant who meets a young lady in a hermitage for the first time. Yet Seetha does not realise his evil intentions, that he is not a pious mendicant. This is rather strange. Seetha is an intelligent girl. Yet she replies thus (Sloka 35,36) She began to talk to him as though he was a good mendicant. She offers him hospitality "Oh Brahmin! Here is Cushion (seat) Take Arghya and Padhya. Here, these foremost fruits are offered.." In chapter 47 of Aaranya she introduces herself thinking that this 'Brahmin' will curse her if not properly talked to. She narrates her story (slokas 2 to 26).

Vaalmeeki perhaps is justified. Seetha was worried about Raama who had gone chasing the golden 'deer' for her. She perhaps did not at first sight itself realise that the "guest" before her was no a true Brahmin mendicant but an evil man because her mind was very agitated. Normally she would never have allowed any one to talk to her like this. ***Vaalmeeki presents Seetha as a simple girl!***

But the moment Raavana reveals himself when Seetha asked this "pious mendicant" about his lineage, gothra etc she treats him with contempt. Her personality reveals itself. We can narrate the sequence. (Sloka 24) Seetha is bold enough to ask this 'pious mendicant', "such as you are, announce yourself clearly, your name, gothra, your family" And Raavana reveals himself (and his evil intentions thus. (slokas 27 to 32) 'The pious mendicant' Ravana tells Seetha "Oh Seetha! I am the lord of demons, Raavana by name, by whom three worlds including Dhevas, Asuras and Pannagas have been terrorised... When I saw you with complexion of gold, ***dressed up in petticoat of silk, I did not have any desire in my wives*** "(At the outset itself Raavana reveals his intentions. and continues) "You therefore become the first and foremost queen to me and to all the foremost women, many who were brought from here and there....."

Seetha rejects him outright. She condemns him (slokas 34 to 50) Her strong character reveals itself. We may give the gist " ....I am totally devoted to Raama who is like lord Indra. who is unshakable like a great mountain, unfathomable like the deep ocean.... the lion among men..who is a Delighter (of one and all)....You, a female jackal, now desire to have me who is a Lioness, unapproachable. You cannot touch me like the Sun's rays cannot be touched...You are indeed a fool (living in a fool's' paradise). (How dare) you desire to take away Raama's wife.... What difference there is between gold and brass, that is the difference between Raama and you. What difference there is between a falcon and crow, between peacock and chicken, between a swan and vulture... between nectar and jujuba juice (.that sums up) is the difference between Raama and you. ...(remember) I will be like a diamond swallowed by a bee...." The 'Delicate' Seetha although facing such a vile, terrible demon, speaks firmly, strongly, pungently. Her character again reveals itself. Seetha did not "Beg" Raavana. (chapter 48, slokas 20, to 24) admonishes and warns Raavana thus. She is terribly angry. "You boast that you are the brother of Kubhaera (is vain) how could you be like this to desire me.... you are a fool, having no self control.. It is possible to be alive after kidnapping (Indra's wife) Sachi from Indra... but after kidnapping me, the wife of Raama, there will be no life in you...There will be no salvation for you even if you drink life saving Nectar..." We see Seetha, the noble, strong, woman of character. She kept her fear to herself facing this terrible demon king Raavana who is about to kidnap her.

While depicting character of a person, Vaalmeeki described the basic character But in various situations and trying circumstances, the person's character undergoes some change. This is human nature. Vaalmeeki, throughout his epic never fails to indicate this. Seetha is a very noble, strong, virtous woman.

And Vaalmeeki presents yet another reality of human nature..

When a person is under stress, under terrible suffering it is but natural for even a very strong willed person entertaining thought of suicide. Seetha was no exception. Vaalmeeki brings this out in various places in his epic. The monkey army in the search of Seetha under the command of Angadha, contemplate suicide when their efforts to find whereabouts of Seetha fail in the South.(Kishkinda-chapter 53) Why, even the great Hanumaan is so dejected in not finding Seetha at first in Lanka, he feels no useful purpose would be served in prolonging his life. (Sundara kaanda-chapter 12 &13) & (particularly slokas 41 to 45 of chapter 13) Thus Seetha who is kept prisoner in Lanka. unable to tolerate the pressure from Raavana to become his wife, contemplates suicide. (Sundara - chapter 26 - sloka 38) "If some one offers me poison, I will be glad to meet the Lord of death, as I am now without Raama" (chapter 28 - slokas 5) " I will kill myself.... there is no sin in this..." (Sloka 18) She toys with the idea of choking herself with her long dark trusses. But later after Raama's emissary. Hanumaan finds her in the Asoka forest as a prisoner and offers her solace, Seetha utters a truth. We can remember the words of wisdom of a very great scholar of the 3/4th century in India, Bharthruhari who said that good and bad are like the spoke of a wheel. In trying circumstances of a person's life, faith and patience are called for. Good, will have to come by: Vaalmeeki expressed this truth long ago through the lips of Seetha before Barthruhari and the like. (Sundara-chapter 34- sloka 6) Seetha affirms "When a person keeps alive, eventually happiness come by to him (or her) although after (may be). 100 years. This worldly 'Saying' has become efficacious in my case "***Thus poet Vaalmeeki expresses another truth. Suicide is no solution.*** In India, it is customary for elders to always bless the young ones "May you live long = Chiranjeevi Bhava, Dheergaaushmaan bhava".

Before we take 'leave' of Seetha and go to other important characters of Vaalmeeki, we should note that Seetha never gave any encouragement to Raavana during her captivity in Lanka. She treated him with utter contempt. Raavana exhibits his wealth, power to entice her. (Aaranya - chapter 55). He exhibits, pearls, costly gems never seen before. Shows his extensive palace, with (swimming pools) oblong ponds, gardens, and what not. He boasts :(sloka 14 to 17). "Oh Seetha. I am lord of 100 million demons. And 22 million demons are of terrible power and deeds. 1,000 demons drawn from them serve me (personally). The rule of my kingdom is entrusted with you. My life likewise. You are more precious than my life." Raavana talking the language of a religious man, says The suffering she had undergone upto now (under Raama) is all gone!! (sloka 28) "Whatever (sin/ karma) by the evil deed (done by you) previously (in your previous birth) (all) that has gone away with your (wretched) forest life (you had with Raama). You now enjoy the "Fruits" of Dharma caused by the (good) deeds (only) done by you (with me as my wife)..."

She is kept prisoner at Asoka forest in Lanka. Raavana gives her 1 year time to change her mind when Seetha places a Dharbha grass and treats him with utter contempt. treats him like a blade of dry grass. Seetha does not take bath, nor eat any luxurious food placed before her by the demonesses who guard her, threaten her, and 'work' upon her to change her mind. But Seetha is a strong, virtuous, woman of Dharma, whose devotion to Raama is total.

6: LAKSHMANA

Every personality in Raamaayana is unique, distinct. Dhasharatha's four sons Raama, Lakshmana, Bharatha and

Shathrugna have distinct personalities. But they have a lot in common. Lakshmana is one of the greatest of men. He was born to the second queen of Dhasharatha, the noble and wise Sumithra. Vaalmeeki uses this expression frequently while talking about Lakshmana = Oh! son of Sumithra =Sowmithri = In the case of Raama, rarely uses the expression, Rama the son of Kowsalya excepting in a few places like in (Bala-chapter 23-sloka 2) when Vishwaamithra wakes him up in forest. Lakshmana is a noble, wise man, born to a most noble, philosophical lady Sumithra. It is Oh.Lakshmana the son of Sumithra!

To say that Lakshmana was always with his brother Raama is to state the obvious. When Vishwaamithra takes Raama with him to his hermitage for protection of his "yaga' and "vows", Lakshmana, even uninvited, goes along with his brother although Vishwaamithra had not requested Dhasharatha for Lakshmana's services also (Baala- chapter 19- sloka 9) Vishwaamithra wanted only Raama. This is very significant. Vishwaamitra could not tell Lakshmana " I don't need you. Your brother is all I want".Vishwaamithra is a very angry man! But he knew Raama. Raama was always with Lakshmana and he did not stop Raama.

Lakshmana, as his name suggests is Lakshmivaan, Lakshmi vardhana and so on. Very auspicious, sign of prosperity., increases prosperity and luster. Association with Lakshmana brings lustre and prosperity. Lakshmana is true to his name.

When Vishwaamithra had taught Raama divine weapons during his tutelage in forest, Raama teaches Lakshmana the usage of the very same divine weapons Vishwaamithra had taught him. Raama's affection for Lakshmana is such. (Bala

Bala - chapter 28 - sloka 16). Raama must share with Lakshmana. Lakshmana's devotion to Raama was such. And Raama being = Krithagnya = a man of gratitude, he shared 'all' with Lakshmana. When Raama hears the news of his being anointed as Crown prince-Yuva raja to succeed his father Dhasaratha, this is what Raama tells Lakshmana (Ayodhya - chapter 4 - sloka 43 and 44) "Oh Lakshman! This resplendent kingdom belongs to you also, who are my very soul (in another body), you are my 'double' ***You rule the_'earth' with me..*** ..Oh son of Sumithra! As fruits of the kingdom , you enjoy pleasures desired...(Because) Life and kingdom I desire for your sake..." Raama even suggests joint rule with Lakshamana! Such was Lakshmana's devotion and loyalty and love to his brother Raama, that Rama could not resist making this offer. Readers ofcourse know that as Raama's coronation did not take place, Lakshmana enjoyed only the 'pleasures of exile' in forest. with Raama! It is interesting that after 14 years of exile when Raama returns to Ayodhya and is crowned King of the kingdom, when Raama as king offers positions to his brothers, Lakshmana alone declines to accept any royal position (Bharatha accepts a position) Yudhdha kaanda - chapter 131- sloka 91) "Yet, in spite of being induced with all his heart by (Raama) and impelled by entreaties, Lakshmana, the son of Sumithra, declined any position...therefore the great soul Raama offered the title of Crown prince to Bharatha, instead..."

Lakshmana had only one goal in life. To serve his brother Raama. As Raama was the embodiment of Dharma, in effect Lakshmana served Dharma.

But we should remember that Lakshmana was first and foremost, a great warrior. He was a Kshathriya warrior belonging to the great Ikshwaaku lineage (of great kings). The Dharma that was foremost in his mind was the Kshathriya Dharma. This is not to say that he did not value other moral values. We will see later what a great noble man he really was, a man of many virtues. When Kaikeyi had effectively put a stop to Raama's coronation just on the day he was to be crowned and Raama was to go on 14 year exile, Lakshmana was terribly angry. He gave went to his feelings. (Ayodhya - chapter21 - slokas 1-20) We give the gist "That Raama should go to forest just to honour the words of a 'woman' is not desired-approved by me. The king (my father) is old and perverse. So, in the affairs of the state, he transgresses norms. Enamoured, instigated by Kaikeyi, what will he not do? By what reason is Raama sent out to forest (what is his sin)....***I will kill this aged father***, the king who is consumed by passion, dominated by a woman...he has lost his sense, no shame at all...he is not devoted to Dharma..." And Lakshmana goes on, a tirade against his father, all because the Kshathriya Dharma of Ikshwaaku lineage was not followed by his father. By tradition, the eldest son takes over the kingdom. Here it is topsy-turvy. But Raama, who had no second thoughts about his going on exile to obey his father and honour his father's commitment to his step mother Kaikeyi, expounds Dharma as he sees it. (Ayodhya – Chapter 21 - sloka 57 to 62) "Oh Lakshmana! I know of your eternal devotion to me. I also know your valour..." Raama makes two points. No wonder Lakshmana is angry. After all his Raama was denied the crown. Secondly, Raama knows that when Lakshman gets angry he can restrain his father to go through with

Kaikeyi's idea of crowning Bharatha instead. Lakshmana possesses such a valour. After all he had taught him all the divine weapons Vishwaamithra had taught him. And Raama continues "..Oh Lad (Lakshmana)! In this world, Dharma, Artha and Kaama are perceived when the fruits of Dharma manifest. All these manifest in one, like a wife blessed with a long desired son. There is no doubt on me whatsoever..." By this Raama affirms that he will follow Dharma rather than go after Artha (Kingdom) and Kaama (pleasures of royalty) / And Raama talks about tight situations like the one facing Lakshmana "///When (in a situation) all three are not found together, one must take recourse to Dharma (from which the other two like Artha and Kaama follow) One who is intent on Artha alone becomes despised. And so is one who is bent on Kaama.." Raama rejects Artha-kingdom He rejects Kaama=pleasures. all because he is bent on following Dharma. of following his father's command (however much it may hurt) to keep his father a man of truth and commitment It is the son's duty to honour his father's commitment, he had made long ago to his step mother Kaikeyi. And his father is a king of Ikshwaaku lineage. Lakshmana had to accept Raama's arguments however hard it was for him to take, particularly when he could set it all right (make Raama the king) by killing or imprisoning his father, taking recourse to his concept of Dharma, the Dharma of a warrior, Kshathriya Dharma. He is so devoted to Raama, he can conceal his feelings. Difficult to know whether Lakshmana really was convinced by Raama's concept of Dharma. But Lakshmana will never go against the wishes of Raama. So devoted was he.

But wrath again seizes Lakshmana. He is not able to reconcile to Raama's fate. We see him in wrath (Full chapter 23) again. He was passing through sorrow and joy. (sloka- 1) Joy because Raama was such a noble man, a man of commitment to his father; Sorrow because he surrendered to the whims and fancy of his father and was choosing the hardship of forest life. Vaalmeeki says he became angry like a cobra in a pit.(sloka 2) ...He was breathing hard and deep. Unable to stand this nonsense of his step mother and father. (Slokas 5 to 42) Lakshmana gives vent to his feelings. He could not accept Raama's concept of Dharma, Karma and Fate. Elsewhere we come across Vaalmeeki's concept of these as seen by Raama, and others like Hanumaan. Here, this is what Lakshmana says: The gist. "Oh Raama! Because of your indulgence and your devotion to this faulty Dharma, and fear that you may cause to the world, great confusion has seized your mind (This will make our kingdom) fall into wrong hands. Such a composed man like you, how can you fall into clutches of the so called) Fate. Fate is unmanliness. There are many slippery characters who pretend to be men of Dharma. Why don't you realise that that this well executed plan of our father and our step mother Kaikeyi) by which the kingdom was snatched away from you, was done by fraud. ....You should not make me (press me) to bear all this...Your decision (to go to forest) is perverse.....contrary to Kshathriya Dharma. ...So much attached are you to this Dharma of yours that you are stupefied. ..When you are capable of setting this (evil of) Adharma all right, (by your valour) why are you fulfilling your father's words which are contemptible, which is Adharma.The Dharma that you follow now is despicable, to all the world. As you dont accept my view, grief overwhelms me. How can you fulfill the wishes of our father and (step) mother who are our parents only in name? That all was caused (decision on your exile and Bharatha's coronation) due to ***Fate*** does not please me. In any case you must investigate the matter further (before you accept your father's command of going on exile). Oh Raama! (Don't you realise that only a weak man timidly follows (the so-called) Fate. Brave men (like you) with inborn qualities of self-reliance do not sit 'around' Fate. Only strong men by manly effort drive away impediments caused by the so called Fate....." After saying all this Lakshmana is so exercised and so angry he threatens action " Let the world witness now the power of man's effort over Fate, the True nature of manliness vis a vis Fate. The people will now witness the knocking down of Fate by ***manly prowess, the Fate by which your royal coronation*** that was ***fixed, was frustrated. I will suppress this work of Fate by my own manliness"*** After affirming "to set it right' by the use of force, Lakshmana says that he will send his father and stepmother, on exile instead.. On one point Lakshmana was factually wrong when he talks about 'pact'. His father did not have a 'pact' with his stepmother Kaikeyi to send Raama on exile or crown her son Bharatha. All that his father had done was he had given two open boons and Kaikeyi had exercised her options at this time and this way. Continuing Lakshmana says "Oh Raama! My two hands are not for beautification (of my body) My bow is not an ornament, My sword is not a piece of attachment..." Lakshmana is very clear. He will kill his father or send him away on exile if Raama is not crowned. Lakshmana loved Raama so much. And Lakshmana being a warrior, a follower of Kshathriya Dharma, will set all this right. By force.

But in one word Raama justifies his acceptance of exile and rejection of violence. Raama's concept of Dharma is beyond Kshathriya Dharma. (Sloka 42) "Repeatedly consoling and calming Lakshmana, wiping tears from Lakshmana's face, Raama who increased the glory of Raghu dynasty says "Lakshmana! You must know me as a man of conviction, the righteous path is in (obeying) words (of command) of our father" No Uncertainty in Raama's Dharma. His father is foremost to him.

When finally he is 'reconciled' to the reality - that his beloved brother Raama will go on his 14 year exile immediately as per the wishes of (his step mother) Kaikeyi and his father's commitment to her by way of the two boons he had given her long, long ago, Lakshmana gets ready to leave with him on his exile. Raama tries to restrain him. He wants Lakshmana to remain in Ayodhya to take care of their father, his mother Kowsalya and other mothers and all. But Raama knows Lakshmana cannot be stopped. We can give the gist of Lakshmana's entreaties (Ayodha - chapter 31 - slokas 3 to 8) "Oh Raama. As you have decided to go to forest, I will also go along with you. Together with me, you will spend the time in the mighty forest abounding in birds, animals. Without you, I care not for life even in heaven. nor even eternal life....." When Raama was still not happy with his coming along, Lakshmana pressed him thus. Lakshmana quoted a precedent. In Vaalmeeki we find references to precedents. In the modern world, even the judiciary, in spite of well written laws, take recourse to precedents. ***Vaalmeeki talks***

about precedents at every opportunity. So Lakshmana justifies his request to go along with Raama thus. "Oh Raama! Even earlier, I had received your permission. Therefore why this restraint upon me this time" Lakshmana was referring to his sojourn with Vishwaamithra when he had accompanied Raama although the invitation by Vishwaamithra covered only Raama. (Baala kaaanda - chapter 19)

Raama could not resist Lakshmana's arguments. Raama was happy to take him along with him to the exile. No Raama without Lakshmana and vice-versa!

An observation we should not lose sight of, but which is worthy of mention. When Raama accompanied by Seetha and Lakshmana takes leave of his father King Dhasharatha just before leaving Ayodhya this is how Raama presents Seetha and Lakshmana. (Ayodhya kaanda –chapter 34 - sloka 23) "Seetha is accompanying me to the forest. And you must give permission to Lakshmana .In spite of being restrained by me with many reasons, he does not desire to remain here....."

Vaalmeeki always remembers protocol. Raama does not seek 'formal' permission for Seetha. Afterall she is his wife. But his brother Lakshmana is a prince, under the command of his father king Dhasharatha. So 'clearance' for his accompanying him must be sought. Vaalmeeki never misses out on details, however insignificant it may appear.... Ofcourse, Raama in the next sloka, formally requests leave to go on exile. .... Back to Lakshmana......

Lakshmana's life is so entwined with Raama's, that when we 'read' their character together we certainly notice certain similarities but they are complimentary as well. In the entire epic, we find these two brothers together always. In Baala kaanda, in Ayodhya Kaanda, in Aaranya kaanda, in Kishkindha kaanda and in Yudhdha kaanda...in all these "books" of Vaalmeeki we 'read about them' together. Even in Sundara Kaanda, which is Hanumaan's kaanda, if we may say so, we find reference to them together. In Sundhara kaanda, chapter 63, when the glorious "Search for Seetha" army under Angadha having achieved the objective of finding Seetha (in Lanka by Hanumaan) was on a celebration spree of wild drinking in Madhu forest of wines belonging to king Sugreeva, and when the Curator of this wine forest took the complaint to his boss, Sugreeva 'waved' him off and told him to 'lay off'. Sugreeva knew that his army would never indulge in wild drinking unless its mission was successful. While Sugreeva and this curator and protector of the wine forest were conversing, Lakshmana who was always vigilant throughout his exile, day and night, who kept his ears and eyes wide open, overheard the conversation, and Sugreeva tells the curious Lakshmana that his Southern army must have found Seetha, judging by the complaint of his curator of his (now) ravished wine forest. (Sundara–Chapter 63-sloka 11 to 24). Raama who was at a distance also hears the news and is extremely delighted. (25). Lakshmana was always 'hearing', 'observing' everything around. But let us get back to their early days of exile. "Sundara" is far away, yet!

As they begin their exile, Raama feels that Lakshmana and Seetha should have no misgivings. After all they chose exile voluntarily unlike him who was commanded. (Ayodhya - chapter 53 - sloka 2.). "Oh Lakshmana! This is our first night (in the forest) away from habitation; and without (our chariot or charioteer) Sumantra. You should have no regrets" Then Raama talks wildly, wailing, so that he can dissuade Lakshmana to get back to Ayodhya even on the first night of their forest life (Slokas-3 to 26). At one point (sloka 16) Raama says "Oh Lakshmana! Your mother (Sumithra) should not suffer (at ayodhya) all on my account Therefore you get back to Ayodhya tomorrow morning".. And Lakshmana is quick with his reply (Sloka 32) "Oh Raama, the tormentor of enemies! Without you I do not desire to 'see' my father, my mother, nor brother Shathrugna. (Why) I dont like to 'see' even heaven " Vaalmeeki says. (Raama) heard such numerous noble words of Lakshmana with respect = Aadhara)= (and consideration.) He decided (then) to complete their entire stay in the forest of 14 annual seasons-years-in a state of **Dharma-** a long time .Raama had a great respect for Lakshmana although he loved him ***deeply*** as a brother as well. ***Vaalmeeki is very choosy about*** usage- ***The word used is = Aadhara= respect, consideration)*** Raama had respect for Lakshmana. Lakshmana was noble, a man of wisdom.

Surprisingly on a few other occasions, when Raama is dejected, he asks Lakshmana to cut short his exile and get back to Ayodhya without him. His love for Lakshmana is such. He can't bear Lakshmana suffering. Neither can Lakshmana bear to see Raama in pain.. So there is no question of Lakshmana leaving Raama in forest. Raama knows it well.

When Raama's friend Guha, a chief of tribals-hunters, after offering hospitality to Raama and Seetha on the banks of the Ganges with the comfort of a grass bed and when Raama is fast asleep, Guha requests Lakshmana to sleep and get some rest. This is what Guha says Ayodhya-chapter 51 - slokas 2 to 7) The gist: "Oh Lakshmana, the royal prince! There is a comfortable bed set up for you. Please refresh yourself.....As I am constantly wandering in the forest there is nothing that is not known to me here. (Why) we can even conquer a mighty army...." Guha sets Lakshmana's mind at rest. He and his folks will be on guard throughout the night. So Lakshmana can also sleep in comfort through night, free of any danger. Now Lakshmana's character reveals Where is the question of sleep and comfort for him He tells Guha thus: (Sloka s 9,10,11) 'When Raama is lying down on bare earth, along with Seetha, how can I obtain or seek comfort. (Oh Guha!) You are seeing such a man who cannot be overpowered by Dhevas, Asura-s in war. (Such a one) is lying on bare earth - on grass along with Seetha! (Ah! What a sight for me to bear) '

Lakshmana rejects hospitality from his dear friend Guha. Throught out their exile Lakshmana never slept or sought comfort for himself. His only concern was the well being of Seetha and Raama. Can there ***be any character nobler than Lakshmana. Service was his motto***. He gave up Ayodhya, comforts, his mother, and even his wife for 14 years to serve Raama.

Lakshmana never considered any service to Seetha and Raama mean or unworthy. When Bharatha vows to get back Raama to Ayodhya and force him to cut short his exile in spite of his father's (and mother Kaikeyi's command) and wants to crown Raama in the forest itself, he takes a large army along with VIP-s, ministers, mothers (Raama's mother, Kowsalya, Lakshmana's mother Sumithra and his mother Kaikeyi) to Raama's hermitage. As Raama's mother Kowsalya goes to meet Raama in his hermitage, she becomes sad, not because her son Raama is leading such a life but because she observes something on the way disturbing her terribly: (Ayodhya-chapter 103- 4 to 7): Kowsalya to Sumithra. "This is the obscure bathing place in forest for these fatherless brothers (Raama and Lakshman) who are never wearied in (good) actions, who are exiled by Kaikeyi. Oh Sumithra! Your son (Lakshmana) son of Sumithra, is carrying water by himself for my son Raama from here, never tired of service to him. Your son will never be censured, even if he indulges in mean acts, because it is decreed that all (good) service done to a brother is meritorious" At least now, your son (Lakshmana) who is not used to such suffering, will he give up this inferior, menial tasks he is doing? (as service to his brother Raama) ...".

Kowsalya like her step son Bharatha and a host of others including citizens, VIP-s, ministers who have all come to the forest to take back Raama along with his wife Seetha and Lakshmana are living in a fool's paradise. Raama will not cut short his 14 year exile. And for Lakshmana, no service is menial if done for Seetha and Raama. Lakshmana did not approve of Raama's exile. Infact he wanted Raama to disobey his father and Kaikeyi's command. But once he accepted Raama's decision as Dharma, Lakshmana will never do anything that will bring ignominy to Raama. He will serve Raama all the 14 years in forest. This is

Lakshmana. By this we are revealing here only a fraction of his great and noble character, as we shall see presently.

It is amazing and remarkable that a prince of Ikshwaaku lineage who is ever used to comforts, who is not expected to do work that involves manual labour, whose concern is only administration of state and its safety, whose only physical labour is military training and bearing arms (bow and weapons), should be such a dexterous man, that he could fell trees, cut the logs, and construct a cottage in forest all by himself. And he can build a raft as well. This is ***Lakshmana for you***. He ***is an architect and a builder***. And he does not need assistance. He designs, procures materials and constructs a hermitage for Raama and Seetha all by his manual labour. (In Ayodhya - chapter 56 - slokas 22 to 33) We see him build a cottage at Chithrakoot. Again, (in aaranya - chapter 15 - slokas 21 to 27) at Panchavati, Lakshmana builds such a lovely cottage, that he receives what Lakshmana cherishes most - Praise from Raama! (Sloka's 29 and 30) "Oh Lakshmana the destroyer of enemies! I am pleased with you. This is great work done by you. My only present is this "hug" for you! Oh Lakshmana! the noble soul man of Dharma! Our father Dhasharatha is ***not dead, because of you***, who are his son, a knower of Dharma, a man of gratitude, who knows mind and heart of others ..." Yes. An architect should know the mind and heart of the lady of the house who is going to live there. Lakshmana knows the mind of Raama and Seetha. So his cottage fully satisfies Raama and Seetha. No wonder, he earns high praise from Raama.

Yes. Lakshmana is also an architect.!

When under advice from Sage Bharadhwaja, they go to Chithrakoot to establish a hermitage for their stay in the beginning of their exile, Raama and Lakshmana had to cross the fast moving river Yamuna at a point. They construct a make shift raft. Their versatility is obvious. Princes they are, yet they are experts even in making boats! (Ayodhya - Chapter 55 - slokas 15 to 23). Lakshmana even prepares a nice seat in this make shift raft (In sloka 16) "Then the brave Lakshman cut sticks of Ratan (botanically= Calassus Rotung) from Jambu tree (Eugenia jambulina) and made a comfortable seat for Seetha". Point is Lakshmana was ever keen to see Seetha in minimum of discomfort in their exile. Seetha should not cross over Jamuna in fear, standing on raft. She must sit in comfort. Thus, Seetha, while crossing Jamuna could offer her prayers when they were in the middle of the river (Slokas 20 to 22) The gist. "Oh Lady Jamuna! Swasthi! (bless us). I am crossing you. May Raama fulfill his vows. When Raama blessed with (your) Swasthi returns (after completing his exile,) to Ayodhya, I will worship you..."

Yes. Lakshmana is a boat builder of some merit!

Lakshmana's life is entwined with Raama's. We have often heard it said that Lakshmana is given to anger and wrath and generally Raama who calms him down. Lakshmana's wrath is because of his profession. He is a Kshathriya. But Raama has the greatest regard for Lakshmana. The only time he admonished him was when Lakshmana had left their hermitage, leaving Seetha alone there, when he was away on the hunt of the golden deer. Lakshmana had never disobeyed Raama's command. But we know that Lakshmana disobeyed Raama and left Seetha alone because no one would tolerate such a character assassination that was indulged in by Seetha. of Lakshmana. This is what Raama says (Aaranya - chapter 59 - sloka 23) Oh Lakshmana! You came here on hearing the harsh words of a woman who was angry. You came here leaving Seetha alone. I am not pleased with you" And follows this up with sloka (24) "Seized by the clutches of wrath, goaded by Seetha, ***you have violated my command. This is quite contrary (to your usual conduct) in every way"***

Perhaps, this is the only time Raama was displeased by Lakshmana's conduct. And as events turned out, Raama was justified in admonishing Lakshmana. (Seetha was kidnapped by Raavana, when she was alone).

Let us look at it this way. Lakshmana treated Seetha as a Goddess. Raama is 'God' to Lakshmana and so Seetha is Goddess. Infact he worshipped her. So he could not restrain Seetha or talk back to her when she went on a tirade against him, using foul language. But she was still a "Goddess" to him. In Kishkinda kaanda, there is a master piece of a sloka by Vaalmeeki which sums up it all. When Seetha was being taken over the sky by Raavana, she had discarded her jewels and thrown them down from the sky. Seetha being an intelligent lady, hoped that someone might find these jewels and show them to Raama when Raama would be making a search for her. As events turned out, Sugreeva's monkey chiefs found these on the cliffs of the mountain they were staying and when Raama and Lakshmana meet him, Sugreeva exhibits these jewels for identification that these were all Seetha's and she was borne over the sky by some 'demon'. Raama wails. And he wants to share his grief with his 'shadow' Lakshmana (Kishkindha – Chapter

6 - Sloka 20 and 21) "Oh Lakshmana! See these ornaments thrown away by Seetha as she was being carried away. See her upper garments. These ornaments were scattered on the soft fresh (grasslands) earth, thrown by Seetha as she was abducted. Surely that is why they are in the same condition"...

Now dear readers. You are in for a surprise. Raama expected Lakshmana who was ever with him, to recognise his wife Seetha's jewels. ***Here comes a master piece from Vaalmeeki. (sloka 22)*** When told by Raama thus, Lakshmana said (to Raama) "I do not know nor have I seen Keyoora (forearm ornament). Nor do I know of her Kundala (Ear drop ornament) But I do know (and do recognise) the Noopura ornament (her - anklet ornaments). Because I have ever served her at her feet (have worshipped her at her feet)" This is how Poet Vaalmeeki describes Lakshmana's devotion to Seetha.. Lakshmana had never looked up, at her. He looked down at her feet, always in reverence. He had never stared at her face! ***Vaalmeeki at his best. It is such a Lakshmana, Seetha abused.*** Raama's admonishment of Lakshmana on his failure to obey his command may be justified. But Lakshmana was heart broken. His Goddess had 'failed' - at least temporarily. This was not the Seetha he knew. This is not the Seetha we all know. But fate had struck her down, the first casualty was her character. And she suffered, suffered terribly for her transgression on Lakshmana who treated her as a Goddess.

In our ancient land, the Bhaaratha Varsh, there never was and perhaps never can be another man like Raama. That Lakshmana was a shadow, a companion, a mentor, and a conscience keeper to this greatest personality, can be attributed only to Divine 'Sanction'. Who can ever be a mentor to Raama! Yet, time and again, in Raamaayana, it is Lakshmana who offers solace to Raama, consoles him, reminds him of his greatness and his incomparable virtues. Infact, once, when Raama was so dejected that his grief overpowered him, Lakshmana, after reminding Raama about his noble qualities and valour, says (in Kishkinda-chapter 27-sloka 40) "..Oh Raama! Time and again I have to remind you about your bravery that seems to go to 'sleep'. Like (rekindling) Holy Fire with pure oblation....of Ahoothi when it is covered by ash. Is it not?..."

Vaalmeeki brings home a truth. However great a man may be, unless he is served by another noble man, depression and dejection might strike him down.

During his entire life with Raama during their exile, poor Lakshmana had not only to bear physical suffering (he did not sleep even at night to keep vigil), he had to offer solace, comfort, even advice to Raama. Lakshmana had to put up a brave, cheerful face even when calamity had hit Raama in the form of his wife's abduction.

In Aaranya Kaanda we see Lakshmana offering solace to Raama.We shall refer to Kishkinda kaanda - chapter 1-. Raama grieves over Seetha. The sight of the beautiful Pampa river basin only adds to his grief; as without Seetha everything appears distasteful to him. Lakshmana is worried that Raama will be 'consumed' by grief and be led into a state of inaction, unworthy of a warrior of the Ikshwaaku clan.

It is worth writing about all that Lakshmana says to Raama, when he grieves about the abducted Seetha. (Kishkinda - chapter 1 - slokas 122 to 143) We give the gist 'Oh Raama the Kaakuthsa! Like a kinnara (worrying over) a female kinnara which is (temporarily) dislocated because of floods, are you tormenting yourself over Seetha, as a feeble person. A woman with such qualities is rare. Yet, Oh Raama, you must (ever) worship (and honour) Dharma alone abandoning everything else." Lakshmana speaking about Kshathriya Dharma says further "There is nothing that is unattainable here (in this world) for one who makes effort (with zeal) through Dharma. Only resolute men prosper. The resolute is foremost. A base man, not knowing the essence of life cannot bear anything, being petty minded. A man like you who has deep understanding (significance) of and the "course of Time" (Kaala pramaana), always 'bears' (temporary suffering) Having renounced the kingdom and the pleasures that are not easily attainable (by even great) men, you have incurred various sufferings (and borne) like a mountain (hit) by hurricane. You are tormenting yourself like a cheap person who is 'covered' by darkness (ignorance). Getting back to your old natural state, you should "harness" yourself to the utmost (to retrieve Seetha and punish the abductor). Like a charioteer with his good (obedient) horses, welfare will (always) be there for you in joy and sorrow. ***You should not direct your mind on grief which only causes (increases) distress (and is purposeless.)*** Like the fiery (turbulent) ocean, harnessing your srength, exhibiting your resolve (and intentions), completing the life in forest and then obtaining 'the earth' (kingdom)...you are going to obtain then after the foremost satisfaction, fame (fruits of) Dharma. And he who stole Seetha, must now be searched for (and found now itself).. The thief, (who stole Seetha) is ' touching the rod of death' Killing him and retrieving Seetha, may you become happy.

And Lakshmana emphasises the urgency of the task at hand. *"Oh Raama! The 'lion' among men! The Urgent And Foremost Task Is This* "And Lakshmana adds. "Oh Raama! Take On Courage! Welfare to you. Do not Lament. The 'Wisdom' of men like you whose mind is never impure, never becomes feeble (never dull). Give up this grief caused by (temporary) separation. The wick, even when wet, burns (when lots of oil are poured). (Likewise you will waste away in torment) when excessive passion and attachment, 'embraces' you (seizes you)....Whether he this Raavana, is in Pathaala (Underworld) or in Upperworld, he will not be alive...But let us obtain the 'presence' of this sinful person and he will obtain death (the moment he is sighted). Seetha, he will give up. Without effort, success never comes. Finally, he says "Oh Raama! Take recourse to perseverance, Because, perseverance (effort) only is strength, powerful (yielding results). There is nothing greater than perseverance, nothing difficult to obtain for a man who has perseverance" ....Lakshmana always had to use his ingenuity to console and 'stir' Raama for action.

Every now and then the most composed Raama gets into a state of 'despair', totally divorced from his character. ***The wise and noble Vaalmeeki expounds yet another Truth.*** When calamity hits us, we are terribly human and we lose our composure and even a strong man of character succumbs to grief and a sense of helplessness. What would have been the fate of Raama if this noble, wise Lakshmana had not been with him as a mentor, as his shade and shadow, and companion. Raama ofcourse recognises this.

Lakshmana was such a man.

Lakshmana, what a great humanitarian he was! As an Ikshwaaku prince and warrior, he bore arms. Weapons he wielded as a 'tool' for protection of citizens. But he would never use the 'tool' for disturbing ecology or harming innocent subjects. We take readers to Aranya kaanda- chapters 63 to 65. The search for Seetha around forests by Raama and Lakshmana naturally turns futile, because Seetha was taken away by the king the of demons, over the ocean, 1,000 miles away to his island kingdom of Lanka. Raama is in wrath as he gets no response when he questions even rivers, mountains, trees and what not, about the whereabouts of Seetha. (chapter 64 - Sloka 31 to 34) In those days, Nature had power of communication through "signs". Getting angry, Raama addressed the mountain like a lion before an ordinary animal. "If you don't want that I should crush all your ridges and plateaus, then show me the golden hued Seetha." And when there was no "sign" or movement in the mountain, Raama gets so furious he says" "Burnt up by the fire power of my arrows, devoid of any grass, trees, and plants, deserted in every way, you will be reduced to ashes. His wrath is never wasted. He could crush even mountains. And Raama threatens rivers. "If this does not inform me about Seetha whose face is like the moon, this river also, I will dry up ".... Raama goes ....talking to Lakshmana in fury... **(In sloka 56) Raama tells Lakshmana a truth** Generally people mistake kindliness for weakness. "Perhaps the celestial lords think of me as one totally lacking in bravery...because I am soft, a man of patience, and restraint ..." ... Finally Raama decides to show his power. Raama in wrath is deluge. (In sloka 69) "Oh Lakshmana! when the three worlds are destroyed by my wrath, Dhevas of heaven will not be there. Nor Daithyas, nor Pishaachas ..." (Aaranya – Chapter 64 - sloka 75) Raama says without uncertainty "Oh Lakshmana! Like fever, death, Time, Fate, all which cannot be warded off by all beings, I, who am in wrath, cannot be restrained in any way (by any one) .....I will make the world topsy turvy...."

Now this is the Raama that Lakshmana sees, confronts for the first time. Lakshmana has never seen Raama in such wrath. And he knows Raama's wrath is never wasted and is verily deluge, total destruction. But Lakshmana is a humanitarian. He cannot tolerate mountains, rivers and trees destroyed by Raama's wrath. He begins to pacify Raama with some sound reasoning. Aaranya-Chapter 65-slokas 5-8:

"Oh Raama! Having been a man of restraint, a tender man who is good to the world, you should not (now) abandon your (inborn) natural good qualities, afflicted by this power of wrath. Like graciousness of the moon, brilliance in Sun, pervasiveness in Wind, forbearance and composure of (mother) Earth, all the foremost qualities are inherent in you." Having described The Raama we all know, Lakshmana gives the reason why Raama should control himself "...Oh Raama! ***Because of a single transgression (by one) you should not destroy the worlds*** Oh King! Instead I am (now) speaking about another original view that is most acceptable (most agreeable) in all actions.. Between the two, Non Dharma never scores victory over Dharma. The Virtuous Seetha who is most auspicious (like Goddess Lakshmi) will never come to harm." And continuing Lakshmana says (Aaranya – Chapter 65 - slokas 12 to16). "Raama! Kings (who are lord of earth) should be tender (kind), tranquil, and give only proper punishment.

For the sake of one transgressor, (for one sin of abduction) you should not destroy the entire world. You are ever the foremost Refuge for all living beings. They seek refuge. Who will ever justify as proper the abduction of your wife? Lakshmana finally affirms (sloka 19) "Oh Raama! Oh the lord of men! If you do not get back Seetha graciously with due respect and in proper conduct to you and in good shape, then you may make everything topsy turvy with a shower of arrows that are gold tipped and comparable to Lord Indra's Vajra." Lakshmana is firm. Raama along with him must make every effort to search for Seetha and catch hold of the criminal. Punishment and wrath should come later.

Vaalmeeki expounds a truth. Justice must be done. Justice may take time. But only the culprit has to be punished. There is no room for wrath when we seek justice.

Lakshmana being a humanitarian and conscience keeper of the noble Raama enlightens us all.

In the art of persuasion, Lakshmana has few equals. When a man is in wrath, it is very difficult to bring him to his senses. In Aaranya-chapter 66, we find this quality in Lakshmana. For instance, he knows that Raama has great affection for their brother Bharatha. So he gently mentions Bharatha by name to him to soften him up! (sloka 4,) ".....this is well known to your brother Bharatha as well..." And in next sloka he says "Oh Raama! If this suffering that has befallen, if you cannot bear, tell me, which other man can bear "(You alone can set an example, says Lakshmana). Raama is the refuge for all. When that is so " ...Oh Raama, the 'tiger' of men! If in anguish, you 'burn' up everything by your power, to whom will the afflicted citizens go to, for removal of their suffering." And Lakshmana quotes precedents. (Slokas 7 to 12). Gist. "This (the suffering) is natural in the world; Yayathi, son of king Nahusha who had kept company with Indra in heaven, fell down on earth.....Our family priest Vasishta had 100 sons. But he lost all of them in a single day. ....And She is The Lady, the mother Earth. Yet she is shaken up by Earthquakes...And the Eyes of the World, Sun and Moon...Even they are eclipsed by Raahu and Kethu..The Dhevas.(of heaven).. cannot escape Fate Why! Even Lord Indra undergoes suffering - good and bad exists among him and his celestials.... So you should not grieve unduly, Oh Raama..." Lakshmana uses the 'Trump' card (slokas 17/18) "Oh Raama! many times, you yourself have advised me. (Tell me) Who will and can reveal all this to you, even if he be a Brihaspathi I say this because. your mind is unfathomable....even by Dhevas...I am merely arousing and waking up your mind and understanding that has gone to sleep due to your grief.." Lakshmana is a man of modesty. even when he presses and arouses Raama with reasons, he says "I am no Brihaspathi to advise you".

Taking leave of Lakshmana for the time being, we must recognise that in Lakshmana we have a character whose qualities of service to the cause of Dharma, is unique and we cannot do sufficient justice in our write up. When Lakshmana left Ayodhya on exile along with Seetha and Raama. his mother knew her son. Sumithra did not exhibit her sorrow of separation as Kowsalya did towards her son Raama. She knew. In following Raama. Lakshmana followed Dharma.

We will conclude our disertation on Lakshmana's character with what his mother told the crying Kowsalya by way of consolation (Ayodhya-chapter 44- sloka 5) "Lakshmana who has always been compassionate, is now with him, as a sinless man, always doing service in this noble course of action (of going on exile with Raama). To this great soul - to this my son Lakshmana-this is gain (of fame, wealth and all).

7: BHARATHA

As his name suggests, Bharatha has enormous capacity to 'bear' and sustain. (from root Bru-Bar = to bear, sustain). All the sons of king Dhasharatha (Raama, Lakshmana, Bharatha, Shathrugna) are noble men of character. They have many things in common; but their character is distinct.

We may be excused for some diversion. This land of ours (so called India) is named Bhaaratha Varsh. It is said Manu himself chose this name for the country. Bharatha is a hallowed name. This land is the sustainer, is the Karma Bhoomi. Not a land for mere pleasures, but a land devoted to Dharma and values. Its citizens are supposed to 'bear' and 'sustain', 'foster' Dharma.It is also known as AaryaVartha, land of the noble. No wonder, Vasishta named this son of Dhasharatha, Bharatha. Appropriately so, as we will see when we proceed. Bharatha brought glory to this land of ours. Infact, the great Tamizh poet and author, Kamban, who wrote his version of the Raamaayana, has this to say about Bharatha when Bharatha turns down the kingdom of Ayodhya which was offered on a'plate' (so to speak) ..." If, at the behest of the mother, the father gave the kingdom to you, and you ***rejected*** it as (it was) evil, and sorrowfully came (to meet) and see Raama (to press him to take the kingdom), can a thousand Raamas be equal to you,

(Bharatha)." Valmeeki ofcourse would not go this far to praise Bharatha and compare him with thousand Raamas. His sense of proportion will not justify such praise and such a comparison indulged in by Kamban. But there is little doubt that Bharatha was a great noble man of Dharma. He did everything possible to set right the Adharma of his mother Kaikeyi who snatched away the kingdom from his brother Raama to make him king.

We should be and circumspect in offering our criticism against observations made by authors. We have to take note of the circumstances under which an author makes his observation. Kamban was no ordinary man. He was a 'divine' Tamizh poet. No doubt very few would turn down kingship; And the kingdom we are talking about is the most prosperous and powerful Ayodhya. Yet, in as much as Kamban has compared Bharatha with a 1,000 Raamas, we should refer to Vaalmeeki and talk about a ***single Raama***. In Yudhdha kaanda, chapter 128-sloka 17, when Raama after completing 14 years of exile as per the command of his father and (Bharatha's mother) Kaikeyi, is on way to Ayodhya to take back the kingdom from Bharatha who had ruled it as a care taker 'king', this is what Raama tells his emissary Hanumaan " ...The resplendent Bharatha, the darling of Raghu-s, if he is desirous of possessing (and keeping) this kingdom because of his association with it (for 14 years), ***then let him rule the vast entire earth (our kingdom)***"

As we said in the beginning, all the four sons of Dhasharatha had similar qualities, they were noble men of Dharma. There is no need for Bharatha being compared with a 1,000 Raamas. To enlighten the world about

Bharatha's greatness and nobility, comparison with one Raama is more than enough. He was as noble as Raama.

Bharatha is such a sweet person he had no enemies. (In Ayodha-chapter 70-sloka 30) Vaalmeeki says "...the great soul Bharatha, who had no enemies = Apetha shathru = ..."

If we can find any fault in his character, it is when he condemns his mother so much, that he would have liked to kill her for her vile deed.. No son should ever entertain such thoughts. But we are ahead of our story......

We know that Bharatha had gone on a holiday to the Kekeya kingdom to spend pleasant days with his maternal grandfather and uncle, along with Shathrugna. A great Drama had taken place in Ayodhya during his absence. His mother Kaikeyi, pressing her husband king Dhasharatha with two boons, had sent out Raama on a 14 year exile and was awaiting Bharatha's return to take over of Ayodhya. And Dhasharatha also had died in utter grief over the separation of his beloved son Raama. This was the scenario when Bharatha under urgent summons from Vasishta, cuts short his holiday and returns to Ayodhya.

Bharatha is a very intelligent prince. When he drives into Ayodhya he knows that there is something seriously wrong with Ayodhya. (In chapter 71 of Ayodhya) he shares his thoughts and grief with his charioteer who had brought him from holiday. As he enters his father's palace, he gets the first shock. His father is not there. Then he visits his mother Kaikeyi. After exchanging a few pleasantries, Bharatha asks her about his father (Chapter 72- slokas 12 and 13) "Oh mother! Mostly at this time, the king my father, will be at my mother's place. (at your palace). I came here desirous of seeing him. But I don't see him. I must prostrate and touch his feet. Perhaps he is with the eldest queen (Kowsalya) ... As I am asking you, you must tell me..." Now comes the second shock for Bharatha as Kaikeyi tells him (slokas 15) "Your brilliant father, the great soul king who had ***performed yaagas*** and who was the Refuge for all good men, has gone the way of all beings"

Vaalmeeki expounds a truth even here! Death strikes one and all, even if he is a mighty emperor with an accumulation of the fruits of Yaagas. So (poetically) Kaikeyi says = Oh my son Bharatha, your father is dead and gone = And when Bharatha swoons and had to be lifted up, Kaikeyi addresses him thus. (Ayodhya – Chapter 72 - sloka 24 and 25).

Vaalmeeki's master piece as usual. Kaikeyi addresses Bharatha not as "Oh son, but as, Oh most famous king!" For Kaikeyi, Bharatha is not just her son any more but the King of Ayodhya although he is still to be royally crowned.

The third shock for Bharatha is to come when he tells his mother (sloka 32 and 33) "Please inform at once of my arrival to Raama who is never wearied in (good) service, ***who is my brother, father, and a friend To this wise man I am but a devoted servant.*** To me who understands Dharma, an elder brother becomes father to him. I will catch at the feet of this Aryan, noble Raama,. Indeed he is now my Refuge "Ofcourse his father is dead and his brother Raama is gone far away on exile. ***Vaalmeki reveals Bharatha's devotion to Raama here*** and with his father gone, it is Raama, Bharatha will look up to. And when Kaikeyi tells him how his father died, wailing Oh Raama, Oh Seetha, Oh Lakshmana Bharatha is shocked and asks her (slokas 40)

"Where is this noble man of Dharma, who increases the joy of his mother Kowsalya, Accompanied by Seetha and Lakshmana where (have they gone)" Kaikeyi replies calmly that they have gone to Dhandaka forest. Bharatha is shocked. Only criminals are sent out to forest as punishment. His Raama is a pure soul. Why had he to go. Bharatha gives vent to his thoughts thus entertaining fear about his brother's conduct (slokas 43 to 46). ***Vaalmeeki through the lips of Bharatha lists some sins here.*** Gist: "Oh mother! I trust some poor Braahmin's wealth was not seized by Raama! I hope no sinless man, poor or rich was harmed by Raama in any way? I hope Raama has not desired (considered in his mind) another's wife. Then for what reason has he been sent out as though he had killed a pregnant woman ". (Incidentally these are some of the sins for which a person could be put away.) When Kaikeyi describes the Drama of the night at Ayodhya, how she exercised her options of the two boons she had obtained from Dhasharatha long, long ago to make his son Bharatha ascend the throne, Bharatha is stunned. Kaikeyi had replied thus (Ayodhya – Chapter 72 - sloka 48 to 55). "No brahmin's wealth was coveted by Raama. No sinless man, rich or poor was harmed by Raama. And you know very well Raama never sets his eye on any woman other than Seetha. He went on exile to fulfill my two boons..."

Bharatha falls unconscious. Was stunned for one hour. (Ayodhya-chapter 73-) Now comes Bharatha's tirade against his mother. We had said before that the only failing-fault in his noble character is his cursing his mother and entertaining thoughts of killing her as well. Bharatha has no enemies, remember. But his mother was not just his enemy.

She was the enemy of all the good folks of Ayodhya. For once Bharatha loses his composure and starts showering abuses on his mother whose 'crime' was her passion for her son, to make him king by any means. Bharatha admonishes her "Shame on me that I spent 10 months in your womb. I stand condemned in the world. Because you 'killed' your husband and you sent away my beloved Raama. For mere pleasures, you have made the king a dead body and Raama (the warrior), a man of penance. Oh you stupid woman. Hang yourself. Take poison or take to water to drown yourself." "Oh Kaikeyi! I would kill you rightaway. But people will say of me that Raama's younger brother is a killer of a woman, his own mother" Bharatha would never want Raama being talked about like this because of his (Bharatha's) crime of killing a woman. A kshathriya never kills a woman. Never a mother.

Bharatha continues his tirade. "What purpose is served for me by this kingdom, without father and with Raama gone. My father had not realised when he used to hug you that you are hot charcoal......"

But Bharatha knows that his mother is not entirely a sinful woman. She must have been instigated "Oh wicked woman. What is all this. Whose work was done by you. By whom were you advised?" Finally Bharatha vows (sloka 28,37,38 of Chapter 72 - Aydhya) "If perchance, there is found in me that strength by (some) method and power of judgement (to rule) I will not see you, who are greedy for the sake of your son, fulfill your desire...I will at once bring back this sinless brother who is beloved of all....most disagreeable though it may be to you, Kaikeyi! ....Bringing back Raama I will become a devoted servant of a Raama who possesses burning brilliance. ..I am fully resolved..."

If poet Kamban had talked so highly of Bharatha it is understandable. Bharatha did not entertain the thought of enjoying the kingdom even for a second. A great, noble man of Dharma, who knew the Norms of Ikshwaku dynasty, he knew that eldest son was always the successor. It is Raama and only Raama who is fit to succeed the throne.

Bharatha was firm. After performing the Last Rites for his father whose body had been preserved, he would go to the forest and bring back Raama after crowning him in forest, forcing him to cut short his exile! (In chapter 66 -sloka 14 and 15 of Ayodhya) we find that even those days, they knew the art of preserving a dead body for days. As all the sons of Dhasharatha were away from Ayodhya when he died, his body was preserved so that Bharatha may perform his Last Rites on his return from his holiday.Bharatha is so disgusted, that he says (Ayodhya – Chapter – 74 – Sloka 31) "After bringing back Raama, I will go to forest on exile instead'

No wonder authors extol Bharatha so highly.

Bharatha is a sweet person he would not harm any one, even people who cause him injury. His tirade against his mother is understandable. Kaikeyi was no ordinary woman. She is a princess, born to the king of Kekeya. Her father is known as a man of Dharma. How could she indulge in such a sin and connive to make her son, the king. When hunch back Manthara, who had instigated Kaikeyi to go through with such a scheme, appears in the Council hall dressed up in jewellery Bharatha's brother Shathrugna, who is normally a man of composure, who has 'conquered' his passions, becomes so angry that he is about to attack the sinful Manthara. (Ayodhya-chapter 78) The door keeper introduces her thus (Sloka 9) "This is the vile sinful woman. By whose actions Raama is in forest now and (your) father is dead. Teach her a lesson...). Shathrugna in wrath, drags her, her jewellery etc were scattered on earth (sloka 12). It is then that Bharatha restrains Shathrugna and calms him (Sloka 21, to 23) Gist: "A female should never be harassed. Therefore may she be forgiven." And Bharatha warns Shathrugna. So much respect and love he has for Raama, Bharatha tells him (slokas 22,23) "If the man of Dharma our brother Raama will not be annoyed with me as a killer of mother, I would have killed this sinful mother Kaikeyi.And if Raama comes to know about the harassment to this hunch back woman, he will not talk to you, ever" Valmeeki had described Shathrugna (Ayodhya- chapter 1-sloka 1) "Shathrugna = the Nithya Shathrugna = meaning that Shathrugna is one who had conquered passions, wrath, jealousy and what not. Yet it is Bharatha who had to remind him about non injury, particularly to a woman., restrain him, and presses him to control his emotions.

No wonder authors extoll Bharatha so highly.

We have repeated this many times. Vaalmeeki wrote the epic without fear or favour. He was factual. But he wrote with devotion, Dharma in his mind. He never spared any one. Even as Bharatha had vowed to bring back Raama from the forest as king of Ayodhya, it is the rather strange that his (step) mother Kowsalya, should wound him like this (Ayodhya- chapter 75- sloka 10,11) "Kowsalya who was in great anguish, addressed Bharatha thus: By the cruel deed of Kaikeyi, this kingdom was 'given' to you, who ***was greedy to possess the kingdom***. It was obtained so quickly by you without hindrance "Poor Bharatha. What a shame he had to hear such character assassination from Kowsalya. Bharatha, being greedy to obtain kingdom! (The poet uses the word = Raajya- Kaama =) It is at that time Bharatha vows, that if he was really 'greedy' to possess the kingdom as charged by his (step) mother Kowsalya, may all the sins (of the world) afflict him. ***Vaalmeeki through the lips of Bharatha, lists some*** sins. We wanted to write a separate chapter in this Guide on what all constitutes sin. The concept of sin is tricky. But we cannot but write about this now, as the noble Bharatha talks about what he considers to be sin in the world. Bharatha begins by begging Koswalya "Oh Aryan lady! Why do you censure me who am sinless, ignorant as I am (I was away at my grandfather's place when all this had happened). You know my strong attachment to Raama the Raaghava" Then he begins. If because of me Raama the Raghava was sent on exile, may the following sins afflict me: We give the Gist (chapter 75 of Ayodhya - sloka 21 to 57): Sins of such men, as under:

1: May that man's mind and perceptions never conform to norms of Shasthra-s. (sinful man's conduct against norms)

2: May he obtain slavery due to sinners. (slavery is the worst.

3: May he defecate in open before Sun (No bath room!)

4: May he kick a sleeping cow with his feet. (Cow is docile and a good animal, most beneficial, sacred)

5: May he harm a good king who protects subjects like his own sons. (A sinful man will go against the law of the land)

6: Having extracted hard labour from servants, may he not pay dues, decent emoluments.(Worker not a slave)

7: The sin that a King commits when having extracted a Sixth as Taxes, does not offer protection to his subjects

(Duty of a good king is to account for taxes he collects)

8: Having performed Yagas and Rituals with the assistance of priests, having agreed to pay fees, cheats them, by skillfully debating that they did not do a good job. (Breach of 'contract' by cleverly finding fault after the work is done)

9: May he be a coward in war, calling himself a warrior

10: May he deny the Holy texts. (In our land one may deny God & Religion But it is sin to deny Vedhas/Scriptures. This is the basic difference between our religion and other religions. Sanathana Dharma as contained in the Holy Texts is our religion, our God.)

11: May this man never see Raama's face. (Religious readers interpret this as Raama is Vishnu on earth. Not being able to see Raama is equivalent to not 'seeing' 'perceiving' God Vishnu)

12: May he devour cakes, sweet milk and products, meat (gluttony is sin)

13: May he cheat friends (cheating a trusted friend is sin)

14: May this wicked man spread false accusations, told partially in secrecy. (Rumour mongering is sin. Particularly when only part facts are known. And told in confidence)

15: May he be ungrateful (Raamaayna itself begins with the word =Krithagnya = gratitude)

16: May he be shameless, lazy, most hated by all.

17: May he eat all by himself in his own house. (Food is to be shared with the members of his family without discrimination, even in a poor man's abode)

19: May he perish without a good wife without progeny

20: May he be without son to do his last rites

21: May his life be short

22: May the sin of killing a king, a woman, a child, an old man, afflict him

23: May the sin of abandoning those who serve him afflict him

24: May sin afflict him who should offer gold to servants who serve him duly but gives them only resinous and putrefied food.

25: May he be slain as he flees from enemy when the battle is raging. (To turn your back in war is sin)

26: May he wander in rags, like a beggar with a begging bow

27: May he be overwhelmed by passion and wrath, always indulge in liqour, women and gambling

28: May his mind ever be in Non Dharma.

29: May his pursuits ever end in failure/worthless

30: May all his accumulations be plundered by robbers

31: May sin afflict him that befalls one who sleeps during Sandhyas

32: May the sin of arson afflict him

33: May he obtain sin of violating his teacher's wife

34: May sin afflict him when one commits treachery on his friend.

35: May he not serve his mother and father duly

36: May he not 'serve' deities with offerings

37: May he be thrown out from 'world' of good men.

38: May he not share glory of the good

39: May he cast away traditional practices

40: May he be so worthless as not to serve his mother

41: May he be with innumerous children, poor, always suffering with diseases.

42: May he be false to the expectations (of promised assistance) to those who seek help, who are feeble, and look up for help, with eyes raised in expectation. (Insincerity is a crime)

43: May he live by fraud, fearing King (and country),

44: May he violate his own virtuous wife after she had just finished her (monthly period) and taken menstural bath. (Violating wife is also a rape)

45: May he abandon his virtuous wife and have intercourse with another's wife

46: May he obtain the sin of one who makes drinking water dirty

47: May he with an impure mind disturb one who is doing prayers, particularly set up by a Brahmin(priest)

48: May he milk a cow that has just given birth to calf (milkmen should not be so avaricious)

49: May he refuse water to a thirsty man

50: May he, during a debate, although he 'sees' the path (of righteousness) refuse to accept this but steadfastly holds on to his own.

In effect, Bharatha swears, that if he had a hand in Raama's exile to take over the kingdom for himself, all these sins enumerated by him should afflict him

It is an irony that this noblest man of them all, should curse himself thus for no fault of his. But a purpose is served, Vaalmeeki through lips of this sinless man lists some of the sins in the world.

Kowsalya regrets she had accused him (of treachery to her son). But she makes amends when she says (slokas 61 and 62) after addressing him as Oh my son! "At this moment my sorrow is even more aroused. By your curses, you are tormenting me. Oh my son! (Bharatha) who is endowed with noble qualities. ***Blessed with divinity***, you will attain "The world of The Good"

Is there any wonder authors extoll Bharatha so high. All the four sons of king Dhasharatha are of strong personality and character. When ministers press Bharatha that as the kingdom will be ruined without a king, and as Raama is in exile, he should straight a way crown himself. Normally Bharatha would never go against the advice of his ministers or by the advice of sages like Vasishta, the priest of Ikshwaakus. Ministers press him (Ayodhya -chapter 79- slokas 3 to 5) Gist:" Oh famous Bharatha. You be our king. Because this kingdom has never been without a king. Your citizens are awaiting you. Coronation materials are ready. The entire multitude is standing by. So accept the kingdom of your forefathers" But Bharatha is firm Will not go by advice of even Vasishta where norms are concerned. Vasishta says (Chapter 82-slokas 6 to 8) Gist: "Your father having gone to heaven has bequeathed this prosperous kingdom to you. And Raama being steadfast in Truth. & Dharma, went on exile. Therefore you must take on the kingdom left by your father and your ***brother Raama***" But Bharatha simply went round the 'Fire Mound' and said (chapter 79-Slokas 7 to 10) Gist; "Men like you well versed in royal norms should not talk to me like this. Because the kingdom for the eldest son, is The norm of our race....I am going to bring back my eldest brother, Raama. from forest.... He alone should be our king....May the army drawn from four services be got ready, may it be huge!...I will crown Raama there itself..." Some critics question Bharatha's right to command and commission the Royal army. After all he is no king. But we must realise that Bharatha is a prince and as such has certain royal privileges. So he has right to the Army. We know, as we shall see later, Bharatha fails in his mission but only partially. He could not bring back Raama.from forest But Raama's Sandals are enough to rule the kingdom in Rama's absence. **He crowns Rama's Sandals. Is there any wonder when Bharatha is extolled!**

After performing his father's Last Rites, Bharatha leaves Ayodhya for forest. As he had decided to crown Raama in the forest itself as king of Ayodhya, he takes a huge army along with an entourage of ministers, VIP-s, artisans, professionals. He even takes along with him the mothers -

his mother Kaikeyi, Rama's mother Kowsalya, and Sumithra, the mother of Lakshmana and Shathrugna. His brother Raama must be befittingly crowned. The coronation in forest, must be exactly as in their capital. Bharatha does not want to waste time. A kingdom cannot be without a king. The king is dead, long live the king. And readers know, how, in modern times when President Kennedy was shot in Dallas, his Vice President Johnson took the oath almost immediately. ***Vaalmeeki thus brings home this point.*** No country can be without a head even for a moment. And second point he ***brings home is this.*** An Ikshwaaku prince must be crowned with due honours wherever he may be. So Bharatha takes a huge entourage with him to give Raama a befitting coronation in forest. Not only that. Bharatha sends an advance party to make roads etc from forest to Ayodhya smooth for Rama's journey back. The Ayodhya-chapter 80 is very interesting reading. **Vaalmeeki gives a good description of Bharatha's organisational** capacity. From the assembly hall at Ayodhya, Bharatha swears (Chapter 82-slokas 18 & 19) Gist: "If I am unable to bring back Raama from forest, I will also, like Lakshmana, live in forest with him. But I am going to put in all my efforts to bring Raama back" When Bharatha goes out with his vast army and all, and when he reaches river Ganges, in spite of his anxiety and uncertainty over Raama, he does not fail to do his duty by his dead father. He gets down from the chariot, offers ritualistic waters for his dead father (chapter 83-sloka 24 of Ayodhya)

This is Bharatha for you.

Now when an army moves out of the capital into forest, there will be speculation. And Bharatha's army was drawn from the Four services (Akshowhini) and very huge. No wonder Raama's friend Guha, the chief of hunters sees the army across the river Ganges with suspicious eyes "Is this an army of peace or an army of war' (Chapter 84- slokas 4 to10) Gist: "He (Bhartha) is going to enslave us all: Or even kill us....now that Raama has been sent away by his father on exile...To kill Raama this son of Kaikeyi (Bharatha) has come here now, desirous of accomplishing (his objective of taking full control of) the resplendent kingdom.....(But) Raama the son of Dhasharatha is my master and friend. (So all of you, my fishermen comrades) be prepared (for any assault) and stay near Ganges...." Here is a case of deep attachment and friendship blinding a person. Guha is such a friend of Raama he suspects even Raama's beloved and most noble brother Bharatha! So much so he does not want Bharatha's army to cross Ganges river to the other bank.(Sloka 9) It is charioteer- minister Sumanthra who sets Guha's mind at rest. He accosts him when Guha goes out to meet them in advance. (slokas11 to 13) Gist: "The glorious Sumanthra who knew protocol and laws of the territory, seeing Guha coming towards them, enlightened Bharatha about Guha with reverence thus = This eminent man is the chief (of this territory) He is served by thousands of his tribesmen. Well conversant about forest. ***And he is your brother Raama's friend."*** Guha, hearing what Sumanthra had said about him to Bharatha, was happy. And when Bharatha hears pleasing words from Sumanthra, he says (sloka 14) "May Guha see me" And in the next sloka, Guha who was happy, having received permission, approached Bharatha with his folks. Incidentally throughout Vaalmeeki Raamaayana, ***protocol*** is always observed. To meet

Bharatha, one must have his permission! He is an Ikshwaku prince!

And Guha addressed his friend Raama's brother Bharatha (slokas 16 to 18) Gist: "This territory is your pleasure garden. (Having said this, Guha adds) We have been cheated by you in as much as we have not had the pleasure of receiving you here as our guest till now...(***Vaalmeeki's master piece. as usual)***. We have brought tubers, fruits, meats,(dry and fresh)....Let your army stay here for the night in comfort...I beg you to leave only tomorrow after enjoying our hospitality...."

Even at this point, Bharatha did not disclose to Guha, the purpose of his visit. He merely asks Guha (Chapter 85 - sloka 4) "Oh Guha! By which route can we go to the hermitage of Sage Bharadhwaja. This area is impenetrable, Further, Ganges is difficult to cross" This was too much for Raama's friend Guha. He could not conceal his fear. Has Bharatha come in peace or in war.? So he replies to Bharatha thus: (Slokas 6 to 7): "Oh Bharatha, the famous prince! Devoted fishermen, wielding bow, will come along with you. And I will also be with you.. (And Guha in no uncertain terms expresses his fear thus) ...I trust you are going on this journey without thinking of harm to Raama, who ever does (good tasks) without any weariness. (Because) This mighty army of yours raises some fear and doubt in me....."What a shame that any one can have any doubt about this great noble and virtuous man Bharatha. Yet Vaalmeeki puts such words into the mouth of Guha and Bharatha has to hear such cruel words.

(In slokas 9 &10) Bharatha sets Guha's mind at rest "Oh Guha! You should never entertain doubt about me. This is cruel (for me to hear.:) (God forbid) Such a situation should ever arise.(Because, you should know this) ***My eldest brother Raama, is equal to my father in (my) esteem***. I am going to bring back Raama who is now in forest. There should be no other thought in you....."

This is Bharatha for you.

And Guha is so pleased that he speaks what Kamban wrote about Bharatha in his Tamizh epic. (Ayodhya-chapter 85-slokas 12 and 13) "Oh Bharatha! I do not see any one in the world equal to you. You desire to reliquish the kingdom that came by you without exertion. You are indeed the most virtuous. Your Fame will follow you and stand eternally in the world. You desire to bring back Raama who is in hardship in forest"

This is Guha's Bharatha. This is Kamban's Bharatha. This is the Bharatha the world extols.

When the huge army of Bharatha was rested for the night on banks of the Ganges, Guha the tribal chief, by way of the extending his hospitality to prince Bharatha, offers him a bed. But Bharatha could not sleep. Vaalmeeki says (chapter 85- slokas 21 and 22) "Being in a state of deep melancholy, affliction, his heart burning with 'fever' (of grief over Raama) this Bharatha the 'bull' amongst men, having lost his sense of understanding, did not obtain any sleep at all. He was breathing hard and deep. He was like a goat, strayed away from the herd.....A man of experience and understanding, normally a man of composure, Bharatha kept company with Guha ...Although he himself was depressed, Guha consoled Bharatha (through the night)"

Bharatha naturally was concerned about Raama Seetha and Lakshmana, how they spent their first night of exile. And the faithful friend Guha narrates the conversation between Lakshmana and himself. And he talked about Raama as well (Ayodhya-Chapters 86 & 87)

How Lakshmana had refused bed and did not sleep at all while Raama was asleep along with Seetha. How Raama refused hospitality of food and drinks from him. How they spent the night under the Ingudha tree with mere water of the Ganges as their night meal. All this was too much for Bharatha. And he vows again (chapter 88-Sloka 30) "If he this Raama, begged by me in many ways with my head bowed in utter reverence does not accept, I will live in forest along with Raama the Raaghava for a long time." Bharatha is so sure of himself that he is certain Raama will not deny him. Raama is always the delighter, the munificent and magnanimous So Bharatha continues " But ***he (Raama) will not deny me*** (he will fulfill my request to get back to Ayodhya and accept kingdom)"

This is the Bharatha about whom Kamban and Guha talked about. Bharatha never for a moment, even in dream thought about kingdom. It is Raama and only Raama who is the king after his father. If Raama does not return, he will live on like Raama in forest. He has no separate existence apart from Raama.

Going in search of Raama, using the services rendered by the tribal chief and friend Guha, Bharatha after crossing Ganges, goes towards the hermitage of sage Bhardhwaaja. Bharatha is sure that the sage will give him direction to Raama's abode in the forest nearby. On sighting the hermitage (Valmeeki says- in Ayodhya - chapter 90 - sloka 1) Bharatha halted his army entourage at a distance of a Krosha (about 3 miles) from the hermitage but went along with his ministers and Sage Vasishta on foot, casting away his ornaments ***Vaalmeeki brings home a point here***. A king should never disturb the peace and tranquillity of a hermitage. And ofcourse when you 'see' a sage you are only a common man, no matter. And Bharatha stops his ministers from entering the gate of the hermitage but takes along with him only Sage Vasishta, the family priest of Ikswaakus.This is significant because, as we have mentioned before, Protocol was strictly observed those days. And when Sage Bharadhwaaja saw Vasishta entering, he was treated to the hospitality of a sage with Arghya and Paadhya by Bharadhwaja's disciples. (In slokas 6 to 7) Vaalmeeki observes "The knower of Dharma (Sage Bhardhwaaja) after offering Arghya and Paadhya and fruits, tubers, asked about the welfare of his (Bharatha's) family, about Ayodhya, about his army, about the state of finance, about his friends, about his ministers." But knowing about the death of Bharatha's father, Dhasharatha, he did not refer to him. Normally he would have asked about welfare of the king as well. And Vasishta and Bharatha in turn asked about Bharadhwaja's health, welfare, fire rituals, his disciples, trees, birds and animals around the hermitage.

In a different place in a different context, we will be referring to this. We may be pardoned if we make a few observations here and now. It is a mistaken notion that a sage ceases to be a sage, if he takes interest in mundane matters. When you visit a hermitage of a most pious sage, he may even ask you about your physical needs when he extends his hospitality. A spiritual leader going by car is no less spiritual than one taking to foot. Vasishta always rode on a (royal) chariot provided by Ikshwaaku kings. And

Vasishta was a Saptha Rishi (one among the exalted 7 Rishi-s). Spiritual men have no 'attachment'. They are 'attached' only to The Supreme Soul. No wonder Bharadhwaja and Vasishta exchange mundane matters with Bharatha. Sometimes even sages are human! Readers may know that when Raama, accompanied by Seetha and Lakshmana left the hermitage of Bharadhwaja to establish an abode at Chithrakoot, ***Vaalmeeki says*** (Ayodhya chapter 55 -sloka 2) "...When they were going away (from his hermitage) he (Bhardhwaja) followed them (to a distance) like a father (following a son)"

But let us get back to Bharatha and his meeting with Bharadhwaja. (In Ayodhya-chapter 90-slokas 10 to 13) the sage questions Bharatha why he should have come all the way into the forest and that too with a huge army. Gist: "Oh Bharatha! He who was begotten by Kowsalya, he who destroys enemies, he who increases the joy (of every one), he, who along with his wife (Seetha) & brother (Lakshmana) went out to forest for a long time,...he, the most famous one who was commanded by his father and (bound) by Kaikeyi, was told =You live here in forest for 14 years= ...I trust you do not desire to bring harm (to such a man, to such a Raama) who is sinless...and (desire to bring harm) to his brother (Lakshmana), in order to enjoy his kingdom without hindrance (to you)...." It is rather cruel that the noble and virtuous Bharatha is being suspected of treachery time and again. But there is a difference when Bharadhwaja raises some doubt and questions Bharatha's nobility. We shall presently see, but before we do that, this is how Bharatha replies to Sage Bharadhwaja with tears rolling down his face: Word coming haltingly; Gist of

(Slokas 14 to 17) "I have no apprehension that (any) sin is in me. (But, you my) Lord. if you think like this about me,(if you also) suspect me, then I am done for. You should not chastise thus. What my mother (Kaikeyi) did when I was not at Ayodhya and (subsequently) what words she said to me (that I should be king), was not accepted by me at all. Wishing to win the favour of my Raama and to worship his feet, I have come here to take him back to Ayodhya. Believe me. Where is Raama....." Bharadhwaja unlike others like Guha, knows Bharatha. Yet if he had asked him thus, it is for this reason.@ (Sloka 20,21) "Oh Bharatha! Oh the 'tiger' of men! Born in the family of Raghu-s (as you are) good conduct towards Guru-s (Elders and teachers), restraint, practice of good conduct of the good, all these abide in you. I know this, the nature of your mind. (But) I asked you because of the reason that your great fame should spread (and surpass everyone) and be firmly established" Bharadhwaja is a very great sage, but is human. He never doubted Bharatha. How could he, he is a great seer. But his love for Ikshwaaku princes like Raama and Bharatha is such, that he wants the world to know Bharatha. (chapter 101)

This is the Bharatha of Guha, Kamban, and now Bharadhwaja.

Bharadhwaja knows where Raama's abode in forest is. After all it was he who had directed him some time ago. He tells Bharatha (Ayodhya- Chapter 90-Sloka 22) "I know (the whereabouts) of the knower of Dharma, Raama, who is with Lakshmana and Seetha. Your brother is living in the great mountain Chithrakoot" And in the next sloka, the great sage makes a request. "Oh most intelligent Bharatha who knows about passion (and mundane) matters! You stay here tonight along with your ministers. ***Tomorrow morning you may go to the place (where Rama is). Fulfill, this my desire***

We had already said that even great sages are human. Here is the renowned sage Bharadhwaja who wants to extend his hospitality to Bharatha, the royal prince. He 'loves' Raama and Bharatha like a son!

Bharatha ofcourse accepts his hospitality. He had to. Bharadhwaaja's request and desire is a command for Ikshwaaku princes and kings.. But Bharatha wonders how the sage is going to feed them all in the middle of forest and at night.

Bharatha, who is always considerate to others, does not want to put his host Bharadhwaja to difficulty. (Ayodhya-chapter 91-slokas 1 and 2) Bharatha diplomatically expresses his concern before his host, the great sage Bharadhwaja. "In this forest, (in your hermitage) Paadhya and Arghya and likewise hospitality (befitting a resident of forest) has been extended by you. This (further hospitality) that is (going to be) extended....(Pray) What May That Be"

And Bharadhwaja while setting his mind at rest extols Bharatha addressing him with a smile thus (Sloka 3) "Oh Bharatha! I know you are already satisfied (with my hospitality). ***Because you are satisfied with even a little***" ***This is the Bharatha whom Kamban and Guha extol***

Bharadhwaja does not stop with this observation on Bharatha. (In the next slokas 4 to 6) he tells him firmly dispelling his anxiety: Gist: "Oh Bharatha the 'bull' among men! I desire to feed your vast army. You should satisfy my desire in such a manner I have planned (for them all) ...Oh

Bharatha! Why did you station your army far away, why did you come here without them all..."

And Bharatha gives the reply thus (Slokas 6 to 9) Gist: "Oh Lord! Out of respect and fear for you, I came here alone. Sages (men of penance) should be zealously kept away from and guarded against kings and princes on matters pertaining to their daily rituals.....I came here alone to your hermitage because the vast army of mine might cause harm to trees, waters etc around your hermitage and also hermitages around here"

Vaalmeeki expounds yet another Truth Kings and army should stay away from places of peace and harmony. In those days the army was either confined to the barracks or drawn out into the battlefield.

What followed is unbelievable. We shall describe the hospitality extended by Bharadhwaaja to Bharatha's army and his entourage later in this 'Guide'. In Ayodhya-chapter 91 - slokas 11 to 84 a full description is given by Vaaleemki. The peaceful hermitage of Bharadhwaaja was transformed into a place of merriment with wine, women and song, so to speak. Chauvinists will be aghast reading this. But we repeat. A sage does not cease to be a sage if he takes care of mundane needs of people who visit him.

Ofcourse great spiritual men like Bharadhwaaja have nothing to do with wine, women and song! ***Vaalmecki expounds this Truth in many places***

Let us get back to Bharatha.

Bharatha had to put up with all this, all this hospitality of Bhardhwaja because he was going to inform about Raama's whereabouts and abode in forest. Bharatha had nothing else in mind. He wanted to go to Raama quick, and quickly get him back to Ayodhya as the king of the land. And Bharatha asks the sage (Chapter 92-sloka 7) " Oh Lord-Bhardhwaaja! Oh foremost Rishi! I beg you to please give me leave who has started (on this journey) to go and meet my brother (Raama). You (please) 'look' at me with your friendly eyes...Oh Knower of Dharma Enlighten me about the great soul Raama's hermitage. Tell me how far is it and route to be taken" Bharatha never lost sight of his mission. He had only one purpose, to get Raama back to Ayodhya as king. And the great sage Bharadhwaaja like any common man gives the full description of the route to be taken to reach Raama's abode in Chithrakoot. Vaalmeeki devotes slokas 10 to 14 in chapter 92 of Ayodha Kanda to enlighten Bharatha about the route to be taken. ***Vaalmeeki again stresses the point***. A sage is like any other when it comes to service for a person seeking his advice. And when Bharatha is about to leave with his vast army to meet Raama, ***Vaalmeeki once again stresses this point*** Sage Bhardhwaja like any other human being, is curious and wants to be introduced to his mothers (his mother Kaikeyi, step mothers Kowsalya and Sumithra.). And this is how Bharatha introduces Raama's mother Kowsalya (Ayodhya – Chapter 92 sloka 21, 22) "Here, whom you see appearing like a deity, who is my father's first lady (and queen), who is now emaciated due to abstinence caused by grief, who is most miserable, is indeed Kowsalya. Like lady Adhithi (begetting Indra), she begot the 'tiger' of men Raama whose strides are like those of a lion" Then Bharatha introduces Sumithra thus (slokas 23 &24) "And she who clings, clutches her left hand and stands by the side of Kowsalya like the branches of Karnikara tree in forest with all flowers fallen down, who is now in low spirits, is the lady to whom two sons Lakshmana and Shathrugna who are very brave, who possess the brilliance of celestials, who are truly valiant, were born" And Bharatha could not contain himself. His wrath on his mother still 'burning' within. He introduces his mother Kaikeyi thus..... (Sloka s 25 to 27) "And she by whose immoral deed king Dhasharatha died and went to heaven due to grief of separation from his beloved Raama the 'tiger' of men who is now wasting his life in forest.....She, who is wrathful, obstinate, proud of her beauty, arrogant, a lover of wealth and power, an ignoble un-Aryan, but appears like a noble woman....is this woman Kaikeyi. You should know her as my mother...A very cruel woman accustomed to sin and its ways. Great calamity I see falling upon me because of her"

And it is here Vaalmeeki brings home another Truth. The difference between a sage, a man of penance and a common human being Bharadhwaja mildly admonishes Bharatha when Bharatha had so cruelly spoken about her (In sloka 29,30) "Oh Bharatha! Your mother Kaikeyi should not be considered (or vowed) wicked by you" And Sages alone know the divine purpose of any event.. Bharadhwaaja knows there is divine sanction to Raama's exile and he knew that Kaikeyi was only an Instrument for The Lord to achieve His objective for the welfare of the world.

Bharatha has still not got over his wrath over his mother! Till Raama returns and takes over as king, Bharatha will not have peace. Bharatha will be 'cursing' his mother till then as she had tried to thrust the kingdom on him!

This is the Bharatha, Kamban and Guha had talked about.

As Bharatha's army goes along the route indicated by Bhardhwaaja on way to Raama's hermitage, it creates 'terror' all around...animals are running a way in fear, fearing a great 'Hunt' is about to take place. A lot of dust rises and from a distance, from the top of a tree near his hermitage, as Raama's ever vigilant brother Lakshmana observes, he is certain that Bharatha is on his way to their hermitage with the sole purpose of completing his task, his unfinished business. = To kill Raama and make sure Raama will never comeback after 14 years of exile. =.It is rather a shame that time and again men have suspected this noble man Bharatha of treachery. Here is his own brother Lakshmana (born ofcourse to another wife of his father) suspecting him. It is the wise and noble Raama who sets Lakshmana's mind at rest In Ayodhya - chapter 97, Raama enlightens the angry Lakshmana when he even threatens to annihilate the army. (In sloka 16) he says" Bharatha is not to be spoken off so harshly by you. Not even with unpleasant words. If Bharatha is displeased (by you), then it would be that I am spoken to, harshly by you."

This is Raama's Bharatha for you.

And Raama adds "Oh lakshmana! If I tell Bharatha = May the kingdom be given to you, Bharatha will say only this= SO BE IT = ***This is the Bharatha of Kamban –Guha.*** Bharaatha, having stationed his army 10 miles from Raama's abode in Chithrakoot, walks up along with Shathrugna, Sumanthra and Vasishta towards the hermitage. As he gets within the sight of Raama, Bharatha was overcome by grief. Picking up some courage and composure, he addresses Raama thus (Ayodhya-chapter 99 - slokas 31 to 36) Gist: "My elder brother who used to be honoured by eminent men in the Assembly hall of Ayodhya, is sitting here 'honoured' by animals of forest. This great soul who was always befittingly dressed up with many thousands of diverse garments, is now dressed up in bark and deer skin materials. How come this Raama who used to wear wonderful garlands of sweet smelling flowers, is now able to 'bear' this braided tuft of hair. He who deserves to 'accumulate' Dharma by 'Ritual Sacrifiices' done as per norms of Shasthras,, such a one is seeking to obtain Dharma by the mortification of his body by living in hardship in forest. How is it, he, whose body used to be 'served' upon by superb sandal pastes, is 'served' by dust. Raama who was ever in comfort and deserves only comfort, is suffering now ***all on my account. What a shame!*** Cruel as I am, fie and shame on me, censured as I am by the worlds" In a short speech, at his first meeting with Raama in forest he has expressed himself effectively. He is the cause of Raama's exile and 'suffering'. And Raama, like a hermit does not have to go to forest and be a man of penance to obtain Dharma. All the Dharma is at his bidding, Because Raama has performed so many Rituals at Ayodhya. and has enough 'accumulation' of Dharma ***Vaalmeeki gives us a Truth. Dharma can be obtained by royal service. as well. And we have this Bharatha, the master of speech!***

Ayodhya-chapter 100- is a very interesting and important chapter. Ofcourse every chapter, nay every sloka of Vaalmeeki, is distinct. But this is particularly important, because, Raama expounds the philosophy of administration. We shall refer to this in detail later. When Bharatha after making such a short and effective address before Raama in great anguish, falls down, unable to bear Raama's life in forest, Raama lifts him up on to his lap, hugs him and consoles him. But Raama is aghast to see Bharatha dressed up like him in the bark dress of a mendicant and sporting "twisted" hair lock. This is not the Bharatha one would like to see as ruler of his mighty kingdom. When Bharatha heard from Guha that Raama and Lakshmana were sporting the style of a mendicant from the first day of their exile, Bharatha took to the same style immediately. He 'became' a mendicant! No luxuries for him. He will have none of the luxuries denied to his beloved brother Raama, ***This is Bharatha for you!*** Raama, not aware of the happenings in Ayodhya after his departure on exile, unaware that his father had passed away, begins a long address. Raama is a prince, even if it be that he is wandering in the forest as a mendicant honouring his father's and kaikeyi's command. So he is concerned with the administration of his kingdom. He is concerned even more because all the four princes are in the forest leaving "the old father King Dhasharatha alone".

(Chapter 100- slokas 6 to 76) Raama gives a dissertation on how a king must rule, and about Dharma. Hearing Raama's words of advice, all that Bharatha could say, in great anguish, is this (Ayodhya-Chapter 101-slokas 1 to 7) Gist: "Oh Raama! What will all this Royal Dharma you have talked about, do for me who has strayed away from Dharma itself. Oh king Raama! When the eldest son is there, the younger son does not become king. Amongst our Ikshwaakus, this is the Dharma that is rooted firmly" Here Bharatha takes a dig at Raama who had expounded the Dharma of Royal conduct, the Dharma of administration.

Bharatha tells Raama when his ascndency (as king) itself is Non-Dharma and is against "Statute" what is the use of Raama talking about Royal norms to him. Rama's advice is misplaced. ***This is Bharatha for you***

Bharatha continues "Oh Raama! Therefore you should come along with me to our prosperous Ayodhya. : For your family's sake: For the welfare of the world, you should crown yourself king." And Bharatha knows who Raama is when he tells him. "They, who talk about you and your conduct as enjoined with Dharma and Artha...talk as though you are a human being...As far as I am concerned, you are to be honoured as Divinity"

Yes. For Bharatha Raama is living God. This is Bharatha for you!

Finally Bharatha reveals the saddest news, and why he has really come. "When I was away at Kekeya on holiday and when you were away on exile in forest, the noble Aryan, our father the king, passed away. He went to heaven, leaving us all, unable to bear separation from you, overwhelmed by grief".

Raama is shattered. So are Lakshmana and Seetha. Raama wails. And citizens who have come along with Bharatha also wail. (Ayodhya- chapter 102-slokas 48 and 49) Vaalmeeki says that Rama hugged the crying citizens as though he was like a father and mother to them. And as per protocol he greeted them all. Even in utter grief, Raama has a word or two for his citizens. Raama is ever The Delighter, remember. Bharatha had only one objective when he went to forest along with his mighty army. Raama must come back, cutting short his exile and become king of Ayodhya. In (Ayodhya - chapters 104,105,106,107) Vaalmeeki narrates the conversation between Bharatha and Raama, their arguments and counter arguments. Bharatha presses Raama to return. Raama is firm. Will go through with 14 years of exile as per the command of his father and stepmother Kaikeyi.

Raama begins to question Bharatha at the very outset thus (Chapter 104-slokas 2 and 30) "Oh Bharatha! I desire to hear from you why you have come here and that too dressed up like a mendicant? You must tell me all. Why did you leave the kingdom sporting a mendicant's hair style"

Bharatha narrates the events leading to their father's death, leaving the kingdom 'kingless'. (slokas 5 to14). And why he had refused to accept kingship. He begs Raama (Sloka 8) " As I am your humble servant (a devotee) you should do me ***this favour***. Now itself you should be anointed king of our kingdom" Bharatha is clever. He knows that Raama will always favour those who seek refuge. Here Bharatha seeks his refuge, as a loyal citizen before 'king' Raama. Bharatha advances another argument. All his 'mothers' including his mother Kaikeyi (who had 'kicked' him out of the kingdom earlier), are praying for his return. Bharatha knows Raama will never refuse the mothers, (his mother and step mothers).

We have here two personalities, both strong men of character, both sticking to their own concept of Dharma, pressing their views strongly. Bharatha argues from the Dharma of the Statute of Ikshwaakus. Only the eldest son takes over and the lineage continues, with his eldest son taking over later. And Raama is equally firm. His Dharma is above the man made laws of Dharma under statute. Under normal circumstances he would have accepted the Norms of the Ikshwaaku kings. But for Raama, (Sathyam vadha-= Speak truth: Dharmam chara =-follow Dharma: Maathru Dhevo Bhava = Be devoted and follow Mother: Pithru Dhevo Bhava = Follow Father:) are the Commandments. This Dharma, overrules the Dharma of the Royal statute. His father and (step) mother have a right to command him: their desire, wish must be honoured by a son. He is not to question the validity of their order, or the justice of their order. And Raama is firm. Just as he is commanded to go on exile, so is Bharatha commanded by his mother to rule the kingdom for 14 years. Bharatha also should ignore the Royal Statute. He should without question accept kingship during his exile. Readers should read the chapters 104,105,106,107, and 111 of Ayodhya because two tricky laws of Dharma are being thrashed out by two of the noblest men this Bharatha varsh-India has seen.

Later, in another context, we will be writing about the verbal exchange between the renowned minister Jaabaali, the atheist and Raama. Jaabaali presses Raama to give up his so called Dharma but return to Ayodhya. Raama is angry He will not give up Dharma.(chapters 108 & 109)..

Let us get back to Bharatha and his resolve to get Raama back to Ayodhya as king: Raama is so firm and resolved to go through with exile to honour his commitment to his late father and 'mother' Kaikeyi, that Bharatha gets exasperated and resorts to Gandhian technique of Sathygraha. (Ayodhya-chapter 111-sloka 13)

"Oh Charioteer Sumanthra! On this bare earth, spread at once a bed of grass. Till Raama favours me (by coming back with me to Ayodhya as king) I am going to "BESIEGE" him. I will lie down, fast unto death..."

This is the Bharatha of Gandhian ways

Not content with this terrible resolve, Bharatha like a true democrat (yes, kings those days were democrats, in mind and spirit without ballot and indelible ink), takes his stand before the citizens who had come along with him to forest. He appeals (Sloka 19) "Why are you not directing this Aryan Raama to return to Ayodhya". Here again Bharatha knows that Raama being the delighter of all, would not make his devoted citizens miserable by turning down kingship, as this is what all his citizens want of him. Finally, when everything fails and Bharatha knows his appeal and entreaties will have no effect on Rama and when he is fully convinced that under no circumstances Raama will return to Ayodhya without fulfilling his obligations, ***Bharatha hits upon a grand, noble idea. Only Bharatha can think of such a magnificent idea.*** (Ayodhya chapter 112 slokas 20,21) "Oh Aryan! Oh noble Rama! Please Put On The Gold Decorated Sandals On Your Feet. Because These are Going to Bestow Welfare Upon All The World" By this, Bharatha formally accepts the inevitable and as a compromise accepts to 'rule the kingdom' as a Caretaker, with the authority of Raama's sandals on throne. And before he leaves Bharatha affirms, (Slokas 24,25,26) "Oh Raama! Awaiting your return (after 14 years) I will stay on, outside the city of Ayodhya, sustaining myself on tubers and fruits, Having invested the governance of the kingdom in your Golden sandals, if after completion of your exile, I do not see you return to Ayodhya, that very moment I will enter fire".

Bharatha, during his entire 14 years of 'rule', denies himself all the luxuries of a Royal ruler. He sports the dress and hair style of a hermit, just like his brothers Raama and Lakshmana. As far as he was concerned, only Raama had the right to enter Ayodhya as king. So he chosen to rule from a village

Bharatha crowns Raama's Royal sandals He rules for 14 years as a Caretaker from a village near Ayodhya, Nandhigram.

How did Bharatha consider himself during his rule. (In sloka 26) Valmeeki says ***"The resplendent Bharatha ruled over the kingdom always as its subject"***

This is your Bharatha, the first citizen

How did Bharatha treat The Royal Throne? (Sloka 25 and 27) "He 'placed' all his 'Acts', all the day to day Government decisions and acts at the feet of Raama as represented by Rama's sandals on throne Even if it was a small event that happened or a costly gift from a vassal, Bharatha first 'placed' them before the throne occupied by Raama's sandals"

This is Bharatha, the Caretaker ruler for you.

This man of modesty rules the kingdom so well, that Vaalmeeki says (Yudhdha- chapter 130-slokas 56,57) that when Bharatha returned the reign of power to Raama, he says "Oh Raama! This kingdom was protected by me on your behalf during your exile. And this kingdom is returned to you. Only now my life is worthy...has achieved some purpose....my desires are fulfilled..."

Bharatha always considered himself a devotee and servant of Raama Even as a ruler he was but a servant of Raama

This is the Bharatha of Kamban and Guha.

Man must be modest. Never haughty. But must be proud and hold his head high, always. Bharatha finally tells Raama (Chapter 130 sloka 57) "Oh Raama! May you please behold our Treasury, Stores, Ware houses, City, Army all these have been multiplied by me Ten fold, thanks to your brilliance and power"

Can there be a Bharatha other than Raama's Bharatha.

The Three Queens: (Kowsalya, Sumithra and Kaikeyi)

8: KOWSALYA

According to Vaalmeeki, King Dhasharatha had 300 wives. But as royal queens with status, there were only three. The eldest was Kowsalya, the mother of Raama. Sumithra was the mother of Lakshmana and Shathrugna. The youngest was Kaikeyi, the mother of Bharatha. We do not know much about them but we read about them as 'players in the drama'. Particularly, Kaikeyi. Kowsalya is depicted as a noble, religious woman. One sloka that is considered a holy sloka by the deeply religious is this (Bala - chapter 23 - sloka 2). This sloka is recited as part of worship even today "Oh Raama, the good, well begotten son of Kowsalya! Get Up, Oh the 'tiger' of men! Early morning is up. You have to perform the morning rituals" There is thus the reference to Raama as the son of Kowsalya here. But surprisingly in the entire epic, Vaalmeeki rarely 'calls' Raama as son of Kowsalya. This is significant as we shall see when we write about Sumithra and Lakshmana. Raama is called, Raaghava, Dhaasarathi, Kaakuthsa, Bharathaagraja Raghu nandana and so on.

During the Ashwamedha Yaaga performed by Dhasharatha, the honour of sacrifice of a ritual horse falls on Kowsalya. (Bala-chapter 14- 33 and 34) Gist "Kowsalya with great devotion and care smote with just three strokes of sword, the ritual horse, in joy. And bound by Dharma, she spent the night, kept vigil, over the slaughtered sacrificial horse" By this, Vaalmeeki gives her a special place amongst Dhasharatha's queens. First she is the eldest. But more important, she is deeply religious and ever observes strict religious norms during her daily prayer. Ofcourse Sumithra and Kaikeyi join the yaga rituals.

Elsewhere in this 'Guide', we will be referring to Kowsalya's daily 'Prayer' in some detail.. But let us study her from the time her son Raama gets ready to leave Ayodhya on exile to fulfill his father's commitment to his 'step' mother Kaikeyi. When Raama gets ready to leave on 14 year exile, he visits his mother Kowsalya to take leave of her. Naturally any mother would be totally in grief. This is understandable. Kowsalya, is no doubt a woman of prayer, but she is also human and a mother, with only one son Raama. When Raama informs his mother that he has been asked to go on exile for 14 years, and he is about to leave. Ayodhya, Kowsalya loses her composure and falls down unconscious. (Ayodhya - chapter 20 - sloka 32). Raama lifts her up and revives her. And she begins her address of grief and sorrow thus (Ayodhya-chapter 20-slokas 36 & 37) Gist: "Had you not been born to me and thus made me childless, I would not be undergoing such a torture now. For a barren woman there is but one grief, that she has no son" ***Vaalmeeki by this conveys another Truth.*** _Sorrow and suffering is part of Samsaara (family life). Along with joy, a son or daughter brings suffering as well. This is life. Kowsalya then continues expressing her deep anguish over her son Raama's absence of 14 years from her. But she gives herself away, unbecoming of a deeply religious woman. Take for instance (in sloka 48) "Oh Raama! You were brought up by me with great care, through great rituals like fasts. All my suffering in raising you has gone to waste" This is expected of an average mother. But Kowsalya is a royal princess, a queen. And she is deeply religious. This bemoaning does not do justice to her noble character. Kowsalya should never have mentioned about her religious devotion. ***Vaalmeeki brings home yet another Truth*** Religion and philosophy may go together but are distinct, separate. A deeply religious person may not be philosophical when suffering hits him In chapter 20 of Ayodhya, Vaalmeeki devotes about 20 slokas on Kowsalya. Lets us examine (slokas 41 to 45): Gist: "Oh lad Raama! Even when you are here I am spurned " By this Kowsalya says that her husband Dhasharatha spent more time with his lovely Kaikeyi and had been neglecting her. She could look up to only her son for solace and comfort. And she adds "Despised by my husband, totally and eternally abandoned, I will become like one of Kaikeyi's maids or even lower" Two points we may observe. Kowsalya, in spite of living with her husband Dhasharatha for so long, does not give even a little credit to her husband. Quite true he was fascinated by Kaikeyi, his third queen who was very beautiful. But Dhasharatha is a man of Dharma. A noble king. Would never 'abuse' any one. Secondly Kowsalya exhibits some selfishness unbecoming of her nobility and status. Her first reaction is only herself, her suffering being without Raama. In sloka 52, she goes further. "This indeed is grief (your separation from me) Therefore all my vows, fasting, charities, prayers, that were observed well for the welfare of my son, have become purposeless. All the 'penance' done by me have gone to waste like seeds sown in saline soil and parched land" This is expected of an ordinary human being who may be religious. But this kind of "credit" "debit" equation in matters of prayer is unbecoming of such a noble lady. **Perhaps Vaalmeeki**

wishes to bring home the point strongly that religion and philosophy are totally different and religion is just a tool to seek 'union' with the Lord. and not to seek mundane pleasures.

Kowsalya cries out so much, she wails thus (Sloka 50 and 51) Gist: " Is there no death at all for me. Why is Lord of death Yama not taking me away now? Is there no place for me in the abode of death? My heart is rock-a stone. That is why it has not split into thousand bits My body is steel! "***Vaalmeeki brings home another well known Truth***. While Yama the Lord of death never takes a holiday, death comes to us only at his appointed time and when he chooses to visit us! Kowsalya thus bemoans!

At one point, Kowsalya tells Raama that as she cannot have peace and freedom in Ayodhya without Raama, she will accompany him to forest. Here again the deeply religious Kowsalya forgot the Dharma of a dutiful wife. Raama had to remind her. (Ayodhya-chapter 21-sloka 62) "......how can lady Kowsalya go away from here ***as though she is a widow***..." A woman's place is by the side of her husband when he is alive. After his death, she may live with her son. **Vaalmeeki affirms this through the lips of Raama again"** (Ayodhya-chapter 24-sloka 19) "....Oh mother! for a woman, her husband is lord and God...." Raama speaks yet another truth that should not have escaped Kowsalya. (slokas 23,24) He tells her " If a woman, even if noble and performs vows and rituals but does not follow her husband, she will go the way of sinners. A woman may not offer prayer to deities. May not even respect elders. But if she serves her husband, she obtains the world of heaven" ***Again Vaalmeeki brings home a truth***. The Dharma of a woman is not in prayer but in the service of her husband who is the pillar of family. Seetha's Dharma is with Raama. So exile for her. And Kowsalya's Dharma is by the side of Dhasharatha. So it is Ayodhya for her, not exile.

But it should be said to her credit, that when she accepted the inevitable, accepted Raama's going on 14 year exile without her, Kowsalya, like a true devotee of the Gods, invokes various deities and sends Raama away with her blessings. As we said we shall be carrying her Prayers later in this guide. After all Vaalmeeki Raamaayana is also a Book of Prayer.

This noble lady Kowsalya, again loses her composure and this is rather hard to take. After Raama left, Dhasharatha was so stricken with grief, that he was losing his sense of perception. (Ayodhya-chapter 42- sloka 33 & 34) "The king whose condition was like that of his Last Night in this world, addressed Kowasalya in the middle of the night. .... My faculty of sight has gone away with Raama. Ah! It is not coming back. Oh Kowsalya! I can't even see you. Please touch me, stroke me ..." One would have expected that Kowsalya would have controlled her emotions, and tried to console Dhasharatha who was like a dying man. Infact he dies shortly after, unable to bear separation from Raama. But Kowsalya (chapter 43) starts wailing, adding misery to the down trodden, sick husband Dhasharatha. in (Ayodhya- chapter 61) when king Dhasharatha is virtually in his death bed, she talks cruelly to him. Vaalmeeki says in sloka 27, "Hearing her, address which contained the cruel words, he became sad and unconscious, after lamenting his own wrong action" This is rather a shame, a blot on her noble character. One would have expected such a deeply religious woman, exhibiting restraint, and face sorrow with equanimity and take pity on her husband. Ofcourse Kowsalya recovers. She is a noble lady .Profusely apologises and seeks her husband's pardon (Ayodhya-chapter62-sloka 12) "Oh my Lord! Have mercy. I beg of you. I prostrate before you. I stand condemned. But please don't condemn me" ***Vaalmeeki has portrayed Kowsalya's character in proper perspective.***_When calamity strikes us, sometimes our FAITH also takes a beating. Perhaps that is the difference between a human being and a man of penance, a sage or rishi

9: SUMITHRA

We have said this many times. We may be pardoned if we repeat. Vaalmeeki is a master when it comes to choosing appropriate words. Even when he calls Raama by name, he may call him in different ways.in different places. (like, of Raama, son of Dhasharatha, or Oh the scion of the Raghu clan, oh the Ikshwaaki, Oh the Kaakuthsa-the member of kakuthsa lineage) But in the case of Lakshmana, invariably he calls him Oh Lakshmana, the son of Sumithra = Sowmithra =

This is the regard Vaalmeeki has for Sumithra.

Sumithra's son Lakshmana also goes on exile along with Raama and Seetha with this difference. He chooses to go voluntarily. There is no evidence in Vaalmeeki of Sumithra trying to stop her son. And there is no evidence that Sumithra wailed and cried her heart out like Kowsalya. Here we have a different woman, different character. Both without their sons for 14 years. Sumithra reacts differently.

No wonder Vaalmeeki, not infrequently, refers to Lakshmana, as "Lakshmana, the son of Sumithra = Sowmithray"

It was rather hard for Sumithra to bear, particularly as her husband Dhasharatha was terribly sick. She could not bear Kowsalya's wail. Infact Dhasharatha had lost interest in living after Raama left. He was losing his health rapidly. In fact he dies shortly after Kowsalya had treated him cruelly with some sharp words. She could never understand that Dhasharatha was bound hand and foot by the two boons he had given his third wife Kaikeyi long ago. A king never breaks a promise. Her husband was no ordinary king. He was an Ikshwaaki. Honour and Truth were the two pillars of their Statute. Readers may know what he had said (Ayodhya- Chapter 12-sloka 87) "When told - Go to forest - if Raama disobeys me and goes against my command, I will be the happiest man. But my Raama will never disobey me" Infact Dhasharatha in his heart of heart must have wished his son Raama to be a man of doubtful character, and thus stay on in Ayodhya against his command. So much he loved him. And this was the man Kowsalya had attacked Kowsalya is portrayed as a deeply religious woman of vows by Vaalmeeki. But Sumithra is a highly philosophical woman. Knows Dharma of Truth and commitment. She takes on the responsibility of consoling Kowsalya. by enlightening her. (Ayodhya - chapter 44). Sumithra, the woman steadfast in Dharma, addresses her senior co-wife. "Oh Kowsalya! How can you cry and wail so pitiably" (Remember, you are a Queen).... In 28 slokas of this chapter Sumithra speaks words of wisdom. Gist. "This mightily strong man, your son Raama, has gone to forest to make his father a man of Dharma and Truth. He always stands firm on Dharma In fact he is the most eminent, the most superior person.(Word used is=Shreshta= most auspicious God Vishnu is Shreshta!).... my son, Lakshmana, always compassionate, is with him in forest taking to this noble course of action of following Raama and this is going to bring glory and fame in all the worlds...Your son is the Lord of the world. Man of restraint, foremost in Truth, in vows. How can you grieve over such a son, Oh Kowsalya....Even the Sun will not torment him in forest...Wind will be ever pleasant to him in forest..Moon's rays will embrace him at night just like his father at Ayodhya! ...pray, Oh Kowsalya, why does he need protection when the great Vishwaamithra had bestowed upon him all the divine weapons....Enemies dare not face him..." After saying all this, Sumithra, the 'divine' lady talks about Raama as a divine person "He is the source of power to Sun; He gives heat to Fire; He is Lord to all Lords!; He is the First among the Glorious, brings glory to the glorious ! In fact, He is the God of Gods; You are queen, you should not wail thus but console your citizens...." Sumithra cannot contain herself. The mother in her comes out when she says (sloka 20) "Is there anything for this Raama, when the foremost of wielders of the bow, my son Lakshmana, is going before him, armed with arrows and weapons and sword" Indeed Lakshmana was equal to Raama in valour. After all he was taught the divine weapons when he had gone with Vishwaamithra along with Raama. Sumithra is justified in praising her son Lakshmana thus before Kowsalya.

Vaalmeeki says (sloka 30) while summing up Sumithra's address to Kowsalya by the way of consoling her "Faultless in word and speech, skillful in exposition, this lady Sumithra who delighted every one, talked thus with various meaningful words to Raama's mother Kowsalya"

Sumithra's address was so effective that Kowsalya shed her grief, became composed. Vaalmeeki says (sloka 31) "Hearing the words of Sumithra, the mother of Lakshmana, the sorrow of Kowsalya, the mother of Raama, at once disappeared, just like water being shed from the 'body' of cloud, laden with water..."

In the entire Raamaayana, very few knew that Raama was God Vishnu on earth for doing good to the world. Sages like Bharadhwaaja knew.

The "Enlightened" Sumithra also knew this.

10: KAIKEYI & MANTHARA

It is strange that one single event can change the course of history. Stranger still, that one woman can change the course of history. We have heard of wars being fought over a woman. Helen of Troy started the Trojan-Greek war, so it is said But even here, scholars of ancient history, find many other causes, apart from this beautiful woman, for this tragic war, which shook that civilisation. in medieval times. In our other great epiç which came much later than Raamaayana, in The Mahaabhaaratha, there was continued animosity between the two groups, Paandavas and Kowrawas. The wife of Pandavas, Dhraupathi cannot be the main reason for the great war. Nor an event - the gambling - the event where the most virtuous Yudhishtra, the head of

The Paandavas pledges away everything at stake and loses all. Ofcourse, in Raamaayana, it is over the woman Seetha that a bitter war ensued. But then, there would never have been kidnapping of Seetha by Raavana if Raama had been crowned Yuvaraja- and later king, as was planned by Dhasharatha. Raama would have ruled Ayodhya in all glory along with queen Seetha. Raavana would never have dared to attack Raama. He was a 'coward'. We may be pardoned for this comment. But we cannot escape from the fact that one woman (along with her mentor) changed the course of history. We are talking about the beautiful Kaikeyi, the wife and queen of King Dhasharatha, who changed the course of history - in Raamaayana. The irony is that Kaikeyi loved Raama, so much that her first reaction on hearing from the vile, evil woman Manthara, the confidant of Kaikeyi, that Raama is to be crowned as Yuva raja by her husband, Dhasharatha, is one of sheer ecstasy. She gets up from her bed and tells (Ayodhya-chapter 7-slokas 32 to 36) Gist: "Oh Manthara! You are telling me such a good news." Saying thus, Kaikeyi at once offers her a most precious ornament as gift to her, indicating there will more of such gifts for her. She is wonderstruck by the news brought by Manthara. She continues "The King is going to anoint Raama in the kingdom. That is why, I am extremely pleased. ***Because, I don't make any distinction between my son Bharatha and (my co-wife's son) Raama***... Oh Manthara! This is most happy (news). There cannot be any news happier than this for me....." This is the Kaikeyi, the step mother of Raama, the beloved of Raama. In just under 12 hours, it is this very Kaikeyi who will drive away Raama to forest on exile. Can there be anything stranger? First, let us proceed with the story leading to Raama's exile, the midnight drama. Dhasharatha, having decided to perform Raama's coronation as Yuva -raaja, the successor to the throne and having given instructions for preparation for the Royal ceremony set for the morning, visits his most beloved and favoured wife, Kaikeyi, early night to personally convey the happy news of the Royal event. But he is in for a shock. Kaikeyi's mentor and confidant, the hunch back Manthara, had already 'worked' upon her, poisoned her mind, so much so Kaikeyi is determined to stop Raama's coronation forthwith, banish him on to the forest, and install her son Bharatha who was on a holiday in her father's house at Kekeya capital, instead. Manthara, had even worked out a foolproof strategy to achieve these two objectives. Dhasharatha had given Kaikeyi two boons, when, during a war long, long ago, Kaikeyi had saved his life. Manthara presses Kaikeyi to exercise the option of asking for and utilising the two boons, as the right time had arrived. Dhasharatha, being a ruler of honour and Truth will never deny these two boons, however hard it may be for him to take it. By the first boon, Raama is to be banished for 14 years. By the second boon, her son Bharatha must be crowned instead (after being recalled from his holiday).

A genius is one who cannot excel himself. A genius is a genius, is a genius.. We may be pardoned if we say that Vaalmeeki excels himself (Ayodhya-chapters 8 & 9) Till Manthara enters the scene, Raama was the most beloved (step) son of Kaikeyi. In just under an hour the scheming, wicked hunchback Manthara, works upon her, to such an extent that Kaikeyi is determined to get rid of Raama! Vaalmeeki is in his elements. This is a master piece of writing as Vaalmeeki takes us through the 'Drama' of the night at Kaikeyi's palace. Let us justify our observation.

When Kaikeyi had received the news of Raama's coronation set for the next day, from her mentor Manthara and had even presented her a costly ornament to her as a gift for bringing her the most happy news, Manthara becomes disheartened and 'sick' Manthara begins to 'work' upon her (Ayodhya-chapter 8) The Gist: "Oh the childish Kaikeyi! You are not aware, that you are about to be submerged in Ocean of sorrow, What is this. You have obtained happiness at a wrong time. A great calamity has befallen you. I deride and mock you for not realising this. Who, if she is in 'right' mind, will obtain happiness at the prosperity of a co-wife's son. I grieve at your stupidity" ***Vaalmeeki through the lips of this wicked Manthara, expounds a mundane truth "Fear is caused by the feared***"

(According to Manthara, fear for Raama is from Bharatha as both are princes) Manthara is a very clever woman. She knows that there is no love lost between Kaikeyi and the co-wife Kowsalya. So she 'hits' Kaikeyi where it will wound her most. " She, whose son is going to be anointed as the mighty crown prince (as successor to the throne) tomorrow, on the Pushya star, by purohits, that woman ***Kowsalya indeed is the most fortunate one"*** Continuing, she tells Kaikeyi "Your son Bharatha will be disinherited, having no chance of wielding power" Manthara says that it is not necessary for a king to appoint only his eldest as successor. She is very clever, although she knows the norms of succession of Ikshwaakus, she says "Oh Kaikeyi! All sons of king are not installed in the kingdom. If it were so, then great mismanagement will be there in a kingdom.

A King appoints only the foremost among them possessing qualities in the affairs of the kingdom." By this we have to understand that Manthara implies that Bharatha is equally eminent like his brother Raama, to fill in as Yuva-raja! Citizens will accept him without question. She taunts Kaikeyi who had presented her a precious ornament. "I came here to advise you. I came here for your welfare. But the irony is that you, merely a co-wife to be reduced to a servant maid like me, are offering me gifts! Raama will drive away your son Bharatha after getting power, even to the other world of heaven, to be free from worry and obstacles" (Manthara knows this is absolutely not true. The four brothers are totally devoted to each other Manthara must be talking about the familiar Mughal rulers of India that we have read in our history books!) Manthara touches a very important point, to indicate that her husband Dhasharatha is not such a clean man but a scheming scoundrel. "Bharatha is but a 'boy' (a simple lad) He has been sent away to his uncle's place for a holiday." Thus implying that Dhasaratha had planned all this to eliminate Bharatha. Finally Manthara says by way of advice "Oh Kaikeyi! You must think about the ways of obtaining kingdom for your son Bharatha" Kaikeyi is an impulsive woman. Easily excitable. Given to passion. When Manthara had finished talking about the 'consequences' of Raama's coronation, she gets so excited that she jumps up from the couch and exclaims (Ayodhya chapter 9 - sloka 2) "Oh Manthara! I will myself send Raama today to forest. I will crown my son Bharatha instead" We may observe a point or two in her character. She still loves Raama. She knows that Raama would do anything for her. So this outburst. Raama will go away if she asks him to do so. This is the irony. In a few minutes, when the strategy is worked out by Manthara for her, Kaikeyi becomes wrathful, indignant. And that is exactly what Manthara wanted of her. Kaikeyi quickly realises that it is not that easy to banish Raama. She asks "Oh Manthara! By what means can I send away Raama and make Bharatha the successor" Manthara is in her elements. She is pleased because Kaikeyi is slowly coming round to her wish- of making Bharatha the ***successor in the place of Raama. She knows Kaikeyi is serious.***

Manthara begins enlightening Kaikeyi about the strategy to be adopted by her to achieve these two objectives. (Ayodhya chapter 6 slokas 6 to 35) Gist: "Oh Kaikeyi! Have you forgotten or remembering it, you have chosen to forget ....." (This is Vaalmeeki's master piece! Manthara telling Kaikeyi that she is an intelligent lady and nothing is unknown to her! Manthara flatters Kaikeyi thus, so that she can have her sway over Kaikeyi and have her way) and she continues "Long ago, in a war between Dhevas and Asuras, your husband Dhasharatha, took you also with him, when he went to help Lord Indra in this war......At that time, Dasharatha fought a mighty war. But he was wounded in battle. Was unconscious. But you 'carried' him away from the battle field and saved him thus....Mightily pleased with you, he had offered you two boons.....And your husband was told by you thus = Whenever I desire to make use of your boons to me, I will ask for them from you = And you were told by your husband = So Be It =

Oh Kaikeyi! I was told by you about this. Out of my love and friendship, I had always remembered this incident..." Now Manthara is specific. What Kaikeyi should do now.

She should press her husband for fulfillment of these two boons he had given her long ago. "You ask for the boons now. Exile for 14 years for Raama and crown for Bharatha. And at once you must restrain your husband from going through with Raama's coronation that is to take place tomorrow"

Manthara had warned Kaikeyi (Ayodhya-chapter 10 &11) what would happen to her if she did not go through with her strategy Gist: "With folded arms, you are going to serve Kowsalya who will be most powerful when her son is crowned......Then along with us, you are going to be her servant.... And your son also will have the same status before Raama...."

As to why Manthara had not asked for more than 14 years, she gives her reason thus. (chapter 9 sloka21). She thinks that 14 years of rule for Bharatha is enough to make him the king permanently "When Raama is exiled for 14 years, your son Bharatha will firmly establish himself on the throne, having obtained the affection and respect of the citizens." ***(Possession is 9 points of Law)***

Not stopping with strategy, Manthara shows Kaikeyi how she should go about achieving her objective. ***Vaalmeeki brings home a point*** here. One may know strategy, but may not know how to execute the same. Manthara does not take any chances. She tells Kaikeyi firmly (slokas 22,23) "Oh Kaikeyi the daughter of king Ashwapathi! Leaving your palace, you enter the House of Mourning immediately. as though you are angry and miserable. Lie down on bare floor. And in dirty worn out dress.When your husband sees you, turn your face away from him." Manthara knows that Dhasharatha is passionately attached towards this beautiful woman. So she assures Kaikeyi "You are ever the most beloved of your husband. He will even jump into the fire for your sake, to satisfy you. No doubt about it. The king cannot bear to see you angry and suffering. And he will never get angry with you. He will even give up his life for your sake".

Manthara warns Kaikeyi that she should not exhibit any shame, pity or consideration for her husband; nor should she be tempted by her husband with mundane stuff. She must remember her objective, always; Crown for her son and exile for Raama. "Dhasharatha may offer you, tempt you, with many wonderful pearls, gems, ornaments...you must have no mind for any of these ...And Oh Kaikeyi, you do not realise the power of your good fortune, the power of your husband's passion for you. Dhasharatha will never go against his word (will honour his boons to you) "Manthara concludes by stating that the time of action is now or never "Oh Kaikeyi! I consider this as the right time for you to act. Discarding your timidity, coercing him, you must first stop this coronation of Raama"

If we have written at length about Manthara in this Guide, reason is Vaalmeeki excels himself .To poison the mind of a woman against a person who had never shown anything but love and consideration for her, and had treated her as his mother, calls for some skill. And all this is done in just an hour. ***Vaalmeeki through this wicked woman Manthara, has brought home a point. How fickle we are.*** 25 years of love, affection, service of Raama to his beloved (step) mother, Kaikeyi, are all rubbed off by the wicked Manthara, an evil genius.

Manthara's evil genius had its effect on Kaikeyi.(Ayodhya Chapter 9 sloka 36 &37) "Made to accept evil as good, Kaikeyi who was convinced totally, addressed Manthara in great joy; like an immature girl, this beautiful Kaikeyi was wonderstruck by words of evil advice of this Manthara" What follows is rather amusing. Kaikeyi indulges in flattery of her mentor and confidant, Manthara the hunch back. ***Vaalmeeki* serves a purpose here,** as we shall see presently.In (slokas 38 and 39) we find Kaikeyi praising Manthara.Gist: "Oh Hunch back! You are indeed foremost among the hunch backs in the world, in sharpness of mind. I had not known you.....that you are one who can express clearly what is most salutary....I had not known the true designs of my husband till you enlightened me. Indeed you are the only one interested in my welfare" Kaikeyi rejects the common view about hunchbacks (sloka 40) "It is said that hunchbacks are very cruel, crooked and of improper conduct. Possessing the most desirable character, you are indeed most pleasing to me like the Lotus!"

Vaalmeeki makes the point that even the most ugly looking will look beautiful before a friend and well wisher. And Kaikeyi starts describing her 'beauty'! the beauty of this ugly, evil woman. (Slokas 41 to 46) "Your chest which is big and goes right up to the shoulders are pretty. And below your pretty waist is slender, as though indicating your modesty. Oh Manthara! How becoming are you! Your back-buttocks are broad. Your breasts, very wholesome. Your face spotless like the moon. Your waist 'shines' with a sparingly sized girdle. your thighs are well rounded. Your feet, long and slender. Oh Manthara! You appear to me as a bright royal swan, even as you are draped in white cloth around your long thighs. You possess all the thousand of the magic art found with magic demon Shambara. It seems, that your knowledge, political wisdom and cunning are hidden in your deformity." And after praising her thus, Kaikeyi assures her that when 'she becomes boss' after her son takes over as yuva-raja, she will decorate her with a golden chain etc. (47 to 50) "I will anoint your hunch back, with costly sandal paste and scents, free from impurities. I will decorate your face with costly cosmetics. I will put on you the costliest of jewelry. And when you wear bewitching dress from me, you will roam about freely like a celestial" And Kaikeyi (in sloka 51) Gist:"Oh Manthara! When you are so decorated. your face will be incomparable, putting to shame even the brilliance of the moon....you will obtain great status, treating people unfriendly to you with utter contempt" (Ayodhya Chapter 9)

We had referred to a purpose being served by Vaalmeeki in all this flattery. Manthara, the hunch back was a slave of queen Kaikeyi, Her antecedents are unknown. She had worked her way up. She became her mentor and confidant. Her loyalty to Kaikeyi was unquestionable. She 'loved' Kaikeyi, having never been loved before in all her life. As a hunch back and a most ugly woman in the city of Ayodhya where it was difficult to find a woman or lady without beauty or charm, she must have come under the taunt of many. Perhaps she wanted to wield some sort of political power through Kaikeyi. But we should think that she wanted to take revenge on society that had considered hunch backs as evil. It is difficult to know why Vaalmeeki devoted so many slokas on Manthara's beauty! But through (Ayodhya-chapter9-sloka 51) Vaalmeeki justifies our observation, perhaps..... "You will obtain status", Vaalmeeki says. Not only status was denied to this (evil) genius, she was a butt of ridicule. Society saw only her ugliness and deformity. If Society had treated her like any other woman, perhaps Ayodhya would have a woman as Minister. Manthara was such a woman, a political genius.

11: KAIKEYI- DHASHARATHA

Let us get back to Kaikeyi and the midnight drama Having been completely swayed by the evil genius Manthara, she leaves her palace and enters the House of Mourning awaiting her beloved husband. She lay on the bare floor, and Vaalmeeki says (Ayodhya-chapter 10-slokas 6 to 8) "At that time (in the house of sorrow) various exquisite and costly jewels and necklaces were scattered on the floor, having been cast away by Kaikeyi. The jewels glittered, making the floor shine like stars in the sky. But Kaikeyi was dressed up in dirty clothes, her hair just tied up in one bunch, In this house of sorrow (house of wrath) she appeared like an ordinary Kinnari woman, bereft of any goodness" Dhasharatha entered the palace but failed to see his most beloved wife. This was unusual, strange for him. (sloka 18) "Never had the king entered the palace, empty without Kaikeyi. Never without being received by this lady" The door attendants told him "Oh Lord, my king! Lady Kaikeyi, in great wrath, has gone away to house of sorrow and wrath" Dhasharatha, naturally was agitated. He addressed her on seeing her down on floor. (Ayodhya Chapter 10 slokas 27 to 39) Gist: "Why are you lying down in dirt, making me miserable. Particularly when I am happy and in splendour. Perhaps you are sick, but you should know I have at my command most able doctors who will cure you and make you comfortable. Dhasharatha wonders whether any one had caused her agony. "Has transgression been done upon you by any one? Do you want me to punish any one." After reassuring her, Dhasharatha forgets himself, forgets he is King of Ayodhya when he rashly and without second thought affirms "Oh Kaikeyi! Tell me who should be favoured and who should receive harm and obtain suffering at my hands" ***Vaalmeeki brings home a point*** When a man is afflicted by passion, fair play and justice takes leave of him. He becomes blind! And there is more of this to come from Dhasharatha "Which poor man must be made wealthy (for your sake) And which rich man must be made to lose all his wealth?" Look who is talking. Here is the very old renowned king, the bearer of rod of justice talking like this, irresponsibly, all because he must please his wife whom he loves with passion. This is no love. This is madness. ***Vaalmeeki brings home this point*** Dhasharatha boasts (sloka 36 and 37) Gist "Wherever the Sun makes his rounds, the entire earth is at my command. ...whether in east, south, or in Sindh, Sowveera region, Sowrashtra, Vanga, Anga, Mathsya, Kaashi...(I am emperor) "We may be pardoned if we draw a parallel = The Sun never sets on the British Empire = (Alas, this is no longer true). Finally Dhasharatha affirms and this is what Kaikeyi wished to hear from him (sloka 35) "Knowing the power of my attachment to you, you should not entertain any doubt I will fulfill your desires. I vow by all my good deeds"

The Die is Cast. The Midnight Drama has just begun.

Kaikeyi replied to Dhasharatha who was struck by arrows of passion over her, thus, with the most cruel words (Ayodhya chapter 11 slokas 2 and 3) ""Oh my Lord! I have not been disrespected by any one. I have not been insulted by anybody. There is one desire in me that I wish for, which can be satisfied by you." ***Kaikeyi is a very clever woman.*** Without disclosing her demand, she makes her husband promise her first. She wants an open commitment from him. "First you give me your promise. Then I will disclose what is in my mind." Dhasharatha, struck by passion, particularly now, unable to see his most beloved wife in such a state, affirms thus (Slokas 5 to 12) Gist: "Oh proud Kaikeyi! You know very well that none is dearer to me than you." And added

"And no ***man*** is dearer to me than Raama" So much affection, respect and regard he had for his son Raama that he swears by him "I swear by that Raama, the Raaghava, the great soul, who is invincible, foremost, and sustains my life. So What you desire in your mind, please tell me. I swear by that Raama whom if I don't see even for a moment, I will lose my life". It is rather an irony. ***Vaalmeeki has put proper words into the mouth of Dhasharatha***. (As events turn out, as told by Dhasharatha, his very life went away when Raama was sent out and when his sight was denied to Dhasharatha) "On such a Raama I swear.to fulfill your demand. I cherish him more than my life. He is even dearer to me than my other sons.and all others. I swear by him to fulfill your wish. You should have no apprehension. Oh Kaikeyi! You will see the power of my attachment to you...."

Kaikeyi being a very clever woman, not satisfied with such an assurance, goes one step further. She knows her husband is a religious person, having performed many Yaagas. Gist "Oh my Lord! You are swearing. As a consequence of which, what boons you had offered me, those, may the 33 Dhevas of heaven and their Lord Indra hear from me. May Sun, Moon, the sky, the constellations, Lords of Day and Night, and the Ten Directions. and Ghandharvas and Raakshasas Let Ghosts, let Fairies. and other celestial bodies, ...May all of them know about your oath to me...This man of Truth, who knows Dharma, who is steadfast and a man of composure, this my husband, is offering me boons...." Thus Kaikeyi bound Dhasharatha knowing fully well that all these are witness to his oath. Then, after reminding him about how she had saved his life in Dheva-asura war long ago, comes out with the two boons she had received from him then, which she had not utilised till now. She binds Dhasharatha thus "If you deny those two boons that were given to me by you as per Dharma. I will give up my life as being insulted by you" Kaikeyi is portrayed as a childish-childlike easy going-pleasure seeking woman. But we must have reservations about this aspect of her character. She plays her card well. She binds Dhasharatha first and then seeks what she wants. She has made the whole world her witness. She has invoked deities, fairies and what not. Even Lord Indra is a witness. Poor Dhasharatha did not realise what he was in for when he gave an open oath, an open commitment. She comes out with her two demands thus (Ayodhya- chapter 11-Slokas 24 to 29) ..The Gist:

"These, the two boons, I am now asking you. Listen to my words. Preparations are going on and materials are being collected for Raama's coronation. With these very same materials, my son Bharatha must be crowned forthwith.

Oh Lord! The second boon that was offered in joy during the Dheva-Asura war, the time has now come for utilising it.

Let Raama, sporting 'tufted' hair locks , wearing deer and bark skin material, live in Dhandaka forest for 10 plus 4 years as a mendicant"

Kaikeyi tells her husband that these are not her new demands on her husband. She is merely utilising the boons given to her by her husband long ago. "I am only asking for the boons already offered. ***I must see Raama leaving for forest today itself.*** This indeed is my foremost wish. Bharatha must be crowned without hindrance (from Raama.)"

Kaikeyi warns her husband in no uncertain terms if he fails to honour his commitment. "As you are king of kings, you must be true to your promise. You must protect the honour of your family, your good birth, your good conduct,. Sages say that for mortals, honouring one's word is foremost, and most salutary to go to heaven."

Who says Kaikeyi is just a pleasure seeking, childish lady who delights herself before the mirror, admiring her beauty.

On hearing Kaikeyi's demands, Dhasharatha swoons and is unconscious for one full Muhoortha of about 48 minutes. Regaining his consciousness he goes on a tirade against Kaikeyi for such vile, obnoxious, immoral demands. As we are now looking at Kaikeyi and her character, we will describe the Drama of the night only in relation to Kaikeyi. Dhasharatha uses the carrot and stick technique, trying to put some sense into her. Ayodhya kaanda - chapter 12 is a long one with 115 slokas. ***No wonder, Vaalmeeki, who has a sense of proportion devotes so many slokas for this midnight drama***. To give an example of the carrot techniique, we may quote sloka 36 "Oh Kaikeyi! I beg you, with folded arms in Anjali, May I touch your feet. May you give refuge to your Raama...." And for the stick technique, we have as example sloka 112, "Oh Kaikei! Torture yourself, as much as you like.! Perish!. Be cut up into thousand parts.! Oh the wicked woman of Kekeya kingdom! I Will Not Fulfill Your Wishes Which is most Cruel..."

Now we have a case of the devil quoting scriptures. Kaikeyi admonishes her husband and quotes precedents. How great kings had behaved before. (Sloka 43, 44) Gist: "Long ago, King Shibi offered his flesh for a mere bird. Royal sage Alarka, pulled out his eyes and gave them away for a blind Brahmin.. The ocean does not cross the shore because it honours an agreement and is on oath. And so, Oh my husband be true to your oath"

Again (in the next chapter 13) Dhasharatha begs and tries hard to change Kaikeyi, make her withdraw her wish. One sloka is particuarly significant (sloka 7) Dhasharatha pleads. "If I maintain that Raama was sent to forest by me desirous as I was to be truthful to you Kaikeyi (to honour your boons), then it would be that what I said in my assembly before the citizens, VIP-s and Purohiths, that I am crowning Raama, will be false." Poor Dhasharatha. Either way he will be a man of Untruth.

Vaalmeeki by this sloka expounds the difficulty faced by a human being, tossed between two 'Dharmas'

But Kaikeyi is no child. She is a strong woman. We see a different character. Nothing can change her. Offer of jewelry, wealth, and what not cannot attract her. When Dhasharatha realises that Kaikeyi will not accept anything less than Raama's exile, in sheer disgust, and grief, he asks his minister.in.waiting Sumanthra to fetch Raama at once from his palace. As Raama enters, he is shocked by the condition of his father (Ayodhya chapter 18- sloka 3) When Dhasharatha sees his son, he could not speak "The downcast king whose eyes were blurred by tears, just uttered = Oh Raama = and fell down unconscious." Raama is horrified and asks Kaikeyi why his father is reduced to such a pitiable state unaware of the drama of the midnight.

Kaikeyi enlightens Raama why his father is downcast (Ayodhya-chapter 18- slokas 20 to 41) Gist:

""Oh Raama! Your father is not angry with you, he is not in any evil predicament. A matter bothers him in his mind which he does not speak about because of the fear that may cause you. He is speechless because he cannot speak unpleasantly to you. What was promised by him to me, that must be done by you and you only." Kaikeyi narrates how his father had offered her two boons long ago which she wants to avail of. She does not disclose what she wanted from his father out of the two boons. Kaikeyi is clever. As usual she gets Raama to vow before she tells him. "This man will not tell you Therefore, if that which was expressed and commanded by the king does not come to naught at your hands, then only I will tell you and disclose what I want" Kaikeyi knows who Raama is. He affirms "By the king's command, I will even jump into fire.I will drink poison if that is his wish. I will drown myself. Oh my lady! You should not speak such words to me. Fie (What a shame that you dont know me). I am always 'bound' by my father who is my Guru-teacher, ever seeking his welfare." He is not a tongue twister He tells Kaikeyi "Raama never speaks in two ways. So Oh Lady! Please tell me the words of command of the king. I swear, I will faithfully execute and fulfill." That is exactly what Kaikeyi wanted. An open acceptance of her wish. **Kaikeyi the clever one!**

When she disclosed the two boons and how she wanted to utilise them, Vaalmeeki says that there was no change in his demeanor "In spite of hearing such cruel words, (of being forced out of the country for 14 years) the magnanimous Raama did not allow grief to 'enter' him and seize him. But the king who heard all this became even more depressed".

As Raama had said that he is not used to speak in 'two' ways, he is quick with his reply to Kaikeyi (Ayodhya-chapter 19- sloka 2) "So Be It! Wearing a mendicant's robe, and sporting unkempt hair locks, honouring the king's command, I will now itself go away to forest to live 14 years" Dhasharatha is semi-unconscious, did not have the strength or heart to speak And so in sloka 23, he says " Although I am not directly told, commanded by this noble man here, this my father, because it is your words of command, I will live out the 14 years in exile in forest" And Raama is very sad, not because of the 14 years exile, but because his (step) mother Kaikeyi had not really known him all these years. (But Kaikeyi did know him!) By sloka

24 "Oh Kaikeyi!! I regret that you who are a Goddess to me, did not expect even a little of the good qualities in me. Perhaps that is why you spoke to the king. (Because, I would have gladly fulfilled your wishes even without his bidding)". So the Die is cast. One woman, Kaikeyi, changed the course of history. Raama is to leave. Bharatha to take over.But we are not through with Kaikeyi yet. The Midnight drama is still to be concluded. The morning saw a barrage of advice-curses-insults on Kaikeyi from various sources. Vasishta, Sumanthra, Sidhdhaartha all these noble men of wisdom advice her, admonish her. The carrot and stick technique. All their words go to waste at the hands of this most remarkable woman, Kaikeyi. Who says a pretty woman is dumb! All these men carry years and years of wisdom. That Kaikeyi was not shaken at all but was firm in her resolve to get Raama away to make way for Bharatha, shows what a woman of 'character' Kaikeyi really is. We ought to read Vaalmeeki in the original or in stanza by stanza in translation. ***Vaalmeeki wrote without fear and favour. Wrote about reality. And wrote Dharma***.

Before we conclude, there is a sad moment. Not because Raama and Seetha along with Lakshmana leave on 14 year exile, making every one shed tears. Not because Kaikeyi wants Seetha also dressed up in Bark/deer skin. The scene is more poignant. Raama's love for Bharatha cannot be expressed in words. As he is going away on 14 year exile, he tells Kaikeyi that he is looking forward to see Bharatha return from holiday and be crowned. Now comes the unkindest cut of all. Kaikeyi treats Raama with contempt (Ayodhya-chapter19-slokas13 & 14) "Oh Raama! The couriers will of course go forth to fetch Bharatha from his uncle's place. But I dont think you should delay your departure" **This wicked *cruel KAIKEYI* is a very clever woman.** She knew. if her son met Raama, that would be the end of her ambition.

12: HANUMAAN

It is difficult to write about this divine personality. When Dheva-s and celestials beg of God Vishnu to descend on earth in human form to destroy Raavana and all the evil forces, Vishnu had sought enlightenment from them about the strength, valour, power of Raavana, the king of Lanka and Lord of the evil demons. (Baala - chapter 16 - sloka 2). The celestials assure God Vishnu that when HE is 'born' as Raama, the son of the Dhasharatha, they will all be 'born' as monkeys and bears or create divine monkeys and bears by their celestial power to assist Raama in war against evil forces, particularly Raavana. Thus we have Hanumaan as a monkey, born to Anjana and Kesari. and as foster son of Lord of Wind. Hanumaan's mobility is just like his 'father', the Lord of Wind As there is no restraint in movement of Wind, so there is no restraint in movement of this divine monkey Hanumaan. In Kishkiinda chapter 66, slokas 8 to 21) there is a description about his divine birth. And even as a child, enamored of the rising sun, he rose up and flew towards the sun, trying to seize it! When Lord Indra saw him going towards the sun, he hurled his Vajra-weapon on him and Hanumaan fell down on earth. His cheek got bruised. Thus he got the name Hanumaan. (One whose cheeks are hit). (Slokas 22 to 26). It is said that Lord of wind was so furious when his 'foster' son was bruised thus, that he threatened to stop blowing air! God Brahma pacifying Lord of Wind, gave this foster son Hanumaan, a boon = Freedom from being killed in war by any weapon = (Sloka 29 & 30). Lord Indra, gave the boon of boons to Hanumaan = Death for Hanumaan will be at his pleasure, not at the pleasure of the Lord of death, Yama =

This is the Hanumaan we are talking about.

When the King of monkeys, Vali, owing to an unfortunate misunderstanding, drives away his brother Prince Sugreeva in wrath, from Kishkinda, Hanumaan and five of the monkeys chose to go along with prince Sugreeva and offer protection to him. We meet Hanumaan as a Minister to Sugreeva. There is no reference why Hanumaan did not stay on with Vaali. It must be that Hanumaan had felt that grave injustice was done to Sugreeva by his wrathful brother Vaali. and Hanumaan being a good noble person, remained with Sugreeva. They seek refuge in the peaks of Malay mountain, not far away from Kishkinda. Vaali cannot trespass into this region owing to a curse on him. When Raama and Lakshmana who were on Search of Seetha when she had been abducted by Raavana to an unknown destination, try to reach Sugreeva to make friendship with him on the advice of Kabhandha for assistance in searching for Seetha, Sugreeva, looking at them from the mountain top from a distance, gets scared. He is convinced that Raama and Lakshmana are spies of his wrathful brother Vaali, who are approaching him to harm him. He expresses his concern thus to his ministers-monkey chiefs... (Kishkinda-chapter 2-sloka 6) "These two presumably in disguise, who have come to this forest, wearing bark and deer skin dress, are roaming about, sent by the hostile brother Vaali. It is certain." Now we are introduced to this great, divine personality, Hanumaan. Hanumaan is a very wise person. He has the instinct. He assures Sugreeva on looking at Raama and Lakshman from a distance thus (Sloka 15 to 18) Gist:

"Oh Sugreeva! I do not see here the cruel Vaali from whom you are running away in fear. The character of the monkey in you, is evident! "But Sugreeva is not convinced. He expresses his fear again thus. (Slokas 20, 21)

Vaalmeeki brings home a subtle point when he uses the word Kapithvam, (character of monkey) to characterise Sugreeva. One cannot escape one's natural nature. However wise Sugreeva may be, and although he could take on any form he wished, being born a monkey, Kapithvam does not leave him. So he says. "How can there be no fear for any one when he sees these two, who are like celestials, who have long hands (reach), and whose eyes are large (and piercing), who are wielding bow and arrow....I suspect they are sent by Vaali. ..." Sugreeva adds "Kings have many friends "We know that wise kings use many friends to destroy enemies. ***Vaalmeeki through the lips of Sugreeva brings home a truth*** (Kishkindha – Chapter 2)

"Kings destroy enemies with great prudence, choosing various means, various men" Sugreeva sends Hanumaan to Raama and Lakshmana to find about them. (sloka 24 to 27) "Oh Hanumaan! Going there, disguising yourself as an ordinary human being, these two must be 'recognised' as to who they really are....by you, through conversation, by their behaviour and reaction....if they are in a happy state of mind, you may then repose confidence in them..by laudatory speech, by good gestures...learn about their true intentions.... ask them about their purpose of visit to this forest...if they are pure souls, then you 'see' them as friends" Everything is fine, what all Sugreeva had said to Hanumaan. Only with this difference. Hanumaan does not need any advice or 'teaching' ***He is indeed the wisest of them all.***

And as a first step, Hanumaan discards his monkey form, takes on the form of a ordinary human being, and presents himself before Raama and Lakshmana. (Kish-chapter 3-sloka 2) intending to 'cheat' them. Then he addresses them (slokas 5 to 20): Gist "Looking like royal sages, having the most radiant complexion, why have you come here.you are like sages performing vows causing fear among birds, animals by your presence...Possessing valour like that of lion, strength of tough bulls, wielding a bow that shines like Lord Indra's, hands and thighs like the trunk of an elephant, why are you roaming about here. You bring lustre to this area...you are fit to rule the earth. you resemble each other...you are like the sun and the moon...With broad chests, appearing like celestials, you are here as though by accident from heaven...your hands are worthy of being ornamented, yet you wield arms and bow. Your swords are shining. While Hanumaan was talking thus, he was surprised that there was no response from Raama and Lakshmana. They are stunned by the way Hanumaan spoke. He narrates the tale of woes of his chief Sugreeva (Some commentators are surprised that Hanumman continues his address without any response from Raama & Lakshmana)..

Slokas 21 to 24: "A brave noble soul, leader of monkeys, Sugreeva by name, driven away by his brother, is now wandering in great sorrow. Sent by Sugreeva, I, who am a monkey, named Hanumaan, have come before you. The noble Sugreeva seeks friendship with you and you should know me as his minister. I am the foster son of the lord of Wind.. Desirous of doing good to my chief, I am in the garb of a mendicant" It may appear strange that Hanumaan, without knowing anything about Raama, should talk about friendship. The truth is that ***Hanumaan has the wisdom, the instinct to judge persons, a quality rare even among very wise ministers.***

When Hanumaan had stopped his address, Raama was beaming with joy. As per protocol, he does not address Hanumaan straight away, but talks to his brother Lakshmana thus (slokas 27 to 36) Gist: "Even as I was desirous of meeting Sugreeva, his most eminent minister Hanumaan has come to me. Oh Lakshmana, you talk to him, who speaks sweetly and who desires friendship." Raama has a word of praise for Hanumaan, in fact praises him sky high even at first sight.

He tells Lakshman further "One who is not educated in Rig vedha, cannot speak like this. One who is not sustained by Yajur vedha cannot speak like this. One who makes jest of Saama vedha, cannot speak like this. And surely, the 'grammar' of speech must be well known to him, he must have studied this many times. Nothing wrong in his speech, although he spoke many words. No blemish, not even a trifle, was perceived either in his face, his eyes, or in any part of his body, as he spoke" ***Vaalmeeki by this says that not only a person should speak well, and clearly, his general demeanour must be striking***.

Raama justifies his observation of Hanumaan when he continues "Moderation in voice, speech short and crisp, unambiguous, no faltering, no tardiness, firm, absence of tremor in voice, words coming out of heart but through lips. Correct Samskar- correct sanskrit- proper pronunciation, proper format- (what to say first) ...." "And listening to these wonderful words that came from three parts of his body, (head, heart and mouth), tell me Lakshman, whose mind will not be pacified? "***Vaalmeeki through Raama expounds the prime quality of speech, music*** The mind conceives, words and music should touch the heart, and come out of the mouth pleasantly. Finally Raama says "Oh Lakshmana! If such an ambassador is not there for a king, how can there be any success at all for him"

Yes, coming as it does from Raama who is a master of speech, ***Hanumaan is a Vaagmee- Master of speech***.

And Vaalmeeki describes here through Raama the qualities of a good ambassador

Yes. Hanuman is an Excellent Ambasador ***as well.***

Vaalmeeki always observes protocol. ***So too Lakshmana who replies to Hanumaan. When Raama had praised Hanumaan thus before Lakshmana, Hanumaan being a wise person, thinks that his mission was already successful. (Kish-chapter 4-sloka 2) "He, Raama also, has come on business (with us). Therefore the tesk of getting back the kingdom by the most eminent Sugreeva has become feasible." We may make a point or two. Hanumaan is such a devoted minister, that his thoughts for his 'boss' Sugreeva never leave him. His wisdom and understanding of the situation is remarkable. This is why in Raamaayana, Hanumaan has a unique place. He feels that if Sugreeva forms friendship with Raama, there is nothing Raama would not do for them. Hanumaan had judged Raama and Lakshmana in a trice even before***

Lakshmana addresses him for the first time. The quality of an ambassador is this. When you are 'abroad' you must discern who is who. Hanumaan goes further by this reasoning. Friendship between two good men will always be fruitful, more important, when they have mutual problems and interests. Vested interest carries us a long way.

Hanumaan thus is a Dheerga dharshi, who looks far ahead!

When Lakshmana addresses him thus, Hanumaan is certain, his judgment is correct. (slokas 6 to 24) Gist "A king named Dhasharatha who was most majestic, who was devoted to Dharma, ruled and protected all the four castes as per Dharma, always. None was hostile to him. He was hostile to none either. He had performed many yaagas. His eldest son is this one, Raama by name. He is a refuge to all. He considers his father's command foremost. But he was driven out of his country. His wife Seetha accompanied him to the forest, like the evening sun.

I am his younger brother. Possessing some merit.. I have entered forest for service to him....I am called Lakshmana. I am serving him who is used to comforts but now suffering forest life...his mind is always directed to do good to all...but is deprived of wealth and kingdom..When she, Seetha, was alone, she was kidnapped by a demon: .....By whom she was kidnapped, we do not know... by Kabhandha we were told that the monkey chief Sugreeva is the fit person to help us find Seetha..." Lakshmana tells him how desperate they are, not in so many words, but by the use of one word, Refuge= Sharanam. Sloka 17: "Raama and I Have Come To Seek Refuge Under Sugreeva" Lakshmana does not say that Raama seeks Friendship = Sakyam. Nor

Help = Sahaayyam. from Sugreeva. But he uses the strong word Refuge=sharanam. We have already written about this earlier. In sloka 19, Lakshman says "His father Dhasharatha, a devotee of Dharma was the Refuge to all before, his son Raama who used to be the refuge for all like him, is seeking Refuge under Sugreeva". Lakshmana is so concerned with Raama who is totally submerged in grief not being able to find the whereabouts of his beloved wife Seetha, that he uses this word Sharanam = Refuge. Lakshmana knows it is Sugreeva who will find Seetha for Raama and thus save him from further agony. Deeply religious people have questioned the use of the word Sharanam = Refuge, by Vaalmeeki. How can a royal prince and a mighty warrior like Raama seek refuge under a monkey. Further how can Raama, God Vishnu on earth, seek refuge under Sugreeva. So goes on the debate. But Vaalmeeki can never be found fault with. When we are down, we have to seek Refuge, even if we are men of power and substance. ***Vaalmeeki brings home a Truth*** here.

Finally Lakshmana pleads before Hanumaan (sloka 24) "As Raama who is overpowered by grief has come ***to seek Refuge***, the foremost monkey Sugreeva must show favour to him"

The master of speech Hanumaan replied to Lakshmana who had spoken pitiably and with tears (Sloka 26 to 29) "Such people like you who are endowed with wisdom, who have controlled their anger must be 'seen' highly (valued highly) by the lord of monkeys, Sugreeva. You have come to meet him. Most fortunate, for Sugreeva. Assuring Lakshmana thus, Hanumaan tells them further "We will go to Sugreeva.

(I will take you there). Driven away by his wrathful brother Vaali due to animosity, and his wife also seized by Vaali, Sugreeva is in great distress. But he will offer you all ***help and assistance*** along with us, in the search of Seetha" Hanumaan does not say here that Sugreeva will offer Refuge to Raama. The great wise Hanumaan knows who he is talking to. Here the expression used by Vaalmeeki is help-assistance = Sahaayyam

Vaalmeeki cannot be found fault with. Remember he is the author ordained by God Brahma, the Vedha personified

And as he carries Raama and Lakshmana on his back to meet Sugreeva, Hanumaan has successfully concluded the object of his mission. Sugreeva wanted him to just find out about Raama and Lakshmana. Hanumaan is no ordinary emissary or ambassador. He must go beyond his brief and will act accordingly, unless it is detrimental to his chief Sugreeva's interest. As we proceed further, this unique quality in him will be seen and recognised.

Hanumaan, The Ambassador.

And Hanumaan The Blessed.

Because he carries on his back the divine beings, Raama and Lakshmana.

When Hanumaan takes Raama and Lakshmana to Sugreeva, he introduces them to him, as only Hanumaan can. (Kish- chapter 5- slokas 2 to 7) He advises Sugreeva thus "These two brothers Raama and Lakshmana are to be honoured. They are desirous of friendship with you. So must be accepted and honoured" Sugreeva has such high regard for his minister Hanumaan that he readily accepts his advice.

No one can ignore Hanumaan, so great and wise is he. By sloka 10, Sugreeva tells Raama "Your noble qualities were narrated by Hanumaan. You are obedient to Dharma, endearing to all" And in the next sloka he says "Oh Lord Raama! That you desire to 'form' friendship with me, a mere monkey, is indeed an honour for me. And is good for me as well" We may observe two points. Sugreeva addresses Raama as =Oh my lord=and uses the term Sowhardam= friendship. There is no question of Sugreeva offering - sharanam= refuge - to Raama. He knows his limitations and that too before Raama. Raama and Sugreeva, before holy fire, ***affirm their friendship***. And they converse in great joy...discuss their mutual problems. Here we may observe, although a triviality, the Protocol. (Kish chapter 5 slokas 20 and 21) "And breaking up a branch of a saala tree with plenty of flowers, leaves, Sugreeva spread it on the floor and sat along with Raama. Hanumaan who was exhilarated with joy as his mission had succeeded, pulled out another branch and sat along with Lakshmana "

Hanumaan the philosopher is a diverse unique personality. The scene is this. Vaali was killed by Raama to make way for Sugreeva as king of the monkey world. Vaali's wife, the wise lady, comes to the field and looks at her mighty husband lying down dead and she cries her heart out.

It is Hanumaan who consoles her not by the usual mundane words of consolation, but by expounding Life's nature. (Kish - chapter 21- slokas 2 to 11) Gist:

"Even after death, a living being, surely obtains good and bad, all of it, obtained by 'fruits' of his own Karma, unaffected (by other's actions)" Vaalmeeki uses the word avyagraha= unaffected This is the traditional Indian view. As you sow, so you reap. If you do good, even if you dont get good results now, you will get reward later, in the next birth. The Dharma- Adharma theory..

Hanumaan expounds yet another Truth known to philosophers when he says. "Oh Thaara! You who are in a state of lament, are lamenting for another -for your dead husband! Miserable as you are, which miserable person is to be lamented for? In the matter of mortal body, that is like a mere 'Bubble', who is to grieve for whom?" Life is a mere bubble. Body 'bursts' and only the soul remains. But we grieve over body!

"You know very well that for all living beings, birth and death are like this, uncontrollable. Your husband, on whom thousands of monkeys, nay millions of monkeys, lived upon, such a one has reached the 'appointed' Time."

Hanumaan's nobility, and magnanimity are seen as he praises Vaali who was not particularly his 'friend' Infact, he had defected from Vaali's kingdom and joined Sugreeva as his minister. "Vali, your husband, knew the essence of Law; he was foremost in the art of Saama- Conciliation: art of giving =Dhaana; in quality of Kshama = Forbearance, forgiveness. He has gone to the world of men who have 'conquered' Dharma - he has gone to heaven. So why lament over him? "Here we may note a few points. Death is not the end of life. It is life again, perhaps in heaven. Every one knows how badly Vaali treated his brother Sugreeva. He never entertained any thought of killing him. He never forgave his brother. He did not administer 'fair justice' to him. Yet Hanumaan praises Vaali. Vaalmeeki through Hanumaan expounds Dharma. Once a person dies, however bad he may be, we should never talk ill of him. Ofcourse, it is difficult to observe this. Once an enemy, always an enemy. Later in the Yudhdha Kaanda, we find the noble Raama expounding this Dharma before Vibheeshana when on the death of Raavana who was slain by Raama in the gruesome war, refuses to perform Funereal Rites for his brother Raavana. Raama admonishes him saying "All enmity ceases with Death" (Yudhdha -chapter 114 slokas 105 and 106 and sloka 112)

Vibheeshana tells Raama "I am not 'worthy' enough to do the last Rites for my brother Raavana, who had abandoned all norms of Dharma, who was most cruel, who violated other's wives, who was a liar, who was my enemy in the garb of a brother ...." Raama chides him "Oh Vibheeshana! Remember this. Enmity is only till death. Our purpose has ended with death. As he is to you, so is he to me ...Perform his last rites with due honours for a king" Raama says that even though Raavana was his sworn enemy in as much as he kidnapped his most beloved wife, after he killed him, thus offering him the punishment due to him, he will not carry animosity further. Readers may forgive the writer if we repeat this in detail later in this Guide. We referred to this here because

Hanumaan is a True follower of Dharma. Dharma of the dead. Hanumaan would never carry animosity. Ofcourse he would not spare an enemy or evil forces. ***He being a deeply religious person as well***, he advises the weeping Thaara thus (slokas 10,11) Gist "King Vaali must be cremated with due honours and the Last Rites. For what purpose, progeny is considered necessary, may son Angadha perform the Rites for his father Vaali"

Hanumaan, the minister

A good minister is one who should give sound advice at the proper time. He should not seek favour but concern himself with what is good for the king and the State and have no reservations to express clearly and firmly even though it may be un-palatable to the king.

After Vaali was killed by Raama and Sugreeva was installed king of the monkey world, it is all wine, women and song for Sugreeva. Raama had kept his oath - that he would kill Vaali and install Sugreeva as king. It is the turn of Sugreeva to send armies to find Seetha.all over the globe. True, Raama had given him 2 months for Sugreeva to take steps. The weather was not conducive for such an operation, it being the heavy rainy season. He expected that Sugreeva, like a true friend, without being reminded, would be taking steps after the season was over. But Sugreeva was so consumed by liquor and passion, that he had no 'time' for 'time'. The deadline for action had passed.

It is then Hanumaan started worrying about Sugreeva. He approached the king of monkeys and addressed him with the most salutary words of advice that will lead him to the right path and conduct. Hanumaan knew the reality of the situation; the consequences of inaction by Sugreeva. (Kish-chapter 29- slokas 9 to 28) Gist: "This kingdom, Oh Sugreeva, was obtained by you with fame and glory going with it. What remains is the favour to be done, the requital, for Raama, as per your oath." Hanumaan warns that he should not be a man of ingratitude, particularly before the mighty Raama. ***Vaalmeeki expounds another Truth --- the Importance of Time-Place ---- for action.*** If we don't take action at the right time, the objective will be lost. We must choose right place as well for action.

"One who knows the proper Time and acts promptly for friends, to such a king, the kingdom flourishes, fame and wealth as well. You, Sugreeva is endowed with good conduct, steadfast in path of Dharma, of restraint, should, as a gesture to your friend Raama, act now (to find out about Seetha). Only he is a true friend who abandons all other work for his friend's sake. And if work for a friend is not done at the right time, any number of other good acts done later, may not turn out to be of purpose to him. Timely service is help rendered. Therefore, Sugreeva, may the search of Seetha be undertaken right now. This is our service to friend Raama. The rainy season is gone. Yet no action is taken. Raama is wise and has sense of timing - he had given you time because he wanted the rainy season to be over - You now give the command at once. If you do this without being impelled by Raama, without being reminded by Raama, it would mean that you have taken the proper step and 'time' had not elapsed" After advising Sugreeva, Hanumaan has this to say about Raama.***Hanumaan knows who Raama is*** "Raama, the Raaghava is The Motive Power. And his power is incomparable." Having warned Sugreeva about the consequences of neglecting his task for Raama as requital, Hanumaan, the Vaagmee, the master of Speech uses the Carrot technique "Oh Sugreeva! I know you. You are one who will do service for another even if he does not do anything for you.. When that is so, will you not do this much for Raama who has made you king "Sugreeva should not think that Raama is his 'slave' awaiting and soliciting favour from him. Hanumaan makes sure that

Sugreeva knows who Raama really is when he tells him "Raama, the son of Dhasharatha can subdue even celestials.. Yet, there must be a reason why he looks forward to you to fulfill your commitment of finding Seetha for him "Offcourse Sugreeva "Wakes UP"

This is Hanumaan, the Minister

It is in the judgement of men one distinguishes between the remarkable and the ordinary. Raama has this extraordinary ability to judge human beings even at first sight. We know that in modern business, unless the top executive has the right 'eye' to spot talent, he cannot command a good administrative force in his office and business. The Degree qualification gives a person merely an introduction. But the top executive must have the ability to choose and choose quickly. Success or failure may depend on the personnel.

When finally, Sugreeva decides to send various armies to the different parts of the Globe in search of the 'lost' Seetha, Raama's judgement becomes obvious. He knows that it is Hanumaan who has the capacity, brilliance, wisdom among them all, to find Seetha. We know from Kishkinda-chapters 40 to 43, various armies headed by different chiefs of the monkey army are sent out; to Eastern part under Vinatha, to the Southern region of the globe under Hanumaan and Angadha, to the West under Sushena, and to the North under Shathabali. Raama, had already marked out Hanumaan as a very wise person when he had first met him as the emissary of Sugreeva. When Sugreeva addresses Hanumaan before he leaves on the search mission to the South, Raama took note of this as he was watching armies leave one by one from Kishkinda. (Kish chapter 44-slokas 2 to 7) Gist: "Oh Hanumaan, the 'tiger' of monkeys!

I have not seen any restraint in your movement, whether on the surface of the earth, or the sky above the earth or the underworld of the ocean. You know them all, the Ghandarvas, naagas, Asuras, human beings. Your unrestricted movement, speed, brilliance, the ease with which you move about, in all these qualities you have taken after your foster father, the lord of Wind. So prepare and 'harness' yourself to find Seetha"

This is the Hanumaan as seen by his king Sugreeva.

This is the confidence Hanumaan generates in his king

Raama is a shrewd observer. When Sugreeva had concluded his special address to Hanumaan with (sloka 7) "Oh Hanumaan. you are an expert in polity. Strength valour, intelligence, right action at right time and place, have all taken 'root' in you", Raama ponders, over Hanumaan's unique qualities, thus (slokas 9 to 11) Gist; "This lord of monkeys, Sugreeva has formed his opinion in every way. ....so in the matter of finding Seetha, Hanumaan is indeed sure to accomplish the task, will find Seetha. It is certain, as he sets out on a long journey." Raama was so delighted by his thoughts over Hanumaan that Vaalmeeki says "...the most brilliant Raama, who had become exhilarated with joy, felt that success had already come by that Seetha was found by Hanumaan" Raama's judgment is so quick, and had to be, because Hanumaan was getting ready for the long journey, that he decides to hand over his Signet Ring, as a token of remembrance, when Hanumaan finds and meets Seetha. Raama is sure. His instinct told him so .His judgement had rarely failed him. By sloka 13, Raama tells Hanumaan "Oh foremost monkey, Hanumaan! By this token, Seetha, the daughter of Janaka, will recognise you without doubt, that you have come from me" And handing over his Signet ring to Hanumaan, Raama finally tells him (sloka 14) Gist: "Oh brave Hanumaan! By Sugreeva's words and his special 'commission' to you, by your well known valour...by your determination to fulfill the task...all these 'tell' me of success in mission"

Such is the regard and respect Hanumaan commanded from Raama. Hanumaan, receiving the Signet ring, held it over his head in Anjali, in utter devotion..

Hanumaan had the privilege of carrying Raama and Lakshmana. Now he 'carries' Raama's Signt ring.

Can there be any one more blessed than Hanumaan

We know that Seetha was kidnapped by demon king Raavana and had been taken away 1,000 miles away over the ocean in the South, into his island kingdom of Lanka. When the 'Search for Seetha' army of monkeys under Angadha and Hanumaan, search the entire south region of India, naturally they could not find Seetha and the entire army was in a state of dejection. The leader Angadha, son of Vaali, is desperate. He feels that if he got back to Sugreeva without finding Seetha, his life would be in peril at his hands. He suggests that they all live in a cave where they can be without fear of Sugreeva and Lakshmana. Hanumaan ridicules this idea. If they think that they will be safe there, they would be living in fool's paradise. And Hanumaan the wise, knows the prowess of Sugreeva and Lakshmana. He gives a bit of advice to Angadha (Kish- chapter 54) and Hanumaan the clever minister brought about a split, dissension, in the army, to ensure that the search army rejects Angadha's suggestion but continue with the search of Seetha. (In sloka 6) Vaalmeeki says "Using the third of the four strategies, Hanumaan brought about a split among the monkeys" We know that there are normally four strategies, in order. Saama = conciliation, talks. Dhaana = Gift away, bribery Bhedha = split, threats and lastly, if all these fail, use of the rod, Dhanda = the stick, war. Hanumaan chose the third strategy to see to it that the search army does not give up hope but continues the search of Seetha. If Hanumaan had not been there, this Southern army of monkeys on search, would have given up long ago, the mission would have failed. Hanumaan ridicules Angadha (sloka 13)

"Oh Angadha! You consider this impenetrable cave will give you sanctuary. In the matter of tearing this to pieces, it is just a moment's work for Lakshmana" ***The Greatness of Hanumaan is not that he found Seetha ultimately. But he had immense faith, the instinct, the drive***.

One of the weakness of Hanumaan, perhaps, is that he is not aware of his greatness. May be due to his modesty. When the "search for Seetha army" of monkeys reaches the southern tip of India and face the mighty ocean, and their search is to take them far away in the Southern Ocean, into the island kingdom of Lanka, the question arose who among them could swim or fly such a long distance. Under Angadha, the monkey chiefs hold a council, facing the ocean. None is sure of crossing that distance and get back safe. This is the Sceneario.When Angadha offers to go, it is rejected by the old and wise Jaambavan. A chief of army, or a prince or king, never should take a risk because if he dies, the army will wither away. ***Vaalmeeki here brings home another truth. (Kish-Chapter 65- slokas 22 to 25) Gist***:

Oh lad, prince Angadha! You are our chief, in a position to command any one to take on this onerous task. You are our Citadel. our master, the chief of our army.You should remain with us to protect us all, at all times.You are also the chief. 'The Root' of this mission. Your life is precious and must be guarded for our sake. This is the doctrine, of the army, the code. Remember, only when the root is firm and flourishes, fruits and flowers issue forth.... so no question about your flying over 1,000 miles. Your capability is not in question"

It is then Jaambavan casts his eye on Hanumaan. (sloka 35) "The most distinguished Jaambavan began to 'goad' Hanumaan, who was 'resting in a solitary place'..."

Hanumaan was staying away, from the discussions among monkey chiefs as to who should fly 1,000 miles over the ocean to find out about Seetha, as though unconcerned, feigning ignorance. In an oblique way, ***Vaalmeeki brings home the well-known Truth. of the importance of advisers.*** Indeed Jambavan was one such.

Hanumaan was his choice, none other.

The old, wise noble Jaambavan stated the obvious when he compared Hanumaan with Sugreeva, Raama and Lakshmana thus to press him to fly 1,000 miles on the Search for Seetha mission. (Kish-chapter 66-sloka 3) "Oh Hanumaan you are indeed equal in strength to Sugreeva, Raama and Lakshmana" As we are now about to write about Hanumaan's decision to fly 1,000 miles, all alone, by himself, and take on the most difficult task of searching for Seetha in the island of Lanka, we might as well describe Hanumaan's birth and deeds as described by Jaambavaan. (Kish-chapter 66) Gist

"He, this Hanumaan, is the son of Arishtanemi who was son of Vinata. Foremost among all birds. Mightily strong, he is known as Garuda. This 'winged' bird was seen by me many times, carrying mighty serpents from the ocean. Oh Hanumaan! Such strength you possess in your arms, as he had it in his wings! Between you two, you are not lagging behind in power and strength." After beginning to talk about Hanumaan, Jaambavan is vexed that there is no response from Hanumaan as he continues "Oh foremost monkey, Hanumaan! When such is the case, how is it you are not aware that qualities of strength, wisdom, brilliance, goodness, distinguish you from the rest of beings? "***Yes Hanumaan is Unique***............And now Jaambavaan narrates Hanumaan's origin, his birth.

"Once there lived Punjikasthala, who was foremost among celestial Apsara ladies. She was renowned as Anjana. She was the wife of Kesari. She was a celestial, yet due to a curse, became 'born' in the world, as a female monkey of extraordinary beauty. Ofcourse she could take on any form on earth when she pleased. On earth she was known as daughter of Kunjara. And once, taking the form of a maiden, wearing lovely garlands, wonderful dress, she roamed about over the mountain peaks, sky. As she rested on top of the mountain, the Lord of Air blew off her lovely dress and this Lord saw her pristine beauty, her well formed body, lovely thighs and legs. At once this Lord was seized with passion over her. He lost control of himself and hugged her. (taking on human form). Anjana being a woman of impeccable conduct and devoted wife being totally bewildered by this, exclaimed in exasperation = Who is trying to snatch away my modesty and virtue, who is trying to destroy my vow of being faithful to one only, my husband = Hearing her wail, Lord of Wind replied = I have not 'spoiled' you or your virtue There be no fear in you. But being Lord of Wind with the right of entry unrestricted by my nature, I have 'entered' you. A very brave son is going to be born to you who will be endowed with wisdom. He will be most brilliant, noble, good mightily strong and valiant. In movement, like me there will be no restriction, can fly very fast. = Hearing this, your mother was pleased and she begot you in a cave". After narrating this Jaambavaan talks about Hanumaan's prowess even as a child. "Oh Hanumaan. You were but a child! Seeing the rising Sun, considering it as a 'fruit' to be had, you jumped up and flew to seize it! Even after flying 300 yojanas = 2,500 miles in the sky, you never got tired or burnt. Lord Indra was worried and hurled Vajra on you. You fell down on the slopes of the mountain with your left cheek bruised. From that time you became renowned as Hanumaan = one with bruised cheeks. Your foster father, Lord of Wind became terribly angry when you were hit by Vajra and he threatened to stop blowing air. God Brahma realising the fate of the world if the Lord stopped his service, pacified him by offering his foster son, you, Hanumman, a boon, by which you have no death by any weapon. Even Lord Indra offered his boon, by which your death is at your pleasure and convenience."

Readers know that none in the world can escape Yama, the lord of Death. He is Time, He chooses the Time. Yet, he has no business with Hanumaan!

Hanumaan is indeed most blessed, is Unique.None like him

The very old, noble, wise Jaambavan, almost begs Hanumaan. Seeing the total dejection of all the monkeys and monkey chiefs of the army stationed on the shore of the ocean as none could fly over 1,000 miles into Lanka, Jaambavan 'begs' Hanumaan (Kish-chapter 66-sloka 39) Gist: "Oh Hanumaan! Why are you indifferent? All these monkeys are totally dejected because none else can do this job" After begging him thus, Jaambavan compares Hanumaan with God Vishnu. Earlier he had compared him with Raama and Lakshmana "Like God Vishnu who became Three-ThriVikrama, you also traverse the Ocean" We know from Baala kaanda(chapter 29), how Vishnu, to humble the arrogant King Bali, came down on earth, as an ordinary Brahmin with a begging bowl, and measured the Universe with just Three steps.

Who else can be compared with Vishnu. Hanumaan It Is
When Jaambavan had goaded and praised Hanumaan thus, the foremost of all monkeys, this Hanumaan, stretched himself, began to augment his strength, began to get ready for the solo flight across the mighty Mahodhadhi ocean (Indian ocean).. All the monkeys gave up their grief when they saw Hanumaan getting ready. Such was the respect Hanumaan commanded. They all extolled him, praised him sky high. No wonder! Hanumaan brandished his tail. He was going to fly into Lanka only in the form of a monkey although he could take on any form. Rising up, bowing to respected elders of the monkey army, he got up and addressed the entire army formation -The Search for Seetha Army, thus as he climbs the Mahendra Mountain on the 'tip' of India, to take off for his flight over the ocean to the island of Lanka, in search of Seetha, Hanumaan 'reveals' himself thus (Kish- chapter 67) even as the entire army of

monkeys, don't take their eyes off him Gist "As I am the foster son of Wind, none to equal me in 'jumping and flying. I am capable of going round even the entire Meru mountain which is wide and which scrapes the sky. I can traverse the sky, over the constellations. I will bring back Seetha the Vaidhehi, the consort of Raama. Like God Vishnu's form when he measured the universe with just three steps, I will jump over taking on a mighty form." When Hanumaan had spoken thus with authority, the monkeys were exhilarated with joy. And Jaambavan's 'goading' had done this 'trick' He had reminded Hanumaan who he really is. He addresses him (Kish-chapter 67-slokas 34 to 37) "Oh Hanumaan, the brave son of Kesari! Oh the foster son of lord of wind! The great torment and worry of your folks here, has been destroyed by you as you have taken on the mission of flying 1,000 miles over the ocean. These monkeys here offer you benediction with devotion for the success of your mission" Jaambavan offers his blessings to Hanumaan thus" By the blessings of sages, and elders, with the permission of elderly monkeys of our army here, May You Cross The Great Ocean". By this he expresses his concern for Hanumaan thus "Till you come back again after finding Seetha, we will be on one feet, will be on our toes. The lives of these monkeys here depend on you "

Thus Jaambavan states the obvious. If a mission depended on one person, surely that person is Hanumaan.

Hanumaan composed himself. His thought and mind already on Lanka, 1000 miles away as he prepares to take off for his flight over the mighty ocean.

Religious people acclaim that among all the 6 "Books" =Kaandams of Vaalmeeki Raamaayana Sundhara Kaanda, the Fifth Book stands out. It is even maintained that if one does not have the time to read the entire epic, reading Sundhara kaanda is sufficient to give solace. Some even go further. They say that even if a chapter of Sundhara kaanda is read, that is enough to offer us spiritual comfort. Why is this so?

Sundhara Kaanda as its name suggests, is a very sweet 'book', it is Hanumaan's all about Hanumaan.:

Such a divine being is Hanumaan. His solo flight over the mighty ocean into island of Lanka, 1,000 miles away. His overcoming obstacles during his flight. His finding the whereabouts of Seetha. His 'secret' conversation with Seetha in spite of her being guarded in isolation by demons in the Ashoka forest. His building confidence in Seetha that he is really her husband Raama's emissary. His meeting with Raavana and giving him a sort of ultimatum to restore Seetha to Rama. His wrath upon Lanka when his tail was set fire to. He returns to Kishkinda to report to Raama and his king Sugreeva, gloriously, having accomplished the mission of finding Seetha. His, no mean task, as Lanka was so closely guarded by the demons of the mighty Raavana.

And Hanumaan achieved this all by himself

The solo flight from tip of India towards South over the ocean is beautifully described. Poet Vaalmeeki excels himself in almost every other sloka of this chapter, he goes 'Poetic' (Sundara - chapter 1) This Guide cannot do full justice to Vaalmeeki through translation. Yet, let us list some of these here.

We must however make some 'allowances' for mythological treatment. Before he takes off from the peaks of mountain, Hanumaan offers prayer to the Lords of Wind, Sun, God Brahma, the Bhoothas, and ofcourse, he prayed silently in his mind to Raama and Lakshmana. (Sundhara-chapter 1- slokas 8 to 10) to his father, rivers and the lord of the oceans. Hanumaan is a religious person. Applying fierce pressure with his feet, Hanumaan takes off with a jump. He augmented his body. Vaalmeeki says he grew to such a size his 'shadow' on the surface of the ocean, was many Yojanas = miles. As he had used the word "Plava" which can mean even -Swim-, some commentators feel that perhaps Hanumaan swam across 1,000 miles. This is because Hanumaan's body is full of salt water. This theory is rejected for many reasons. Hanumaan perhaps flew low and the suction pressure of his vast huge body, created mighty waves which constantly hit his body. Secondly Hanumaan is son of Wind and it is his flying power that could take him over to Lanka in just under 7 or 8 hours. He must have flown at 250 KMP. for overcoming obstacles during flight. (Sundhara-chapter 1- sloka 76) "His body over the top of the ocean, his huge shadow 'pressing' the surface of the ocean...." (Sloka 78,79) " Warding off huge waves with his chest which was like a mountain, the great monkey, Hanumaan crossed over. The fierce wind that issued forth as he dragged it on with him and the wind of the sky, made the ocean very, very turbulent" We should not be surprised at this mythological extravaganza. (sloka 85) "The shadow cast by Hanumaan's body on the ocean, was 10 by 30 yojanas" Readers may prepare themselves for a mild shock- or surprise. A Yojana is about 8 to 9 miles!

No question about it. Hanumaan flew and flew low over the ocean.

Vaalmeeki goes poetic in this chapter. (sloka 81) Flying over the ocean, it appeared as though Hanumaan was taking 'Count' of the ceaseless number of waves that was hitting his chest" If you want more of Vaalmeeki's artistry, here is another (sloka 64) "The appearance of the sky with its rising clouds and the appearance of the ocean with rising waves, were similar" One could not know where sky ended and the surface of the ocean emerged. As the mighty Hanumaan was flying at his will, the ocean appeared like a vast swimming pool! Students of poetry can the read this chapter with some satisfaction. Ah! Vaalmeeki the poet!.

Ofcourse Hanumaan faces some obstacles during his flight. We will only say that by sheer dexterity and wisdom, he overcomes them and reaches Lanka in late evening the same day of Takeoff.

When Hanumaan reaches Lanka and takes a look from the sky he thinks thus (sloka 222) "Seeing the bigness of my body, these demons of Lanka will be seized with curiosity about me" As he descended on the peak called Lamba on Thrikoota hills, on the outskirts of Lanka he reduced the size of his body. Hanumaan being on a delicate mission, did not want to be conspicuous. He enters Lanka by night fall. Is confronted by a mystical demoness guard, protecting entire city. He overwhelms her. But this woman who had turned out to be a vile woman because of a curse, is emancipated from the curse and blesses Hanumaan for the success of his mission in Lanka.

Hanumaan had thus achieved 'miracle' Flying over 1,000 miles all alone, ***Only Hanumaan could do it***. Jaambavan was right. Sugreeva was right. And ofcourse Raama. They were all very wise persons, wisdom. personified

Hanumaan never fails.

Hanumaan is on a difficult and delicate mission. He is in fierce demon land. Lanka is crowded, and tightly guarded. Even if he sees Seetha, it will be difficult for him to convince her that he is not a spy, a demon in the form of a monkey. Who can believe that a monkey can enter Lanka 1,000 miles away from any land.

Hanumaan sets his mind to some thinking. (Sundhara-chapter 2) He ponders over the terrible enemy Raavana. (Sloka 27,28) "Here, even if all the monkeys and the entire army come over, no purpose will be served, because, even by Dhevas, Lanka cannot be conquered by war. What is this strong limbed Raama going to do even after reaching this place to attack, when it is ruled and guarded well by Raavana....very dangerous to tread "This was Hanumaan's first reaction when he took a look at Lanka. Hanumaan, does not know his own power; his diffidence is uderstandable. He even doubts Raama's valour! Hanumaan is made this way. He ponders further. Vaalmeeki through Hanumaan discusses the Four Way Strategy = Saama, Dhaana, Bhedha and Dhanda =

"There is no room for conciliation with these demons. No purpose will be served by 'peace' talks. Nothing can be achieved by gifts, offerings, bribery. Lanka is so prosperous that no demon needs anything from any one. And threats will be treated with contempt. As for the last strategy War= Dhanda, stick, this cannot be 'seen' as an option. The demons are terrific."

Hanumaan quickly recovers from his despondency. He is a master of timing - knows the proper time and place for any endeavour. He realises that this is not the time to ponder over strategy. So (by sloka 31) "First, I will find out whether Seetha is alive at all. After meeting her, I will think and worry about strategy"

This is Hanumaan, the wise, master, Time-Place Doctrine

Hanumaan, starts worrying about how to find Seetha in this vast city of Lanka (Sundhara – Chapter 2 - slokas 37, 38)

"By what strategy will I find Seetha, without being found out? This task for Raama should not come to nought".

Vaalmeeki through Hanumaan brings home the importance of considering the pros-cons of an action taken after a good deal of deliberation and choosing the right time and place for action. (slokas 39,40) "Even if a task is possible to accomplish, if it is undertaken by an emissary who gets 'confused', comes to naught, like darkness after sunset..... when done at wrong time and place....In the matter of right and wrong course of action, even after a good deal of deliberation, the mind is not clear. When that is so, some emissaries think they are 'pundits', the 'Know all' "

Hanumaan is always diffident. Although he is clear in mind, and is the master of action, has the sense of timing Hanumaan is indeed a Pundit. But is too modest.

Taking the form of an ordinary monkey, Hanumaan roams around Lanka, at night, in search of Seetha. unobserved, unseen. Elsewhere in this Guide we shall describe Lanka by the night, its night orgies, its palaces, the lovely women sleeping. We owe this to Hanumaan. We are now concerned as Hanumaan was, about finding the whereabouts of Seetha in Lanka. Hanumaan, like any other ordinary being rejoiced by the sight of Lanka at night (Sundhara-chapter 4- sloka 8) Gist "Roaming around the city for the purpose of Raama's mission of finding Seetha, he saw everything, and he rejoiced by the sight of Lanka" He jumped from house to nouse in search of Seetha. As per Sundhara kaanda chapters 4 to 11, Hanumaan exhausted his search over the city. He had even gone inside of Raavana's chamber, saw him sleeping and when he saw his wife and first queen Mandodhari, for a moment, Hanumaan thought that this could be Seetha, but soon changes his mind (chapter 11, slokas 1 to 3) Gist: "Great monkey shook off this thought. Without being with Raama, Seetha would not sleep so soundly and peacefully. She will not be dressed like this. Nor wear jewelry like this. She will have nothing to do with any other than Raama, even if he be the Lord of the celestials" Hanumaan being a devotee of Raama and Seetha, could never think of Seetha but as the purest and noblest of women. An interesting or a somewhat painful thought, seizes Hanumaan, as he visits the inner apartments of palaces past midnight. Justifiably so as Hanumaan is the purest of human beings. This trespassing and looking at ladies in 'bed room'. Privacy is sacred. And Hanumaan has violated the code, norms (Sundhara-chapter 11 -sloka 35) "Having looked at the ladies at night stealthily, this great monkey was seized with remorse, anxiety, alarmed by the fear of having transgressed Dharma" But Hanumaan does not need to consult anyone else. He contemplates thus (slokas 36 to 45) Gist" My looking at these wives of Raavana and others, particularly when they are asleep, is an act of violation of Dharma, very serious! But then, my mind is not for carnal pleasures as I look at them. Indeed my sight is directed towards women, only because of my reverence to the wife of another man Raama." ***Vaalmeeki expounds a great Truth through Hanumaan.***

When a modern surgeon operates a lady for say appendix removal, no transgression of Dharma takes place. Looking at a woman is not sinful. It is how you look at them. Hanumaan is pleased with himself. So many lovely ladies there, some almost naked, yet there is no amorous thought in Hanumaan, his sight is for search of a noble and pure lady, Seetha. nothing else "Indeed no change in my mind at all. Further where will Seetha be unless she has company of some women" So Hanumaan had rightly decided to stealthily search for Seetha in various harems and women's chambers at night. ***And (by sloka 42)we have another Truth from Hanumaan***

"Indeed, it is The Mind, that causes the 'stirring up' of all senses, passions etc....whether good or evil...in all situations... Fortunately for me, 'This' abides well by me!"

Hanumaan for once talks well about himself. For once he knows his strength. Hanumaan is indeed a man of Restraint

Unable to find Seetha so far, Hanumaan is somewhat disappointed. But feels that he should put in more effort. And Hanumaan expresses another Truth. Incidentally, this has been expressed by a very great scholar and philosopher, ages later, by Bharthruhari, who puts this Truth even more strongly. ***Bharthruhari says "Forget*** God, Fate & all that. Put in your effort. If even after you perform your duty and work by the power of ***your manliness***, success does not come by, so what" We are here referring to Bharthruhari only to indicate how much Vaalmeeki has influenced us all. Every scholar or philosopher in India that is Bhaarath has extensively drawn from Vaalmeeki. In (Sundara- chapter 12-sloka 10 & 11) Hanumaan exclaims "Root of prosperity lies in avoidance of despondency. Avoidance of despondency will lead to success and happiness. Avoidance of despondency, promotes all activities, indeed so. That which yields fruits to ***man's effort***, this is what it does, this avoidance of despondency.. Therefore, I will not give room for despondency". Thus Hanumaan the man of wisdom, augments his effort to search for Seetha with even greater zeal and effort, in Lanka.

Hanumaan the most devoted and dedicated to duty. Untiring, unwearied in Action

Hanumaan renews his effort with even greater zeal. But Seetha's sight is denied to him. He ponders. Perhaps Seetha is dead and gone. But the great 'seer', the old divine bird Sampaathi had assured him before he took off on 1,000 miles flight from India, that Seetha is in Lanka. How come? So many thoughts pass through this wise Hanumaan. Vaalmeeki writes in such a detail in chapters 10,11,12 of Sundara kaanda. because Vaalmeeki Raamaayana is for all ages and for all. And Vaalmeeki treats even Hanumaan as a human being! Vaalmeeki writes always in a matter of fact way. What all thoughts pass through this wise man when his ceaseless effort turns to naught. So much so, Hanumaan even contemplates suicide Failures and suffering may bend even a very strong resolute person. Vaalmeeki writes about Seetha as a woman who almost committed suicide, unable to find escape from Raavana and demonesses, the guards. Even Raama, the man of restraint, feels so low and depressed that he feels no useful purpose is served by prolonging life. He even begs Lakshmana to get back to Ayodhya, leaving him in forest. But Hanumaan is a man of wisdom. Even at such a failure, he could get back his will power. And he argues with himself (Sundara-chapter 13-sloka 40) "If I stay on here in Lanka without getting back, these two mighty warriors Raama and Lakshmana who are men of Dharma will hold on to their life, with hope and expectation that I will bring them news" And Hanumaan rejects suicide outright although this crossed his mind earlier. (By sloka 50) ***Vaalmeeki expounds a Truth*** as Hanumaan affirms "In destroying one's self, the sins and disadvantages are many. Only when one lives on, he attains good, good fortune. So, I will hold on to my life, come what may "***By this Vaalmeeki tells the world through the wise Hanumaan.***

Suicide does not solve any problem.

Being deeply religious, Hanumaan takes to prayer. Lord Tennyson had said, "More things are wrought by Prayer than this world dreams of" This English poet only followed what was expounded by Vaalmeeki centuries ago. Hanumaan prays for success in his mission of finding Seetha. (Sundara-chapter 13- slokas 69 to 71) "God Brahma, the self created, and lords of the celestial kingdom, Lords Agni-Fire, Vaayu-wind, Indra must bestow me with success. Likewise Lord Varuna, who holds 'the Noose' Lord Sun and Lord Moon, the Maruths, the Ashwinis, must favour me with success. The Bhoothas and their lord, The Deities-the Gocharas, and The Sharva-GodVishnu, likewise must bring me success in finding Seetha" He prays also to Raama, Lakshmana, Seetha, Lord Rudhra as well.

Having rejected suicide as an option, Hanumaan ponders. What are the places I have still not searched? Jumping on to the rampart of Raavana's palace, his thought and sight direct him to a forest nearby, The Ashoka forest. Finally, Hanumaan's instinct tells him, if at all Seetha is to be found, it is in this most beautiful forest that befits Seetha. (Sundhara- chapter 14-sloka 50) "The pleasant Ashoka forest is the most befitting place for Seetha, the wife of Raama ..."

As events turn out, Hanumaan's faith and reasoning is justified. It is in an isolated part of this delightful Ashoka forest of the suburb of Lanka that Seetha is kept as prisoner, guarded by demonesses.

At last Hanumaan sees Seetha, from the covered branches of a tree, hiding himself, unseen. Even Hanumaan, a person who could control his emotions, is shocked at the first sight of noble lady who is squatting on the foot of a large tree, surrounded by women guards..

Yet doubt lurks in his mind, whether it is Seetha whom he is seeing. Vaalmeeki puts it so beautifully as only he can, about Hanumaan's doubt whether the lady is really Seetha! (Sundhara-chapter 15-sloka 36) "In spite of seeing Seetha, it was like Vedhic Knowledge, hardly becoming perceptible by lack of application and without repeated study" If Vaalmeeki had introduced this analogy, we must consider this carefully. Here is Hanumaan, who almost gives up hope of finding Seetha in this vast city of Lanka. He has seen many, many lovely ladies. He had even seen the lovely and majestic lady, queen Mandodhari, wife of Raavana. Hanumaan must make sure that this is Seetha. How can he be sure. Only by systematic reasoning - the pros and cons.

Vaalmeeki compares this difficult task, with the study of Vedhas. Unless you study Vedhas repeatedly and with proper step by step understanding Vedhas wont mean anything. Like the study of Vedhas that is extremely difficult and calls for concentration and application, Hanumaan who is a master of Vedha, puts his mind into deep thinking to make sure that it is Seetha he is 'seeing' at the base of the tree. And in sloka 37, we find .

"With great difficulty, Hanumaan finally recognised her as Seetha, .It was like taking time to understand speech which caries diverse meanings, when words are not embellished properly nor 'decorated'- well constructed, well enjoined" Vaalmeeki merely confirms how difficult it is for a person who is on search of another whom he had never seen nor met before.

Vaalmeeki goes poetic, to describe this difficulty Ah!

Hanumaan, before making sure that this is Seetha, starts questioning himself, giving himself the reasoning for such a conclusion. (Sundhara-chapter 15) describes all this.

By sloka 39 "All those ornaments that were described by Raama as worn by her on her body, were shining on the branches of the tree" Seetha, when she became captive in Lanka had no heart to wear them. She had thrown them away, on to the tree and they were safely lodged there! Hanumaan thus concluded that this is the virtuous Seetha who would not care for jewelry on her without her beloved husband Raama. (By Sundhara- chapter 15 - sloka 48 to 50) "This is indeed 'She', on whose account Raama is greatly tormented by four fold reasons, of compassion, kindness, grief and love. Compassion to Seetha because she lost her freedom; Kindness because she was ever kind to him; Grief, because she was lost, her sight to him denied; Love, because he loved her passionately" Hanumaan after seeing Seetha, is not at all surprised why Raama is so devoted to her and is somewhat surprised how Raama is able to 'keep' himself alive. (Sloka 53) "Raama is somehow 'bearing' his body, separated from her! Raama is doing what is most difficult to do! " Yes! Hanumaan is right. If Lakshmana had not been there with Raama always, Raama would have lost all zest for life. Without Seetha, even a 'muhoortha' will be like a year for Raama.

Hanumaan has thus achieved yet another grand success. First ofcourse was his solo flight over the ocean and landing in Lanka after overcoming all obstacles during his 8 hour flight. Now his mission is successful. He has seen Seetha. She is very much alive. But, for Hanumaan, success is only partial. His mission will be complete only when he "meets" Seetha, talks to her, consoles her and assures her that Raama has not forgotten her but will take steps to retrieve her. He is shocked by the treatment handed over to her by the demonesses, the guards who use the 'carrot'-stick' technique on her.

While Hanumaan was passing through mixed thoughts of joy and sorrow - Joy because he was blessed by the sight of Seetha, and sorrow because such a divine lady was undergoing torment. - Raavana makes a routine visit to the Ashoka forest, to press Seetha to give up grief and accept him as his wife and queen. After all Hanumaan is also human! Seetha treats Raavana with contempt. Raavana is terribly angry. (Sundhara chapters 20 to 22). Hanumaan was witnessing this terrible scene- Seetha- Raavana confrontation - hidden under the branches of a tree, unseen.

(Chapter 22-slokas 8 & 9) Raavana gives Seetha an Ultimatum Gist: "OH Seetha! The time limit set by me for you is two months. You will till then be protected. Therefore get on to my bed now and be my wife But if at the end of two months you do not desire me as your husband, my cooks will cut you into pieces and serve you for my morning breakfast." This is the scene Hanumaan had to watch. After Raavana had left, the demonesses 'work' upon the miserable Seetha. They threaten her, coax her, revile her, all to make her accept the inevitable, to become his wife. But Seetha will have none of this. In sheer desperation, she even tries to choke herself to death with her long hair. For Hanumaan this is painful, terrible. Hanumaan ponders. He is master of Time-Place syndrome for action. He knows if he did not act now, anything might happen to Seetha.and his mission would have served no purpose.

Now the 'Genius' of Hanumaan comes into play. He must meet Seetha. He must have a conversation with her. How to do all this with demonesses-guards watching her?

Further, as a monkey, Seetha might be suspicious if he straight away jumps from the tree and presents himself before her. She might think that he is a 'demon' or even Raavana in disguise. Did not demon Maareecha entice her as a deer.

And was she not kidnapped by Raavana, the "Brahmin mendicant" Hanumaan is not a man who will act on impulse. Although a monkey by birth, he had no 'monkey business' nor the character of a monkey in him. It is indeed remarkable. Only Hanumaan could hit upon such a strategy. By (Sundhara-chapter 30 -slokas 42 to 45) Gist Hanumaan decides thus "By singing and extolling about Raama, I am going to make Seetha, free from shudder and fright.....With laudatory words embellished with Dharma., I will make her listen to everything.....Invoking...speaking sweetly.... I will present all this to her in such a way that Seetha will have confidence....will not suspect me as a spy of Raavana" In chapter 31, Hanumaan begins to sing in a low voice, hidden behind the tree even as the demonesses were sleepy. We do not know in what language, whether Paali or Sanskrit or in an 'associate' language Hanumaan 'sang' Vaalmeeki has not indicated this. But knowing Hanumaan as we do, he must have used a language which Seetha alone understood, not the demoness-guards there! Let research scholars worry about this! By slokas 2 to 16, Hanumaan briefly narrates the events leading to Seetha's kidnapping, Raama's search, his killing Vaali, making friendship with Sugreeva and how he was sent out to find her by Sugreeva, and by divine grace he was able to see this fine noble lady, wife of Raama at the Ashoka forest.

Hanumaan's strategy works. Naturally. his strategy will always work! Seetha, on hearing all this is wonderstruck. Who would not be. In demon's land, who is talking about Raama! And 'singing' so beautifully. (Sundhara-chapter 31- sloka 21) Seetha looks up. "Looking all around, sideways, up and down, Seetha saw Hanumaan of inconceivable intelligence, shining like the rising sun.

Thus did Hanumaan draw the attention of Seetha. Indeed most remarkable. This is no mean achievement. It is as great and wonderful as his solo flight of 1,000 miles across the ocean. A delicate 'operation' in his mission. And as remarkable as his success in finding Seetha in this terribly guarded Lanka.

Can any one be compared with Hanumaan?

But Seetha thinks it is all illusion. She can't believe her eyes. In fact at her first sight, she becomes unconscious (Sundara-chapter 32-sloka 8) "As soon as Seetha saw him clearly, she became unconscious, as though her breath had departed from her body. But regaining consciousness she began to think" In Sundhar- chapter 32. Vaalmeeki describes the conflicting thoughts passed through her mind. This is what Hanumaan had feared. Yet he had no choice other than to use this strategy of 'singing' Raama's story because he knew that only through this, Seetha's attention may be drawn towards him, hidden as he was in the branches of a tree nearby. Hanumaan had considered various options but being wise, he was prepared for the initial 'setback'. Having broken the 'ice', Hanumaan prepares to 'speak' to Seetha in a low voice. (Sundhara-chapter 33-slokas 3 to 14) being a Vaagmee, master of speech, like Vaachaspathi, he knows ultimately he will win her confidence These slokas again reveal what a perfect conversationalist Hanumaan is. We ought to remember the circumstances under which he is trying to have conversation with Seetha. Any other person would have caused such a fear in her, that she would simply have closed her ears and eyes. Such was the state Seetha was in. No bath, very little food, no change of dress. and constantly threatened by guards. All she was doing was remembering Raama and Lakshmana.

When Hanumaan finished his speech and wants to make sure that he is addressing, Seetha, she replies. Not that

Hanuman was not sure. But protocol calls for such response. After all he is the emissary of Raama and king Sugreeva! An ambassador or emissary must await a response! Hanumaan is no ordinary emissary!

In Sundhara-chapter 33, Seetha introduces herself and narrates her tale of woes to Hanumaan who conveys the welfare of her husband and Lakshmana, how Raama is tormented not being with her. They begin to converse. But once again fear seizes Seetha: Perhaps this monkey is trying to deceive her being a very clever monkey. So he describes the personal attributes of Raama, and his physical features, Seetha is convinced that monkey is Hanumaan, Raama's emissary.

Having made sure that it is Seetha, Hanumaan fulfills a pleasant task that was entrusted by Raama before he left Kishkindha in search of Seetha. (Sundhara-chapter 36-slokas 1 to 3) Gist: With a view to building total confidence in her that he is from Raama, Hanumaan says "Oh Illustrious lady Seetha! I am the emissary of Raama and am a monkey. Please 'see' this Signet Ring with Raama's name engraved upon it. This was given to me by Raama to be given to you as a token of remembrance, and proof.. So comfort yourself, drive away your sorrow" Shedding tears of joy Seetha converses with Hanumaan freely.

But what follows is rather a shame. But then it is Fate. ***Vaalmeeki never shies away from reality.*** So Vaalmeeki writes about this incident. He could well have 'covered' this shameful incident With all his self control, restraint and wisdom, Hanumaan is a sensitive man. When he sees Seetha in such a most pitiable state, withering away, with her life itself in danger, grief seizes Hanumaan. So much shaken is he, that in Sundhara - chapter 37- slokas 19 to 28, Hanumaan tells Seetha Gist: "OH Seetha! Alternatively, if you care to, you get on my back. I will thus free you from agony. I can cross the ocean back to India, carrying you on my back. I will deliver you to Raama who is now in Prasravana- India

Like Rohini with Lord of Moon you will be enjoined with your husband. Just as I came here by 'flight' so can I get back by flight, carrying you on my shoulders".

Now comes the 'Unkindest' cut, a shame, rather cruel. Seetha could have rejected this kind offer with a simple 'No' Elsewhere, in a different context, in this Guide, we have referred to this. Seetha tells Hanumaan thus (sloka 29) Gist: "Oh monkey chief, Hanumaan! That you desire to carry me, over a very long distance, indicates the flippant character of a monkey - monkey business =Kapithvam = " For once Hanumaan was 'hurt' not by weapons, but by one word = Kapithvam = and that too from the lady he venerated as a Goddess.

And the world must know what happens when Hanumaan is insulted. Vaalmeeki is in his elements when Hanumaan takes on his Vishwa -Roopa, When he hears this expression Kapithvam from Seetha and humiliation at the hands of Seetha, he decided to present his "form" to Seetha. What this monkey is really like when it chooses to! (Slokas 34 to 38) Gist "Jumping from the base of the tree, Hanumaan, by the way of reposing confidence in her, began to increase his form As he stood before Seetha, he appeared like 'burning flame' He was like Mandara and Meru mountain. His teeth and nails were like Indra's Vajra weapon". Then he addressed Seetha this form " There is power in me to carry Lanka itself. And along with its mountains, gardens, forests etc. And Also Its Lord Raavana" ***Can any one dare compare any one with Hanumaan.***

Hanumaan ofcourse is a magnanimous person, of a charitable disposition. When Seetha gives reasons for rejecting his offer to carry her back to India and to Raama, ***Hanumaan accepts her reasons with grace***. Her main reason seems to be that as a Kshathriya warrior Raama should punish the sinner Raavana, and take her back after killing Raavana. In Sundhara -chapter 37 Seetha gives many reasons why she cannot ride on his back. One is that ***voluntarily*** she will not 'even touch' another's body. She bemoans (Slokas 60 & 61) " I do not desire to touch voluntarily another's body other than Raama's. I am totally devoted to him. But what could I do when I 'touched' Raavana's body, virtuous though I am, I was seized by force, was powerless, destitute as I was".

By this Vaalmeeki brings home a point. Even in rape, a woman does not lose her virtue. Society must accept her.

Hanumaan recognises this Truth. Seetha is ever The Pure & Virtuous So he never questioned Seetha's rejection of his offer. He was only hurt by her use of the term, Kapithvam = monkey business. He accepted all her reasons. ***Hanumaan is such a man He can 'see' other's views.***

He expresses this clearly (Sundhara-chapter 38-sloka 2) "Oh lady Seetha! What all was spoken by you, befits you, indeed! It conforms to a virtuous person's nature and discipline" They converse. Having accomplished his mission, as Hanumaan was planning to return to India and Raama, with good news, Hanumaan asks Seetha (sloka 54)

"Please tell me! what all is to be told to Raama Lakshmana and my king Sugreeva?" After Seetha had conveyed all to Hanumaan, she, like her husband Raama, wishes to hand over a costly ornament as token of remembrance = The Choodamani, the 'Hair pendant'.

Hanumaan receives this Ornament with utter devotion.

But Hanumaan is very wise. He does not want anything to happen to the ornament, does not want to lose it. The scene is described (Sundhara-chapter 38- slokas 70 to 73). Gist: "Taking the extraordinary ornament studded with gems, the brave Hanumaan put it on his fingers. He then bowed to Seetha, went round her with his hands cupped in Anjali in reverence. His body stood there, but his heart was already with Raama as he had found Raama's beloved Seetha."

Hanumaan is ever The Blessed. Now he 'carries' Seetha's ornament. He had carried Raama and Lakshmana on his back. He wanted to carry Seetha on his back. So what! He is now carrying her most precious ornament!

This is Hanumaan for you.

The character in Hanumaan is such that he will even present himself as an average person if that would serve a purpose. When Seetha expressed her concern how Raama and his monkey army could come to Lanka and conquer this terrible army of demons and Raavana, Hanumaan by the way of assuring Seetha, belittles himself.

(Sundhara-chapter 39-slokas 38,39) Gist: "Oh Seetha! In Sugreeva's 'assembly' there are monkeys equal to me! Nay, even more distinquished than I am. You know, only 'ordinary' men are sent out as emissaries, couriers. When, an ordinary monkey can come over, need I say about monkeys who are stronger "Imagine a man who has crossed over ocean 1,000 miles facing obstacles and accomplishing this difficult and delicate task, talking about himself thus. Thiis is no modesty. This is travesty of truth. Here the man of modesty, Hanumaan, is not just being modest. He is a Vaagmee who must convey effectively. He ***must leave Seetha in peace as he gets back to India. So he 'rated' himself.thus Ah! Hanumaan!***

Taking leave of Seetha, Hanumaan ponders. (Sundhara-chapter 41)Gist; "Seetha has been found and seen by me. But I feel there is balance of work to be done by me here at Lanka. So leaving aside the first three strategies, the fourth is seen to be the best under the circumstances" Hanumaan is contemplating the use of violence, the last strategy one resorts to after the first three fail. Saama-talks, conciliation: Dhaana- settlement through gifts, bribes Bhedha- threat, creating dissension in enemy ranks. The last is Dhanda - the stick, war, violence Now what possibly could be Hanumaan's 'unfinished task' in Lanka. that he contemplates the use of 'The Stick' here. His 'brief' was clear when he left Kishkinda with the "search for Seetha army". Sugreeva had clearly stated that within a month they should find about Seetha. Hanumaan had not only discovered the whereabouts of Seetha, he has talked to her and offered her solace. Infact he was carrying her message to Raama with her token of remembrance His mission is thus complete. All he has to do is to get back to Sugreeva as a faithful emissary. Yet, he not only talks about 'unfinished' business but the use of violence. The question is did Hanumaan exceed his 'brief'?

Vaalmeeki does not touch this directly but only obliquely.

Let us continue with Hanumaan's thoughts as he ponders. "With these demons, Saama-conciliation does not merit consideration. Dhana - Gifts, bribery - of what use are these when they are all so affluent. As for threats and dissension, the demons are too brave and united. The only 'language' they will understand is the language of the stick-force-violence. If some brave demons are killed, others may become 'compliant'." ***Hanumaan, being a master tactician, knows the importance of preparation and preliminary work***.

"When one is directed to do a job, he can complete it satisfactorily only if he accomplishes all the preparatory work thoroughly." ***Hanumaan expounds yet another truth. One must keep the options open, always***. "Even for an ordinary job, a single strategy, or course of action, may not yield results. He who considers a course of action in many ways, he alone will accomplish".

Hanumaan, like all ambassadors, feels that he should carry to his king Sugreeva, details about the 'strength' and 'weakness' of defense, army etc of Lanka. We all know that an ambassador is also a spy although he 'covers' himself with diplomatic security and status. Hanumaan feels that he is not just an emissary to find about Seetha, but must take on the responsibility of enlightening his king about Lanka and its army and defence, just in case of war. The basic question remains unanswered Did Hanumaan carry at all any brief. Hanumaan is a wise man. Let us also not forget, he is No 1 Minister to king Sugreeva. Vaalmeeki perhaps does not refer to this because Hanumaan is a 'seer' and knows that war is imminent and he has a responsibility to Sugreeva, his other ministers, his army chiefs and Raama. Hanumaan says "Knowing the difference, the relative military strength of the enemy, and ourselves, if I go back to the king of monkeys, then only my task, my mission will be complete" And to know the strength of the demons, he wants a direct confrontation. "How will this confrontation with the demons come about. How will Raavana take note of me? I can then go back in happiness to Raama and Sugreeva" In effect he wants an audience with Raavana. As a monkey he may be treated with contempt. No one will take notice of him. But when he exhibits his power, they may take note of him and present him to Raavana. He wants to give him a sort of an Ultimatum.

Brief or no brief, Hanumaan decides on confrontation. ***Hanumaan never takes a decision without deliberation; deliberation based on Dharma***. (Sundhara-chapter 41-slokas 9 to 13)

Gist; "...then in such an event, facing and confronting the ten headed Raavana, in a fight against his army chiefs, and thus understanding his strength, his reaction, I will be able to go back in happiness......This garden which is like the celestial garden Nandana, which captivates every one's eye, belongs to Raavana.....I will destroy it, like fire on dry leaf.. The ten headed Ravana will be seized with wrath. And then he will assign a large army...... leading to a fight with me.....and I will know their strength....I will kill them and then get back happily to Sugreeva and Raama" Deciding thus Hanumaan plays havoc on the garden of pleasure of Raavana's harem (slokas 15 to 20) Gist: "Hanumaan routed the garden.....it was most unpleasant a sight....fences were in shambles...the great forest garden appeared totally devastated....everything was laid to waste by the mighty monkey Hanumaan...." His ploy works. He augmented his size, strength. The Citizens were astounded. News reaches Raavana, who is furious, And by sloka 23, "Drops of tears fell from the eyes of Raavana." Raavana who makes every one cry, weeps as his lovely garden forest is devastated. He commanded the brave demons- The Kimkaras- to capture Hanumaan, who makes mincemeat of them all.

Hanumaan roars in the name of his king Sugreeva&Raama

In Sundhara-Chapters 42 to 47, we find Hanumaan had destroyed one after the other, even as Raavana sends them out to capture Hanumaan dead or alive. Such is Hanumaan's power. He destroys, a few army chiefs, the demon chief Jambumaali and Raavana's younger son, the brave and educated Aksha.

Raavana realises that this is no monkey as he sends his favourite son Indrajith to capture Hanumaan. He warns his son thus (Sundhara - chapter 48 - slokas 12,13) The Gist "Armies are defenseless before him; Don't think the Vajra weapon will serve your purpose: There is no limit to his movement: He is too clever, so cunning tactics will be of no use before him"

Raavana is too much of a warrior. Even without 'seeing' Hanuman he knows! So he advises his son Indrajith as he leaves to capture Hanumaan.

As Raavana had warned, Hanumaan is 'captured' only when the weapon of weapons, Bramma Asthra is used on him by Indrajith. Hanumaan submits to this weapon of God

Bramma as he is blessed by God Bramma Himself that no harm will however come to him through weapons. The soldiers tie him up and drag him along and present him before King Raavana, precisely what Hanumaan wanted. He wanted to meet Raavana after giving the demon king a dose of violence, through killing Kimkaras, army chiefs, and Jambumaali. Raavana is furious. He asks his Minister Prahastha to interrogate Hanumaan who is astounded by the opulence of Raavana's court, palace. Hanumaan thunders like this (sundhara-chapter 51) **Remember Hanumaan is a Vaagmee-Master of Speech** Gist: "Oh Lord of demons, Raavana! I am here in your presence by the command of Sugreeva, the king of monkeys, who is like a brother to me. He asked me to inquire about your welfare. You must listen to the words of advice of this great soul Sugreeva, which will be most salutary, both in this world and the world to come." After introducing himself thus, Hanumaan narrates various events, Seetha's abduction, Raama's friendship with Sugreeva, killing of Vaali by Raama, Sugreeva's taking over as king, and how he had come over in search of Seetha.

Hanumaan is sharp and clear. By Sundhara-chapter 51-sloka 17, he tells Raavana : "Oh most intelligent Raavana ! You are well acquainted with the norms of Dharma, its subtleties. You have attained fulfillment through austerities and penance. Therefore you Should Not Lock Up Another's Wife". He warns Raavana (slokas 19.20)

"Who, whether he be from amongst Dhevas or Asuras, can stand before the arrows discharged by Lakshmana ***to satisfy Rama's wrath*** Who can obtain happiness after causing pain and transgression upon Raama, not one in all the worlds"

Ofcourse Raavana does not pay any heed to Hanumaan's advice, nor take note of his warning. Infact he is so enraged he wants him executed! But by the advice of his brother Vibheeshana who affirms that an emissary is never executed, Raavana sets a punishment upon Hanumaan. for his having played havoc in Lanka. They set fire to Hanumaan's tail. With his tail burning, Hanumaan ponders. **Hanumaan is so clever** and dexterous, even the burning of his tail will serve a purpose! He decides to set fire to Lanka!

As Lanka burns, his joy turns into sorrow because he is worried about Seetha's safety. What if she is also burnt in the carnage. For once Hanumaan 'curses' himself and his monkey character = kapithvam= monkey business (Sundhara-chapter 55) (Sloka 2) " = The deed of burning of Lanka was done by me. What for? = A great fear seized him. A state of contempt grew upon him. "Then he curses himself ***Hanumaan expounds some Truths, speaks words of wisdom*** (slokas 3 to 20) Gist

"Indeed they are the foremost and fortunate souls. who can restrain their wrath. Who will not commit sin in anger? An angry man will insult even a good man. An angry man cannot differentiate between good and bad, between the proper and improper words.

In a state of anger, there are no improper words! Indeed he alone is The Purusha - The (real) Man, who bears anger and throws it away like a cobra shedding its old skin.Ah! Shame on me! ....who is foolish minded.....who am among the foremost of sinners....all because, unwittingly, Seetha is burnt ..It is certain that as Lanka is burning, Seetha also would have been burnt!" Thus did Hanumaan grieve. ***But Hanumaan, even in grief, can ponder, objectively*** He questions himself. Fire is burning my tail. Yet, I don't feel any heat. All 'The Heat' is turned over upon palaces and gardens of Lanka How come? How can Fire burn Fire. Seetha's chastity is Fire. She can never be burnt by ordinary fire. Confident that Seetha would be safe, Hanuman wants to make sure that she is safe and decides to see her before returning to India.(Sundhara -chapter 56) Bowing to Seetha, who was sitting motionless under Shimshupa tree, Hanumaan addressed her thus "By divine grace, I am seeing you unharmed." Seetha ofcourse was surprised to see him return, but was happy to see him again. Perhaps to make amends for calling Hanumaan a mere monkey with the characteristics of a monkey = Kapithvam= praises Hanumaan thus (Sloka 3) "Oh destroyer of enemy warriors! Indeed ***you are the only one*** who is adequate to complete a task as desired. The greatness of your power is most renowned" Seetha knows that single handed. Hanumaan can destroy the demons and retrieve Seetha. But her devotion to Raama is such that she wants her husband to do it (Sloka 4) "If the dstroyer of enemy forces Raama takes me back after making Lanka topsy-turvy. That Will Befit Him" Vaalmeeki by all this and through Seetha clubs Hanumaan with Raama.

Does Hanumaan need any "Certificate" from anyone?

Having completed his mission totally, Hanumaan flies back to India, but carries with him some memories of Lanka. We shall ofcourse refer to this when we write about Raavana's character. Hanumaan was struck by the opulence of Lanka. He could not resist making this observation about Raavana, the king of demons and Lanka.Hanumaan is a wise man. He will give credit where it is due. But he will view everything from the stand point of Dharma. He was so charmed by Raavana when he saw him in his Court that he says (Sundhara-chapter 49-slokas 17 to19) Gist "Ah! What a form. What courage. What brilliance, what strength! Oh! All the royal qualities are found in him. If only this lord of demons was not a person of Non Dharma, he would have been (fit to be) the protector of all the world, including the world of Indra!"

Hanumaan will praise even an enemy, will give the devil his due. Hanumaan is made that way!

As he lands at the Southern tip of India where the southern army under the command of Angadha is eagerly awaiting him with news about Seetha, Hanumaan, greets them with just one crisp "word" Brevity is called for when in anxious moments one wishes to convey something very, very important. Hanumaan is master of speech. First, he bows to Jaambavaan. Then tells them, (Sundhara-chapter 57-sloka 36)" Seetha Seen". Then he observes Protocol by first greeting Prince Angadha. Hanumaan then gives the description, the scene at the ashoka forest where Seetha is kept a prisoner by Raavana. Then Hanumaan narrates his mission in great detail (by chapter 58)

By nature Hanumaan is retiring type reticent. But when he has to communicate something important, he is expansive and will not shy away from even details. Thus the Southern army of Search for Seetha, has found Seetha

All because of one monkey, Hanumaan.

Before the monkey army returns to the headquarters to inform Sugreeva and Raama about Seetha, an interesting thing happened. The army is always an army. So they celebrate their success. And No celebration without liquor. It was so then. It is so now. It will be so in the future as well! When the monkeys lay waste a wine forest on their way, the guards and the protector of this forest of wines, try to sober them all a bit. We come to an interesting and somewhat unbelievable episode, because Hanumaan is involved. There is no evidence that Hanumaan indulged in "booze". But he is no joy killer. Imagine him exhorting them all thus (Sundhara- chapter 62- slokas 1 & 2) Gist Hanumaan assures his comrades "Oh monkeys! You drink wines with an undisturbed mind = drink, drink and drink. And those who come up against you, I will cover them "

Vaalmeeki's greatness is this. He portrays reality. Never covers up. This side of Hanumaan's character can never even be imagined. He is such a pure noble soul. deeply religious. Yet in two slokas Vaalmeeki has portrayed his character. Not only he allows his comrades to drink and devastate this wine forest, but he will offer them all protection when they go on drinking spree.

Vaalmeeki wrote without fear or favour.

When the Southern Army returns to the headquarters_after their Victory celebration, Raama looks at Hanumaan and Hanumaan narrates all. and when he hands over the ornament- choodaamani given to him by Seetha as token of remembrance, Hanumaan's mission becomes complete.

(Sundhara-chapter slokas 63 17) sums up ***Hanumaan's character and achievement as seen by Sugreeva.***

"Succress in a mission, intelligence, effort, bravery, knowledge-wisdom, have all taken firm root in this 'tiger' of monkeys. ***This is Hanumaan.***

Hanumaan narrates his mission in detail to Raama and Sugreeva. ***It is Raama's turn to extol Hanumaan.*** (Yudhdha-chapter 1-) Gist "The most difficult task was done by Hanumaan in this world, which cannot be conceived even in mind by any one else. Who can cross 1,000 miles over the ocean, visit Lanka and return alive? None equal to Hanumaan in valour, bravery." **Raama the master of personnel management,** differentiates between various types of men (slokas 7,8,9) " When a servant who is entrusted with a most difficult task by his master completes the job totally, with love and attachment to his master, he is spoken of as the noblest of men. When a capable servant, does not do the job to the full satisfaction of his king, (but does some work) he is spoken off as an average person. But when one does not do anything at all, he is considered as a base person" Raama ofcourse puts Hanumaan in the first category, and more. (By slokas 10,11)Gist: "In this task of finding Seetha, what all was expected to be done was done by Hanumaan. No lack of dignity was brought on to himself. And his King Sugreeva was pleased and fully satisfied" Raama as we all know is a Krithagnya = man of gratitude. So he bemoans (sloka 12,13) Gist: " It is a pity I am not able to repay him befittingly.....I am very much distressed by this....However, at this moment, placed as I am in this situation, this my only ***Fond Embrace*** is being offered to him"....... Saying thus, Raama hugged great soul Hanumaan. Raama knows the consequence of not finding Seetha. He expresses his gratitude to Hanumaan (sloka 11).

"I, my race of Raghu-s, and the mighty Lakshmana, are all 'saved' (from ignominy) as Hanumaan has seen Seetha and found her devoted to Dharma".

What better "present" or 'Gift' can there be for Hanumaan than Raama's Hug.

It is going to be war. Raavana has no intention of giving back Seetha. After Hanumaan had told him all about Raavana, Raama vows (Yudhdha-chapter 4- sloka 2) "I am going to destroy Lanka and rid at of the terrible demons. This I truthfully affirm" And when the huge army of monkeys of Sugreeva reaches the tip of India, an incident happens.

Raavana's brother, Vibheeshana accompanied by his five trusted demons, defect. They leave Lanka and are about to land near the shores of the ocean where Raama and his huge army under Sugreeva, is stationed. This, you may say is the first "war" casualty for Raavana. And what a loss for Raavana. There is the debate. Should Vibheeshana be accepted by Sugreeva and Raama, or be treated as a war prisoner? We shall be writing in detail about the debate amongst monkey chiefs, Raama and others elsewhere. As we are now on the character of Hanumaan we have to refer to Hanumaan's views on Vibheeshana. Let us not forget that only Hanumaan knows something about demons and about Vibheeshana. He had been to Lanka. He is shrewd, and knows who is who there. Hanumaan expresses his view thus (Yudha - chapter 17- slokas 51 to 69). We may write about the main reason why Hanumaan feels that Vibheeshana had to be inducted into their army and not treated as an enemy in disguise. He also knows how Vibheeshana had pressed Raavana not to execute him as he was only an emissary and how he spoke Dharma of International Norms and Affairs when Hanumaan was 'captured'.

"Vibheeshana has chosen the right time and place to defect to us. Hearing about your prowess, Oh Raama, and about your crowning of Sugreeva after killing Vaali. Vibheeshana has come here. So it is the right time and place for defection" It is interesting, that none of them wanted to take a risk. But only Raama was with Hanumaan. Vibheeshana was accepted.

But a question arises. Did Vibheeshana think about the Crown of Lanka for himself when he defected? This question is debatable. Even Shoorpanaka, the cousin of Raavana, had told Raama and Lakshmana (Aaranya Kaanda - chapter 17-sloka 24) that Vibheeshana did not possess any characteristic of a demon. He was a Vishnu Bhaktha. ***Yet, Hanumaan talks about his defection for some consideration for himself***. Let us leave it at that. But our purpose here is served. That is, ***only Raama sides with Hanumaan.*** Vibheeshana joins Raama and Sugreeva along with his five trustworthy demon chiefs who defect with him. No wonder, thanks to Hanumaan and to Raama.as well!

As war preparations are going on, as the Army of Raama-Sugreeva preparing to cross 1,000 miles of the ocean to invade Lanka, Raama the Ikshwaaku prince and warrior, asks Hanumaan about the army and defence of Lanka.(Yudhdha-chapter3- slokas 2 to 6) Hanumaan describes everything he found in Lanka. (Slokas 7 to 30)

We had talked about 'Brief'! Hanumaan's job was merely to find the whereabouts of Seetha. The wisdom of Hanumaan is revealed again! Hanumaan the Chief minister to his King Sugreeva knew that as war was imminent, he was pondering over some 'unfinished' business in Lanka after he had seen and taken leave of Seetha. So when Raama questions him about the Army and defense, Hanumaan is able to enlighten him. We had said that Hanumaan would never act without some deliberation. Our observation is justified. Raama can now plan an attack on Lanka when he invades it.

Hanumaan, the Seer, the Dheerga-Dharshi, had thought about it all.

And Vaalmeeki never fails He has presented Hanumaan in proper light even here.

We will not describe the Great War here. Hanumaan's bravery is well known and does not call for extensive description. But we have to make a few special references about Hanumaan's great service in this war that was fought with terrible ferocity. In (Yudhdha-Chapter 74) when Raama and Lakshmana fall down and were motionless, struggling for breath in the battle field and the monkey army was in disarray, and when there is chaos, the old and wise Jaambavaan asks for the great Hanumaan thus (Sloka 19 to 21) "Oh Vibheeshana! Only by your voice, I am recognising you. Tormented as I am by the shower of arrows, I am not able to see you. And he, by whom his mother Anjana became endowed with such a brilliant son, and likewise, his foster father, Lord of Wind,

is that foremost monkey Hanumaan still alive?" Vibheeshana was surprised that Jaambavaan was showing special concern about the welfare of Hanumaan even as Raama and Lakshmana were struggling for their lives. Jaambavaan was quick to clear Vibheeshana's surprise. (slokas 21 to 26) Gist: "Oh Vibheeshana! You listen as to why I am specially asking for and asking about Hanumaan and his welfare. If this Hanumaan is alive our army will never be destroyed. But if he loses his life, we who are alive now are as good as dead"

Such was Hanumaan's prestige in war.

When Hanumaan meets Jaambavaan in battle field at the summons of the old and wise Jaambavan, this is what is told to him by Jaambavaan who felt as though he was reborn when he saw him! (Slokas 28 to 37) The Gist:

"Oh Hanumaan! Come close! ***You should save us, the monkeys. No one else has adequate bravery.*** This is the time for you to exhibit your power. You fly to Himaalayas quickly. There is a mountain called Rishabha. Amidst the peaks, you will find a hill called Oshadi, which is ever luminescent and full of life saving herbals like Mrithasanjeevini, Vishalyakarni, Saavarnakarni, Santhanakarni.

Taking all these with you, you come back quickly and save all the dying monkeys"

For Hanumaan long distance flying is almost a habit, like some top businessmen with international connections!

When he reaches the peak of Kailash, Hanumaan not having graduated from a medical school with an FRCS and the like, not knowing the difference between betel leaf and a herbal leaf, pulls out the mountain peak itself and brings them to the battle field at Lanka where the medical core can have their choice of medicines. In effect it is like one, who, when asked for an antibiotic, uproots the medical shop itself and offers the sick patient his choice!

This is Hanumaan for you! After herbals had done its service, he takes back the peaks the mountain and restores it in the Himaalyas.

We all know that in War, everything becomes important. Not merely arms and ammunition. Food supplies, clothing. transport, medical facilities are equally important. The service of Hanumaan is unique. No wonder, the old wise, Jaambavan had praised him and picked him for this life saving job.

During this war, this is not the only occasion Hanumaan is pressed for this kind of service. (Yudhdha- chapter 102) again to revive Lakshmana (By slokas 23 to 33) the chief of medical core Sushena says, the Gist "Oh Hanumaan! That place Jaambavaan had told you about as auspicious, you go to that Oshadi hills from here at once. To revive the noble Lakshmana, you go at once and brings the herbals..."

Again it is Hanumaan. And this time he saves Lakshmana. By saving Lakshman with these drugs, Hanumaan had saved the life of Raama itself. Ah! Hanumaan!

When war ended, with Raavana killed by Raama and the evil demons of Lanka slaughtered by Sugreeva's army of monkeys, Vibhheeshana is crowned as Raavana's successor as king of Lanka. It is Hanumaan who is sent by Raama to inform the news to Seetha about all this. We mention this because in all delicate missions it is Hanumaan! When Hanumaan presents himself before Seetha who was sitting under the tree in Ashoka forest, she extols him. Hanumaan in a short, crisp, effective address which comes out naturally to him, narrates all the happenings. Seetha tells him (Yudhdha-chapter116 -slokas 23 to 26) Gist "I am speechless by the news. Oh monkey Hanumaan! I cannot see, however much I think about, a befitting 'salutations' of thanks to you....I cannot see anything befitting as a present to you no gold, no costly gems....all these are not even to be thought of as present to you....such is the news you have brought me" Seetha extols Hanumaan thus (slokas 32 to 34) gist

"Indeed, Hanumaan, you alone can speak couched with words of quality, words 'ornamented' with sweetness, and with the 'Eight Way' wisdom of mind. You are the foremost man of Dharma, strong, very brave, You have knowledge of Shruthi-s, Smrithis, vedhas. You are a man of character. Foremost in skill and dexterity. You possess brilliance, forbearance, firmness, unweariness, modesty, a good education. ***many more noble qualities shine in you "Seetha has said it all. Yes. Hanumaan's character can never be fully described".***

When the victorious Raama, along with Seetha and Lakshmana, after completing his 14 years of exile, flies back from Lanka in Pushpaka Aircraft accompanied by Hanumaan, Sugreeva and his entire army of monkeys, rests near Bharadhwaaja hermitage, it is again ***Hanumaan who is sent out on a delicate mission***. Raama sends Hanumaan in advance to Ayodhya, to inform his brother Bharatha that he will be back shortly. The mission is delicate because, Raama feels that in as much as Bharatha had ruled Ayodhya for 14 years, he may like to continue. After all "Power Corrupts" even with the noblest. It is Hanumaan who must find this out for Raama. Raama did not want to embarrass his brother. Ofcourse whole world knows that Bharatha was only waiting to hand over the kingdom to his brother. Indeed he had waited long enough. Yes, 14 years is a long wait! And when Hanumaan met Bharatha, it did not take him long to realise that Raama's 'doubt' had no substance. He knew that Bharatha is afterall Raama's brother. Like Raama, he was totally 'detached' Bharatha had merely said after hearing everything from Hanumaan (Yudhdha-chapter 129-sloka 57) "Indeed, my desire that has ever been with me, and for a long time, has now only been fulfilled".

After the coronation of Raama at Ayodhya, when Raama offers gifts to every one and when he offers a costly Necklace with diamonds and gems, to Seetha, Seetha looks around for a while. She accepts this (Yudhdha chapter 131) Raama had given her the option, if she chose, to offer it to any one worthy enough, any one possessing qualities like brilliance, steadfastness in duty, fame, dexterity, ability, modesty, prudence, norms of good conduct, valour, virility, Seetha had no second thought. She offers this to Hanumaan. Who can possess so many qualities, so diverse? ***It Is Hanumaan and Hanumaan Only.***

Lastly, when the entire army of monkeys returns home to Kishkinda, Vaalmeeki mentions about Sugreeva and Vibheeshana being given leave by Raama.We would like to think that Hanumaan stayed back. We cant imagine a life for this noble divine person without Raama and Seetha.

Ah! Hanumaan, The Maaruthi, The Aanjaneya!

Monkey Brothers (Vaali-Sugreeva)

13: VAALI

He was the king of monkeys and the lord of Kishkindha.He was 'foster' son of Lord Indra His younger brother Sugreeva, was 'foster' son of Sun. By natural birth they had the same parents. Both were great warriors, could take on any form they pleased, but they were monkeys. In the early days of his rule, Vaali was very much attached to his brother. So was Sugreeva. But a most unfortunate incident in which Sugreeva was not to be blamed at all, made Vaali so wrathful, that he not only drove Sugreeva away from the kingdom but also kept his brother's wife to himself. This, even in the animal world is a crime. And Vaali was a king, supposed to protect other's wives. But this much credit we can give Vaali. At no time did he try to kill Sugreeva. (In Kishkindha, chapter 16- sloka 7) he assures his wife Taara that he will never take away Sugreeva's life, only his insolence! When Raama, after making friendship with Sugreeva, kills Vaali with a single arrow, we have a never ending debate, whether Raama was justified in killing Vaali. Elsewhere we will be writing about this in detail.

About his strength and valour, it is but natural that Sugreeva talks about him. He knows Vaali. He has been with him in all encounters with terrific demons like Dhundhubi and Maayaavi. (Kish-chapters 10 & 11).

As Vaali dies, he makes a dying declaration. He addresses his brother Sugreeva This does him great credit. Indeed merit worthy. (Kish- Chapter 22-Slokas 3 to 15) Gist: "Oh Sugreeva! You must discharge me from my sin. I was dragged into sin by the confusion of my mind, caused by the arrogance of my power. You should not reproach me." Vaali bemoans that although they had good times in the early part of their lives, it did not continue.

"Oh my dear brother! It is not ordained that between us, there can be that brotherly happiness that is associated with brothers, which we could ***enjoy together.*** (Fate separated us) You take over our kingdom. Oh Sugreeva the king! In this state as I am, what I am going to tell you, that must be acted upon by you, even if arduous. My son Angadha is but a boy, you must be his protector. I know like me you are a 'Giver' "Vaali is thus human, although given to wrath as a warrior. He has high praise for his wife Thaara whom he wants to protect as well "Thaara the daughter of Sushena, is a highly accomplished woman in every way. When she says a job can be done, it is done without much·difficulty. When it meets with Thaara's approval, it will not be other wise." Vaali does not forget Raama. He advises (warns) Sugreeva. "Raama's task, of retrieving Seetha, must be undertaken by you without any hesitation. If not done it will be Non Dharma. Further, if Raama is slighted, he will harm you" And Vaali finally gives him a present. He takes off his divine chain. "Take this, the divine chain and put it on before I give up my life".

Sugreeva is so much seized with grief by all this, that he loses zest for life, even as Vaali gives his son Angadha his last advice "You must pursue the proper Time & Place for any action. You must bear bad with good. Be obedient to Sugreeva. You were, always fondled by me. But you are no longer a boy, dont expect Sugreeva to fondle you. Don't go near Sugreeva's enemies, be ever restrained. There should be no excessive manifestation of affection, nor lack of it. The 'Middle' course is the right path.".

Yes! Blood is thicker than water as the saying goes. Every one cries his heart out, including Sugreeva whom he had hurt so much. Yes! Vaali is a very great personality. But Fate chose Sugreeva for Raama!

14: SUGREEVA

Sugreeva is a fortunate person in as much as he is served by Hanumaan. Behind all great men, you will find persons endowed with wisdom to offer counsel. King Janaka, the father of Seetha, has Shathaanand, a very pious and noble sage as his adviser and principal minister. The Ikshwaaku kings are blessed. They can seek counsel from any number of men of wisdom, like Brahma Rishi Vasishta.

No business can thrive unless its top executives have consultants who can offer wise and timely advice.

When Sugreeva who had taken refuge in the peaks of Malay mountain which is out of bounds for his wrathful brother Vaali, sees Raama and Lakshmana at a distance, he is seized by the fear that these two may have been sent out by his enemy Vaali, to harm him. When a man is seized by fear, he will suspect everything. ***Vaalmeeki expounds this truth***. Even a warrior like Sugreeva loses his composure. But the wise Hanumaan sets his mind at rest.

When Raama and Sugreeva form their friendship with Fire as witness, Sugreeva is so happy that he says (Kish-chapter 5-sloka 10 to 12) Gist: "Oh Raama! Your noble qualities were narrated by Hanumaan, that you are 'obedient' to Dharma, and you are ever endearing to all. That you desire to form friendship with me, a mere monkey, is indeed an honour to me. And further it is most advantageous to me. If you desire friendship with me, here is my extended hand "A point or two may be recognised. Sugreeva had such faith in Hanumaan, that he did not need time to consider friendship with Raama. Secondly, basically Sugreeva was a man of Dharma and although he had a vested interest in this friendship (he was seeking Raama's help to save him from his brother, Vaali), it is this that made him accept Raama so quickly. Sugreeva had affirmed (sloka 19) "You are my hearty friend, happiness and sorrow are common to us" to which Raama responded positively.

There is always a lurking doubt whether Raama and Sugreeva would have become such friends had they not been tormented by a common problem and if they had no vested interest. We know about Raama. Raama will give refuge even to an enemy if he 'seeks' him! But what about Sugreeva? ***Vaalmeeki sets our mind at rest***. (Kish-chapter 8-) Gist "Oh Raama! You are my friend, so I am blessed with the favour of Dhevas totally! With your assistance, even the kingdom of Dhevas is not beyond me; need I say about my kingdom of Kishkinda, which I had lost." With such an address one may come to the conclusion that Sugreeva's friendship with Raama is purely selfish. This is only a partial truth. In the next sloka, he is proud to say "Oh Raama! Such as I am, to whom a person born in the Ikshwaaku - Raghu family has become friend, and that too before Fire as witness, ***will now share honours with my friend and relatives***." A person is judged by the company he keeps. As the saying goes "Tell me who his friend is, I will then talk about him" Sugreeva values Raama's friendship because it is by divine hand that a monkey gets the hand of friendship of such a noble man like Raama. (By slokas 5 to 9) Sugreeva talks about what constitutes real friendship. "In course of time you will come to know ***that I am also a befitting friend to you,***" As events turn out it is Sugreeva, who serves Raama till the end and Raama is able to retrieve Seetha. Friendship is no one-way traffic. And Sugreeva adds "Whether it is silver, gold dresses, good men consider these as undivided wealth with their friends "A friend in need is a friend indeed!".

"Whether poor or rich, in happiness or in distress, whether wicked or good, a friend is a foremost refuge" Sugreeva views friendship as beyond status. A true friend does not run away from his friend who is in distress

Thus we come back to the debate. Was Sugreeva a true friend? Did he accept friendship with Raama only because he was going to serve his purpose? Vaalmeeki had no doubt. Sugreeva was a man of Dharma basically. So his friendship is true, although he may have Raama's assistance in view. And to confirm this view, we have in (Kish-chapter 29- sloka 21) Hanumaan says "Oh Sugreeva! You are the one, who will do good to even those who do not do anything for you." As the noble, wise Hanumaan has spoken thus of Sugreeva, we need not extend the debate further. Yes Sugreeva is a true friend. And Raama himself confirmed this when he had included Sugreeva amongst his four brothers and Guha, the chief of hunters. Raama in (Kish-chapter39-sloka3) compares Sugreeva's friendship with the rays of the moon "People like you always do good for their friends, like the Moon doing good to all by its pleasant rays."

On the subject of Friendship, we may proceed further. After Vaali was killed by Raama and Sugreeva was installed king of monkeys by Raama, it was expected that Sugreeva, as requital, would send the army of monkeys to search for the abducted Seetha. Raama had asked Sugreeva to lay off for two months as it was rainy season but start the search immediately after. But during the rainy season Sugreeva was so consumed by wine, women and song that he was not even aware that the rainy season had gone by that he should start his work for Raama. Lakshmana who was in wrath because of the insolence of Sugreeva visits him to convey the warning,

(Kish-Chapter - 32-slokas - 44 to 49)

"Having set the time limit, for the search of Seetha, Sugreeva is not even aware that the time limit is over, all because he is indulging in liquor, and is enjoying himself with cheap pleasures" Lakshman states a truth "Drinking and the like is not commended for Dharma and Artha. Objectives fail. Ultimately even Kaama one may not obtain" Kama- is a general term for all pleasures. Drinking will take away even the very pleasures you seek through drinks. "It will be great violation of Dharma for a person who fails to repay his debt particularly to a friend who has done service. In a noble friend's ruin, there will be great loss for him later. Sugreeva is not steadfast in Dharma- (he is no friend). A friend is one who abides by Truth and Dharma. Sugreeva has no such qualification, because he has abandoned these two. He is ungrateful" Lakshmana having talked about friendship and about Sugreeva's lack of it, Lakshmana issues a sharp warning (Kish-chapter 34-slokas 18,19) "The path treaded by his brother Vaali that took him to another world, is not closed for Sugreeva as well."

We write about this because Sugreeva had talked about qualities of friendship. And we were also debating about Sugreeva being a true friend. Inspite of his carelessness, Sugreeva is still a sincere, devoted friend.as he says (Kish-chapter 32- slokas 3 to 8) Gist "Nothing wrong was done nor uttered by me. I am thinking why Lakshman is angry.! Perhaps he has been told by unfriendly enemies of mine and by those who always try to look 'wrong' done by me, about all sorts of inconceivable faults in me. I have no fear from Lakshmana. That my dear friend is angry with me, causes me grief" Thus Sugreeva who feels he is a sincere friend, thinks that his enemies are trying to break up his friendship! Sugrreva (by sloka 7) expounds a truth "Friendship is easy to form, but difficult to sustain".

In the next sloka, he expresses his gratitude thus ***"The help and service rendered for me by Raama, can never be repaid by me befittingly"***

Events proved that Sugreeva was not only a friend of Raama. He was treated by Raama as a brother.

Sugreeva's knowledge of geography of the world is indeed most remarkable. He knew every 'nook and corner' of the world. But this was not by his 'study' or by regular visits but be sheer accident and due to fate. When Raama asks him after Sugreeva had sent separate armies to all the four directions of the globe on search of Seetha, Sugreeva narrates how he knew so much about various regions of the globe. (Kish-chapter 46- sloka 1) "Oh Sugreeva, how is it you know so much of the globe" Then Sugreeva tells him Gist "Oh Raama, I will narrate how I came to know the globe.. This evil brother of mine, Vaali who was terribly angry with me, chased me out while I was running away with my ministers. To escape from him, I ran hither and thither and thus I saw various rivers, towns, forests,. I went towards the East. I saw Udaya mountains, even the Ocean of Ksheeroda. In south the entire Vindhyas in the western region, even the mountain of Astha where Sun rests at night. And in North Himaalayas, the Meru mountain and Northern sea.".

Vaalmeeki brings home a truth. If one is wise, even fear and suffering may be put to good use. Sugreeva remembered all the places he sees, out of utter fear from his brother. Knowledge never goes to waste. Sugreeva is thus able to give minute details to the monkey chiefs who were going out to various directions in search of Seetha.

The brothers Vaali and Sugreeva have many 'qualities' in common. Both are mighty warriors. Both are addicted to wine, women and song. Vaali had problems with a demon on account of a woman (Ref: Kish-Chapter 9-sloka 5) After driving his brother out of the kingdom, Vaali keeps his brother Sugreeva's wife, Ruma, as his! Sugreeva is no different. After Vaali was slain by Raama and he had become king, Vaali's wife Thaara whom he should have considered as his 'sister', becomes his mistress. But we should suppose that it is all in the game in the monkey world.

Sugreeva's fondness for liquor is well known. So much addicted to drinks that he almost forgets his commitment to Raama to search for Seetha. We write about all this in the context of an incident in Kishkinda kaanda. We know that the monkey army of Southern command under Angadha, returns after achieving a great 'victory' by finding Seetha in Lanka through Hanumaan, and starts destroying The Madhu-Wine forest belonging to Sugreeva, as part of their celebration. When Sugreeva was informed by the chief curator about the devastation to his favourite Wine-Forest, Sugreeva for once does not exhibit anger. He knows that his Army is celebrating their victory. Being fond of Liquor, in what better way can his army celebrate!

The brothers have yet another 'quality' -Impetuousness.

(in Kish-chapter 15-) we find Vaali's wife restraining him from going out to fight his brother Sugreeva without deliberation. (Slokas 7 to 9) Gist: "Oh Vaali! Give up this wrath that is gushing forth like flood of river in spate. You can do battle with Sugreeva tomorrow. No slight or insignficance will be there for you by postponing the fight. Your going out in the hurry & your impetuosity, disturbs me" Thaara warns.that this time Sugreeva must surely have come with support. Ofcourse we know the consequence of Vaali's rashness. He paid with his life at the hands of Raama as he ventured to fight

In the case of Sugreeva we have a similar exhibition of rashness, impetuosity. (Ref Yudhdh-chapter 40) Along with Sugreeva, Raama, from the top of the Suvela mountain in Lanka, surveys the battle ground as armies are getting ready for war on both sides. Suddenly, Sugreeva jumps out from the cliff, flies over to where Raavana was standing, looking all around. (Sloka 7 & 8) Gist:"As soon as Sugreeva 'saw' Raavana from a distance, he at once rose, even while foremost monkey chiefs of his army were watching, and even as Raama was looking on. Rising up from the tip of the Suvela mountain with great force and courage, he flew over to the tower from where Raavana was surveying the armies. He rushed towards him, wrath speeding him up" There was a combat between Sugreeva and Raavana. Fortunately, Sugreeva got back with minor injuries after his fight with the demon lord. So upset was Raama he admonishes Sugreeva. Wars are not won by skirmishes like this. (Yudhdha- chapter 41-sloka2) "Oh Sugreeva! Without any deliberation and without consulting me, this action was done by you in haste. Kings will never do like this"

Once a monkey, always a monkey! ***Vaalmeeki presents Sugreeva as a monkey here***, although Sugreeva is a mighty warrior and is a man of wisdom normally. Fortunately, unlike his brother Vaali who had acted in haste and thus paid with his life at the hands of Raama, Sugreeva was wise enough to escape with minor injuries on his body that were inflicted by Raavana in the One to One combat.

Yes. The brothers, when in wrath, lost their cool and acted impetuously.

Under friendship, we had referred to Sugreeva, that Raama considered his friend as a 'brother'. Justification for this is not far to seek. We all know that Lakshmana was not only his brother, but was a mentor to Raama. Time and again it is Lakshmana who consoles, cheers and 'activates' Raama. When friendship grew between Sugreeva and Raama, we find, not infrequently, Sugreeva taking on the role of Lakshmana. In Kishkindha kaanda, chapter 7, we find Sugreeva saying thus; Gist "Oh Raama! Enough of this despondency! Remember only your inborn quality of firmness, courage. Such light hearteness is unbecoming of great men like you. Great sorrow afflicts me as my wife was snatched away by Vaali. But I have not abandoned courage. And I am a monkey, an ordinary monkey. I am not 'teaching' you. I am telling you as a friend. A man of firmness always critically examines a situation, never withers away in grief. When one wastes himself in grief, nothing good comes to him. So I beg you. Take on to courage ...."

Although impetuous in wrath, Sugreeva is a wise man. Grief over the temporary loss of his beloved wife Ruma did not shatter him His zeal never diminished.

Again in Yudhdha, chapter 2, we find Sugreeva consoling and cheering up Raama. Gist "Oh Raama! Why are you tormenting yourself like some ordinary person. You are wise. You have complete knowledge of all weaponry. You are very intelligent. Infact you are a Pundit. An agitated mind is not conducive to activity." And Sugreeva is clear about priorities. He is wise. He knows that all are not Hanumaans to fly over 1,000 miles to Lanka and carry war in Raavana's citadel. So he says firmly (Sloka 11) "Oh Raama! You must act in such a way that a bridge can be constructed so that we can 'see' the city of Raavana (we can face Lanka and do war with him).. Once our army is in Lanka, Raavana is as good as killed".

The DEMONS

The Brothers: Raavana, Kumbakarna & Vibeeshana

15: RAAVANA

He was the eldest son of Rishi Vishrawas. His cousin demoness Shoorpanaka while trying to make love to Raama and entice him, introduces herself as 'sister' of Raavana, Kumbakarna and Vibheeshana (Aaranya chapter 17 slokas 2 & 24) "The Lord of demons, Raavana who is very brave, is son of Vishrawas. He is my brother. Likewise, the strong Kumbakarna who is given to long slumber, is my brother. I have another brother Vibeeshana who does not possess any of the qualities of a demon" We all know that the main purpose of God Vishnu being born as Raama to king Dhasharatha, is to destroy Raavana who was the 'epi centre' of all evil in the world. In Baala kanda chapter 15, the celestials beseech God Bramma who had given boons to Raavana. Raavana was not born a demon. By birth he was a brahmin, but by sheer arrogance, power madness, and total lack of good conduct, became a demon and lord of all demons of the world. The celestials address God Bramma (slokas 6 to 11) Gist: "Oh God Bramma! By your grace and boons, Demon chief Raavana is harassing us. We are unable to restrain him. If we are enduring torture at his hands, it is because of the respect we have for you in as much as he has come under your grace by being blessed by your boons. He terrorises all the three worlds. He has no respect for 'elders'. He desires to embrocate Lord Indra. Arrogant because of your boons to him, he attacks pious rishi-s, yakshas, ghandharvas, asuras and brahmins. The Sun does not burn him up nor torment him. The Wind blows always softly, fearing him. Even oceans are tranquil when they see him. Fear is spread all over.

Therefore may you, Oh Bramma, find a way to destroy him".

Thus Raavana unwittingly becomes a principal character of Vaalmeeki Raamaayana. Raama is to destroy Raavana!

Good must overcome Evil Dharma must conquer Non Dharma (A-Dharma).

A Diversion:

Raavana was the son of Vishrawas. Vishrawas was the son of Pulasthya who was created by God Bramma Himself when He conceived him in His Mind. Pulasthya is listed along with Prajaapathi-s, the first of human beings. Pulasthya had thus divine birth. We write this by the way of introduction to Raavana. Ofcourse Vishrawas had another son, the famous Lord of wealth, Kubhaera. With such a lineage, one would have expected Raavana to be a man of Dharma. Yet, he turns out to be a terrible demon, to prove that caste, lineage have nothing to do with a person's conduct and nature. Caste is mere division of labour. Here Ravana fails to do his duties as a brahmin. He is the vilest among brahmins. He is a demon, a terrible demon, by his conduct has become a demon. Who says the caste system is rigid? One cannot claim status merely through caste or by caste. No wonder Shoorpanaka had talked about Raavana to Raama thus.

Raama and Raavana are the two main characters in Raamaayana. We may observe a similarity. Two women have had a hand, unwittingly, to draw Raama and Raavana in war. Fate has played a hand, for the welfare of the world. In Ayodhya Kaanda, we find the evil genius, the hunch back Manthara changing the course of history by 'working' upon her protege, queen Kaikeyi, to drive away Raama into a 14 year exile in the deep forest along with Seetha.

In Aaranya Kaanda we find the clever demoness Shoorpanaka working upon her cousin Raavana, to abduct Seetha. Raavana kidnaps Seetha. Thus the divine purpose of the celestials is served. Raama wages war with Raavana, destroys him along with his evil demons and the world once again is blessed with peace and tranquillity.

There is thus a divine sanction for any event in this world.

In the modern world, we should take comfort when certain events happen to us which may even cause some sorrow to us, by remembering that everything has a divine purpose and we are only a tiny part in the scheme of The Lord. We have to submit to The Lord. Back to Raavana.

When Shoorpanaka finally takes her complaint to Raavana after Raama had killed the demon warriors Khara, Dhooshana and Thrishiras who fight Raama at her bidding, just as we saw Manthara 'working' on Kaikeyi, she 'works' upon Raavana. She knows that Raavana is a 'womaniser'. She wants to take revenge on Raama and Lakshmana who had cut off her nose when her amorous advances were rejected by both of them. The best way for revenge is by exploiting Raavana's weakness for women. (Aaranya-chapter 34) Shoorpanaka to Raavana Gist "Seetha, is not a celestial, a ghandarva, a yaksi, or a kinnara woman; but such a lovely woman has not been seen by me before! If you take one look at her, you will be stricken by arrows of the lord of love. He, to whom she becomes wife, to such a person pleasures will be eternal" Raavana's passion for women is well known. He had been 'collecting' women for his harem like a gem or a stamp collector! He falls for this bait. And the rest is history. With the assistance of Maareecha, ***through magic and duping***, he abducts Seetha when Raama & Lakshmana were away from her hermitage. Weakness for women, makes Raavana even a coward, a great warrior though he is.

Raavana & Shoorpanaka.

We had said that two women had changed the course of history. The hunchback Manthara who had queen Kaikeyi under her clutches and thereby made Raama go on exile with Seetha. And Shoorpanaka, 'working' upon her cousin Raavana made him abduct Seetha. We had said earlier that Manthara was an evil genius. Shoorpanaka being a demoness, her approach was somewhat different. But both women got what they wanted. When Shoorpanaka who was stricken with passion over Raama, failed to make Raama (or) Lakshmana to fall in love with her, and when her nose was chopped off when she became aggressive and tried to molest Seetha, Shoorpanaka goads Khara to kill them. But single handily, Raama kills demon chiefs Khara, Dhooshana and Thrischiras, and their 14,000 strong army of terrible demons at Dhandakaaranya forest in Central India. Shoorpanaka could not take it any longer. She is a vengeful person. So flies into Lanka and takes her tale of woes and complaint to Raavana. The news of the killing of his demon chiefs had already reached Raavana through his spy, Akampana. Shoorpanaka is a clever woman and knows that Raama cannot be conquered. We are writing in detail mainly for two reasons We get to know Raavana better. Secondly, Vaalmeeki through the lips of this wicked woman brings home some truths. Gist (Aaranya-chapter 33),: She addresses her cousin Raavana in wrath "Intoxicated by sensual pleasures, acting without restraint, without taking control over activities in your realm, not knowing what is going on, you are not aware of the calamity that awaits you about which you should have known" By this Shoorpanaka expounds a truth. Kings should not be consumed by passion, women, wine and song. They should always be aware of what is going on in the state.

"The citizens will have no respect for a king, who is steeped in passion and indulges in vulgar pleasure. If a king does not know the time and place for action, he gets destroyed. A king must be seen, must give audience to citizens, should not be found in the harem always. He must have an independent mind and judgment. But alas! Fickle as you are, how are you still a king, having made enemies of Gandharvas, Dhevas, and not worrying about it? Childish as you are, Oh dear 'brother', how can you be a king? When movements, finance, management are not under his control, he is just an ordinary man, not a king at all. Kings should know happenings all over, through their spies. Then only kings are known as 'Far sighted' "Shoorpanaka having reviled his cousin, king Raavana tells him that he is not aware of the seriousness of the happenings at Dhandakaaranya forest where his chiefs-vassals were slain by Raama. She warns him "A king who is haughty, considers himself as an all knowing pundit, who is not trusted, who merely gets angry will be rejected by his citizens. He will end up as a blade of grass." A king is one who keeps 'awake' always, and alert even while asleep. A king is honoured and respected only when his anger or favour is properly directed".

It must be said to the credit of Raavaana that he did not get angry with his 'sister' but (as in sloka 24) "...he contemplated in his mind, about his failings enumerated by Shoorpanaka.".

Like Manthara, Shoorpanaka distorts truth: about happenings in Dhandaka forest. when Raavana questions her (Aaranya-chapter 34) Gist: "Who is this Raama about whom you are talking about?. For what purpose has he entered Dhandaka forest?. By what valour and weapons were my chiefs Khara, Dhooshana and Thrisharas were killed by him?" The clever Shoorpanaka, with revenge in her mind, after describing Raama's valour and Lakshmana talks about Seetha. No wonder! Her purpose cannot be served unless Raavana sets his mind on Seetha. It is through Seetha, she must and will have her revenge upon Raama and Lakshmana. She knows her 'brother' well. He will go after any pretty woman. (By Aaranya-chapter 34-slokas 20,21) she tells a blatant lie "..... ***When I undertook to bring Seetha to you to make her your wife***.....I was disfigured by Lakshmana" And Raavana falls for the 'bait'! But Raavana being warned by Akampana earlier, wants to 'steal' Seetha rather than face Raama and Lakshmana in combat.. ***Raavana with all his bravery behaves like a coward***.

Raavana and his friend Maareecha:

Raavana falls for the bait. Shoorpanaka had done her work. Raavana must have Seetha at any cost. But Akampana had warned him about Raama. About the havoc played by Raama in Janasthana. (Aaranya-chapter 31-) "The glorious scion of the royal family is enjoined with his brother Lakshmana, like fire with wind. The gold shafted feathered arrows discharged by Raama, became five headed cobras, and ate up all our demons there. They are all so gripped by fear, they see only Raama" Having put fear in Raavana, Akampana had advised him how to destroy Raama. It cannot be through combat with him So he says (sloka 31) "You can take away his wife Seetha and as Raama is passionately in love with her, he will give up his life without her" So the die is cast. Raavana flies to India and meets his demon friend for assistance to kidnap Seetha through deceit and trickery. Maareecha being a master of magic, should wander as a 'golden' deer around Seetha's hermitage and as Seetha is fond of deer will beg her husband to capture this deer. When Raama goes away on hunt, Maarecha should imitate the voice of Raama and cry out as though Raama is in great trouble and needs the assistance of his brother. Lakshmana, on hearing this cry for help from 'Raama', will rush out of the hermitage and when both are away it should be child's play for Raavana to kidnap Seetha. This is the crooked strategy conceived by

Raavana. When his friend Maareecha refuses to go through with this. (Aaranya-chapter 31- sloka 49) "Oh Raavana! Have mercy. Be tranquil. Go back to Lanka. May you enjoy life eternally with your other wives" When Raavana threatens him, Maareecha speaks a truth which is a master piece from Vaalmeeki (Aaranya-chapter 37- sloka 2) "Oh Raavana the king! It is always easy to find flatterers who speak sweetly but not what is salutary. But rare indeed to find one who may speak unpleasantly but speaks what is good and salutary. And rarer still to find one who will listen" The Chapters 35 to 41 describe Vaalmeeki's artistry. Maareecha refusing to go through with this crooked strategy at first. Finally Maarecha takes on the form a of magical golden deer and Raavana has his way. We will only narrate a few slokas how Raavana had threatened his friend (Chapter 40 sloka 26) "If you don't do this, I will kill you. So even under duress you must do this for me" ***Raavana has scant regard for friendship.. Friendship for Raavana means only this much. Slavery under him.*** Earlier Raavana had told Maareecha. "There is some chance for you to be alive when Raama hunts you as a deer. But rest assured. There is no chance for you to live even for a moment if you refuse me."

The character of Raavana and Raama is one of total contrast. Even on friendship Raama's was based on Dharma. But Raavana's was A-Dharma.

Raavana and Seetha.

Taking on the form of a mendicant, Raavana visits Seetha's hermitage when she was alone to go through with his most dastardly act of kidnapping her when both her husband and Lakshmana were away on 'hunt of the golden deer-Maareecha' Dress may cover up one's body, but the character of a person cannot be. It reveals itself soon enough. No sage or a mendicant will look at a woman and describe her physical attributes. Yet Raavana as he enters Seetha's hermitage starts talking about her beauty. Perhaps he was so consumed by her beauty he could not resist even for a moment. Vaalmeeki thus brings home a truth. A crooked man with a dirty mind, 'disrobes' a fully dressed up woman through his inimical eyes. (Aaranya-chapter 46) He describes their first meeting. Gist: "Oh Lady with lovely eyes! Lady with fine hips. Your teeth are well set, and white! Spotless eyes! Your buttocks are broad. Your thighs are like the trunk of an elephant.

Your two breasts are round and firm with distinguished nipples. Your waist is slender. You have compact contiguous breasts. ...." Now these are not the words of a mendicant or a sage of the forest. Surely Vaalmeeki must have introduced these words only to tell the world that a crooked man cannot hide his dirty mind even if he tries hard. Raavana was not only a bad man but before a lady he has no restraint when he sets his mind on her.

But what is surprising is. Seetha calmly replies to him. Perhaps she felt that as a sage or mendicant, he may curse her if she did not reply. (Aarany- chapter 47-sloka 2)

"This one is a guest. and a Brahmin. If not replied to he will curse me" Vaalmeeki can never be wrong. That is why, although Seetha is an intelligent woman, and has a lurking doubt about the credentials of this 'brahimn guest' she does not want to take chances but goes through with a formal reply about who she is and what brought her to the forest. Raavana reveals himself and rest is history. He has his way and kidnaps her.

Raavana is totally rejected by Seetha. Even as a captive in Askoka forest in Lanka. Seetha treats him with contempt. Raavana is a romantic person. He has a way with women. But with Seetha, he meets with his nemesis. Further, due to a curse, Raavana cannot force a woman to submit to him.

(Yudha-chapter 13 -slokas 1-15): Gist "I seized a woman Punjikasthala by force once and 'raped'' her. God Brahma who was enraged cursed me thus = From now on if you 'approach' any woman by force, at once your head will burst into pieces. = Because of this curse, I am not forcing Seetha to my bed".

With all his charm and brilliance, Raavana used to force women against their will before this curse upon him. ***Raavana is a base person unworthy to be a king.***

Yet_Vaalmeeki gives this devil his due. Not all women were forced into his harem. True, many lovely ladies were kidnapped or brought through victory, to Lanka They all submitted to him voluntarily after Raavana had exhibited his charm and favour upon them in his palace. Vaalmeeki says that in 'collecting' women for his harem, the only yardstick was their diverse beauty (Sundhara-chapter 9-slokas 70 to 73) "Women were from families of sages, various lords, ghandharvas, and demons. These women were seized by force after war. But some came to him voluntarily out of passion and by his charm. None, after life with him, ever loved any one else!" Vaalmeeki pays a compliment to Raavana! Raavana was highly 'cultivated' as far as his mistresses were concerned. "None became his wife who came from a low lineage. None who was not pretty.

None who was not intelligent. None without character. He pays again a compliment. None he treated with contempt or disrespect.

No wonder Raavana wanted Seetha at all costs. Even at the cost of giving up his bravery. Even by being a coward and stealing her like a common thief. Seetha ofcourse is the embodiment of womanhood. In all characteristics attributed to a woman, Seetha stood apart from the rest of the world of womanhood. This much credit we must give Raavana. He knew he cannot be a cultivated 'lover' unless he had the gem of gems. Seetha, as the rarest and unique 'collection' in his harem.

But Raavana is a coward. 'The Gem' was obtained only as a thief and through trickery.

Before we leave Raavana and his women and pass on to his other character, and leave Seetha 'alone', we should mention that Raavana's charm and his 'carrot and stick' technique totally failed with Seetha. At one point he is so exasperated he tells her (Sundhara-chapter 22- sloka 2)

"The more one placates a woman, the more he comes under the'will' of a woman. And more endearing he is, the more he is despised" For the carrot technique, as an example we have "Oh Lady! you enjoy freely all comforts with me. You may bestow land, wealth as you please, to any of your folks. The entire earth, if you want, I will hand over to your father, king Janaka" and so on......As for 'The stick' . we have "I am not killing you, although for every word you said to me, I would have given punishment of death to you."

Raavana is a man of wrath. But he is also man of passion, and he would never kill Seetha because she is worth waiting for!

Yes. This is Raavana, the lover!

We had said in our introduction to Raavana that he was a descendant of God Brahma Himself, through Rishi Pulasthya. Even Raavana could not 'escape' from his lineage although by his conduct he had become a demon.

We refer to an interesting but a significant incident. When Raavana was carrying away Seetha over the sky to his capital Lanka 1,000 miles away in the southern ocean,

the son of Sampaathi, the Lord of Birds, sees him near the tip of India. Thinking that Raavana would be good meat for him and his father, he approaches Raavana for the kill, but could not get close to him. Supaarswa, Sampaathi's son, who is as brave as his old father, narrates this (Kish-chapter 59- slokas 13 to 18) Gist: ".....At that time, a man who looked like a lump of a broken mountain, was seen by me and he was carrying away a woman. I decided to use them for our food. But I was beseeched by him, in humility, in a conciliatory manner. Indeed, there cannot be any one anywhere, even the basest of beings, who will attack a man well versed in Saama Vedha" Thus Supaarswa let him off and Raavana continued his journey to Lanka, carrying Seetha with him.

Yes Raavana was master of Vedhas. Particularly Saama Vedha! Blood tells. Demon he was. He could not escape from his lineage. He used to be a man of penance although his purpose was anything but spiritual. We shall be referring to this when we are on Lanka later.

Almost the first thing he does after imprisoning Seetha in Ashoka forest in Lanka, with a command to the guards that "without my permission, no one male or female should see Seetha" is to send trusted spies to India to keep an eye on Raama and Lakshmana (Aaranya-chapter 54- slokas 14 & slokas 20 to 29), with following Brief. Gist:

"Armed with various weapons, you go to Janasthana in India which used to be administered by Khara..The army under Khara was destroyed by Raama. Unable to endure this, wrath overpowers me. Revenge on Raama is what I seek. Only when I kill Raama I will rest content. Living in Janasthana, the activities of Raama must be watched and communicated to me. Dont move about carelessly. Every effort must be made for Raama's destruction" Vaalmeeki has written in detail to bring home a point or two.

Although Raavana had acted in a cowardly manner to steal Seetha, which he had never done as he had hitherto won women only as prize for valour, now feels that somehow

Raama must be slain. Following the advice of Shoorpanaka, through spies he is to watch the enemy, Raama. Remember, she had taunted him earlier! Not that Raavana needed advice. We should rather say that Shoorpanaka merely reminded him about some of his royal qualities that had gone to 'sleep'.

In spite of all this, Hanumaan finds Seetha as prisoner in Lanka, totally isolated from any being other than guards. Security was tight. Lanka is an island 1,000 miles away from the 'tip' of India. Through Vaalmeeki we can draw a lesson. When ceaseless effort is made, no one can be safe in this world. You may hide in the thick of the Himaalayan range, inside a cave or live in South pole in an Ice Box, and if you think you are safe, you are not living in Himaaalyas or South pole but in fool's paradise. Through Hanumaan, Vaalmeeki has brought this up poetically, mythologically but effectively. (Kish-chapter 67) Gist: "I am capable of following the Sun, there will be no sunset for me. I can go to and around, Meru mountain. Why! I can even find and bring Life saving Nectar from Indra himself..." Yes No one can isolate himself in this world and feel safe! ***Even the mighty Raavana could not isolate Seetha.***

It is rather difficult to understand human behaviour at times. We know that Raavana is wrathful. His favourite pleasure garden was destroyed by Raama's emissary Hanumaan. When Hanumaan was presented before him, no wonder Raavana hands out the punishment of death to Hanumaan. This befits his character. But when Vibheeshana pleads with him and reminds him about International Law on emissaries and ambassadors, surprisingly Raavana accepts his advice, and Hanumaan gets a milder sentence, the burning of his tail (In Sundhara-chapter 52) By sloka 1 & 2 of chapter 53 Raavana accepts this: Gist: "Hearing the words of Vibheeshana, that suited 'Time & Place' and met with justice. Raavana said. = What was said by you is proper. ***Killing of an emissary is contemptible*** - "'

Raavana listened to his brother Vibheeshana, accepted his counsel in the case of Hanumaan. Yet, when the question of return of Seetha to Raama came up to avoid war and bloodshed, Raavana's true colour came to light. Passion and arrogance of his might and power clouded his thinking...

Vaalmeeki projects man's character in proper light thus.

When war with Raama was imminent, and Hanumaan's advice and unofficial 'ultimatum' were rejected by Raavana, with Hanumaan's tail being set fire to. Raavana seeks counsel from his ministers and chiefs. (Yudha-chapter 6 and 7). Gist: "Thinking about the terrible deed of Hanumaan in Lanka, Raavana who was somewhat ashamed of himself, addressed his chiefs with his head down" Vaalmeeki says that even the mighty Raavana was humiliated by a mere monkey! Raavana bemoans "Our Lanka that cannot be 'trespassed' was 'entered' by Hanumaan, a mere monkey.....city devastated... And Seetha was also found out.

What further steps are to be undertaken by us.. What should I do now? "A cruel demon though he may be, Raavana speaks words of wisdom now and then. He says (Yudh-chapter 6) "The wise and noble say, victory is obtained through deliberation and counsel" He proceeds further when he differentiates between men from whom counsel can be had. "In this world there are three types of men: Foremost, average and inferior." With capable ministers who are ever concerned with your welfare, and who are experts in tendering sound advice, and with friends who have common objectives, and with relatives who are devoted to you, if one deliberates with these persons, and then commences the task putting in all his efforts, and placing ***Faith in God***, he is indeed the foremost." It may

not be out of place to make an observation or two in this statement by Raavana. Not only a master of Vedhas, he is a man of Faith and religion. Vaalmeeki expounds a truth, however hard it may be for us to bear. A man of religion, need not necessarily become a virtuous or good man. We have Raavana as an example. He is a man of penance. He has received Grace from God Brahma Himself. We have a noble virtuous man ***Jaabaali, who is an atheist***. Unlike in other religions, Sanaathana Dharma is the Religion of ancient India, that is Bhaarath. Even Gods are bound by Shruthis and Smrithis. the unwritten truths. The first sloka of Raaamaayana begins with the celestial Lord Naaradha = Thapas Swa-adhyaaya Niratham, Naaradham = Naaradha was ever in meditation and contemplation of Vedhas. We have written at some length because, in spite of Raavana's faith in religion, he caused immense suffering to the good and innocent and weak men in the world. The truth is that he had only 'studied' the Vedhas but never really 'learnt' Back to Raavana and his classification. And Raavana continues. "He deliberates only with himself! Directs his mind only on Dharma (as he sees it) He does everything by himself. Such a man, is only an average person, so elders say! "We may observe here that even if a man does his task with Dharma, but without faith in God, he is only an average man. Raavana is indeed a man of religion and has faith in God. The great 'seer' Bharthruhari who lived about 2,000 years ago, even goes to the extent of saying thus: Gist = Forget God etc. Do your task by your manliness. If you still don't succeed, with all your effort, so what?=
Raavana now talks about the inferior type "Without deliberating about what is good, he jumps into action saying to himself = I will do the task I please = forgetting even GOD This person is indeed inferior of men" ***Vaalmeeki thus projects Raavana as a man of Faith.***

Raavana now differentiates between Counsels: What is foremost counsel, what is average counsel and what is inferior counsel "When counsellers, after perceiving through the view point (through 'eye' of) Shaasthras, arrive at unanimity, indeed this is the foremost counsel" Vaalmeeki says that unanimity among noble men who have 'digested' shaasthras is foremost. Counsel from such a galaxy of men is indeed foremost.

"In a matter where there are many views among ministers and men, but in the end they reach a consensus, this counsel is only average counsel." This is the democratic way of arriving at a decision, not always good though.

"When there is no unanimity at all, when everyone speaks differently, speaks against one another, standing firm on their own view point, counsel then arrived at will be very inferior." You choose counsel by lottery!

It is rather sad that such a gifted man who had spoken for kings, administrators, top executives, such words of merit, lacked good conduct himself.

Hanumaan had expressed this before (Sundhara-chapter 49-slokas 17 &18) "Ah! What a form, what all royal qualities Raavana possesses. If only Raavana was not a man of A-Dharma and of bad conduct, he would be the ideal ruler & protector of the world, including Indra's world!" ***Yes, the great Raavana failed the world! Alas!***

Vaalmeeki thus expounds a truth. Knowledge and intelligence must be backed by good conduct. Bharthruhari expressed this, most beautifully, in his 'collection' of poems.=Neethi shathakam= when he used analogy thus. "A five headed king cobra with 'jewel' on its head may be pleasant sight (for the artists and the like), but is dangerous all the same".

We can give credit to Raavana only to the extent that he condescended to seek counsel when war was imminent. But he failed miserably to take in the right advice. When a man is arrogant of power & when passion seizes him, he loses whatever qualities he may possess. Unfortunately, he was surrounded by ministers and chiefs, who were not only demons but whose thinking was based on wrath and passion. Thus (Yudha-chapter 7) they all praise Raavana sky high. Demon chief Prahastha, Nikumbaha, son of his brother Kumbakarna. and others justify Raavana's action to bring Seetha to Lanka.. Only Vibheeshana and Kumbhakarna give him sound advice. They are the brothers of Raavana We shall write about their advice when we discuss the character of Vibheeshana and Kumbhakarna later. Vibheeshana advises Raavana to hand over Seetha to Raama and thus avoid war. But Raavana, seized with passion and going by the advice of his chiefs, rejects his advice. Thus war becomes inevitable.

Raavana's character is thus one of Frenzy and passion. Frenzy because his chiefs like Khara, Dhooshana were killed in India by Raama & Passion, over Seetha.

Raavana is worried. as Raama is getting ready with Sugreeva's army of monkeys, planning to invade Lanka. Through spies he receives the shocking news. His brother Vibheeshana had defected to Raama and joined the enemy camp at the southern 'tip' of India. (Yudha-chapter-20) Gist: "The very brave demon Shaardhoola approached and saw the vast army in the southern shores of the ocean, in India. Seeing all this, this demon spy rushed to Lanka" And he said these words quickly to Raavana. "The multitude of bears and monkeys vast like the ocean, cannot be estimated, or penetrated. It is approaching Lanka. You should accept the reality of the situation. Oh great king Raavana, your emissaries should look into this."

Raavana is a clever man. Thinks that he should attempt some dissension within the enemy camp. After all Sugreeva is a monkey. What purpose is served for him to risk a war on behalf of Raama! So he commissions demon chief Shuka to go and tell Sugreeva thus (Yudh-chapter 20 slokas 11 to13) Gist: "Oh great king of monkeys, Oh Sugreeva who is born in a noble family! Oh son of Rikshiraja! Oh the mightily strong one! "Even the introduction by Raavana is striking. After all he has been a king for so long, he knows how to address another 'king'! Raavana continues his message through his emissary Shuka thus "***You are like a brother to me*** There is neither gain nor loss for you in this matter of war, and the abduction of the wife of Raama. Therefore please go back to your kingdom of Kishkinda" Having said this, he gives a warning "Lanka cannot be reached in any way Even by Dhevas. So how can monkeys!

"Ofcourse Shuka's message to Sugreeva is treated with contempt. Raavana's effort to prevent war through dissension in enemy camp, fails.

This is Raavana's second defeat in war as Sugreeva taunts Raavana in his message to Raavana by way of a reply through Raavana's spy-emissary The first defeat or casualty for Raavana is the defection of his brother Vibheeshana to Raama's camp. But Raavana never really appreciated the calamity that is about to strike him and his Lanka through Raama. He boasts. (Yudha-chapter 24) "I will never give back Seetha even if Dhevas and Asuras do war with me. Raama does not know my prowess in war. Like the Sun taking away the brilliance of a multitude of stars, I will take away the strength of this man Raama My force is like that of the ocean, in ferocity. My mobility is like wind. Whether Indra, or Yama, or Varuna or Kubhaera, none can face me...."

When Sugreeva's army of monkeys along with Raama and Lakshmana cross the ocean through a fantastic bridge constructed by architect-monkey Nala and are stationed at the outskirts of Lanka, ready for attack, Raavana could not believe this. (Yudha-chapter 25) For once he is shaken "The army of monkeys has crossed the ocean. Somehow I cannot believe about a bridge being constructed over the ocean. Surely I will now have to reckon with this army" After telling this to Shuka and Saarana, his two demon-spies, he commissions them "You two enter the Army without being seen and find out about the extent of the army, their bravery, and about monkey chiefs ......" He thinks he is clever. We know in modern war, spies are all over. Nothing strange. It was so those days.

But Raavana failed to take note of his own stupidity. He should have been conciliatory to his brother Vibheeshana and should never have allowed him to go away from Lanka. When Vibheeshana had defected to Raama and Sugreeva, he had taken along with him only a few of his chiefs and had not carried any armaments.. Yet, when an enemy joins you from the enemy's camp, you have a double advantage. The enemy's strength diminishes but more important all the secrets of the enemy are available to you 'free of cost'! Moving about amidst a million monkeys is not difficult when you have taken the form of a monkey. But these two were easily caught thanks to Vibheeshana. After all Vibheeshana is an erstwhile prince of Lanka and knows about his ministers, spies. When these spies were presented before Raama, he did what is expected of Raama! This is what he says (Yudha-chapter 25-slokas 19 to 28) "If our entire army has been 'seen' and investigated by you two (spies) and if your mission is accomplished as per your brief, you may go back" This is Raama for you! Raavana had wanted to kill Hanumaan, remember. But he satisfied himself with burning his tail. The only thing common between Raama the Ikshwaaki and Raavana the demon, is that their names begin with "R"! Even in such trying conditions with war preparations going on in a foreign land. Raama did not lose his sense of humour (By sloka 20) he adds "If there is anything further and more not seen by you, please do see them" Adding insult to injury he says "Perhaps (your erstwhile prince) Vibheeshana will take you around and show you" This is war-humour for you! Raama being a practical man, sends a sort of ultimatum to Raavana through the two spies who are let off. Gist: "Going back to Lanka, Raavana, the brother of Kubhaera, must be told exactly these words of mine."

Raama begins his address to Raavana with a taunt. "The might & power with which you became the abductor of my wife, Seetha, you may now exhibit before me" ***Vaalmeeki's poetry here!*** We all know Raavana acted as a coward, like a common thief, when he abducted Seetha, when neither Raama nor Lakshmana was around. Whatever be Raavana's glory as a mighty king or warrior, ***History will always judge him as a coward by this obnoxious act of his, unbecoming of a warrior.*** Raama says further "I am going to discharge my terrible wrath on you, tomorrow morning. So get ready, bear yourself with your army."

When these two spies convey Raama's message with an advice to Raavana ".......enough of enmity with Raama. May Seetha be handed back to Raama. May you seek peace with Raama" no emissary could have spoken the truth so strongly for the welfare of their king and Lanka.

But Raavana's, arrogance, wrath and passion totally blinded him while facing realities. He had talked about counsel and all that. But he failed to appreciate his own sermon. Fate ofcourse had decided on war. Fate had decided that he and his evil demons must be annihilated.

He had no intention of returning Seetha and his mind is well set on war, he takes a look at the formation of the enemy's army with demon Saarana (Yudha-chapter 26) "I will never give up Seetha." Climbing on to the Rampart, he surveys the vast army of monkeys at the outskirts of his lovely Lanka. Saarana points out to Raavana from there, various chiefs of Sugreeva's army. (Did they have binoculars those days. Ah! who knows?)

In Vaalmeeki Raamaayana, not infrequently we have reference to a basic character a person must endeavour -.

Restraint. A man given to wrath and passion, comes to grief. Raavana, a great warrior, backed by boons by the Grace of God Brahma, falls into and clutches of passion and frenzy. A king must keep his cool and control anger. Raavana who had been a king for a long time, is consumed by wrath and passion reducing himself to a cheap and base person. After taking a look at the vast army of monkeys at the outskirts of his Lanka from the rampart and after he was enlightened about this army by his demon chief Saarana, Raavana, was so shaken, that he began to deliberate. One would have expected Raavana to ponder over various options like a peace mission-treaty with Raama. Or deliberate with his army chiefs for defence of Lanka. But this great warrior who had caused terror to Dhevas and who had made Sun's rays cool in summer and warm in winter and who had made his Lanka 'Airconditioned' with wind blowing softly and cool, resorts to a silly and cheap strategy, unbecoming of a powerful king. All because of his passion. He must have Seetha at all costs. She will come to him if he proves that Raama is dead Wishful thinking, indeed. Raama is very much alive and is about to strike, strike hard. (Yudha-chapter 31) And he 'takes' it on poor Seetha! (Slokas 6 to 8) Raavana's strategy to dupe Seetha! A master magician, he went to the place where Seetha was, taking with him the expert magician Vidyujihva He told him! "We shall stupefy and dupe Seetha by magic! By Magic, Oh Vidyujihva, bring with you quickly, Raama's head along with his broken bow and arrow, and see me." Entering the Asoka forest, he addressed Seetha thus (Yudha-chapter 31-slokas 17 to 39) the coward Ravana.

The entire chapter, Raavana describes how the army of monkeys were destroyed, how one after the other of their chiefs was slain, and finally how Raama himself was killed. Ofcourse all this is to dupe Seetha. Raavana's wishful thinking! Gist of a few slokas: "Oh blessed Seetha! He who killed Khara, he, abiding by whom you leap in joy, that Raama. your husband, was 'killed' by me. Your root is totally destroyed. Your pride and arrogance are removed. You will now have to become my wife" Saying this, Raavana narrates the names of all the chiefs killed when they were all very sleepy after their 1,000 mile tiring journey! **Ah! What a 'Sell'** To prove that Raama is no more, he calls the magic demon Vidujihva "Place the head of the son of Dhasharatha at once before Seetha. Let her take a (good) look at her husband's last journey!" When Vidhyujihva had exhibited 'Raama's head' Raavana again addresses Seetha "Oh Seetha! This is your Raama's bow, strung up, having killed Raama at night, my chief Prahastha had brought this to me." Finally he tells the weeping Seetha ***"Now, You Be Obedient To Me"*** Soon enough,, Seetha realises that this is all magic and Raama is not such a man who will be careless to be slaughtered while asleep or his army slain..

But how can Raavana the great warrior and mighty king who had humbled even Lord Indra, stoop so low?

Raavana's cowardliness shows up now and then. All because he can't think straight. Wrath and passion had totally consumed him. ***Ah. This stupid Raavana!***

Sometimes Raavana's character is rather intriguing. How stupid can he get? Even if Raama had been killed, did Raavana really believe that Seetha would accept him. She would place a blade of grass and treat him with contempt and then kill herself.

To give Raavana a final chance to redeem himself, Raama following International Law sends an official Ultimatum through prince, monkey Angadha. (Yudh-Chapter 41). This is a long chapter but we will present only slokas 64 & 67: "Oh Raavana! As I who am emaciated by the abduction of my wife Seetha by you, am standing at the gates of Lanka as The Bearer of The Rod of Justice and punishment to you bringing with me a mighty army, now your pride and arrogance arising out of the Grace and Boons offered by God Brahma is gone (will be gone)" **This is the ultimatum of Raama: "If You Do Not Restore Seetha, And Seek Surrender, I Will Make The Entire World Free Of Your Demons".**

But the foolish Raavana failed to take advantage of this Raavana failed to remember Hanumaan and his havoc on Lanka single handedly. Raavana failed to take note of the killing of his chiefs in India by Raama, all by himself when 14,000 demons were destroyed in a couple of hours along with the terrible demons Khara, Thrisharas and Dhooshana. He failed to take note of the vast army of Sugreeva overcoming the Ocean that separated India and his Lanka by 1,000 miles. Even an ordinary man with a little brain would have pondered. But Raavana indulged in only self praise and was not aware of his limitations. No wonder he was annihilated by Raama.

Raavana did not deserve to be king of Lanka any longer.

And Raavana did not behave as a king when Angadha presented Raama's Ultimatum. He does not treat him with consideration due to an ambassador. He merely exhibits his wrath. Further there was no Vibheeshana with him to advise him about royal norms. (Yudha-chapter 41-slokas 86 & 87) "As this monkey was speaking, Raavana was seized by wrath and he said to his ministers = This one, this monkey must be seized and 'hit', repeatedly (tortured) = "And so the war begins. Sugreeva's army of monkeys fighting for Raama. Raavana's army of demons trying to save Lanka and its demons. A terrible war and we have already referred to Vaalmeeki's description of this war - No comparison with any other war! One after the other, chiefs on either side are killed. Monkeys by thousands and demons as well, are slaughtered every Muhoortha, by the hour! War is fought against (Geneva!) Convention. They fight even at night Later we will describe the war and the list the demon chiefs killed.

We see Raavana entering the war front ***in earnest*** only in Yudha-chapter 100 seeing his army commanders killed. But he enters the field even earlier though. (chapter 58) Raavana, who is in terrible agony and wrath, vows: "Killing these two, this Raama and Lakshmana, I will remove totally the suffering of Lanka that is under siege now. I will cut in battle This Tree that is Raama which offers fruits like Seetha....." Vaalmeeki goes poetic! Even here, in the thick of war, Seetha is The fruit to be had for Raavana. ***Vaalmeeki does not waste his words nor his poetry***!

In (Yudha chapter 59) we find this mighty, proud, arrogant Raavana was totally humiliated by Raama in the battlefield. But chivalry was the order of the day. Raama was an Ikshwaku prince. A royal man of Dharma, son of Raaja Rishi Dhasharatha. (slokas 150 to 157) Raavana had never been shaken up before. Even by Lord Indra's vajra,. Yet he could not stand the arrows of Raama.and Lakshmana. He was in great pain, feeble. Raama observing his enemy in this state says "As I consider you as being very tired, ***I do not wish to send you*** to ***the dominion of the dead now***. I give you leave to go back. After refreshing yourself, you may return. only to see my power and the ferocity of my weapons".

(By Yudh-chapter 60-slokas 1 to 3) Vaalmeeki describes Raavana's plight when he was humiliated thus by Raama.

"Entering the city of Lanka, Raavana became afflicted with fear; His pride gone, his mind totally confused and he told his chiefs = I, who am equal to Lord Indra, have been 'conquered' by a mere man =. In spite of all this Raavana does not see what is coming to him. Ah, Fate!

At one point in the battle between Raama and Raavana, seeing Raavana very tired, (a very rare sight indeed!) Raavana's charioteer drives him off the battlefield, away from Raama. Raavana is furious and admonishes his charioteer for this insult. But he could not realise that his charioteer had 'saved' him, atleast for the time being.. Ofcourse he comes back to do battle after being refreshed. thanks to his clever charioteer. Yet he does not realise what he is in for. Ah Fate!

Let us list a few slokas where Raama taunts Raavana as he is face to face in combat. (chapter105-slokas 11 to 25) Gist: "Oh Raavana the very brave warrior, one who steals other's wives like a thief! Yet, you are thinking = I am a warrior = Ah! After a long time you have come within my sight. By divine grace! I will now release my wrath caused by the abduction of my wife" We have written these slokas to justify what we had earlier said about Raavana. (Coward, a thief).

Having taunted him Raama offers a terrible fight to Raavana, an unbearable fight for Raavana.

We must give the devil his due. Even after losing all his chiefs commanders, and his sons and the 'prince of Wales', Indrajith, Raavana never tried to run away or seek peace or volunteer surrender.

He saw the writing on the wall, surely. Perhaps he was so ashamed that death was better than living as a vassal.

Indeed, knowing Raama as we do, he would even then had given Raavana 'refuge' if he had surrendered to Raama We must give this much credit to Raavana. Infact after his death at the hands of Raama, when Vibheeshana refuses to perform his Last Rites, Raama admonishes Vibheeshana and has this to say about Raavana his enemy. (Yudha-chapter114-slokas109 to 113) "Oh Vibheeshana! Surely he was a man of Adharma! But he was very eminent, brave, a warrior in battle. He made the world cry in fear of him. and as a warrior, one has never heard of his being conquered by even Dhevas or Asuras."

We will conclude this write up on The Character of Raavana by saying that he was indeed lucky that it is Raama who killed him. No other enemy would have been so magnanimous like Raama and press the case for performing his last Rites. Let us not forget that Indians believe that with the Last Rites all our sins are 'quenched'. Who Knows! If Vibheeshana had not done this, perhaps Raama would have performed Raavana's Last Rites! Yes. Lakshmana who was keeping count of the persons who had the good fortune of their Last Rites being performed by Raama, would have one more to his List..

Jataayu, Kabandha, Viraadha, why not Raavana?

16: KUMBAKARNA

We may read Vaalmeeki Raamaayana as a mighty story book or an exercise in mythology. Even if you dont look beyond this, we will be well served by Vaalmeeki. But Vaalmeeki's epic is like the first 'Naama' of Vishnu Sahasra naama. =VISH= To enter, to permeate. This epic permeates, covers us all, totally. It touches all our activities, relationships, Dharma and so on. If this analogy is not taken literally, if we are content with this Epic as a mere story book, it is like a top business man investing his profits in Government 4% bonds.! But a wise businessman knows better! We crave your indulgence for beginning this write up on Kumbakarna this way. You will appreciate why we have begun like this, when we write about his other brother, Vibheeshana also that follows.

Kumbakarna is brother of Raavana, younger to him. When Raama sees this giant of a demon from a distance and asks him thus (Yudha-chapter 61-slokas 6 to 8) Gist: "Oh Vibeeshana! A person is seen, who is wearing a crown who is like a mountain, whose eyes are reddish-brown, who is like the cloud with a streak of lightning. He seems unique to me. Our monkeys are terrified by his sight"

Vibheeshana describes his elder brother Kumbakarna thus (slokas 10 to 36) Gist of s few slokas "He, by whom, Lord of death Yama, was conquered, by whom Indra also was conquered likewise, is the son of Vishrawas. This majestic person is Kumbakarna. There is no demon comparable to him in stature. He was born brilliant ...... unlike other demons who got power through boons! Once, in sheer wrath he pulled out from Indra's elephant, a tusk and with this hit Indra himself. The celestials and their Lord Indra became so terrified that they sought grace and protection from God Brahma. Kumbakarna was swallowing all, like some fruit. They feared thus.

"If Kumbakarna eats us all like this, in a short time, the world will be empty." God Brahma hearing all this from his celestials, cursed Kumbakarna (sloka 26) "From now on, Oh Kumbakarna, you will sleep on as dead" When Raavana heard of this curse he begged Brahma thus (sloka 28) "Oh lord of Creation! A golden tree after it has grown well is being cut off when about to yield fruits. To curse your own great grandson is not fair" Here, we refer to what we wrote about Raavana. But we repeat. Pulasthya was created by

Brahma with his mind To him was born Vishrawas. Like Raavana, Kumbakarna is his son and the great grandson of The CREATOR himself. God Brahma taking pity on them, modified this curse thus "He will sleep at a stretch for 6 months. will be awake just for one day" Thus Kumbakarna is given to long slumber. It is difficult to wake him up. When he wakes up he is a terror to all humans. he will swallow every one, drink anything. But only for the day.

This is Kumbakarna. But we will talk about his character in relation to Raavana and all that was happening, even while he was in deep slumber.

When Raavana felt that war with Raama on account of his abduction of Seetha, was imminent, he decided to seek counsel from his chiefs and from his brothers Vibeeshana and Kumbakarna. (Yudh-chapter 12) Hearing Raavana's words, Kumbakarna was seized with wrath. He admonished Raavana (slokas 30 to 42) Gist: "Like river Yamuna taking on to what belongs to Yamuna only, when Seetha was brought by force, at that time itself you should have deliberated, taken a firm decision. You should have realised the consequence before you took this step. You should have discussed this with us even then..

When a king after deliberation, decides and acts, he does not come to grief later. "W***e have this master piece from Vaalmeeki through the lips of Kumbakarna"*** "When one desires to do tasks that should be done first, later, but does tasks first, that should be taken up only later, it means he has no understanding of right & wrong"

After criticising Raavana thus, and later when Raama's army were besieging Lanka and war had begun, he was woken up before his 6 months slumber, Kumbakarna, whose assistance in war was sought by Raavana, again reviles Raavana thus (Yudh=chapter 63) This is a very important chapter because Kumbakarna, although a demon, speaks words of wisdom: Gist: "The danger that was seen by us when we deliberated upon this matter some time back, it is That, that is now encountered by you who are not devoted to follow what is good and salutary. Like fruits of punishment in hell for one who does evil deeds, ruin caused by evil deeds, is approaching you. Your sin is catching up with you. Your 'work' of abduction was not deliberated by you, because of your arrogance. The consequence of your action was never deliberated by you. You do not know priority.You think. and then act But you. Ah! have acted & are now thinking! Deeds done in haste and in topsy turvy manner go to waste eventually. He, who chooses the proper time & place for action after deliberating with his ministers, resorting to three fold principles in action, employing a five fold strategy, never fails" We may broadly elaborate on these here. ***Three Fold actions are broadly*** Going to war with the enemy only when you are stronger. Making treaty when relative strength is almost even. To compromise, when you are weaker. ***The Five fold Strategy*** Deliberating on the first step: then making preparation: choosing a proper time and place for attack: a proper time for retreat & withdrawal,:stopping when the objective is realised.

Kumbakarna criticises Raavana for his confrontation with Raama, inspite of knowing the prowess of Raama.

Kumbakarna continues his attack on Raavana. "A king who desires to do things at the proper time and place according to norms and tradition, who considers the views of ministers and friends, only he enjoys, Dharma, Artha and Kaama. at proper times" Kumbakarna talks about many matters. As we said this chapter 63 of Yudha is very significant. Kumbakarna takes a dig at Raavana's ministers who are not fit to be ministers. "The un-salutary words of advice from those who defile Shaasthras, who have no knowledge of the essence of Shaasthras, who desire only knowledge of the essence of Shaasthras, who desire only ***profit and material gain from their master***, should never be accepted. These men prattle and in arrogance of their position. They destroy the deed and they must be 'watched' by their king. They should be kept away from counsel! Some ministers even 'join' the enemy camp causing harm. A king must therefore identify them who only pose as his friend "Kumbakarna tells Raavana, he has lost the power of discrimination in seeking advice from every minister of his, without investigating about their nature or ability."Finally Kumbakarna exhibiting his brotherly affection affirms, that he will fight for him with his life to save Lanka. "Oh Raavana! All this was spoken by me out of my affection for you as your brother and by my relationship with you. So now, at this moment what all befitting that is to be done, will be done by me. You will see Raama and Lakshmana killed by me in battle. When I bring the head of Raama, you will be in happiness with Seetha. So command me. to war now itself. I will annihilate your enemies totally." Kumbakarna makes a statement which turns out to be true "Only when I am killed, Raama will kill you!" How true it turned out. He fought a terrific battle, but was killed by Raama.

17: VIBHEESHANA

We may recall what Shoorpanaka said while introducing herself before Raama as 'sister' of Raavana

(Aranya-chapter17) (Sloka 24) "The noble soul and man of Dharma, Vibheeshana is my brother, but unlike his brothers Raavana and Kumbakarna, ***he does not possess the behaviour of demons***" By association with his brothers he had to put up with a lot of evil. Under normal circumstances, perhaps he would have lead a nobler life. We find him advising Raavana, that as per norms of International politics, an ambassador or emissary is never killed. Surprisingly, for a change, Raavana had accepted his advice and spared the life of Hanumaan, when Hanumaan as emissary of Raama and Sugreeva, finds about Seetha and destroys Raavana's favourite garden.

When Raavana seeks counsel from his ministers and his two brothers after he had brought Seetha to Lanka and as war with Raama was imminent, we had seen how strongly Kumbakarna had criticised Raavana's action. Vibheeshana goes one step further. He advises him to give back Seetha. and save Lanka and all, including himself. (Yudha-chapter 14) He goes on a tirade against some of Raavana's ministers for tendering wrong and immoral advice to their king. But his arrogant brother Raavana, indulging in self praise and boast, supported by stupid ministers like Prahastha, not only refuses to listen to the salutary advice of Vibeeshana but calls him a traitor, and one who is so jealous of Raavana as only a brother can be! (Yudh-chapter 16-sloka 10) "Oh Vibeeshana! I am honoured and respected in the world. I have obtained all the wealth. I 'stand' at the head of my enemies, always! ***All this is not liked by you"*** What a shame, that this good man is called a jealous man. Vibheeshana realising that Raavana is in terrible wrath, finally gives up and says (Yudh-chapter16-slokas 18 to 25)

Gist: "You are my elder brother. So you may say what all you wish to say about me, I must bear. You are to be honoured by me as a father. But as you are not standing on the path of Dharma, I grieve. I am unable to bear these cruel words against me because they are totally false". Through the lips of Vibheeshana, Vaalmeeki hands out a truth "Those who come under clutches of Yama-death, hasten their end" This was later on expressed by Bhathruhari and other scholars who followed Vaalmeeki, years and years later. = Vinaasha- kaa lay, Vi pareetha Bhudhi = The first casualty when a man's end is near, is his sense of thinking and understanding. Vaalmeeki follows this through the lips of Vibheeshana (sloka21) "Oh King! It is always very easy to find persons who speak sweetly to flatter, but rare to find one who speaks severely but who speaks what is salutary & good. And rarer still to find one who will listen to him" We all know that Vaalmeeki rarely repeats himself. This is one of the two slokas which has been repeated by Vaalmeeki. On both occasions, it is Raavana who ignores this advice, this sloka. Maareecha had said this. (Aaranya-chapter 37-sloka 2) Now it is Vivbheeshana who tells Raavana. If Vaalmeeki had repeated a sloka it must have some 'sanction' ***Vaalmeeki does not waste words***

(Aaranya-chapter 37-sloka 2 & Yudh-chapter 16-sloka 21)
Finally Vibheeshana decides to leave Lanka (Slokas 22 to 27) Gist: "Like one who cannot be indifferent when the house is burning, I cannot look away but must tender counsel, to you who is bound by the 'Rope' of Time. I desire not to see you killed by Raama. Desirous as I am in your welfare always, whatever was spoken by me to you out of my attachment to you, all that may you forgive me as you are my 'guru'."

"I am going from here May there be welfare of swasthi to you May you ever be In happiness even without me" Vibeeshana leaves Lanka for good.

We had remarked why Vaalmeeki should not be treated as merely a story writer of mythology when we introduced Kumbakarna. Vaalmeeki had a problem. Here are two brothers, demons Kumbakarna and Vibeeshana. Both have strongly condemned the action of their brother Raavana in abducting Seetha. Yet, Kumbakarna decides to stay on and fight for Raavana. But Vibheeshana defects. and joins enemy Raama. This is the scenario. Both have justified their actions. How can that be? This is the problem Vaalmeeki had to contend with. That is why we should not read his Epic as merely a story book!

Vibeeshana realises that Raama is a divine person. When he lands at the southern tip of India before Raama where the army of monkeys are ready to cross the ocean and attack Lanka, he introduces himself thus (Yudh-chapter 17) Gist "There is a demon called Raavana of immoral deeds. I am his brother. I repeatedly advised him to give back Seetha with many reasons. But like a dying man he refused my advice" After saying this Vibeeshana justifies his defection thus (sloka 17) "You please inform Raama that I am Vibheeshana, who has come to him, who is a great soul, ***Who Is the Refuge For All In The World***".

Vaalmeeki being a man of few words, with this single line justifies Vibeeshana's defection. Vibeeshana is a Vishnu Bhaktha. Realises that Raama is no man, but divine! A few commentators feel that Vibheeshana should have stayed on in lanka without offering his services in war to Raavana. Others are even more critical that Vibeeshana, having enjoyed the 'hospitality' of his brother should have fought for Raavana. Some are so uncharitable that they attribute a selfish reason. he wanted to be king of Lanka after Raama kills Raavana!

Poet Vaalmeeki brings home a point: Gratitude to a friend or relative is subject to Dharma. If the world will suffer, or if even society will suffer, then you must reconsider your relationship with a friend or relative. Here we are talking about Sanaathana Dharma. Under normal circumstnces, gratitude is a virtue.

They contrast Vibeeshana's action with Kumbakarna's. But the point is that Kumbakarna never went into the question of morality of kidnapping Seetha, with the same force as Vibeeshana did. Kumbakarna is so consumed by his own power and strength, that fight with Raama comes up before him rather quickly! Morality in an action does not exercise his mind as much as in the case of Vibeeshana. Who says

Vaalmeeki is just a story writer? Let them read Yudh-chapters 9,10,12, 14,15,16,17, 63. If they don't know Sanskrit, let them take recourse to stanza by stanza rendering in English or in a language they are conversant with. Flippant observations only hit the 'observer' not the 'observed' Vaalmeeki wrote without fear or favour. He wrote reality. And he wrote with Dharma in his mind. As he is a devotee of Sanaathana Dharma, ***indeed only Vaalmeeki could be called the most religious person in the Universe.***

As Vibeeshana falls at the feet of Raama, Raama who is refuge to all accepts him even against the advice of Sugreeva and a few others. (Yudh-chapter19- slokas5 to 8) "I am Raavana's brother who was humilated. As you are ***The Refuge For All, I Seek Refuge Under You*** Lanka was abandoned by me; likewise my wealth, friends wife. Family. My life and my 'kingdom' are at your service. My happinessis is with you" Vibeeshana does not surrender to Raama. He surrenders to God Vishnu in human form. He surrenders to and for everything that is noble, virtuous and surrenders for welfare of all.

When the army of monkeys reach the southern 'tip' of India and face the Ocean and deliberate how the army should reach Lanka, 1000 miles away, it is Vibeeshana who offers advice (Yudh-chapter 19-slokas 33 & 34) ***This is almost his first service to Raama after his defection***. "King Raama should seek 'refuge' under the Lord of The Ocean" As he had sought refuge under Raama, so should Raama seek refuge under this Lord and offer his prayer. Vibeeshana knows history! He says"The unfathomable Ocean-Mahodadhi, was 'cut up' (was created), by Raama's forefather king Sagara. This wise Lord Mahodadhi, realising the importance of Raama's task will certainly favour him" Thanks to his advice, the huge army of monkeys cross 1,000 miles through a bridge constructed over the ocean, Mahodadhi.!

When Raama and Lakshmana fall down in the battle field struck by The weapon of weapons, The Brahma Asthra, and there was total chaos in the army of monkeys, Vibeeshana keeps calm, and offers sound advice (Yudh-chapter 74-slokas3 to 7) Gist: "Fear not! This is not the time for despondency. Because these two, Raama and Lakshman are now only in languor. This great weapon of Brahma Asthra never goes to waste. Out of respect to God Brahma, these two have timidly submitted to this, and are not dead. As such, how can you all be despondent" Incidentally, Vibeeshana was not at all perturbed or affected by this Asthra although he was close by in the battle field because of a boon from God Brahma. ***Vibeeshana's service in War cannot be underestimated***.

During the fight between Raavana's brilliant son Indrajith and the army of monkeys, Vibeeshana again tenders sound advice (Yudh-chapter 84-slokas13,14)He warns thus: "Indrajith, after terrorising and stupefying monkeys has gone to the temple Nikumbila to perform Homa for success in war. If Indrajith completes The homa, he will be invincible" Thus when Indrajith was prevented from completing his ritual, and when Lakshmana takes him on, after a terrific battle, he is killed by him Earlier there is an interesting dialogue, or rather a hot exchange of words between Vibeeshana and his nephew Indrajith where Indrajith accuses him as traitor. (Yudh-chapter 87) and he warns "You are after all Raavana's brother. Necessarily an enemy of Raama. ...although you may claim friendship with him!" Vibeeshana replies "Although a demon, I do not possess the conduct of demons! I follow the conduct of men, the good. I do not 'enjoy' fruits obtained through Non-Dharma. I was virtually driven out by your father;

Raavana who has abandoned Dharma. Lanka will not exist, nor you, not even your father". Vibeeshana knows that Indrajith being a cruel person, he must be killed. Yet he does not want to kill him. He wants Lakshmana to do the killing He says (Yudh-chapter 90-slokas 17 & 18) "It is not proper for me to kill a 'son'(after all Raavana's son is my 'son') But for the sake of Raama I want him to be killed. Tears are covering my eyes, so how can I kill him. It is Lakshmana who will kill him" Blood is thicker than water! Ah!

Vibeeshana, although a demon is very human

No wonder when his brother Raavana is killed by Raama and war ends, he wails. He remembers only the good of this wrathful brother Raavana. (Yudh-chapter 112) Gist of a few slokas"Oh my brother, Oh the brave! Oh the most renowned in valour! Oh the most learned! Oh the most well versed in Polity! How can you lie down now on bare earth!" Customarily we speak well of a dead person. But what all Vibeeshana says about his brother is not merely by custom, but some of these words are true. Vibeeshana may be forgiven when he says "The embankment of righteousness has given way! The embodiment of Dharma has gone! The epitome of goodness is gone." Here Vibeeshana follows custom. When a man, good or bad, dies, we say only good things. about him. But we should not criticise Vibeeshana too much here. Raavana did possess some of these qualities, although his power, arrogance and passion totally submerged whatever good was in him. We have a strange behaviour when Vibeeshana, who is the sole survivor of Pulasthyas, refuses to perform his brothers's Last Rites. Raama admonishes him and Vibeeshana does perform Raavana's Last Rites in Royal fashion. Vibeeshana's service in war was strategic. When Raama asks Lakshman to crown him King of Lanka after killing Raavana he says (Yudh-chapter 115-slokas9 & 10) "You crown Vibeeshana who is most affectionate, most devoted, ***who has done me great service.*** If I see him crowned, that would be my foremost wish No other certificate is necessary for Vibeeshana

Raama has spoken.

And Raama is God Vishnu on earth for Vibeeshana

Vibeeshana did not defect to a common man

18: LANKA & CITIZENS

We had written about Ayodhya and its citizens. Ayodhya was the capital of Ikshwaakus. Naturally we should talk about Lanka of the demon king Raavana. No comparison is attempted though.

Lanka is an island 1,000 miles away from the Southern shores of India. Hanumaan flies this distance to trace Seetha there. Vaalmeeki states that he covered this distance of 100 Yojanas during the day.. A Yojana is about 8-9 miles. We can thus estimate the distance to be nearly 1,000 miles from India.It all fits in with the flying speed of Hanumaan. Incidentally, what is now called SriLanka is not Raavana's Lanka!

The kingdom itself had a population of over 100 million demons (Aaranya-chapter55- sloka14) Raavana says "Oh Seetha! I am the lord of 100 million demons, 22,000 of them are of terrible deeds" Ofcourse the demon population is spread all over, like in Dhandakaaranya in India with Raavana's chief Khara ruling over it.

We have modern conveniences like air conditioning, heating system in sub-zero weather. But Raavana's Lanka was unique. The entire city and suburbs were totally air-conditioned. Here there was no need for AC-s Sun warmed up in winter and during summer, sent only cooler rays to fall upon on it. The wind not only blew pleasantly, according to the weather, but always carried fragrance. So scared of Raavana, were the 'Elements'! Modern scientists and technologists should take a cue from Vaalmeeki and make our cities, clean, un-polluted, always cool and warm, always, with a total AC-system.

(Aaranya-chapter 48 - slokas 8, & 9).

The city was comparable to the celestial city of Amaravathy, in sheer beauty, structure and totally protected by the mighty ocean. We can appreciate this when we remember that although the island nations, Britain and Japan are not far away from the mainland, by their isolation, they were rarely invaded. Raavana boasts that his kingdom is 1,000 miles away from civilsation as an isolated island. He ruled without care and worry!

The city itself was protected by huge ramparts, with moats, with archways, gates etc. The houses were decorated with costly gems and pearls. Even 'golden' houses you could find there (Aaranya-chapter 48-slokas 10 to 13). It was a city of Culture. Sound of music everywhere, rhythm sounds from Thoorya and Mridunga beats. Trees lining up boulevards. Full of vehicles, easy transport facilities, with plenty of elephants and horses. And by command of Raavana one could enjoy ***fresh fruit*** at all times and seasons. If Raavana was ruling instead, we would be getting fresh mango in January, even in Srinagar.

The city itself was surrounded by any number of mountains. Hanumaan was stunned when after his memorable solo flight to Lanka, he lands at a mountain and takes a look at this glorious Lanka. (Sundhara-chapter2-) Trees and trees everywhere, forests, lovely gardens, ponds and lakes with Uthphala flowers floating and giving fragrance! In the city proper, roads and boulevards were clean, broad, well laid. Hundreds of watch towers so that citizens can move about freely in safety. The rows of houses. Here Vaalmeeki says that they appeared like a constellation of stars, looking like cloud in the autumn. The heart of the city was located in the peaks of a mountain! Vaalmeeki says it appeared that Lanka was in heaven rather than in earth. The city appeared as though it was 'hanging' like a garland!

By the command of Raavana, the moon always gave some light at night. Power failure thus is a rare occurrence in Lanka. Even Ayodhya did not enjoy AC. But then it was ruled by a 'people's man, (Dhasharatha)! like our country ruled by people's men today. Ofcourse Ayodhya is in UP, our politician's paradise, in more ways than one!

(Sundhara-chapter 4) "The city was resplendent with mighty mansions built according to Vardhaman Architecture. (Modern architects can do some research on this!) Some were white like white clouds. (like against the blue sky).Night life in Lanka is indescribable. It will put some of the cities in the "West" to shame. Lovely women who were like celestial Apsara women sang in three tones. Liquor flowed freely. There was always wine women and song. But it was not all wine and song and women. You could hear Holy Chants from scriptures recited in some of the mansions. Let us not forget that Raavana was a master of Saama Vedha. We had already covered this in our character on Raavana. Infact some citizens, that is, some demons were so devoted to Vedhic studies and Shaasthras, that they always recited the Vedhas. There were ofcourse some priests from among demons. We write all this to clear a misconception, that in Raavana's kingdom, it was only wine, women and song and 'butchery' ***Vaalmeeki wrote without fear or favour.*** He presents the citizens, the demons of Lanka in proper perspective. Some of these priests sang laudatory verses on their king Raavana. The city was swarmed by armed demons. The army was always in readiness. Tough soldiers lined up important boulevards. There were any number of' 'foot' soldiers although there were soldiers on horse back, carts etc, They were all armed with diverse weapons.

Vaalmeeki thus has a high praise for this city and the citizens .

Raavana's mansion is so beautiful that Hanumaan is stunned; he says (Sundhara-chapter-9) Gist: "This may be heaven! This may be celestial world! This may be the city of Gandharvas!" Thousands of lovely ladies Hanumaan saw at night, wearing foremost garlands and dresses, with various 'Make-ups' Everything beautiful: Yet as this is demon land, there are any number of ugly, monstrous looking women. We need not waste a description of them.excepting to say that Raavana used some of them when he resorted to carrot and stick technique on persons who did not submit to him. Raavana terrorised them with ugly demons and demonesses.

In Raavana's Lanka you have an Aircraft- Airstation ***Pushpak***. Raavana 'snatched' this divine Aircraft-Air station from his brother Kubhaera after a bitter fight with him. We crave your indulgence, readers! It is difficult to describe this unique transport. This= Vimaana= this Aircraft mansion, can fly at any speed, can fly anywhere, does not need any 3 mile take off strip. It could be a Moth plane or could be a space ship carrying a metropolis! One thing we can affirm:--. You will never be on the 'waiting' list at your airport if Pushpak vimaana is around--. It 'grows' sideways and also upwards to suit passenger traffic!. Our modern scientists and technologists connected with the Air craft industry should give some thought to this unique, mythological 'contraption'! We cannot comprehend such a transport even in our century when we 'reached' Moon and Mars! We will conclude by what Vibeeshana said after becoming king of Lanka when Raama wanted to get back to Ayodhya quickly-that is a distance of 4,000 KM (Yudh-Chapter 124- sloka 8) "Oh Raama! I Will Take You Back To Your City In Just Under A Day" Lanka is glorious, so is their citizens, so is their ruler Raavana.

19: The BRAHMA RISHI -Vishwaamithra

In Vaalmeeki Raamaayana we find references to any number of spiritual men, sages, rishi-s, thapaswins (men of penance). We have Vasishta who was the official priest of the Ikshwaaku kings. We have a great man Agasthya, who put an end to the arrogance of Vindhya mountain when it started growing up, disturbing the ecology and environment of the sub continent. If we single out Vishwaamithra as a subject for discussion here, there is a good reason. (Elsewhere we shall give a list of all sages and Rishis in this epic) If we take the liberty of saying that the first book of Vaalmeeki Raamaayana, the Baala Kaanda, is Vishwaamithra Kaanda, very few can find fault with us. .

Vishwaamithra moulded Raama, the principal character of this epic. He taught him history and geography during his short stay with him in his hermitage. And he also arranged to test his bravery at Mithila. Raama exhibited his bravery by breaking the Divine Bow kept by King Janaka at Mithila. (Bala-chapter-67). And Vishwaaithra, not only arranged the marriage of Raama with Seetha, he made sure that all the sons of King Dhasharatha got married at the same time at Mithila to 'sisters' of Seetha. (Baala-chapter-72-slokas 5 to 9) Vishwaamithra addresses Janaka: Gist "Oh King Janaka! We are seeking the marriage of the two daughters of your brother Kushadwaja for the other sons of Dhasharatha." The marriage of the four brothers into the family of Janaka is thus blessed by Vishwaamithra.

If Vaalmeeki has portrayed Vishwaamithra as a marriage broker, it is with a purpose. A broker profits, but for himself. But great men do this for welfare of the world. Herein lies the difference.

The respect Vishwaamithra commands may be seen in (Baala-chapter 18) Desirous of meeting Dhasharatha, Vishwaamithra on reaching the palace of Ayodhya tells the guards "Inform Immediately, That Son of Gaadhi Of Kushika Family Has Come" We may observe that Vishwaamithra's request is a command for immediate audience with the king! Dhasharatha is no ordinary king, a sort of emperor! And the king ofcourse went at once along with his ministers, his chief priest Vasishta, as though Indra is summoned by God Brahma. Vishwaamithra is never kept waiting!

We all know the purpose of Vishwaamithra's visit to Ayodhya. He wants the assistance of Dhasharatha's son Raama to be on guard when he is performing a yaaga in his hermitage which calls for total abstinence of force by him. The world knows that Vishwaamithra can destroy any one if he chooses to exhibit his wrath. He does not need any protector, But this Yaaga calls for total "Dheeksha", total 'surrender' to Parama-Aathman. He cannot and should not exhibit anger or force on any one. And certain demons are always bent on spoiling his rituals at his hermitage. As Raama is a Kshathriya and a warrior, it becomes the duty of the king to offer protection, particularly to such a great Rishi, like Vishwaamithra. Yet Dhasharatha refuses because he feels his son is too immature to take on demons. and offer protection. We have caste coming into play. It is the duty of a kshathriya! (By baala-chapter 21-slokas 5 to 21), we have the glimpse of the greatness of Vishwaamithra from Vasishta when he presses his king to honour Vishwaamithra's request and send his son Raama: Gist

"Like nectar that cannot be 'touched' by fire, whether your son Raama is mature enough, whether he is proficient or not, when he is with Vishwaamithra, nothing can 'touch' him.

Vishwaamithra is a master of all weapons although a sage" And Vasishta has this to say about him "In all the three worlds, moving and non moving, none really 'know' him.

And none can really know him" Coming from the Great Brahma Rishi Vasishta, this cannot be far from truth. and he adds "Rishi-s know him not, celestials know him not, nor Asuras, nor demons, nor kinnaras, any one in the world. He is The Embodiment of Dharma. He is foremost in wisdom. And foremost in penance" And let not Dhasharatha think that Vishwaamithra needs the assistance of his son Raama because of his incapability. "As for the destruction of these demons who harm his yaaga, he is capable of doing this himself without any one. Yet, for the sake of doing good to Raama, he wants to take him along to his hermitage"

No other certificate is needed. Vishwaamithra is Unique

Raama accompanied by his brother Lakshmana, goes along with Vishwaamithra, quite an experience for the brothers. They learn the art of discharging and controlling the divine weapons. They are taught Bala and Athibala. two hymns that drive away tiresomeness and thirst. They learn history and geography. Their education in such a short stay with Vishwaamithra is thus total.

Vishwaamithra is thus a great complete teacher.

Vishwaamithra planned all this because he wanted Raama to be totally 'equipped' when he takes on Raavana and his evil demons years later.

Thus Vishwaamithra is a Dheerga Dharshi= A Seer

Vishwaamithra did this for the welfare of The world

We had said that Baala kaanda is Vishwaamithra's kaanda. From chapters 19 to almost the end, that is till the 73rd chapter, it is all Vishwaamithra. We may summarise these chapters here or indicate a few events here. (Baala kaanda) Vishwaamithra's first teaching starts with two hymns, Bala and Athibala. (chapter 22-slokas15 to 18) Gist: "When you recite these two hymns, these two 'knowledge' that are God Brahma's daughters, you will command the respect of all the worlds. And there will be no hunger, thirst tiresomeness for you" And in chapters 27 & 28. Vishwaamithra teaches Raama, all the divine weapons come in handy when he fights demons and when he takes on Raavana himself and in the great war.

It is interesting to note that Vishwaamithra teaches these weapons only to Raama. But Raama teaches them to Lakshmana (chapter28-sloka 16) "Then the resplendent Raama, ***by the command of Vishwaamithra***, the expounder of The Supreme 'Brammam', taught all this to Lakshmana"

Vaalmeeki does not give any reason why Vishwaamithra did not teach both of them simultaneously.

In Raama, Vishwaamithra has an ideal student. Time and again Raama's curiosity arises and he must know! And Vishwaamithra is only too glad to teach his most beloved disciple. On their journey through 'thataka' forest, while crossing the river, Raama expresses surprise that there is a terrible sound emanating from the bottom of the river.. (Bala-chapter 24-slokas 8 to 10) The sage tells him: Gist: "Oh Raama! Conceived in mind by God Brahma, a lake was created in mount Kailash. Being created by the mind, it became Manas-mind creation. (Modern Mansarovar in China-India in Himaalayan range). River Sarayu that flows around Ayodhya gets swollen through Manasarovar, and the sound at this place is because of this violent confluence. Sarayu joins Ganges".

When they reach Thataka forest, Raama is astounded by the gruesome looking desolate forest. (Bala-chapter-24-slokas 17 to 28) Vishwaamithra enlightens him about the history of this place, how this region which once was a prosperous one, was called Maladha and Karusha But this was being ravished and destroyed by demoness Thaataka. Vishwaamithra has brought Raama through this territory to free this place from the evil minded Thaataka and

Maarecha. "Oh Raama! Blocking the way she lives about 2 yojanas from here. ***By my command, you should kill*** her" Raama is a Kshathriya warrior, a prince of the great Ikshwaakus. How can he kill a woman? This exercised his mind. Vishwaamithra cannot be challenged or refused. He realises that Raama is 'fighting' within himself. It was a test of chivalry for Raama We have written this story at length only for this purpose-To bring out the character of Vishwaamithra. He quotes precedents. He knows Raama goes by norms and practices. So he tells him (Bala - Chapter25-slokas 22 to 24) "Long ago Indra killed Virochana's daughter Mandara when she desired to crush the earth! The mother of Kavya who was resolute in vows and who was Bhrigu's wife, was killed by God Vishnu when she wanted to destroy Indra." These were women, killed by men, given to chivalry. Raama has no choice. He kills Thataka. Vishwaamithra wants Raama to carry no stain with him as having killed a woman. So he enlightens him with precedents. After all Raama is going to be the king of Ayodhya.

The wisdom of Vishwaamithra is revealed by this incident.

When Vishwaamithra reaches his hermitage to perform his Yaaga, Raama asks him (Baala-chapter 29)

After narrating about the history of this Sidhdha Hermitage, Vishwaamithra (by sloka 46) says "Oh Raama! We shall enter Sidha hermitage" Saying thus, Vishwaamithra adds ***"As this hermitage is mine, it is also yours"***

It is wrong to think that a sage ceases to be a sage if he exhibits his love. Vishwaamithra is a renowned man of penance, without any attachment Yet here he says what belongs to him belongs to Raama as well. Like any one coming into contact with Raama, the delighter, ***Vishwaamithra also has special affection for Raama***!

Vishwaamithra describes his own family to Raama. So much affection he has for Raama..

And when Vishwaamithra having successfully completed his Yaga thanks to Raama, decides to return, he takes Raama to Mithila first, so that Raama could exhibit his dexterity as a mighty warrior by stringing up a Divine Bow. There was also a prize for valour. Janaka had promised the hand of his daughter Seetha to any brave warrior who could handle the divine Bow. On the way to Mithila Vishwaamithra narrates The Birth of India's foremost deity, Kumar or Skandha. He narrates about Raama's fore father King Sagara. The bringing down of Ganges to earth by his forefather Bageeratha, so many stories relating to history and geography. But one story is of special significance because Vishwaamithra being humane, makes Raama visit the territory of Visaala where Ahalya was 'living' as a stone for 1,000 years being cursed by her husband Sage Gauthama for her affair with Indra. Vishwaamithra wanted to resurrect her. He knew that Raama's presence at this gruesome sight will discharge Ahalya's curse and that she would rejoin her husband, her sin washed away by the mere sight of Raama.

And hearing of Vishwaamithra's arrival at Mithila with Raama and Lakshmana, Janaka at once went along with his priests and his chief adviser, Shathaanand, to receive him. Vishwaamithra always commanded great respect. (Baala-chapter 50-sloka 6) Vaalmeeki uses the word = *Vinaya= "Hearing the arrival of Vishwaamithra, Janaka at once went towards him in ***great humility*** accompanied by Shathaanand" Janaka who was in the midst of a yaga he was performing at Mithila, says (slokas 13 & 14) "By my lord's presence, by your very sight, the fruits of my yaaga have already been obtained by me. As you have condescended to visit me, I am indeed most blessed, most fortunate" Vishwaamithra commanded such the respect. Ofcourse purpose of his visit was entirely different. Not to take part in the king's yaaga but for a more important purpose. Raama must exhibit his power by stringing up the divine Bow kept there, and thus he wanted Raama to be wed to Seetha, daughter of Janaka, as prize for his valour. If events turn out exactly as Vishwaamithra wanted, it is not surprising. ***Vishwaamithra was a great sage, a Seer. He does everything for welfare of the world. His name itself is worthy of this = Vishwasya Mithra= friend of the world.***

Shathaanand is a very great man. He is adviser and priest to king Janaka. And he is the son of Ahalya and sage Gauthama. His mother Ahalya had just been resurrected by Raama thanks to Vishwaamithra who took Raama to Visaala territory where she had remained a stone for many many years cursed by her husband for her affair with Indra. This is the scenario. Shathaanand is indeed happy. We will be writing about this incident in detail elsewhere, but we are now on Vishwaamithra Shathaananda by way of expressing his gratitude to Vishwaamithra, tells Raama how fortunate he is that he has Vishwaamithra as his Guru-teacher. He begins to narrate Vishwaamithra's life story, how he was once a mighty king with the army of Akshowhini-s (four some army) and finally became a great man of penance with the title of Brahma Rishi. Chapters 51 to 65 of Baala kaanda, it is all about Vishwaamithra. What it takes to become such a great man of penance. And a Brahma rishi. We have, from Raaja-king, to Raja-rishi, then to rishi, then to Maha rishi, and finally Brahma rishi, the highest... All the 15 chapters, are very interesting reading. They describe the various stages of his personality. It all started with his enmity to Brahma rishi Vasishta, when, as a mighty king, he visits him and enjoys his hospitality. But he abuses Vasishta's hospitality by wanting the divine, holy cow Kaamadenu, as a king's 'treasure', by the divine right of kings! This cow is not an ordinary cow. It is a celestial cow, can offer more than just milk! That is where the trouble started. Vasishta refuses to make a present of the cow. Vishwaamithra 'laughs' at his impudence and uses force to snatch it from his hermitage. Vishwaamithra gets a taste of what this divine cow can do. It 'creates' a mighty army! Vishwaamithra loses his army and his self-respect. Enmity with Vasishta has begun! He must teach Vasishta a lesson. So begins penance. Brahma offers him use of the celestial weapons. Armed with all this, with the knowledge of Dhanur vedha, he demolishes Vasishta's hermitage. Vasishta is furious, rarely he is in wrath. With one ROD, with chants of Brahmam, Vasishta destroys Vishwaamithra totally, sparing just his life. Vishwaamithra realises the power of Brahmam as he expresses thus in sheer exasperation(Baala -chapter 56-sloka 23) "Fie, fie. Shame on the power of Kshathriya. It is only the Power of Brahmam that is real power"

If the analogy is not taken literally, how can conventional and common technological weapons, stand before weapons created by 'sages' like Einstein whose thought equation E=MCC (Energy, E, equals Mass, M, multiplied by square of Velocity of Light- C) releases Energy beyond comprehension.

Shathaanand takes us through the various penances of Vishwaamithra, various obstacles to his penance. Ultimately he gives up his wrath, anger, enmity with Vasishta, and attains Brahmam. He becomes a Brahma Rishi.

He tells Raama while concluding his story of Vishwaamithra and we will also conclude this write up on Vishwaamithra with what Shathaananda tells Raama (Baala-Chapter 65- slokas 28 to 36) "Oh Raama! The state of Brahmam was obtained by this great 'soul'. He is the Foremost of Rishi-s. He is the embodiment of penance. He practices Dharma, ever. He is foremost refuge in 'bravery'."

And Janaka affirms "Oh, the foremost among the foremost, Brahma Rishi! By your very sight I am purefied. By your presence, I have obtained Merit=Punnya Your penance is unparalelled. Your power is unique. There is never full satisfaction to hear your story"

Creation is the work of The Gods! Brahma creates. Yet while concluding a write up on Vishwaamithra, there will be a serious omission if we forget to mention, that Vishwaamithra, in great wrath, created another world, with celestials and all, and he made Raama's forefather Thrishanku.lord of this world when he bemoaned that Indra was not seen there, in this new world! (Baala-chapter 60-sloka 23) gist;"So what? I will create another Indra. But why do you need Indra at all. Let your world be without Indra! "***Yes. Vishwaamithra is a Creator as well!***

20: VASISHTA

Among Rishi's we have Raaja rishi,_Rishi, Maha Rishi, Dheva Rishi, and Brahma Rishi. Vasishta is not only a Brahma Rishi, he is one of the 'Select', among the Seven-Saptha Rishi-s. (Athri, Bhrigu, Kuthsa, Vasishta, Gowthama, Kaashyapa, and Aangeerasa). He is The chief priest of the Ikshwaaku kings. ***His word is law.***

When Dhasharatha hesitates to send Raama with Vishwaamithra to the forest to protect his Yaaga at his hermitage, Vasishta has the last word (Baala-chapter 21-slokas 6 to 21) Gist: "Oh Dhasharatha! You are known in all the worlds that you are a man of Dharma. Having told Vishwaamithra = I will do what you say = if you do not keep your word by refusing to send Raama with him, there will be no fruits for all your previous rites, rituals and yaagas. If Vishwaamithra makes this request to you to send Raama with him to offer protection to his yaaga at his hermitage, it is only for doing good to your son. Vishwamithra does not need any one to 'protect' him or his Yaaga."That was enough for Dhasharatha and he gladly accepts his advice. Such was his influence over the Ikshwaakus.

When God Brahma finally bestows the Title of Brahma Rishi upon Vishwaamithra, this did not fully satisfy the happy Vishwaamithra. He wanted Vasishta to recognise him as a Brahma Rishi! (Baala-chapter 65-sloka 24) Gist "This son of God Brahma, Vasishta, foremost among those wellversed in Brahma Vedha, and Kshathriya Vedha as well, should speak of me as a Brahma Rishi........" Here is a case where a certificate from Brahma Himself does not satisfy a person: from God who is Vedha personified: but wants a certificate from a human being!

Such is the respect Vasishta commanded. And till Vasishta acclaims "So Be It", he would not 'leave' Brahma and the celestial lords!

Vasishta ofcourse performs Yaagas for Dhasharatha. He is master of rituals (Baala- chapter 14). And even choosing proper names for the princes, for Raama and his brothers, is done by Vasishta (Bala- chapter 18-sloka 21).

During the marriage ceremony of his sons at Mithila, this is how he introduces Vasishta to King Janaka (Baala-chapter 70-sloka 17) "Oh great king Janaka! The Lord Rishi, this Vasishta, is 'God' to our Ikshwaakus. It should be known to you that in all our matters, He Is The One To Speak (first)" Such is the respect he commanded.

And during the marriage ceremony Vasishta who presides over all the rituals (Baala-chapter 73-slokas 19 & 20) King

Janaka requests Vasishta:" Oh Lord! You must perform the marriage ceremony of Raama, the delighter..
Oh the foremost among those knowing Brahmam! There is nothing that is not known to you........." Such is the respect he commanded from kings of other territories!
During the earlier years, when Vishwaamithra considered Vasishta as his sworn enemy, when in wrath he curses his 100 sons (Baala-chapter 59) Vasishta remains calm, does not curse Vishwaamithra! Later they not only became friends, but developed great respect and affection for each other
Vasishta is a seer. When Dhasharatha along with his newly wed sons and daughters.in.law was returning to Ayodhya from Mithila along with his army and entourage, he was totally stupefied with fear, at the sight of the terrible Parashu-Raama confronting him with axe and bow in hand. (Bala-chapter 74-sloka 16) Vasishta, knowing before hand what it is all about, tells Dhasharatha thus:
"Oh Dhasharatha! There is ***Divine Sanction*** to this. May this torment of yours be given up! "Ofcourse we know that. Dhasharatha's Raama humbles the terrible Brahmin Raama, The Parashu Raama & once and for all, the caste war ends. This was the divine sanction Vasishta had 'Seen'!
Vasishta being a great man of penance and having seen long, long years, is a man of total restraint and composure. Yet Vaalmeeki portrays him slightly differently on a couple of occasions.
When Raama was all set to leave Ayodhya on his 14 year exile and had even discarded his costly royal robes for bark dress of a mendicant and had put on his wife Seetha, a similar apparel, it was too much for even the saintly Vasishta. (Ayodhya-chapter 37-slokas 22 to 36) He rebukes Kaikeyi Gist: "Oh Insolent Kaikeyi, Oh foolish woman! Oh the evil one bringing downfall of this glorious Ikshwakus.!

Princess Seetha need not go on exile dressed up in these bark dress" This agony of Vasishta is understandable. After all even a sage is human. None would like to see a princess dressed up like a 'beggar' But what follows from Vasishta is rather strange "Let Seetha occupy the royal seat, that is by right, Raama's, (which you have snatched away) "By what norms or royal code can Vasishta suggest this? Ofcourse, we have in India today wife having the 'divine' right to take over her husband's position to rule over a state! But Ikshwaakus are known to be strict followers of tradition and norms.

Here Vaalmeeki portrays Vasishta as having lost his cool!

Vasishta is a deeply religious man. A man of Rituals. A master of Rituals. Sometimes he could be rather severe and 'cruel' when rituals are not done according to procedure and the code.

When Bharatha was in a state of shock at the twin calamity that had struck him, namely the death of his father and a 14 year exile on Raama, and could not direct his mind for performing the last rites of his father, Vasishta admonishes him. (Ayodha-chapter 76=sloka 2) Gist "Oh famous prince Bharatha! Enough of this grieving! You do the foremost last rites for your father at proper time" and again when on 13 th day, when Bharatha was not the directing his mind to the rituals Vasishta rebukes him (ayodhya-chapter 77-slokas 22 to 26) Gist: "Oh Bharatha!

Today is the thirteenth day of your father's death. Why are delaying doing oblations for your father?"

Vasishta was a stickler for Rituals.

Vasishta expounda the philosophy of life and death.

"In all beings there exists three laws without discrimination- The law of duality-male-female happiness and sorrow- birth and death. Inevitable as these are, you should not grieve, Bharatha"

But what is most remarkable about Vasishta is that he is a liberal! Steeped in rituals, totally religious, yet, he could see another's point of view in a different light, forgetting himself. When the old, noble but atheistic Jaabaali who was Dhasharatha's adviser couldn't stand the four brothers Raama, Lakshmana, Bharatha and Shathrugna wasting away their time in forest talking about rituals for their father like Gaya Shraadha without worrying about affairs of the state, without trying to get back to Ayodhya, he went on a tirade against Raama.We will be carrying this elsewhere.in our Guide. For once Raama is enraged, all because Jaabaali had preached atheism to press home his point..When he starts his counter offensive against the old noble and wise Jaabaali, Vasishta is shocked. Normally if one were deeply religious and a believer of Faith and a believer of Rituals that go with Faith, we would expect him to support Raama. Afterall Raama carried most of Vasishta's views. But Vasishta is not only a liberal man but also respects elders and he wants Raama to remember that Jaabaali was no ordinary person to be talked to by him like the way he did.

So Vasishta in a few words stops Raama (Ayodhya-chapter 110- sloka 1 & 2) Gist: "Raama! Remember Jaabaali knows the origin of the world (origin of species)! He had said all this to convince you to return to Ayodhya which is without a ruler now"

Not content with this Vasishta begins the narration; the origin of the world as if to say that Jaabali knows all this. Thus Vasishta warns Raama to be more guarded when he talks to elders with different views!

No wonder the brahma Rshi is a Saptha Rishi

This is Vasishta

21: AGASTHYA

During his exile Raama is blessed by many sages. He enjoys their hospitality. The sages are so fond of him that some of them treat him like a son! Raama is such a man. But his meeting with Sage Agasthya is of importance.Refer Aaranya-chapters 11,12,13):Agasthya's service to Raama is remarkable. He taught Aadithya Hridhaya to Raama. But we shall refer to this later in the Guide.

While on way to Agasthya's hermitage, Raama narrates the sages' greatness to Lakshmana (Gist of chapter11)

"Once there lived two cruel and sadistic demons, Vaathaapi and his brother Ilvala. They not only killed sages and innocent men of penance, but their method was sadistic Ilvala, taking the form of a brahmin, will invite sages to share the 'oblations of his yaaga'. Earlier, Vaathaapi, taking the magical form of a goat, would offer himself to Holy fire and when the oblations, that is, the cooked 'meat' is eaten by these poor sages and men, Ilvala would call = Oh Vaathaapi, come out = And taking back his normal form of demon, Vaathaapi would rip open their stomach and come out, thus killing these persons who had mistakenly joined in Ilvala's yaaga! Thousands and thousands of innocent persons living in forest were killed by these two most evil, cruel demons" Continuing his story to Lakshmana, Raama says one day, Agasthya deciding to put an end to these two, offered himself as a poor Brahmin for partaking oblations. He ate the oblations offered, the cooked goat meat' from the holy fire. When Ilvala shouted = Oh Vaathaapi, come out = Agasthya told him "How can your brother Vaathaapi come out of my stomach ripping it open, when I have digested him along with his goat body!"

And by his 'power' Agasthya burnt Ivala.as well.

This is the Agasthya Raama visits

We have yet another. The foremost mountain Vindhyas, became arrogant, began to grow taller and wider, trying to cover up everything, beating the Himaalayas. It tried to cover up even the Sun. But fearing Agasthya, finally Vindhyas stopped growing, giving thus free movement between North India and South India!

This is Agasthya =Aga-mountain; Sthaa-Sthi-to press, hurl= (sloka 88 of Aranya-chapter 11) Raama says "He is worshipped by the world. He is a Saadhu ever devoted to the welfare of the good. He will bring prosperity to any one who seeks him" Agasthya is considered a Sage of The South.

His affection for Raama is such that (Aaranya-chapter12-sloka 11) Agasthya is rather annoyed with his disciples "Why was Raama who is with Seetha and Lakshmana, not brought before me duly honoured......" thus telling them that Raama needs no invitation, and he should not be kept waiting for an audience with him!

Offering Raama hospitality, the sage begins his 'discourse' Gist: (slokas30 to 40) "Oh Raama! If a sage does not conduct himself properly, then he will eat his own flesh for food. He will be treated with contempt as a ***False Witness!*** You, Raama are the king of the world! Follower of Dharma! Great Charioteer! Most honoured and most worthy of honour!"

It is wrong to think that a sage ceases to be a sage, if he does not think about mundane aspects of life. ***Agasthya is also a practical man***, knows that Raama needs weapons with him even as a mendicant in forest if he has to protect innocent persons living here. So offers Raama "Oh Raama the tiger of men! This mighty celestial bow, decorated in gold and with gems, created by the divine architect Vishwakarma, is God Vishnu's bow.

These foremost arrows are like burning Sun. They were offered by God Brahma. And two quivers, with unlimited supply of arrows, were given by Lord Indra to me. And here is a sword, decorated in gold. Oh Raama! For the sake of victory for you always, please accept all these from me. And Lord Indra had given me an armour which cannot be pierced. Accept this as well".

Having offered all these, the great 'Seer' that he is, Agasthya tells Raama "If and when you entertain doubt about your victory, if you become low spirited, Lord Indra's charioteer, Maathali, will come to you with his chariot and offer you his service". Being very humane, human as well, Agasthya like a good host asks Raama (Aaranay-chapter13-) "Oh Raama! Was the night spent in comfort pleasantly" It is, we repeat, wrong to think that a sage ceases to be sage if he now and then addresses himself to mundane things of life. A sage is human. He is not God. He is not a living God on earth. Raama acknowledges his hospitality thus. "By you, our most worshipful lord, we have been duly honoured! With offer of beds, quilts, etc. With food and all desirables! "And Raama adds this, how he enjoyed Agasthya's hospitality ".....we enjoyed just like in our palace at Ayodhya, of king Dhasharatha......"

Agasthya gives a 'parting' advice even as Raama takes leave of him "Oh Raama, the period of exile stipulated by king Dhasharatha will pass off. Fulfilling your commitment you will then live happily."

But when Agasthya, out of his deep attachment to Raama praises him thus "Your father king Dhasharatha is indeed most blessed as he has you as his son. And like your forefather Yayaathi, is 'saved' by you from ignominy" Raama likes being praised, but not at the cost of such remarks at his father. So he is quick with the rejoinder "Oh Muni Agasthya! I am indeed honoured and most pleased that my lord has such a high opinion of me. But the king my father Dhasharatha was not 'saved' by me, helped to 'cross over the ocean of sin' By his own virtues, by his own yaagas, he was 'saved' and crossed the ocean of sin. My father king Dhasharatha went to heaven by his deeds, not through services done by his son or anyone else" ***We write in detail, because Vaalmeeki always drives home truths, from time to time***.

A sage is also very human. Here is a very great muni, Agasthya whose love and admiration for Raama is such, that he is concerned about the hospitality he extends Raama in his hermitage in forest! Knowing what a great man King Dhasharatha was, his endearment to Raama makes him praise Raama at the cost of his father. ***Vaalmeeki brings home a truth here. Never praise one at the cost of another, particularly when the other one is also a remarkable person***!

Agasthya's affection for Raama is such that he exhibits some concern for Seetha. After all Seetha is a woman and she must be treated with extra consideration particularly in forest. After telling Raama that he should offer protection to those innocent persons living in Dhandaka forest, he says. (Aaranya-chapter 13-slokas 35 to 47) Gist" I am pleased you have come to meet me along with your wife Seetha and Lakshmana. This girl, who is used to comforts, out of her love and devotion to you, has come along to the forest which is abundant in hardships. You must act in such a way, she will be ever happy here" Agasthya differentiates between a common woman and Seetha ***exhibiting his chauvinism***!" Ever since creation, women generally gratify men who are in affluent circumstances! They abandon men when they are down! This is their nature! In fickleness, women are like lightning, In harshness, like sharp arrows, like wind swift to abandon men' ***Agasthya,the male chauvinist!***

22: RISHYASHRINGA

Rishyashringa is a saint. When king Dhasharatha decides to perform Ashwamedha Yaaga for progeny, his charioteer and minister, Sumanthra advises him that for successful completion of his Yaga, he should invite Rishyashringa to preside over the ceremonies. (Bala-chapters 9 & 10). The reason is not far to seek. Once during a severe draught in Anga kingdom, when Rishyshringa set foot in the soil, there was heavy downpour, bringing relief to the citizens. Under the patronage of Rishyshringa, Dhasharatha not only completes his Yaaga, he is also blessed with four children Raama, Lakshmana, Bharatha and Shathrugna.

Rishyashringa was the son of sage Vibhandaka. But unlike other great sages and rishi-s, Vibhandaka was so narrow minded, that from his childhood; he isolated his son totally from civilisation. Even as a youth of teens, he had never known women. Infact he was not even aware that in the human race there were two sexes! But Rishyshringa from childhood was devoted to penance. Vibhandaka's hermitage was isolated, in the deep forest. Rishyshringa even as a young boy, by virtue of his total dedication to penance, had 'divine' powers.

It was at about that time, King of Anga, Romapaadha, was very much concerned about continuing draught in his kingdom, causing misery to all. When he sought advice, his ministers told him that the only remedy lay in bringing Rishyashringa to the capital and offer him his daughter Shaantha in marriage. This was almost a hopeless task as Rishyashringa was 'closely' guarded by his father Vibandaka and totally isolated and could not easily be

enticed to come to the capital. The clever Ministers. They suggested a strategy which from time immemorial was ever efficacious. = Girls= Send lovely damsels, they will 'work' on this innocent Rishyashringa and entice him and bring him to the capital, father or no father! Valmeeki has narrated all this in (Bala-chapters 9 to 12) beautifully and poetically. Ofcourse Rishyashringa falls for this trick and leaves his hermitage and his father Vibandaka and even as he enters Anga territory, poet Vaalmeeki says, rain began to pour. Infact Rishyashringa had 'brought' rain with him! And he was married to the king's daughter. Shantha and lived in the capital for ever! If we write about Rishyashringa at length here, it is to bring home a point.
Vaalmeeki by this episode conveys another Truth.
Censorship and isolation can isolate a person only for some time. Society cannot be controlled for long by isolating it from the world of reality. If Rishyashringa had not been isolated from society and women, he would never have 'fallen' to these dames so easily. He would have been wise enough to think and decide for himself! His father sage Vibhandaka, unlike other sages, tried to 'protect' his son. But he chose the wrong way.

But Rishyashringa was a saint. When one obtains his grace and patronage only good will accrue to him. Dhasharatha, who had no children over long years, is blessed with four noble sons all due to the grace and patronage of Rishyashringa.

Some good demons and demonesses

23: THRIJATA

This Book has carried a number of personalities under the head 'Character' We should not get the impression that every one in the demon land was bad and cruel. In

Vaalmeeki Raamaayana there are quite a few demonesses who not only were humane and considerate, but some of them could foresee the future. One such demoness was Thrijata. (woman with three- knotted hair style) She was one of the guards protecting Seetha at Ashoka forest when she was held prisoner by Raavana. There is a description of the many gruesome, cruel demonesses who guarded Seetha (Sundhara- chapter 17). It is gruesome reading! Poor Seetha not only had to bear their sight, but also their taunts, threats, their cajoling, and what not. Their king Raavana had ordered them to use the 'Carrot-Stick' technique to bring her around, to make Seetha submit to him voluntarily. Seetha did not respond or give them any encouragement. It is Raama, only Raama for her, ever.

When some of these demonesses threaten to kill Seetha and eat her up, Thrijata warns her colleagues. (Sundhara- chapter 27-slokas 6 to 66) Gist: "Oh ye Un-Aaryan demonesses! Eat me up, if you like! But do not eat Seetha, who is beloved of all." After saying this, she narrates about a dream she had 'seen' In this long chapter Vaalmeeki describes Trijata's dream. At one point Thrijata says (sloka 26) "....Raama who delights one and all, ***became himself God Vishnu***, as he was seated in foremost seat" By this Vaalmeeki tells us that Thrijata, although a demoness through her dream knew that Raama was no man but the incarnation of God Vishnu. Only a few in Raamaayana knew Raama as incarnation.

Some sages knew through their spiritual power and far sight. Even Raama was not aware that he is Vishnu on earth! Yet this demoness 'sees' Raama and Seetha as Vishnu & Lakshmi!

Thrijata's vision takes her even far! "He revealed himself as The Supreme Brahmam! The Supreme Reality (truth)! The Supreme Knowledge (Vedha)! The Supreme Penance! The

Supreme Seed (creator)! The Supreme Cause and Effect! The Supreme body!"

God had revealed Himself to Thrijata in her dream Thrijata was a demoness, living in the demon land! God reveals Himself in many ways to many! Did not Krishna reveal Himself to his foster mother Yashodha by opening his mouth, in the other epic, Mahaa Bhaaratha! Deeply religious people who read Vaalmeeki Raamaayana, see in Thrijata's dream, God's revelation!

24: SARAMA

There is another good demoness who was ever kind to Seetha during her captivity in Lanka. (Yudha-chapter33). When Seetha was being duped and was stupefied by being shown the 'head' of Raama as though he was slain in battle, all by magic by Raavana, it is Sarama who consoles Seetha telling her that Raama is well and is ready for war with Raavana to retrieve her and the 'head' that was exhibited to her is only a replica of her husband created by magic to fool her so that Seetha may submit to him. (by slokas 1 to 3): Gist: "Seeing Seetha was stupefied by the exhibition of this magically produced 'head' of Raama, demoness Sarama approached her. This soft speaking Sarama began to console Seetha who was in terrible sorrow. She was a guard appointed by Raavana, But she was compassionate to Seetha. She treated ***Seetha as a friend***!" Sarama knows the prowess of Raama. She affirms "There is no killing of Raama who is 'tiger' of men." Sarama, even at the risk of her own life, (after all she was a guard earning her livelihood at Raavana's hands), had gone out to find what was happening at the battle field. It is Sarama who always used to give news about happenings in Lanka. Seetha was totally isolated at Ashoka forest. Gist: "Oh Seetha! Your grief is all gone. Good fortune is approaching you. Now in war, your husband Raama along with Lakshmana will kill Raavana, displaying his valour on all demons" And Sarama like Thrijata, can foresee "I am seeing Raama's arrival. The falling down of demons. I am seeing you, the most virtuous, on his lap. You will shed tears of joy only." Sarama being a demoness of some capability, assures Seetha (Yudha chapter34) Gist "Oh dark eyed Seetha!

Remember. Unseen, I am capable of flying over the sky, and meet your Raama in battle field, inform him about your welfare and return back to you. Even birds that fly fast cannot follow me in the sky!"

Seetha naturally praises her demoness friend Sarama thus "Why, you are capable of going even up to under worlds = the Paathaala = for my sake! I know what all you will do for me."

We hear from Sarama that there were quite a few demons and demonesses who were good folks, who wanted Raavana to release Seetha and make her get back to her husband Raama. (Yudh-chapter34) "Oh Seetha! The lord of demons was advised by Avidhwa, the most elderly of his ministers, to return Seetha to Raama. Although advised even by his old mother, Raavana refused. Therefore without his being killed by Raama, you will not get back freedom"

Being in service and treated well by Raavana, Thrijata and Sarama should be persons of gratitude. Infact Raamaayana begins with the term 'gratitude' = Krithagnya = Here we find these two demonesses are not only kind to Seetha, they do service for her against their king Raavana. Yet, Thrijata and Sarama are to be considered noble persons. ***Vaalmeeki brings this out. 'Gratitude' must be within the norms of Dharma.*** (In Yudh-chapter 35) we find Maalyavaan, Raavana's mother's uncle, advising Raavana. He expounds Truth & Dharma Gist: "Only when a king follows the righteous path and is educated in Shaasthras, he can remain long in wealth and power. An enemy should never be treated with contempt by a king. When a king is inferior to another, he should seek peace and treaty. The very A-Dharma (non Dharma) of yours is swallowing us all. Make peace with Raama" Raavana did have some noble men in the demon land. Only he did not make use of them!

(Some minor characters)

25: Big Bird JATAAYU

When we talk about minor characters, it is only from the standpoint of the 'body' of Raamaayana. Certainly they are not minor in character! When Seetha was being kidnapped by Raavana, and wails pitiably, big bird Jataayu hears this and puts up a fight. (Aaranya-chapters 50 & 51) Jataayu, although a bird, expounds Dharma befitting a king. Gist: "I am Jataayu, the king of vultures ! How can a king who abides by Dharma, violate another's wife, particularly wife of another 'king' like you? Turn away from this vile deed. The learned and wise illuminate their king even about Dharma, Artha & Kaama that are not discerned clearly in the Shaasthras (Has n't any one in Lanka advised about all this, that you are committing such a vile deed) A King becomes 'Dharma'. Oh Raavana! How come you, who are so fickle, who are of sinful disposition, obtained all the wealth and glory for so long? You do not realise the consequence of your deed, you have tightened your neck with a rope Who will do a deed, which when done, will bring only loss of fame, power, position and all soon? "After saying all this Jataayu gives him a warning "It is 60,000 years since I was born! I have been protecting the kingdom of birds I am very old now. You are young. You cannot carry away Seetha even as I am looking on! So

Raavana, stay for a while and fight with me if you are brave"

By this Vaalmeeki conveys a truth, a Dharma, to all of us

When evil is seen before our very eyes, we should not be silent spectators. As expected, Raavana mortally wounds Jataayu and the demon king is on his way to Lanka, carrying Seetha

Jataayu is indeed a very noble person. No wonder Raama performs his Last Rites with full honours.

26: Charioteer SUMANTHRA

Sumanthra was a minister in waiting to King Dhasharatha.

A great charioteer, he was very close to Dhasharatha. Infact he was a friend to him. Very few could meet the king without appointment. But Sumanthra could visit him whenever he had to see him. (Ayodhya-chapter13-sloka44) "The king's guards did not stop the elderly Sumanthra as they had previous standing instructions".

So in the midnight drama when queen Kaikeyi has her way and the coronation of Raama in the morning is stopped and Raama is asked to go on14 year exile, it is Sumanthra who has lot of work. Kaikeyi sends for Sumanthra, early morning(Ayodhya- chapter 13-slokas 45 to 59) : Although he was close to Dhasharatha, he never forgot to observe norms and protocol. ***Infact, one feature in Vaalmeeki is that he never stopped from mentioning about Protocol!*** This is how Dhasharatha's friend minister Sumanthra observes protocol when he is sent for by Kaikeyi to the palace. Ofcourse Sumanthra had not known anything about the midnight drama. Gist: "Like Maathali, the charioteer waking up his king, lord Indra, I am awakening you early morning. Like Vedhas awakening and beckoning God Brahma, I am waking you up May the lords of Sun, Moon,

God Shiva & Varuna ever bestow success. Oh Royal sage, my king! Wake up. You should do what is to be done. All arrangements for Raama's coronation are made. Vasishta is standing by" Poor Sumanthra! He had not realised the torment his friend and king had undergone throughout the night at the hands of his wife Kaikeyi, who had forced Dhasharatha to countermand his order of crowning Raama in the morning. So when Sumanthra had extolled the king as per protocol (a King is always woken up by praises) Dhasharatha is so depressed, as though salt is being rubbed on the wound, that he says: (Ayodhya-chapter14-slokas 59 & 60).

"Pondering over the future of his son Raama, king Dhasharatha who had lost all joy for life, addressed the charioteer Sumanthra = By your eulogies, the vitals of my body are even more cut up.=" So afflicted by grief was he that he could not speak further. The evil minded selfish Kaikeyi it is, who enlightens Sumanthra thus "Oh Sumanthra! Fatigued by keeping awake at night, but longing to see Raama, the king is subdued and sleepy. Therefore you go at once and fetch Raama.....there need be no deliberation in this matter...."

Surprisingly, Sumanthra in spite of having known Dhasharatha so well, has no inkling of what had happened at night to his king. Believes that Dhasharatha is really sleepy! ***This is rather strange!*** And Sumanthra is an old man with a lot of experience. He rushes to Raama and informs him that his father wants to see him at once. Rest is history. Kaikeyi tells her stepson that he should go on 14 year exile to make way for her own son Bharatha. Raama readily accepts to please his stepmother!

When Raama is about to leave Ayodhya, Sumanthra who could not tolerate to see his dear friend and king Dhasharatha reduced to such a pitiable state because of his beloved son being driven away from Ayodhya by Kaikeyi, rebukes Kaikeyi (Ayodhya-chapter 35) Knowing the feelings of his friend and king Dhasharatha, he spoke cruel words against Kaikeyi Gist: "Oh Kaikeyi! You are a 'killer' of your husband" As events turn out, Dhasharatha dies soon after Raama leaves, unable to bear separation from his beloved son Raama. As no one would like to hear bad about one's own mother, Sumanthra to wound Kaikeyi where it will hurt most, narrates a story about her mother, to tell the world = like mother, so is daughter =

As this is a very interesting story and as Vaalmeeki tries to convey a point or two, we will briefly narrate this. By a boon Kaikeyi's father King of Kekeya kingdom, could also understand the 'language' and conversation of living beings other than human beings.. Once while watching some ants, he burst into laughter. His wife, that is Kaikeyi's mother wanted to know the cause of his mirth! But Kaikeyi's father refused to divulge to his wife because the boon to him was such that he should not share this with anyone else. If he did, his head would burst into pieces! Here comes the cruelty. Kaikeyi's mother was such a wicked woman, she told her husband, that she couldn't care less whether her husband was dead or alive, but she must know.! Aghast by this, Kaikeyi's father, offering her some allowance for her future, drove her away from kingdom. By this Vaalmeeki brings home a point or two. In those days there were men who could 'understand' even tiny beings. Secondly, according to Vaalmeeki, in many cases, character is hereditary. So Sumanthra says =like mother, daughter=

It is Sumanthra who as a charioteer drives Raama, Lakshmana and Seetha deep into the forest to begin their 14 year exile. He is an expert charioteer. Yet when crowds follow the chariot as he drives along with Raama, it is almost impossible for him to control either his emotions or his horses! (Ayodhya-chapter 40) "Oh Charioteer, please tighten the leash, we wish to see the face of Raaama" So the crowds beg Sumanthra. Raama wants a quick get away from Ayodhya to save continued agony for the vast crowd at Ayodhya.He commands Sumanthra to drive fast. (By sloka 46) Poet Vaalmeeki describes this " Raama said = Go, Go = (While citizens and even Dhasharatha) said = Stop, stop = The heart of poor Sumanthra was as though it was caught between the wheels of his powerful chariot"

When Raama, along with Seetha and Lakshmana, get ready to cross the Ganges to go into forest to begin their exile and when he gives leave to Sumanthra to return to Ayodhya along with his chariot, we face a different Sumanthra. He forgets he is minister to Dhasharatha! This old Sumanthra would rather stay on in the forest with Raama rather than get back to Ayodhya! Such is his love for Raama! (Ayodhya-chapter52) Gist: Raama addresses Sumanthra "I cannot perceive a friend equal to you, to members of my Ikshwaaku family. You must do all that in Ayodhya in such a way your king will not grieve at my separation from him" But Sumanthra will have none of this. He is determined to follow Raama on his 14 year exile. Gist: "What am I going to tell your mother at Ayodhya when I get back = I left your son at his uncle's place = Such a lie I can never speak. But if I tell the truth that I left you in deep forest, that is truth, but this truth will kill her" Sumanthra follows this with Vaalmeeki's masterpiece (sloka 51) Gist

"I was denied the pleasure of driving you through the Royal boulevard at Ayodhya during the coronation that was denied to you. Now I will have the pleasure of driving you along these lovely forests during your exile".

When Sumanthra returns to Ayodhya alone in his chariot after dropping Raama in forest, he is in low spirits. But Raama's advice was very clear. He must not add to

Dhasharatha's torment. He conveys Raama's message to Dhasharatha calmly. And he consoles his mother thus (Ayodhya-chapter 60) Gist: "Raama lives in the forest happily, having no torment all. Lakshmana by serving Raama, is achieving great merit and fame. As for Seetha, whose heart is ever with Raama, she enjoys life in forest; so even the forest is Ayodhya for her !"

Sumanthra is certainly no 'minor' in character.

27: Friend GUHA

One of the most remarkable features in ancient India, that is Bhaarath, is that friendship had nothing to do with caste or social status. In India today, you and I, coming from different castes may be friends, thick as thieves, may share a bottle, but when it comes to promotion in our office, our caste will 'out'! In Vaalmeeki's times, it was not so. The blue blood Raama of the great Ikshwaakus, considered Guha as his friend with distinction. Guha was a tribal. A chief of hunters and fishermen.

When Raama reached the Ganges on the first day of their exile, the first man to receive him and greet him is his friend Guha. (Ayodhya-chapter 50-sloka 32) "There lived there, a chieftain ruling that place, a strong man, a man from family of hunters, Guha by name, who was well known as friend of Raama" This is how Vaalmeeki introduces Guha to us. Guha was excited. So ".......hearing Raama had come to this region, he came there, accompanied by his relatives and elderly folks" This is what Guha says on meeting Raama, after hugging him. (chapter 50) Gist: "Oh Raama! This place, is like Ayodhya for you! Who else can receive such a distinguished guest! Pray, what should be done by me for you" After greeting

Raama thus, Guha invites him to a good meal, placing before him wonderful meat and drinks

But Raama declines to partake any of these delicacies! Lest Guha would be hurt by this, Raama tells his dear friend. "Oh Guha! We are deeply honoured by your exhibition of hospitality and consideration as a friend. We are delighted." Hugging him again, Raama continues "Oh Guha! I am happy to see you in good health. My good fortune indeed! Is everything well with you, your citizens, your wealth" And now comes rather the cruel part of Raama's address to his dear friend Guha.

"But I am in no position to receive all these you have brought up for me. All these you have brought out of your deep affection for me, I regret, to leave them, untouched. Because you should now know me as not a prince but a mendicant living in forest, wearing bark material and deer skin." But after turning down all this Raama being a compassionate and considerate person, tells Guha "I will be satisfied with your offer of feed for the horses of my chariot that has brought me to the forest. Dear Guha! At this time, this alone will satisfy me greatly"

We should study Vaalmeeki in proper perspective. We have many things to learn from the dialogue between Raama and his friend Guha. A very orthodox man may not even have even a cup of tea in his best friend's house owing to his rigid (perhaps despicable) orthodoxy. But they were true to their friendship because, in Vaalmeeki's time, Dharma was the basis of friendship. Orthodoxy and caste never stood in the way. Secondly, Raama's acceptance of 14 years exile in forest is total. He is not a prince to enjoy the pleasures of Royalty. The reader should pardon us if we bring in Mahatma Gandhi here. During his imprisonment in British-India jails- indeed he spent nearly 15 years in Jail in his life of Dharma-he accepted all the rules of the Jail with equanimity, one may even say, with pleasure! No wonder Gandhi was a Vishnu Bhaktha, a Raama Bhaktha! Yes, ***we should read Vaalmeeki, thus, in proper perspective***

A true friend he is, Guha accepted Raama's new status and he served Raama in diverse ways. Offering service for his tired horses and providing a boat for Raama to cross Ganges to begin his exile of forest life.

Guha's affection for Raama is so deep that when Raama was sleeping on a bed of grass on the floor and resting for the night along with Seetha, he was keeping vigil through the night. He felt it was unnecessary for Lakshmana to keep awake for Raama. He is rather exasperated! (Ayodhya-chapter 51) Gist: "Oh Lakshmana, the royal prince! There is a comfortable bed for you. Please refresh yourself. All these folks with me who are keeping vigil, are used to discomforts, because they are men of forest." Then Guha explains what Raama is to him. He is a tribal & hunter is the scion of Ikshwaakus. "In this world, there is none dearer to me than Raama! This I affirm, swearing on Truth" Ofcourse Lakshmana rejects his kind offer of bed. If Guha is Raama's friend, Lakshmana is Raama's 'soul' in a separate body! So how could he sleep when Raama is lying on bare earth!

Sometimes our friendship and loyalty to a friend may blind us to accept reality. We may even suspect a good man when he confronts a close friend of ours.. Through Guha, Vaalmeeki brings home this common failing in a man. When Raama's brother Bharatha, after performing the last rites of his father king Dhasharatha at Ayodhya, decides to bring back Raama at any cost, forcing him to cut short his 14 year exile, he brings with him VIP-s, ministers, mothers, and a huge army to the forest to crown Raama in the forest itself. Guha sees this huge army. He gets agitated because he finds from a distance it is Bharatha who is leading the army. His friendship and deep affection for Raama blinds him. He could never imagine that Bharatha could be there for any purpose other than to do harm to Raama. He is quick with his decision.

(Ayodhya-chapter 84) When this king of hunters saw this huge army, he addressed his men "I think the wicked minded Bharatha is coming here to harm Raama. He is going to enslave us all. To kill Raama and thus make certain the kingdom is his forever, Bharatha has come here now. If Bharatha becomes wicked, we should not allow him and his entourage cross the river and come to our side"

Ofcourse Guha realises his mistake soon when Bharatha addresses Guha thus (Ayodhya-chapter85) Gist: "Oh Guha, my guru Raama's friend!" Then when Bharatha, without disclosing the purpose of his visit to forest asks Guha thus "By which route should we go to the hermitage of sage Bharadhwaaja so that we can find Raama". Guha was still doubting Bharatha and he asks him "I trust you are on this journey without any intention of doing harm to Raama". Bharatha affirms and assures Guha. "There should be no other thought in you. I am going to bring back Raama to Ayodhya as king".

Guha is delighted he glorifies Bharatha thus. Infact he rejoices so much that he calls Bharatha unique in the world. "Oh Bharatha! I Cannot See Any One In The World Equal To You As You Desire To Relinquish The Kingdom Voluntarily"

Guha was a noble man, man of his Dharma, born though he was as a tribal, and though his vocation was hunting and fishing.

Yes Vaalmeeki puts everything in proper perspective

It is befitting that with Guha, we end our dissertation on "CHARACTER" in this Guide to Vaalmeeki – The Revelation.

VAALMEEKI RAAMAAYANA
A REVELATION

PART III

A PANORAMA

REVELATION

PART III – PANORAMA

CONTENTS

1: I AM BUT A MAN =

Aham Maanisham Mann yay=

Vaalmeeki Raamaayana is about a man, a fine man, a noble man,.a virtuous man. Raama is the principal character. It is about his life and times that Vaalmeeki wrote. If this epic has withstood the test of Time, (in fact its history is over 5,000 years), it is because Vaalmeeki wrote for us all He did not treat Raama as a God, but as a man. He wanted every citizen to aspire to be like Raama. Infact Raamaayana begins with five questions put by Vaalmeeki to the divine sage Naaradha (Baala-chapter 1-slokas 2 to 5) "Who, in this world, at present, is adorned with good qualities, is brave, knows Dharma, is truthful, is resolute, steadfast in vows, who is a man of gratitude, endowed with good conduct, who is compassionate to all living beings, foremost in knowledge, most capable, whose looks are always pleasant, who is ever a man of courage, who is bright, free from jealousy, who controls his anger but who, when provoked is terror even to celestials".

Vaalmeeki was curious to know whether any man was living at that time with any or some of these qualities. Naaradha, after some deliberation answers him, that although it is difficult for a man to have such diverse qualities in this world, he can think of one man Raama. This is how Vaalmeeki's interest in Raama was kindled and he wrote Raama's life in 22,000 slokas. that turned out to be an epic- a Vedha

But Raama is incarnation of God Vishnu. When celestials unable to bear the suffering of the cruel demons and their king Raavana, take their complaint to God Vishnu, and beg Him to do something about it, the All Merciful God Vishnu decides to be born on earth as a human being, as Raama, and as son of King Dhasharatha and annihilate all evil forces including Raavana.

Now poet Vaalmeeki is in his elements. Even as God Vishnu decides to become a man on earth for their welfare, The All Knowing, All Powerful Lord begins to exhibit the characteristics of a human being! HE is already thinking like a man! (Baala-chapter 16-slokas & 2) When beseeched by these celestials, Naaraayana, the Lord, God Vishnu, ***in spite of knowing everything asks the celestials*** Vaalmeeki uses this expression in sanskrit = Jaanunapi- (to sound as Jaa- None-Apee =)

Vaalmeeki never wastes words. These two words are significant. "What means are there (for us) in the killing of the demon king Raavana?" These celestials assure the Lord that there will be millions of bears and monkeys born when he, as Raama, fights the demons, to assist Him.

When after Raama had slain all the demons and evil forces and had killed the most evil demon king Raavana, and when Raama behaves like a man, not accepting to take back Seetha because she had 'lived' in another's house (even though as prisoner), the Gods Rudhra & Brahma, extol him and remind him that he is God Vishnu on earth and that he should not treat Seetha like this and behave like an ordinary man. And Raama comes out with this famous statement:(Yudha- chapter 120-sloka 12)

"I consider myself as a man. I am Raama, son of Dhasharatha = Aham Maanisham Mann yay."

Vaalmeeki by this brings out a Truth. When one takes on the body of a man and lives on earth, only the characteristics of a human, reveal themselves Vaalmeeki wrote about Raama the man. He did not write about Raama, the incarnation of Vishnu. He presented Raama, and he did not spare this noble and most virtuous man, when occasionally his 'noble and diverse qualities go to sleep'.

2: ASHWAMEDHA - Horse Sacrifice

In the Vedhic times, sacrifices were part of ritual ceremonies and Yaagas. We have reference to sacrificial ceremonies like Vaajapaayi and other sacrificial ceremonies. Even during a house warming ceremony, a goat or antelope is sacrificed. When Raama during his exile enters a new abode, he asks Lakshmana to bring a fat goat for sacrifice in the holy fire ritual he is performing as house warming ceremony. At Chithrakoot.(Ayodhya-chapter 56-sloka25)

"Oh Lakshman! House warming =Vasthu ceremony must be done by those who are to live long in an abode.So we shall perform the Ritual –Vasthu = Homa ***with deer meat***"

Ashwamedha Horse Sacrifice is a different kind of Sacrifice. Only kings and emperors have the capacity to perform this Yaaga. It is said that if one performs 100 Ashwamedhas, he gets the power and position of the Lord of the Celestial world. Apart from the enormous expenditure involved, the rituals are taxing. Very few priests are qualified in hymns and chants pertaining to this sacrifice. If any part of the ritual is transgressed, it may even bring harm to the king who performs it. This is what king Dhasharatha says when he decides to perform this Yaaga.

(Bala- chapter 8- sloka 16 & 18) "If this mighty yaaga, is not done properly, a grievous transgression would result. If the yaaga is a simple one, it could be done by any ordinary king. Clever Braamins- the Bramma-Raakshasas- always find fault. Even a small 'failing' will result in harm to the 'Doer' "When Dhasharatha performed the Yaaga, he was advised by his minister Sumanthra that for successful completion of the Yaga, he should have the patronage of the great saint, Rishyshringa. (Baala-chapter11)

The origin of this Sacrifice is obscure from even pre-vedhic times. We do have some details of the ceremony from Vaalmeeki (Baala-chapters 12 to 14) We may broadly describe what this Yaaga is all about. A horse well groomed & trained by = Upaa-dhyaa-yaas= ((priests) is let loose. It roams about freely. No one dares to stop it. If any ruler or king does this it is at his peril. If any one seizes it, it is obligatory on the part of The 'Doer' to retrieve it by force. Then after a period, it is brought back and after rituals it is sacrificed.

When Raama's forefather King Sagara performed this Yaaga, The Horse was 'stolen'. (Baala-chapters 38 to 44).

A consequence was that King Sagara, sends his 100 sons to search for the horse, retrieve it and also punish the thief. We give the gist of chapters 38 to 44. Sagara's 100 sons perish after they harm an innocent person whom they consider as thief of The Horse. Sagara's grandson Amshumaan finally retrieves the Horse and Sagara completes the Yaaga. The sequel to all this, is that Amshumaan's grandson King Bageeratha, brings Holy Ganges to Earth and to the underworld, to resurrect the 100 sons of Sagara, who were reduced to ashes when they (mistakenly) had tried to punish the 'thief', with the waters of holy Ganges! But this is another story. We are concerned with Ashwamedha Yaaga and Dhasharatha's ceremony. (Baala-chapter 13) Gist: Vasishta takes on the responsibility of organising this great Yaaga. He commissions "experts in construction work, elderly Braahmins well versed in Shaasthras, men of Dharma, accountants, dancers, singers, carpenters, well diggers, decorators may be asked to do their respective jobs. Bricks in plenty for fire mound. May lovely cottages with all features =Gunas= be built for VIP-s and other citizens from outside."

Vasishta orders plenty of food to be made available to all during the Yaaga for citizens attending the Yaaga. Vasishta warns "***Men of all castes should be treated with respect and honour, and without discrimination***. Either out of passion or in anger, no one should be treated with disrespect" ***Vaalmeeki by this brings home to all of us a point generally overlooked***. We had caste, but there was ***NO CASTEISM***. Remember! It is Vasishta, the Brahimn of Brahmins, who gives the warning. None should be shown disrespect. He wants persons of all castes to attend the ceremony. Caste is abolished today. But alas, casteism is not. Caste existed for the well being of society. Caste was a sort of division of labour. Nothing more, those days.

(Baala-chapter 14) Gist: "In the august presence of and under the patronage of Rishyashringa, the yaaga was performed. Rithviks well versed in Shaasthras, who had 'crossed' the 'ocean of ' Shaasthras, performed the Yaaga for the king as per norms. & the code. They did Pravargya., Upaasadh, and other rituals. Braahmins did ceremonies like Praathas savan. They did the evening ceremony of Savana as well. Holy Fire in Mound was burning continuously. Oblations were offered as per custom. Even Indra received oblations." Vaalmeeki now talks about mundane matters. ***Vaalmeeki is human***

"None was seen who was tired or hungry. Braahmins ate well, so did Shoodras! Why even men normally devoted to penance, ate well. Women, old men, children, all ate well. So much food was there and such tasty food, they were never fully satisfied! They all extolled the King by saying food was excellent, tasty, well cooked!" Now we come back to the rituals and the ceremony. "In this yaaga there was no priest who had not studied the Vedha & Shaasthras, scriptures, codes and norms".

"When the time of fixing pillars arrived, 6 masts made of Bilva tree (Aegle-marmelosa - or 'apple'tree) and an equal number in wood from Kadhira (acacia-catechu) and from Parni (Butea-frontosa) was erected. Two masts from Sleshma (Pandarus-odaritismus) and from Dheadhaaru (avaria longifolia) erected. These 21 masts were beautifully draped with 21 meters of lovely cloth. All the masts were well decorated. They were fixed rigidly. And for sacrifice, cows, reptiles, and birds were tied up to please various 'lords' and deities. And 300 cow were tied up, secured on masts. Dhasharatha's Horse -the foremost gem of a horse- the sacrificial horse was separately tied up." After describing all this, the privilege of killing the Sacrificial Horse, surprisingly, goes to Dhasharatha's eldest queen, Kowsalya. Ofcourse she is a Kshathriya princess. (Bala-chapter 14 sloka 33 & 34)

"Kowsalya, with great devotion, and care, smote (killed) the Sacrificial Horse, in just three strokes in great joy! And bound by Dharma, she spent the night (kept vigil) with the Sacrifice, with a resolute mind!"

Oblations are offered by 16 priests. There is a description of Fire rituals. Athiraathra was done. Rituals of Jyothista and Aayush were performed Likewise Abhijith & Vishwajith, Mahaa yaaga, and Aapthoryaama. We are giving here some of these details to show that Ashwamedha Yaaga is a rigorous, taxing ceremony. After completing the Yaaaga, the King must offer Gifts innumerous. Gold coins, cows, lands, territories.

The Yaaga is unique. Only emperors can undertake Ashwameda Yaaga.

No wonder the Kings of Ikshwakus, who were all like 'emperors' performed. ***The Ashwamedha Yaaga.***

3: CASTE, CASTE & CASTE: Ah!

Today, in India that is Bhaarath we have a paper (sorry, written) Constitution which abolishes caste from our life. But in our ancient land, caste was an integral part of society. They were not apologetic, they did not have to be, because, in the first place all the four castes were 'born' from the limbs of the creator, God Brahma. Secondly, there was no social or economic discrimination. The caste division was functional, utilitarian. A sort of division of labour for the welfare of all. It suited those times.

Vaalmeeki brings home this point in many places. We have people from all castes being invited to King Dhasharatha's Yaaga. Vasishta says (Baala- chapter 13) that men from all castes should not only be invited but treated with 'due respect and honour'. We have already referred to this. Time and again, he mentions how Dhasharatha and his son Raama treated every section of society. with due respect. The point is Dharma was the basis of all activity and all men submitted to this Dharma. Even at the conclusion of his epic, Vaalmeeki specifically names all the four castes (Yudh-chapter 131) "The Brahmins, the Kshathriyas, the Vysyas, the Shoodhras, all of them were bereft of covetousness, they did their duties, were devoted to Dharma. Every one of them was endowed with good qualities, none among them were liars" It is not as though only Brahmins should read scriptures. Naaradha exhorts one and all to read Raama's story which is Vedha (Baala-chapter 1-sloka 100) "If a Brahmin reads he becomes a master of speech. If a Kshathriya reads, he will imbibe the qualities of a ruler. If a Vysya reads, he will be a prosperous and if a Shoodra reads, he will attain stature".

By this, indirectly, Vaalmeeki divides caste according to their vocation.

When Seetha admonishes Raama for wielding the bow and arrow on their exile in forest, forgetting that he is no longer prince of Ayodhya but a mendicant in forest, Raama tells her that he is born a Kshathriya and it is his duty to protect innocent people living in forest. The Dharma of the Kshathriya caste is to defend. Raama thus justifies his carrying arms. If need be he will kill. And he does. (Aaranya-chapters 9 & 10) Raama says (sloka 3 to 20) Gist:"Oh Seetha! A bow is held by a ***Kshathriya*** because there should be no cry for relief from pain by sufferers. Protection was offered by me for these sages who are living in constant fear of demons. Even if they had not sought my assistance I would have gladly gone to their aid, because this becomes my duty" A doctor, even on holiday, must attend cases if need be, if he is asked. Once a doctor, always a doctor. The caste system of ancient India merely carries this Dharma. Ofcourse this system may be out of date and perhaps no more useful purpose may be served by adhering to this in the world now. **But trying to cover up all our failings today by blaming caste as a dirty legacy, is just cheating ourselves.**

It was not as though everything was fine with the caste system. Vaalmeeki never shied away from realities. If something was wrong, he wrote about it. Thus we have caste war, reported by Vaalmeeki. (Bala-chapter-75 &76)

The great Jamadagni, while he was in meditation, was killed by one Arjuna. Jamadagni happens to be a Brahmin and Arjuna a Kshathriya. What more do you want for a caste war? Jamadagni's son is a Brahmin, the terrible Parashu - Raama (Raama who always wields an axe) So wrathful he is that he starts systematically eliminating Kshathriyas, till he is humbled by ***Kshathriya Raama. The caste war ends***. There is no room for casteism in Raama's rule.

Before we conclude this dissertation on caste, we have to introduce a noble, spiritual lady. Her only qualification was that she spent all her life serving old, noble sages in the Maathanga forest. She did all mundane and menial jobs for men of penance. (Aaranya-chapter 74) She was an 'untouchable, did not belong to any caste, was a 'tribal'. The sages treated her with great affection and respect. She was not an untouchable to them! Raama honours her by a visit to her although he had an immediate task before him. He was to meet Sugreeva for seeking assistance to locate his abducted wife Seetha. She receives Raama & Lakshmana with great affection and extends the hospitality of a poor lady of forest. (sloka 19) "........when told thus by Shabari, the noble soul Raama told her, who was ever ***considered an outcaste, an untouchable...."*** Here is Raama, the doyen of royalty, condescending to visit a lady, an untouchable at that, particularly when he is pressed for time. Shabari ofcourse goes to heaven, immediately after meeting Raama. Infact she was looking forward to the visit of Raama and Lakshmana. (Slokas 33 to 37) Gist: "Giving up her dress of bark, and desirous of giving up her withered body, and taking leave of Raama, she offered herself to fire in Fire mound and went to heaven. As she went up she appeared most lovely, her face shone like streaks of lightning" Comment is needless. Ah! caste, caste, caste!

4: TRUTH, UNTRUTH, LIE

God Brahma, when he blessed Vaalmeeki, had said that his Raamaayana will be true (to history). There will be nothing untrue and none can find fault with him. (Baala-chapter 2-sloka 36).

Truth is always associated with good. Untruth considered evil. Outright lie, despicable. But a few situations present themselves before us, when we are tested, and our mind gets confused. Is Untruth entirely evil? Can a man speak a lie at all?

Vaalmeeki presents a piquant situation. King Dhasharatha is dead. Raama and Lakshmana away from Ayodhya on 14 year exile. Bharatha and Shathrugna are on holiday at Kekeya kingdom. Ayodhya is without a prince or ruler. The King is dead, Long live the King" So Vasishta decides that urgent summons be sent out to Bharatha and he must be brought immediately from his (maternal) grandfather's place, cutting short his holiday. Ayodhya cannot be without a ruler even for a moment.

(Ayodhya-chapter 68- slokas 5 to 8) Gist "Oh Sidhaartha, Come here! Oh Vijaya, Ashoka, Jayantha! Giving up grief (over the death of your king Dhasharatha here), you go at once to the city of Rajgrigha and tell Bharatha, this, as my command = The purohith (me, Vasishta) inquires about your welfare. Without wasting time, you come back to Ayodhya at once. Because, the work that must be done by you here, is important and pressing. ="

After saying this, Vasishta tells these messengers, the ministers, firmly "Going there, You ***Should Not Report To Him About Raama's Exile or His Father's Death"***

And when ministers reach Rajgriha and carry Vasishta's message to Bharatha, the first question of Bharatha concerns the welfare of his father and his brother Raama. (Ayodhya-chapter 70- slokas 7 to 10): Gist:"I trust my father king Dhasharatha, is well. I trust the great soul Raama and Lakshamana, likewise are in good health!" Ofcourse Dhasharatha is safe in heaven and Raama is in good health in deep forest!

Now comes our dilemma. What should be the minister's reply. Should they go by Vasishta or should they speak the truth? These ministers have always been men of Truth. They had never lied before. But they know Vasishta as a man of Dharma. They know that he is a Brahma Rishi and one of The Seven = Saptha = Rishi-s. They would rather speak Untruth than speak 'against' Vasishta (sloka12)

"Oh the tiger of men! Oh Bharatha! These people whose welfare you desire, ***are all well***"

Vasishta wanted to hide the truth. The ministers also 'connived' to lie. Because Vasishta wanted to spare the agony for Bharatha in a 'foreign' land. Let him undergo torment in Ayodhya. Let him hear all this at his palace.

Vaalmeeki presents us the Dharma of Truth - Untruth equation

And this is not the only place in Vaalmeeki Raamaayana. where the question of Truth - Untruth exercises our mind. In Ayodhya (chapter 13-sloka 7) Dhasharatha wails, helpless

Gist: "If I tell the men of my assembly that Raama was sent out to forest by me on exile, because I was Truthful to Kaikeyi (by honouring the boons I had given her long ago) then it would mean that I spoke untruth- lie- before the assembly yesterday, when I told them that I will crown Raama by morning".

We have a few more instances where our mind gets exercised over truth-untruth dogmas (example-Sumantra's wail- Ayodhya kaanda)

Yes! Vaalmeeki did not shy away from presenting the truth. Even though at times untruth overshadows truth

5: SEVEN STRINGS & SEVEN CHARACTERISTICS

When Vaalmeeki presented his epic, it was as a musical. it was popularised. Lava and Kusha, the sons of Raama set this 22,000 slokas to music format and sang. before sages, citizens and even before his father at Ayodhya. (Baala kaanda-chapter 4): They sang in sweet voice, in various raagas. They sang in three scales and from 'head, and through mouth and with heart' They adopted the 'Maarga' style of singing. Valmeeki's Raamaayana, when sung was like Veena. We shall be writing about various musical instruments in Vaalmeeki, later in part IV.

By slokas 8 & 9, it is said that music was as sweet to the ear like the 7 stringed instrument Veena. Like 7 strings, Vaalmeeki's Raamayana carried 7 characteristics

(1)	Shringaara	=	Romance, pleasure
(2)	Karuna	=	compassion
(3)	Veera	=	Valour, bravery
(4)	Roudhra	=	Wrath
(5)	Bhayaanaka	=	Fear
(6)	Haasya	=	Laughter, jokes, humour
(7)	Bheebatsa	=	Revulsion, Disgust

Vaalmeeki compares the seven strings of Veena to these characteristics. And as there cannot be music without rhythm = laya, and as Veena carries laya = rhythm in its strings, the musical expression of Raamaayana was sung to perfect Thaala = Laya = rhythm.

Incidentally Veena, the ancient lute of India, is supposed to have been invented by the first musicologist, sage Naaradha. No wonder the first sloka of Vaalmeeki Raamaayna carries his name. There is a view that the 7 strings of Veena are fixed on top of the Veena over the frets and the laya strings are fixed below, making this a 10 stringed instrument. In modern India, it is only a 7 stringed instrument. We shall write about a few of these characteristics

HUMOUR

Raama is well settled in his hermitage at Panchavati along with his wife Seetha and brother Lakshmana. They have a visitor. The demoness Shoorpanka, a cousin sister of Raavana (Aaranya-chapter 17) She is so enchanted by the form of Raama she tells him (aaranya-chapter 18) "Beautiful as I am, matching your form, I am indeed your wife! You will enjoy and roam about the Dhandaka forest with me" Even here there is lot of humour because Shoorpanaka is ugly but gives herself a certificate that she is most beautiful!

Now comes the humour in Vaalmeeki. Raama has a sense of humour. He replies "Your ladyship. I am married. My wife Seetha is dear to me. If you marry me you have to be a co-wife. For a distinquished woman like you it is difficult to accept this position. Here is my brother Lakshmana. He has no woman with him. He is handsome. He is the right man for you"

Lakshmana continuing the jest tells Shoorpanaka "Oh lady whose complexion is like that of blue lotus! How can you desire to be my wife as suggested by Raama? Oh lady with large eyes! You have the capacity to take on any form. My brother Raama will soon discard his 'ugly' wife Seetha for you. He is the right husband for you. Besides, I am after all a 'slave' to him. You can't marry me, a slave!"

Shoorpanaka falling for this 'bait' rushes to kill Seetha forthwith to make Raama her husband.for good.

Raama feels the jest and humour have gone far enough. He tells Lakshmana " Oh Lakshmana! I realise that we should not indulge in humour with these evil demons. Teach her a lesson by cutting off her nose and maim her" Lakshmana then cuts off her nose and Shoorpanaka runs away in fear, crying. And the rest is history.

During his exile, Raama has the unique distinction of performing the last rites for people not at all related to him. Infact, although he was the eldest son, it was Bharatha who performs the last rites for their father Dhasharatha. Raama had to deny himself this, but he performs the last rites for others. When Raavana was carrying off Seetha and when the brave old bird king Jataayu was killed by him as he tried to save Seetha, it is Raama who performs Last Rites for this bird as though the bird is his own father (aaranya-chapter 68). When demon Viradha is killed by him and hc secks salvation, Raama buries him. (Aaranya-chapter 4) . Again Raama, cremates Kabhanda who gets salvation and goes to heaven.

Now comes the humour. Lakshmana could not contain himself and must have a joke at Raama's expense. (Aaranya-chapter 72)

Gist: "Oh Raama! Jataayu was cremated. Then Viradha. Now Kabandha. Who is next in your list!"

Humour apart, a comment is called for. The deeply religious men know that all these people could not have obtained salvation without Raama performing their rites. They are indeed the most fortunate ones who have this Punnya=Merit. After all Raama, is none other than God Vishnu.

We have another example of humour-jest.in this epic. (Ayodhya-chapter 32) The Thrijata episode. He was a poor Brahmin, of Gargya family, who, inspite of having a large family, was totally devoted only to prayer, rituals and vows. Mundane needs hardly concerned him His wife, in sheer agony and poverty admonishes him "Do as I tell you! Casting away your spade and shovel, you go and 'see' Raama. You may get 'something' from him." It was the time when Raama was giving away all his personal wealth at Ayodhya, as he was leaving on 14 year exile away from Ayodhya. Thrijata addressed Raama on seeing him thus "Oh Raama! I am a poor man. I have many children. I have not much means in the forest where I am. So please consider me for favour and give me something".

Raama the munificent, could have easily satisfied him and sent him away quickly. But Raama in playing this jest with him, wanted to bring out a truth to the world. Here is a case of jest coming to the aid of expounding Dharma. Raama tells Thrijata who appeared like a man of ridicule."Oh Braahmin! In thousands, I have given away. Yet as you have not received anything from me, I can offer you only this. You throw the pole, the support staff you are carrying with you, to a distance. And all the land and the belongings covered by the distance of your throw, you may have" Even olympic champions cannot throw a javelin to more than a couple of hundred metres or more. And this poor old brahmin has gone without food for days! But "Tying up his worn out ragged cloth around his hips, with zeal and in haste, he swiftly hurled his stick, with full breath and force. And Lo! This pole that was hurled by him, flew, crossed over the banks of river Sarayu, and fell near a cowshed of 1000 cows." Raama hugged Thrijata and offered him all those around Sarayu river with the help of cow boys" Then Raama told him "Oh Thrijata! Forgive me for this jest. I merely desired the world to know this; your power of penance. I swear on truth. There be no restraint in you to ask all you want from me." Thrijata was happy and he went away with a herd of cows and before he left, he blessed Raama with affection and pleasure.

By this jest, Raama proved to the world the power of penance and prayer.

KARUNA: = Compassion

Perhaps, Vaalmeeki would not have written this epic if he was not a man of compassion! His compassion reaches out even to birds. As a bird watcher, when he saw a male bird being killed by a thoughtless hunter while it was making love, Vaalmeeki was seized with compassion. So much he grieved for the female bird which had lost its lover, that he cursed the hunter (Baala-chapter 2) and this curse came out of his mouth as poetry. In many places in Raamaayana we find this quality, compassion, being written about.

VEERA = Valour : ROUDHRA= WRATH

There are any number of brave characters who exhibit their valour. Surprisingly, there are many instances when wrath seizes them before they exhibit their valour! Yet in Baala-chapter 5, we find that there were any number of warriors who were extremely brave but were never seized by wrath. Their bow was never stretched except to protect the innocent and arrows were never discharged in anger.

Yet we find Lakshmana, the most valiant warrior in Raamaayana equal to Raama in valour, is so much seized by wrath on seeing Bharatha's army rushing towards their hermitage. (Ayodhya-chapter 97) he says "The suppressed wrath and disgrace we received at Ayodhya (when we were thrown out of our kingdom), I am now going to discharge on the hostile army of Bharatha, like fire on dry wood" Wrath over shadows valour. Lakshmana's frenzy blinds his valour. Bharatha was not rushing towards their hermitage to harm Raama but to take him back to Ayodhya with full military honours! Raama admonishes Lakshmana for his mistaken wrath.

Raama's wrath is of a different kind. The poet says neither Raama's wrath nor favour is ever wasted! When he gets angry, it is deluge! If wrath overpowers Raama and Raama starts exhibiting his valour, it is terrible. When the elements and nature do not respond to Raama who begs them to indicate where Seetha had gone, wrath seizes Raama so much that Lakshmana prostrates before him, and begs him to give up wrath. Lakshmana's wrath is one thing, but Raama's is different. Lakshmana knows that when Raama starts using force in wrath, there will be total ecological chaos. The world cannot stand Raama's valour when he is consumed by wrath. When the Lord of the Ocean fails to appear before him after he had offered prayers for safe passage across the ocean for his monkeys to travel 1,000 miles to Lanka, wrath seizes him and he exclaims fixing an arrow on his bow (Yudhdha kaanda - chapter 21) "Oh Lakshmana! In this world one cannot achieve results by conciliation. The King of the ocean does not respond to me, because of my friendly approach. ***In wrath as I am*** I am going to shake up the ocean, and I will dry up the ocean!" Raama's wrath is such; his valour is such!

When Sugreeva was seized by fury on seeing Raavana from a distance, he thoughtlessly jumps from the mountain and goes over to Raavana for a twosome combat. A reckless act. Raama admonishes Sugreeva (Yudha-chapter 40) Sugreeva is a brave warrior, most valiant. Yet this act was a reckless one. Wrath had clouded his thinking.

In the great war, we find all the demons and monkeys fight more fiercely when backed up by wrath!

Yes. Sometimes wrath and valour go together.

SRINGARA - Romance (General term)

Raamaayana is full of Sringaara, in which Vaalmeeki excels. At the basest understanding of this term, we have Raavana obsessed by the physical beauty of a woman. (Aaranaya kaanda chapter 46) Raavana is so obsessed with the physical attributes of Seetha, he loses self-control of himself and describes her body! "Oh Seetha! Your teeth are well set, the pupil of your eyes are dark over your bright clear eyes. Your buttocks are broad and fleshy. Your thighs are like the trunk of elephant. Your breasts are alluring and so on" Vaalmeeki says that Raavana was so much in passion that he tells her (Sundara-chapter 20) "Oh Seetha! When my sight falls upon any part of your body, my mind gets transfixed on that part. My sight fails me to look at anything else". All this is vulgar 'sex'. Passion is the basest form of Love. We have Raaama describing the beauty of Seetha but on a higher plane.

But we should talk about Sringaara, the sublime pleasures Vaalmeeki hands out to us at various places. When he describes the seasons, he is in his elements. We will revert to the seasons later. The scenic beauty, the trees in full blossom, the clouds in the rainy season and in autumn, the rivers, the mountains the moon, the animals like deer, all these are poetically described by Vaalmeeki Everything pleases our heart. In Ayodhya-chapters 94 & 95, Raama describes the beauty of Chithrakoot and Mandakini river. So enchanted is he that he tells Seetha " Even if I live for many autumns here, with you, I will not miss Ayodhya"

BHAYAANAKA: Fear, terror

There is no dearth of this term in Raamaayana, with so many demons around! Infact, Vishnu appears as a human being, Raama only because of the fear and terror of even celestials at the hands of Raavana.In Baala-chapter 15, the celestials beg of Vishnu. "This evil minded Raavana terrorises all. He even tries to 'crush' the Lord of Dhevas". Raama was born only to remove fear totally. Fear is the worst enemy of man. Raama was born to remove the fear of all mankind. In Vaalmeeki, Bhayaanaka manifests in many places.

It is not from demons alone, fear was caused. We have the case of the Brahmin, the terrible Parashuraama who had been systematically causing harm to Kshathriyas Finally the Kshathriya Raama subdues him. The Kshatriyas are relieved of their fear, once and for all. (Baala- Chapter 76)

BHEEBHATSA (disgust, revulsion)

A disgusting event in Raamaayana leads to some good to world. Throughout, Vaalmeeki portrays Lord Indra as a selfish person given to evil acts. A notorious lord! When he finds that his stepmother Dhithi pregnant and her sons may challenge his status and even his life, he resorts to a crime, unparalleled crime. He builds up confidence in her by serving her, taking care of her mundane needs. Then one day, when she was sleepy and tired, and her lower garments had slipped away, he 'enters' her womb and tries to kill the unborn children,

Fortunately they are saved. These are born as The Maruths in the world, for welfare of all. This indeed, is a disgusting incident. Total Revulsion (Baala-chapter 46).

6: **PRAANA-THYAAGA** (Suicide):

We make no apology in repeating ourselves. Vaalmeeki never shied away to present reality even if he had to hurt the characters he had portrayed as noble and great. Let us take for instance 'suicide' in the epic. In India, it is customary for elders to bless the young ones with long life. Our elders were wise. They knew that unless a person lives long enough and goes through various stages of life, he cannot obtain salvation. The purpose of birth in this Bhaaratha Varsh (India) is for ultimate salvation. This land is The Karma Bhoomi, land of service. Good or bad, you have to live your full life, take in the suffering in your stride. This used to be the traditional view of life in this country. When Bharatha Varsh came to be known as India, this view has undergone change. We have to accept reality.

Ending one's life is considered evil. Till recently, the Indian penal code stipulated punishment for 'attempted' suicide. Ofcourse we can never put behind bars a person who had committed suicide, as punishment to him!. Man made laws can never reach out that far!. But when a person commits suicide, there is justice above us, the justice of The Lord. The sin of committing suicide, dogs us in successive births.

Vaalmeeki portrays Raama as a near perfect man. Seetha is the jewel among women. There can never be another Hanumaan. Yet at some point in their lives they considered suicide as a means of getting rid of their suffering. In the epic, Vaalmeeki could have avoided reference to suicide and save himself some embarrassment. But he wrote without fear or favour. He wrote reality. He wrote about human failings, weaknesses in character.

When Seetha was abducted by Raavana in the early stages of their search, Raama could not find any trace of Seetha. He wails and asks Lakshmana to get back to Ayodhya as he feels Seetha must have perished and no useful purpose is there for him to continue his life. He will not return to Ayodhya but end his life in forest. (Aaranya-chapter62-sloka20) "Oh Lakshmana! Seetha's death and my death must be told in great detail by you to my mother, (when you get back)"

Who knows? But for Lakshmana who was not only a brother and a companion, but was also Raama's conscience keeper, Raama perhaps would have ended life in forest as a recluse. Lakshmana who from time to time goads Raama to take on courage and effort, to surmount difficulties.

Seetha was undergoing such torment that any other woman would have committed suicide. For Seetha, nothing was more precious in the world than utter devotion to Raama. And this is denied. She represented the noblest and purest of Indian womanhood. Infact if she had committed suicide, unable to prolong the agony at the hands of her abductor Ravana, the world would not have condemned her. Even the Lords in heaven would have condoned her sin.

In Sundara kaanda-chapter 26, we find Seetha crying her heart out "If someone here offers me poison now, I will be the happiest because I will go to the abode of Yama. I cannot live any longer without my beloved Raama" And by sloka 20 in chapter 25, she bemoans. "What a life, that I am not even able to give up life!" Seetha curses herself that she has no freedom even to obtain poison. Seetha goes philosophical. Perhaps even here Fate has a hand. None can die till Yama, the Lord of time and death, decides the appointed hour.

Finding no other options, Seetha decides to choke herself to death using her long bunch of hair as the 'hangman's rope. Fortunately, she sees good omens and hears Hanumaan's sweet voice and thus abandons the idea of suicide.

Seetha speaks of duality of life. (Sundara kanda-chapter 26) Gist: "Indeed, only those who are not affected by joy or sorrow, are great men, illustrious persons, conquerors of 'Self' Sages! no wonder, are honoured.

Light-Darkness: joy-sorrow; birth-death. Such mundane duality of life, they accept with equanimity".

Finally Seetha says what we had said in the introduction why in India our elders bless young ones with long life (Sundara-chapter 3sloka 6) "Only when a person keeps himself alive, happiness comes to him even if it be after 100 years of suffering".

By this single statement by Seetha, Vaalmeeki rejects suicide as a solution to problems.

Vaalmeeki did not spare the noble Hanumaan either! Hanumaan is wise, dexterous, hard working. Searching for Seetha in Lanka, he had gone round thoroughly, systematically, the entire Lanka.Yet, unable to find Seetha, he contemplates suicide! (Sundara kaanda-chapter 13). But being a wise man, he quickly rejects suicide as an option! But not before he talks thus to himself in desperation: Gist "If I do not see Seetha, I will become a recluse, eating only that which falls into my mouth. Why? I will even enter fire mound. Or let crows and animals devour my body." After saying all this, the wise Hanumaan gets back to his natural state and affirms "In destroying one's self, the disadvantages are many. Only when one keeps on living, he can see happiness to him. Therefore, I will hold on to my life". And Hanumaan continues his search with even greater zeal and we know the rest.

Vaalmeeki in talking about suicide, has brought out a Truth. We have to bear everything with patience, and forbearance and put in our maximum effort. Suicide is an option that never solves any problem.

KSHAMA: Vaalmeeki has talked about patience and forbearance. In Baal kaanda-chapter 33 he talks about Kshama = Patience & forbearance. He chooses the right place to describe this virtue. When the 100 daughters of King Kushanaabha, were molested by the Lord of Air, and bore this with great equanimity, their father extols them saying:

"Patience is wealth and charity: Patience is Truth. Patience is Fame. Patience is Yaaga. Patience is Dharma. Infact the World is sustained by patience and forbearance"

The 100 daughters bore this 'injury' on them with equanimity and fortitude. They did not contemplate suicide. They not only married later, but created a great dynasty, renowned in the world.

Vaalmeeki has to be read in proper perspective. Only then we can become enlightened.

7: MARYAADHA, VINAYA REETHI
(Protocol, Norms)

In the entire Vaalmeeki, protocol and norms being observed by all; whether it be a common man, a king, or a sage. By observing protocol, we can avoid embarrassment. By sticking to norms, we pay our respect only to position and status and not to the person. In other words, we are paying our respect only to 'Duty' of a person, not its instrument. Dharma is the basis of protocol. Our army is still well disciplined because the Services follow protocol, even in the matter of taking salute.

The list is endless. But we may offer a few examples. When Brahma appears before Vaalmeeki to ordain him to do this epic, protocol is observed by the sage (Baala-chapter 2-slokas 24 to 26) "Standing up, cupping his hands in Anjali, *modestly restraining himself to a few words* (*the Sanskrit word used is Vaagyatha). He offered Argya and Paadya and offered Him a seat and stood there" Then Brahma directed him to a seat after HE had sat down Then Vaalmeeki sat down" (Vaalmeeki says =so ordered by Brahma, he sat down= In his own house he does not choose his seat. Brahma does it!)

In the council hall Dhasharatha having sat down on the throne, directs the various chiefs, VIP-s to their respective seats as per protocol. (Ayodhya-chapter 1). Dhasharatha was not an ordinary king but was a sort of an emperor. Yet, he directs the vassals, chiefs, VIPs to their seats.

Before the marriage ceremonies begin in Mithila when the four sons of Dhasharatha are married to the daughters of Janaka and his brother, customarily, lineage is described. Incidentally, in marriages in India, even today the bride's and bridegroom's lineage is announced. Owing to constraint of time, nowadays, they announce names, and go back to only their father, grandfather and great grandfather, The public knows who is marrying whom, without ambiguity! When Dhasharatha introduces himself before king Janaka, this is what he says (Bala-chapter 70) "Oh great king Janaka! The Lord, the rishi Vasishta is 'God' to us of Ikshwaaku family, It should be known to you, that in all our matters, ***he is the First to speak*** "Brahma Rishi, Vasishta introduces Dhasharatha by describing his lineage. A long list, Dhasharatha's forefathers who ruled Ayodhya.

When Raama, accompanied by his wife Seetha, gets ready to go on exile and appears before his father, Dhasharatha for taking leave of him. this is what he says to his father

"Oh Emperor! Seetha is accompanying me to forest. In spite of my restraining him with many reasons, Lakshmana desires to accompany me. You must therefore give him permission" Here norms are observed. Seetha being his wife, as per Dharma, she has a right to go along with Raama without seeking permission. But in the case of Lakshmana it is different. He may be his brother, but he is a prince of Ayodhya and necessarily must get clearance from King Dhasharatha.. Vaalmeeki does not waste words. We should read him in the original and then only we will know how effective his writing is. Brevity is Vaalmeeki. But no uncertainty or confusion in what is conveyed. It is norms and norms with Vaalmeeki.

It is well known that among Dhasharatha's council of ministers and advisers, Minister Sumanthra holds a unique place. He was the king's charioteer and minister in.waiting. But more than all this he was his personal friend. Yet protocol was always observed by him. He never said "Hai, Dhasharatha! "although that was the sort of relationship they had. He had access to the king's inner apartments. He did not need an appointment. (Ayodhya-chapter 14-sloka 43 to 57) Gist Sumanthra, the charioteer entered his palace, extolling his king. Dhasharatha. The king's guards, who served their king lovingly, did not stop Sumanthra from entering the inner apartments who was highly esteemed by the king.as they had standing instructions (to allow him to enter). But Sumanthra inspite of all this never failed to follows protocol. He greets his friend, Dhasharatha thus. Gist: "Just as the brilliant ocean 'rejoices' at sun rise, so are you rejoicing this early morning? Just as Vedhas 'wake up' Brahma, so am I waking you up! May lords of Sun, Moon, and may God Shiva, and lords Kubhaera, and Varuna ever bestow you with all!"

When Hanumaan meets Raama for the first time and even when he was struck by Hanumaan's knowledge and wisdom and his demeanour, he asks Lakshmana to reply to him. (Kishkinda-chapter 3- sloka 28) Gist "You talk to ***this 'monkey' who is a minister to Sugreeva*** "

Even in the matter of seating in the mountain slope, Sugreeva spreads a carpet of grass for Raama and invites him to sit, while Hanumaan invites Lakshmana!

After the war ended and Vibheeshana is crowned king of Lanka (by ***Lakshmana),*** Raama has this to say to Hanumaan, to make certain that Vibeeshana is no longer just a 'defector from the enemy's camp' but is now king! (Yudhdha-chapter 115 slokas 22 to 24) Gist:"Oh Hanumaan! You must respect and honour Vibheeshana. As per norms, taking leave and permission of the king etc, etc"

If Raama does not follow Protocol who will. Yes. Vaalmeeki did follow protocol in his epic!

8 PRAMAANA:

POORVA-DHRISHTI (Precendents)

In spite of rapid changes in the world, and although situations facing human beings may not be entirely similar, it is good for us to follow precedents when we are in a dilemma. After all, precedents are out of experience over ages. Vaalmeeki sets a high value for observing norms. When out of chivalry, Raama has no heart to kill a woman, the demoness Thaataka. Vishwaamithra admonishes Raama for wasting time over her killing by him. He quotes precedents (Baala-chapter 25) Gist "Oh Raama! Let there be no aversion in you to kill a woman. Whether the deed is cruel or not, it is always justified when an evil woman causes misery to the world. Lord Indra had killed Virochana's daughter. Bhrigu's wife was killed by God Vishnu "

When Raama's mother Kowsalya wails before Raama when he was taking leave of her to go on the 14 year exile, Raama quotes precedents to justify his action of obeying his father's (and Kaikeyi's) command without question. (Ayodhya-chapter 21 Raama says: Gist: "At the bidding of his father, even an innocent cow was killed by Rishi Kandu, who knew Dharma! In our family, long ago, Sagara's sons tortured earth (and humanity) at the bidding of their father to search for the stolen yaga horse. Parashu Raama killed his mother when he was ordered to by his father in wrath." Raama is so convinced in following precedents that he tells his mother when she begs Raama not to go on exile at his father's command, leaving her 'alone' "Disagreeable though it may be, I am not setting in motion, a new, unprecedented Dharma. In this world, one who follows his father's command never comes by grief."

Even the selfish Kaikeyi quotes precedents to her husband. This ofcourse, is like a 'devil quoting scriptures' Kaikeyi twists precedents to her advantage. But the point is she does take recourse to precedens. (Ayodhya-chapter 14) "King Shibi cut off portions from his body to feed big bird Syena. Alarka plucked out his two eyes to give sight to a Brahimn who was well versed in Vedhas!"

Seetha uses precedents in the form of a parable. Weapons and Violence go together. We see this in the world today. Vaalmeeki had seen this long ago. Seetha could never reconcile herself to Raama wielding the bow and sword in forest. He wanted him to be a man of peace. She narrates a story of how a sage in forest, got so enamoured of a sword presented by Indra, that he soon gave up his penance and started using the sword. (Aaranya-chapter 9)!

Situations may be different. So it is not as though we should follow precedents blindly. Infact Vaalmeeki has brought this out as well. Raama gives the reason why he cannot accept Seetha's advice through her parable and precedent. The Situation is different.

But we cannot ignore precedents.

9: SHARANAM: (Refuge, shelter, protection)

Raama seeking asylum! Ah!

In Kishkinda kaanda, chapter 4, Vaalmeeki uses the word 'Sharanam' coming out of the mouth of the great warrior and prince, Lakshmana, when he meets Hanumaan along with his brother Raama. Hanumaan had asked him about the purpose of their visit to this forest. Lakshmana tells him that they are on a search of Raama's wife Seetha who had been abducted. They are there only for this purpose: To meet Sugreeva and seek'REFUGE=Sharanam' under him in the hope that Sugreeva will find Seetha for them.

Sharanam is a strong word. Raama and Lakshmana are princes. They are no mean warriors. Sugreeva is a monkey although a prince of monkeys. Deeply religious people consider Raama as an Avathar of Vishnu. Why then did Vaalmeeki use this strong word. Lakshmana could have told Sugreeva that Raama seeks Sahaayyam = Help, from Sugreeva. He could have added that they want Sakhyam=Friendship with Sugreeva. Yet, in about 8 or 9 stanzas, Lakshmana uses this word. Raama seeks asylum under Sugreeva! In sloka 20 of this chapter, there is no ambiguity. Vaalmeeki never will deceive you or himself. If he had used this word, it is for a definite purpose. "Oh Hanumaan! Raama has always been a man of Dharma who gave ***refuge*** to all in the world. And that man, my brother Raama, now ***seeks Sharanam = refuge under Sugreeva*** "And in the previous sloka 19, Lakshmana had referred to their father king Dhasharatha thus "Whose father being a devotee of Dharma was The Refuge to all, such a man's son, this Raama now seeks asylum under Sugreeva"

How can Raama the prince of Ikshwaaku lineage, an avathar, a man, seek refuge under a monkey? Rather strange, but not quite. Nothing is strange for Vaalmeeki. When the chips are down you have to bend, no matter who you may be. This is the Universal truth. Vaalmeeki expounds this. Lakshmana is a wise man, and has not used this expression without deliberation. Yes they are seeking asylum under a monkey. No doubt about this. All for a noble purpose.

When Sugreeva in gratitude accepts Raama and Lakshmana, there is no reference to Sharanam=Asylum, refuge. Let us refer to chapter 5 slokas 11 & 12 where in Sugreeva says "Oh Raama! That you desire to form ***Sakhyam=Friendship*** with me. a mere monkey, is indeed an honour to me. If you desire friendship, here is my extended hand" Sugreeva knows who he is and to whom he is talking to. So he never dares to say = Raama, I will give you asylum= And Vaalmeeki also knows Lakshmana quite well. Yes. When the chips are down, you bend. no matter!

On a personal note:

His Holiness Swargeeya Abhinava Vidya Theertha Swamin, the then pontiff of Sringeri, in fact stimulated your author's interest in Vaalmeeki, by enlightening him about the use of this word = Sharanam= in Kishkinda kaanda by Vaalmeeki, that had somewhat disturbed him in ignorance!

10: **MAATHRU-VATHSALA**: Mother's Love

That a mother's love for her child is unique, is to state the obvious. Vaalmeeki has talked about this in a few places.

Queen Kaikeyi's love for her son Bharatha is such that not only she wants her son to be crowned, but drives away her 'step' son Raama to forest forthwith. It is well known, that it is Raama who was very dear to her, treated her like his mother. Kaikeyi's affection for Raama was equally strong.

Infact her first reaction when she heard of Raama's coronation was one of ecstasy. (Ayodhya-chapter 7) "Hearing Manthara's words, while reclining in her couch, Kaikeyi was filled with joy, her face glowed like the full moon. She became extremely exhilarated, and gave an ornament to Manthara, for bringing her the news" Yet, when Manthara 'works' upon her and tells her how her son Bharatha would be reduced to slavery if her step son Raama ascends the throne, she becomes wicked and her love for her son Bharatha blinds her and makes her aggressive.

Kowsalya is a deeply religious person. Yet when she hears her son Raama banished for 14 years, she says (Ayodhya - chapter 24) "Oh Raama! Wherever you go, I will follow you. How can a cow be separated from its calf. Will not a cow (me, your mother) follow her calf (you, my son) to the forest? "And Kowsalya bemoans (Ayodhya-chapter 20-slokas 36&37).

"Oh Raama! Had you not been born to me and thus made me childless, I would not be suffering like this today. For a barren woman, her only suffering is that she is childless. There is no other torment in her!"

By this Kowsalya says that a mother's bond is something different from the rest. 10 months of bearing a child in her womb gives her a special status: It is not just physical but her heart rests with her son/daughter ever after. That is why Bharatha who was horrified by his mother Kaikeyi's action in sending Raama to forest to make him 'king' instead, 'hits' her at the place which will hit a mother most (Ayodhya-chapter 73-sloka 5) "Shame on me that I had to spend 10 months in your womb!"

Mythologically, Surabhi, the celestial cow (Kaama dhenu) is the mother of all cows. Thus she has millions as her children. Yet! She grieves to see two of her 'children' suffering. (Ayodhya - chapter 74) Gist: Seeing two bullocks tired and unable to bear a heavy load at mid day, and whipped by their master, this 'mother' Surabhi who was looking down on earth from sky shed tears! Two drops of her tears fell on Lord Indra as he was flying over the sky and his eyes fell on Surabhi who was crying. He addressed her "Oh! 'We' have no fear or danger or suffering from any one in the universe. When that is so what may be the cause of your anguish?" And Surabhi told him "Yes, Oh Indra! We have no fear from any quarter. Yet, look at my two children on earth, these two bullocks, being tormented by heavy load and sweat at mid-day. I am unable to suffer this, the suffering of my two children!

Indra was wonder struck. Could not believe that Surabhi who had millions of children could grieve over these two children.! We may quote the slokas 25 & 26 of chapter 74 of Ayodhya: Gist: "None is equal to a child in the matter of love.. Therefore seeing these two, my children, my heart bled! "And Indra realised "None is dearer to a mother than her son!" ***Vaalmeeki conveys this universal Truth about Mother.***

11: HASTHA-KRIYA (Manual Labour)

Abraham Lincoln, not only could fell a tree, but could fashion-building materials for a log cabin. It is said that he made a coffin to bury his mother. And he was just 16. Whether The Presidency was in his mind, we do not know but he never shied away from manual work. And he was called Honest Abe!

Vaalmeeki presents Manual Labour, not with such high sounding sophisticated terminology like 'Dignity of Labour', but as part of our duty and Dharma. Lakshmana is the scion of the Ikshwaakus. But no manual labour was below his dignity. Serving his brother Raama and his sister.in.law was part of his Dharma. Lakshmana was not in

Ayodhya, where his legs and hands used to be caressed and massaged by charming ladies of the Royal household. He is in deep forest. He carries loads to their hermitage. Takes care of water needs. Ayodhya in Kaanda-chapter 103, we find Kowsalya, telling Sumithra, the mother of Lakshmana in anguish "Oh Sumithra! Your son, Lakshmana is carrying water for my son Raama, ever unwearied in service, service through manual labour" Kowsalya is so upset that she prays that her step son Lakshmana will not have to suffer any longer as she will beg Raama to return to Ayodhya, cutting short his exile, and save further agony for his brother Lakshmana "At least now, this, your son Lakshmana, who is not used to such suffering and menial tasks, will he give up doing all this?"

Lakshmana not only was never tired of doing manual labour. He was dexterous. Highly skilled with his hands, he must have undergone some training in Ayodhya as a Royal prince! When Raama accompanied by Seetha and Lakshmana, reaches Chithrakoot, Raama who was pleased with that place and tells Lakshmana (Ayodhya-chapter22) "Oh Lakshmana! Bring strong logs of wood, from choicest trees. Build a cottage here. My mind delights living here" Lakshmana, on hearing such words from Raama, brought various 'wood' from trees and he built a small cottage" Again, later on, at Panchavati, Raama tells Lakshmana (Aaranya-chapter 15) Gist: "Build a cottage near a place within reach of water....amidst trees where we can get Samiths etc" Lakshmana replies "Oh Raama! For hundreds of years, I am but your obedient servant! Therefore as you say =Get it done= it becomes your command and I will execute it without delay" Lakshmana built an extensive hermitage, walls plastered in good clay, well supported by strong pillars, using long well split bamboos, using good wood, ropes .....floor evenly laid, ... Raama was so pleased by this hermitage, he hugged him and said: "Oh Lakshmana! I am pleased. This is great work. All I can offer you as my present, is this my hug". And once, when they were crossing river, Lakshmana had built a small raft!

During the construction of 1,000 mile long bridge over the Ocean into Lanka, the monkeys finished this in just under 5/6 days. (Yudhdha kaanda-chapter 22) Some of these monkeys were sons of celestials and had never done this kind of manual work.

Yes. ***Vaalmeeki knows the Dharma of Hastha-Kriya, manual labour.***

12: AADESHA: (Commandments)

By tradition, we have the following Commandments:

(a)Sathyam vadha = Speak Truth

(b) Dharmam Chara= Practise Dharma

(c) Maathru Dhevo Bhava= Be devoted to mother

(d) Pithru Dhevo Bhava= Be devoted to father

(e) Aachaarya Dhevo Bhava = Be devoted to teacher

(f) Athithi Dhevo Bhava = Be devoted to guests

Vaalmeeki Raamaayana covers all this comprehensively at all places and in diverse situations. Thus, this epic becomes a 'Book' on Commandments.

In today's world, it is not necessary or possible to follow all this totally. The world has changed beyond comprehension. We must however recognise that these were the basic values, recommended for good life. We will just skip through these in this Guide.

(a) ***Truth*** For our modern sage, Mahatma Gandhi, Truth was God. He was a Vishnu Bhaktha and Raama was God Vishnu on earth. Raamaayana rests on Truth as God Brahma ordains Vaalmeeki thus (Bala-chapter 2-sloka 36) Gist: "In this, your epic, words will never be false, but ever Truth........"

In describing the character of Raama, Poet Vaalmeeki says (Ayodhya-chapter 12-sloka 30) Gist: "***Truth,*** charity, Loyalty-friendship, Sacrifices- rituals, Integrity, sincerity abide in Raama ....." Truth gets the first place. In chapter 4,sloka 7, surprisingly through the lips of selfish Kaikeyi we have this on Truth "Truth is one word for Brahmam, Dharma itself rests on Truth, Only through Truth, we can obtain salvation".

Raama is the embodiment of Truth. Today we are very clever, we say something, later retract. This is not what I meant! = But Raama is not such a slippery character. He means what he says. In Ayodhya chapter 18 sloka 30 he affirms "Raama never speaks in two ways"

(b) Dharma;

There is no equivalent for dharma in any language. Dharma has to be 'realised', experienced. It is difficult to comprehend. Dharma comprises a range, a gamut of all activity. When we read Vaalmeeki, we go through this 'experience'. The word has its origin in root 'Dhar', to bear, to sustain, to preseve. Dharma could mean statute, law, decree, usage, duty, right, justice, virtue, morality, norms and so on. Mere understanding this term could make one, a man of Dharma. Practice of Dharma is difficult because Dharma is so complex and has to be adapted to situations and circumstances. If not properly followed, the very Dharma may hurt you. Infact when Vaalmeeki seeks enlightenment from divine sage Naaradha, he asks him. "Who is a man in this world who ***knows*** Dharma" (Bala kaanda chapter 1) Even knowing Dharma is so difficult, let alone practising Dharma. The Kshathriya has his Dharma; The sage has his own Dharma. and so on. And in describing Raama, Naaradha has this to say about him. (Sloka 12 & 13) "He ***knows*** Dharma, protector of Dharma, and is ***protector of his own Dharma..."*** Dharma follows

Vaalmeeki throughout this Epic. Vaalmeeki follows Dharma. It is said that only the study of Vedha can enlighten one on Dharma. Thus, Vaalmeeki's epic becomes Vedha at his hands because Dharma chases him and Valmeeki does not run away but follows Dharma throughout.! Your author craves pardon that he cannot enlighten you more, except to request you to study this Vedha, that is Raamaayana, in text or in translation.

(c) Mathru Dhevo Bhava

(d) Pithru Dhevo Bhava

In India the mother has a greater place than even a father! She bears you and sustains you in her body for 10 months. She brings you out and sustains you during your early years. In ancient times before Bhaarath became India, service and devotion to mother and father was considered equivalent to devotion to God. There are many places in Raamaayana where this is brought out. Today, owing to vast changes in our lives, this is dying out. At one point Raama tells Seetha (Ayodhya-chapter 30 slokas 33 to 35) Gist: "Oh Seetha! When we have before us father and mother, who are living 'gods' is it not strange that people go and 'seek' Gods that are not before them, and unseen? For me there is no means of purification than service to father and mother. Even (other Dharmas like) Truth, Rituals cannot yield the same results as service to father and mother" Vaalmeeki through Raama even treats visits to temples as of no consequence for a man who follows. Commandment- Mathru-Pithru Dhevo Bhava.

Time and again Vaalmeeki brings home the importance of this Commandment. In Ayodhya Kaanda, Dhasharatha narrates a story of how he became accursed because he had accidentally killed a young man of penance whose whole life was in the service of his infirm, old, blind parents. This young man went straight to heaven! (Ayodhya-chapters 63 & 64).

But we cannot ignore Bharatha when he rejects his mother Kaikeyi's bidding that he should take over the kingdom. The question arises why Bharatha did not accept his mother's request (or command) to take over the kingdom. Whatever may be Kaikeyi's design, she is his mother. Should he not have followed her and accepted her wish or command that he should become king? Here we are confronted with another Dharma. Bharatha cannot accept kingdom because it is against all norms of Dharma. When the eldest son is alive, the crown should go only to him and not to his younger brother. This is the traditional custom, the Dharma of Ikshwaakus. So Bharatha countermands his mother's order and tries to bring back his eldest brother Raama from forest to make him king instead. In the order of Commandments, Dharma precedes Mathru Dhevo Bhava! Bharatha follows the traditional Kshathriya Dharma.

Incidentally, when Bharatha starts talking ill of his mother Kaikeyi before Bharadhwaja, the sage reprimands him. A mother is a mother, should never be spoken ill of! (Ayodhya-chapter 92) This is how Bharatha introduces his mother Kaikeyi: Gist: "She, by whose immoral deed my father passed away, unable to bear separation from Raama, she, who is wrathful, obstinate, proud of her beauty, arrogant, she who is lover of power and wealth, an Un-Aryan, is this woman, my mother Kaikeyi!" Sage Bharadhwaja reprimands him at once thus "Oh Bharatha! Your mother should not be talked about thus, never considered wicked by you". The sage, proclaims Dharma, Commandment. = Maathru Dhevo Bhava =

(e) & (f) Aacharya Dhevo Bhava- Aththi Dhevo Bhava

A Teacher must always be respected and honoured. We find this throughout Vaalmeeki. So is a guest. A guest is not to be treated as a burden. Infact, he does service for us by blessing us. Even when she was alone and nervous, Seetha honours Raavana, little realising that he had come as a Brahimin only to deceive her and kidnap her. She offers him Arghya and Paadhya and fruits! (Aranya-chapter 46 & 47) She talks to this 'guest' thinking that this 'sage' may curse her if not properly spoken to!

The entire epic of Raamayana carries these commandments. We need not write more.

13: VIDHI-KRITHANTHA (Fate)

This is rather a difficult topic to write about. Yet, as we find reference to this at various places and in different situations in Vaalmeeki, we must take note of this. Fate is the ultimate agency or power that predetermines the course of events. No matter how powerful you are and how sure you are, fate ultimately decides the course of events and you realise that you are powerless. The poet, philosopher Bharthruhari who lived in this land some 1,800 years ago, no doubt believed in Fate. But he could not stand his countrymen sitting idle, doing nothing and bemoaning = What does it matter. Fate takes care of everything = So he wrote as admonishment against these good for nothing folks. We give you the gist "Forget about God and Fate. Take to manliness and put in your effort. And if you don't succeed, so what" Infact Bharthruhari uses strong words = Deivam-Nihathya = Kill God and fate! We make no apology to begin this topic by referring to that great Indian, Bharthruhari. Because we shall presently see such a noble man Lakshmana talking in this vein about Fate!

As this is only a Guide and not a dissertation on Indian philosophy, we shall just enumerate reference to Fate as it is written about in Vaalmeeki.

Thrishanku was a great Ikshwaaku king, a forefather of Raama. Somehow it got into his head that he should go to heaven in his mortal body! Vasishta's sons curse him to become an untouchable. Still he wanted to go to heaven as a human being and approached Vishwaamithra to do yaaga for this purpose. In Baala kaanda, chapter 58. we have the story: Gist: "Oh Vishwaamithra ! 100 yagas I have performed. Yet this is what I have received as fruits of my penance!" He bemoans thus before the great sage "Everything is caused by Fate. Fate is supreme. Fate is the universal Refuge! I consider man's effort worthless before fate" As a passing reference, we may make a few observations. King Thrishanku failed in observing Dharma. Heaven is the abode for those who have no physical attachment. Heaven is the abode for the spiritual. But Thrishanku failed to realise this. Fate acted as justice and punished him thus. The lovely, handsome body with which he wanted to seek abode in heaven was reduced to ugly, deformed body, associated with an untouchable! It is with this body, Vishwaamithra sends him to a heaven of his creation! (Baala-chapter 60).

Fate-Raama & Lakshmana

Raama is to be crowned successor the next morning. All preparations are over at Ayodhya for this great event. Something happens at Dhasharatha's palace. You may call it The Midnight Drama, if you like. Kaikeyi has her way. Raama is to be banished for 14 years and it is her son Bharatha who is to be crowned instead. All this happened in a matter of couple of hours during night!

Raama accepts this without any ill will to any one. His stepmother Kaikeyi, is still his 'mother' whom he venerates! But Lakshmana cannot accept all this. He is in wrath. This is the scenario. (Ayodhya-chapter22) Raama expounds the philosophy of fate!

"Lakshmana! You must look at all this as the work of Fate. My losing the kingdom that was offered, in just under a couple of hours. My exile as well." And Raama makes an interesting reference to Fate. It was well known that his 'step' mother Kaikeyi loved Rama just as much, if not more, as her own son Bharatha. Raama loved her as much as her own mother Kowsalya.

Raama talks about Fate thus (Ayodhya-chapter 22) Gist "Oh Lakshmana! If what has happened to me is not the work of destiny and Fate, how else could Kaikeyi have caused all this, my exile. You know very well never before there was any distinction between my mother and 'mother' Kaikeyi. For Kaikeyi also, there was never any distinction between her son Bharatha and me, I perceive clearly that there can be no reason other than Fate ......that she should utter such cruel words .....that she should send me away for 14 years".

We have Lakshmana. The Kshathriya in him comes out. Ofcourse Raama is just as much a kshathriya warrior as Lakshmana. Only with this difference. Raama could perceive. Lakshmana had no such eye at that moment!

By sloka 20, Raama expounded the truth about fate in a nutshell. "Lakshmana! When, unexpectedly, inconceivably, certain occurrences are not hindered, that, is the work of fate. This is manifested, in me, in Kaikeyi, in diverse and perverse ways "

Lakshmana refuses to accept fate & all that stuff " Oh Raama! Your opinion that the action of Kaikeyi and Dhasharatha are the work of Fate does not please me at all. In any case this must be investigated, deliberated further by you" By this Lakshmana wants a discussion on the so called

Fate. And Lakshmana, pressing home his own views in this matter starts talking! "Oh Raama! He who has no bravery, who is weak, submits to Fate timidly Brave men of self reliance don't sit around -Fate- and do nothing. He, who, by his manliness drives away impediments caused by (the so called) Fate, only that man never gets disheartened and achieves results." If we had mentioned the great philosopher Bharthruhari earlier, it is only as support to Lakshmana.

Lakshmana gives vent to his feelings in this matter of Fate

"Oh Rama! Let the world witness the power of man over Fate! People will witness the knocking down of Fate by my manliness. Like seizing an unmanageable wild elephant, I will suppress this Fate which denied you the crown. Oh Raama, listen! The suffering to you caused by Fate, will pale into insignificance by the suffering caused by the power of my arms. My two hands are not for beautification with armlets and unguents. My bow is not a piece of jewelry. My sword is not a load, an attachment. I will suppress the 'agents' who caused harm to you" The tirade goes on. Chapter 23 Ayodhya is interesting reading. Fate versus Manliness.

Raama knows that it is difficult to convince Lakshmana particularly when he is in wrath. Instead of entering into polemics, he merely says "Lakshmana! You must know me as a man of conviction, that the righteous path is in obeying the command of my father" Without going into the question of Fate Raama effectively answers Lakshmana through Dharma.The Commandment.Mathru-Pithru Dhevo Bhava.

Raama's mother is a deeply religious person. It is not surprising that she accepts Fate as divinity. (Ayodhya-chapter 24-sloka 33) "Oh Raama! In this world, the work of Fate can never be apprehended. It is this, I feel, that has made you reject my prayer that you should not go on exile"

By this Kowsalya tells Raama that although he is the most dutiful son and will never go against the wishes of his mother (Maathru dhevo Bhava), if now he is going against her wishes it is because of Fate. Fate separates them now!

Even demon Kabhandha has this to say about Fate: (Aaranya-chapter 72-sloka 20) "Oh Raama! Fate can never be overcome. What happens inevitably, that, cannot be stopped or changed"

Vaali-Sugreeva-Thaara on Fate.

Vaali was mortally wounded by a single arrow from Raama. Just before his death, Vaali calls his brother Sugreeva and tells him that although he really loved him, it was Fate that had separated them. (Kishkinda-chapter 22-sloka 4) "Oh Sugreeva! It is ***ordained*** that between us brothers, there cannot be that brotherly happiness that is associated with brothers, and it is ordained, that we cannot live happily together, enjoy happiness together. That is why it has happened this way!"

And when Thaara, wife of Vaali was wailing in the field over her husband, Raama has this to say to her. (Kish-chapter 24-sloka 44) "Oh Thaara! All the Three Worlds are under His (God's) control! None can transgress Fate as decreed by Him" Here Raama says that The Lord is The Cause, the Fate that predetermines our destiny.

Seetha's view on Fate is coupled with Time-Kaala. Fate takes its own time and acts. When she was undergoing imprisonment at Lanka, and she could not bear the suffering any longer, she contemplates suicide, she bemoans (Sundara- chapter 28-sloka 3) Gist: "Venerable people say that, Death does not come by till the 'appointed' time." Seetha thus affirms, even if a person decides on suicide, he will die only when the time for death arrives. Fate will decide this. Fate will chose the time!

The great Hanumaan, grieves over the miserable Seetha thus at Asoka forest (Sundara-chapter16-sloka 3) "When even Seetha, the wife of the lord (Raama) and who is honoured by Lakshmana, should be in this state of suffering, we can only conclude, that none can overcome Fate"

Yes! Fate is an integral part of our philosophy.

Vaalmeeki brings out this throughout.

Bharatha and Fate

It is befitting we conclude this topic with reference to Bharatha. Bharatha considered his brother Raama as God on earth. Ayodhya kaanda - chapter 101- sloka 4, is of great significance. We give the gist of this. This is what he says. "They, who talk about his conduct as enjoined with Dharma and Artha, and talk of him as a divine being, also talk about him as though this king is just a human being! But as far as I am cocerned, he is to be revered and considered only as Divinity":

So, when Bharatha hears from Guha that such a Raama slept on bare earth during his first day of exile, he grieves and gives vent to his feelings thus (Ayodhya-chapter 88-sloka11) "If Raama, the son of Dhasharatha should lie on bare earth, it only means that that even God is not stronger than Fate!"

Yes! Fate is an integral part of our philosophy. ***Vaalmeeki brings out this throughout.***

14: PRAJAA - PRABHUTHVA (Democracy)

There is this apparent contradiction. In modern India we are to believe that there can never be democracy under a king. We call ourselves a republic, of the people, by the people, for the people and what not! The Ikshwaku kings would never qualify for this political title. Democrat.

Dhasharatha was the ruler of Ayodhya kingdom. In those days Ayodhya had a pride of place and Dhasharatha was a Mahaa-Raaja. = emperor! He had the divine right of kings, he could rule as an absolute dictator. We began this topic with an 'apparent contradiction' How can a ruler armed with absolute power be a democrat.

Before Bharatha Varsh became India that is Bharath, one thing stood out and that was Sanaathana Dharma =Eternal Norms. Even our religion was not Hinduism but Sanaathana Dharma. Based on our scriptures, Vedhas and Ithihaas. Dhasharatha although a 'dictator' would not violate the unwritten laws, the Sanaathana Dharma. Vaalmeeki, throughout the epic stresses that all our actions should be for the welfare of all. Vaalmeeki even talks about restrictions on kings while they go on hunting sport in forest. (In Ayodhya-chapter 49) Raama says "In this world, hunting in forest for amusement for royal sages (kings) who are expert wielders of bow, is accepted as proper, ***only at proper times***.........." By this Raama, a great marksman and 'hunter' rejects indiscriminate hunting although none can question his action. He is emperor's son. The kings those days were democrats, not dictators although they had the divine right to be so!

When King Dhasharatha contemplates handing over the kingdom to his crown prince Raama as he was old, and 'tired', by the divine right of kings, he could appoint his eldest son Raama to the throne. He could even appoint any one he likes? But Dhasharatha being a democrat in spirit as most of the kings were those days when there was never a written constitution of the people, by the people and for the people, he calls not just his ministers but calls an assembly of citizens drawn from all castes and communities. (Ayodhya-chapter 1) "Leaving out people living in far away cities and places, king Dhasharatha, asked such of those citizens and lords to assemble before him in his council hall. He appeared like Lord Indra, when he was thus surrounded by men from cities and villages"

What is Vaalmeeki all about? It is Dharma that you strive through Vaalmeeki. No written constitution, absolute right for people in power, yet it is Sanaathana Dharma that they all practise. Readers should forgive us when we grieve thus The Indian constitution is a beautiful essay, but it is only a scrap of paper= There is no heart or spirit in it!

This is how emperor Dhasharatha who had ruled for thousands of years addresses (Ayodhya-chapter 2) Gist: "You are aware that this kingdom was ruled and protected by my forefathers like a son. Following my forefathers, the citizens were protected by me also, without sleep, to the best of my ability. My body is decayed. I wish to give rest to this body of mine that is physically worn out. I therefore seek retirement after appointing my son Raama" After giving reasons and after announcing the name of his successor, Dhasharatha, the democrat says "This is my desire. ***But if you have any alternative. may you deliberate*** upon it" And now comes the master piece ***from Vaalmeeki through Dhasharatha "Only when a matter is examined by those who are neutral (who have no vested interests), great prosperity to all results***"

No comment is necessary! This is the democracy of our ancients.

Even in the matter of marriage of his son, Dhasharatha seeks counsel. Afterall, whoever marries his son, will become queen. The citizens have a right to know and accept her as such. (Baala-chapter 68) Gist: "My son Raama has been found by the king of Mithila, the great Janaka, as truly brave! He desires to offer his daughter Seetha in marriage. ***If this pleases you***, we shall go to Mithila "Only when all his ministers and Rishi-s and sages there accept this,

Dhasharatha goes to Mithila with a large retinue for the marriage. Vaalmeeki thus affirms that a prince just cannot marry whoever he likes unless it is approved by the council of ministers and by elders.

Interestingly even the demon king Raavana exhibits some qualities of a democrat! Only with this difference. He had no character. He had no understanding of Dharma. His counsellers were men of A-Dharma. (Yudhdha-chapter 6) Raavana asks his Council. Incidentally this chapter is interesting reading. Raavana speaks words of wisdom. Alas he merely speaks but does not follow! "The wise and noble say, that victory comes by only when the matter is deliberated by wise men"

Yes. They were liberal. They were democrats. Vaalmeeki thus brings this out in many places.

15: HETHU-VRITHAM (Cause-Effect Syndrome)

Ours is a scientific mind. We cannot timidly accept events without assigning the cause. Quite a few who are of a scientific mind and upbringing have raised this issue. Why should three of the noblest of human species, undergo such a suffering. Raama, Lakshmana and Seetha. You cannot easily satisfy these men of science by saying that it is ordained thus. Bearing this in mind, we have attempted to give Hethu-Reasons for the Vritham- Effect- suffering undergone by these three during their exile. This write up is meant for those who cannot accept Fate and Karma so easily. So we have ventured to go 'scientific' We crave your indulgence!

Seetha is kidnapped. Suffers torture in Lanka. Raama cannot be without his beloved Seetha even for a moment. His suffering is terrible. As for Lakshmana who had accompanied Raama only for the sole purpose of protecting these two during exile, the suffering is even more. This is the situation. What is the cause of such suffering for these noble, pure human beings.

We may attempt to give reasons. We repeat, this exercise is only to satisfy men of scientific mind who are obsessed by the Cause-Effect syndrome. Vaalmeeki does not say nor have to say all this. For once your writer has strayed from Vaalmeeki! We refer to Aaranya kaanda-chapter 43. The demon Maareecha is trying to allure Seetha by taking on the form of a Golden deer of exceptional beauty. Seetha is enticed, allured. She must have this deer as her pet in her hermitage. She presses her husband. Raama succumbs, even though he is warned by Lakshmana that this is no deer but a demon in disguise.

Raama who is living the life of an ascetic and celibacy, suddenly loses his composure when he tells Lakshmana

"On this most excellent 'golden' skin of this deer, Seetha the Vaidhehi will sit by my side" ***For the sinless Raama, the ascetic, this very thought becomes his sin and he pays for the desire of enjoying company with Seetha in luxury of a deer skin.*** Thus he is drawn away by the deer (demon Maareecha) and Seetha is kidnapped while he is away.

What was Seetha's sin. Most unbecoming cruel words, words of character assassination pour out of her mouth on Lakshmana who considers Seetha as a Goddess, when he refuses to leave her alone in the hermitage. This was the sin of the sinless Seetha here. The result of her sin was that she drove away Lakshmana and was left alone for Raavana to kidnap her easily.

What was Lakhshmana's sin? Well. He disobeyed his brother Raama who had ordered him not to stir out of the hermitage under any circumstances. A soldier never disobeys a command, even under trying circumstances or under provocation. Here, this was the sin of sinless Lakshmana.

We have thus three sins, these sins were the Hethu-s for the Vrithi-(consequence) suffering of all the three.

We repeat. All this is not Vaalmeeki's. We have written this only for satisfying the agnostics who go by Cause-Effect syndrome.

16: **RAAJA DHOOTHA** (King's ambassador)

We covered a part of this topic when we described Hanumaan's character. Yet we wish to write a few more lines on this topic as is seen by Vaalmeeki.

Hanumaan is a near perfect ambassador. In Kishkinda-chapter 3, we find some qualities of a good ambassador listed: Gist: "An ambassador must be highly educated, must have knowledge of the Shaasthras. He must have a good command of language. Must have studied grammar. He must be a good speaker, not only speak well and clearly but his demeanour must be striking. His address must be short, crisp, effective. No ambiguity in his speech. Words should come out unhaltingly. No tardiness. Moderation in voice. Words must come out of his heart, to give the impression that he is conveying with sincerity....." Vaalmeeki says that if a king is not endowed with a good ambassador, he will stand to lose. With a good ambassador, a king's task gets a nice beginning and good results follow...

Even when an ambassador goes on a serious mission like giving an ultimatum for war like what Angadha did before Raavana, he must have some basic qualities. He must be brave, without fear, being in enemy's territory, with war imminent. And if he fears that the enemy will violate the International Convention of not harming an ambassador, he must be quick to 'get away' and save himself from harassment.

Whatever one may say about an ambassador, even in modern times, an ambassador is also a sort of spy. He must have a sharp eye. No wonder Hanumaan is considered a great ambassador.

17: MITHRA -THVAM (Friendship)

Vaalmeeki has touched this topic from diverse angles. Let us begin with a base form of friendship. Friendship of demon king Raavana and his friend, the terrible demon Maareecha. There can never be friendship when it is based on A-Dharma. When Raavana, on hearing from his spies that his chiefs like Khara were destroyed by Raama in Janasthana in India, he rushes to India in wrath and seeks assistance from Maareecha to help him in the abduction of Seetha. (Aaranya-chapter 31-sloka 42) Maarecha gives him sound advice "Oh Raavana!

By which enemy of yours, ***appearing as your friend,*** was Seetha informed to you" When Maareecha advises him not to have anything to do with Raama, Raavana gets back to Lanka. He accepts Maareecha's advice as from a friend and well wisher.

But not for long. Again he gets back to him. But this time he approaches Maareecha as the king of demons! But he begins his plea by saying "Oh Maareecha! Suffering as I am, you ***are indeed my refuge***" Raavana has a scheme by which his friend Maareecha, through his magic should roam around Raama's hermitage as a golden deer of exceptional grace and beauty, entice Seetha, make Raama and Lakshmana go out of hermitage to capture this 'deer' for Seetha and Raavana would then kidnap Seetha when she is alone. Maareecha reacted instantly to this obnoxious scheme and poet Vaalmeeki expresses the universal truth, by the famous sloka (2) in Aaranya-chapter37-"Oh Raavana! It is always easy to find flatterers, (friends) who speak sweetly. But rare indeed is to find one, who speaks unpleasantly, but speaks what is salutary (for his friend) And rarer still to find one who will listen to him". Maareecha tells Raavana, that as he is his friend and well wisher, he is advising Raavana strongly not to have anything to do with Raama if he knows what is good for him. His advice may sound harsh to Raavana. But this is the advice that he would give him because it is good for his friend Raavana.

The rest is history. Raavana forgets himself. Threatens to kill his 'friend' Maareecha if he does not help him. Maareecha realising that his friend Raavana is in wrath, goes through this scheme, and gets killed by Raama but not before Raavana abducts Seetha, as per the strategy. Friendship did not save Maareecha. Raavana also is killed by Raama in war not long after.

The friendship between Raama and Sugreeva begins through a common cause of woes between them. Raama had 'lost' his wife Seetha and Sugreeva had lost his wife Ruma to his brother Vaali. Both ofcourse have lost their kingdoms as well! Both need mutual support. But their friendship grew with time and was based on Dharma and not on mere self interest. Quite true Raama tells Sugreeva soon after forming a friendship over fire as witness (Kish-chapter 5) "Oh great monkey Sugreeva! It is well known to me that true friendship is in bestowing service to a friend in need. I will kill your brother Vaali who abducted your wife" Sugreeva is a wise monkey and realises what friendship with Raama means to him. This follows the old adage = Tell me who his friends are, then I will know him truly= In chapter 8 of Kishkinda, we have a few slokas wherein we find Sugreeva talking about friendship; Gist:

"Oh Raama, as you are now my friend, I am blessed with the favour of Dhevas. No doubt. As you of the great family of Raghu-s, are my friend, I will share honours with friends and relatives." By this Sugreeva tells Raama that he will no longer be a monkey of ridicule, as he has now the great Raama as his friend. Vaalmeeki brings home this point. Sugreeva wants Raama to know that he is an honest man, his friendship is sincere "In course of time, Oh Raama, you will come to know me as a true friend. I am not competent to talk about myself!" By this Vaalmeeki says that friendship may begin under different circumstances, Even with selfish interests. But between noble men, friendship would keep growing. Friendship is beyond status or society. "Whether poor or wealthy, whether in happiness or distress, whether wicked or good, a friend alone is his refuge! Whether gold, or ornaments or property, friends consider these as undivided property." Sugreeva is so happy he tells Raama. "The affection of great men of pure souls like you, is ever abounding, firm, and steady, like the courage of a man of firmness and composure" Later, when Lakshmana visits him in wrath, Sugreeva expounds another truth about friendship."It is easy to form friendship, but difficult to sustain, nourish, and flourish" As events proved Sugreeva became a close friend of Raama.

We had observed that friendship is beyond status or society. We have the tribal chief, Guha who perhaps was closest to Raama as a friend. The scion of Ikshwaakus- rubbing shoulders with a rustic! Ah.! Vaalmeeki brings home this point beautifully in his epic.

Vibheeshana defects to Raama just before war. But friendship marks their association. He is never treated as a defector from the enemy camp. When he is crowned king of Lanka after Raama had killed his brother Raavana, this is what Raama tells Lakshmana (Yudha-chapter 115) Gist:

"Oh Lakshmana! You will crown Vibheeshana, who is most affectionate, devoted and who has done so much for me. If I see Vibheeshana crowned as king of Lanka, that would be foremost to me!" Raama ofcourse is an ideal friend. He treated even vassals as a friend. We should read Vaalmeeki to get a total view on friendship.

18: **RISHI-s, SAGES**: (Men of penance, mendicants)

It is rather a shame that in India today quite a large number of men of religion go by external appearance and extraneous consideration. A religious and spiritual leader taking to car as a means of transport invariably falls down in their 'esteem'. Their 'living Gods' should be above all these mundane things. There are sages and sages, there are rishi-s and rishi-s in Vaalmeki Raamaayana and it is worthwhile for us to read about them.

Sages are human and humane. What makes the difference between us and the sages is in the total detachment. We have Dharma, Artha, Kaama, Moksha. In practice of Dharma if they use mundane things (Artha) it is without Kaama (passion and attachment). Their goal was only Moksha. This is the basic difference between us and spiritual men.

When Dhasharatha commands his ministers to provide a (first class) chariot for Brahma Rishi Vasishta to go to Mithila to attend his son Raama's marriage, Vasishta, the Saptha Rishi did not turn down the offer because his spirituality would not accept the comfort of a chariot.(Bala kanda-chapter 69). It is Vasishta and Vamadheva who should go first to Mithila.Vasishta did not walk to Mithila!

Vaalmeeki, at many places has brought out this point. How human and humane are these sages at times and behave like ordinary men. Raama asks Vishwaamithra "Oh Lord, whose place is this?" Vishwaamithra replies "It is my abode" And does not stop with this but his affection for

Raama is that of a father towards his son. So he adds "Oh Raama, As this is mine, it becomes yours as well!"

The man of 1,000 penances, this Brahma Rishi, this creator of another 'universe', Vishwaamithra who had abandoned family, talks like this as though Raama belongs to him! (Bala-chapter 29).

We have Sage Bhardhwaaja at Prayaag (modern Allahabad). We will be writing separately about his feast, his hospitality, to Bharatha's army. After indicating a place for stay in forest to Raama, when they leave, this is what happens to the great sage Bhardhwaja who, in his life time on earth had realised 'Brahmam'. Vaalmeeki in Ayodhya-chapter 55-sloka 2, says "The great sage Bhardhwaaja blessed them (blessed Raama, Seetha and Lakshmana) with Swasthi. ***When they were going away, he followed them to a distance like a father** !"*

Again, when Bharatha with his huge army visits him at Prayaag, Bharadhwaja like an ordinary man wants him to introduce his mothers to him (Ayodhya-chapter 92)- Bharatha introduces Kowsalya, Sumithra and Kaikeyi!

Whenever a great sage visits a king, almost the first questions he puts him is about the welfare of The State. (Bala-chapter- slokas 44 & 45) Vishwaamithra asks king Dhasharatha about king's welfare, about city and towns, about state of finance, friends and relatives etc = Oh Dhasharatha! Are the feudal lords obedient to you? Are your enemies kept under check? Are your mundane and spiritual activities being properly observed? = And Brahma Rishi Vishwaamithra, observing strict protocol, only after enquiring about the welfare of the king, directs his enquiry on the 'fellow' Brahma Rishi, the great sage Vasishta! And then he successively enquired others.

We have the great and most powerful sage Agasthya, who teaches Raama the prayer of prayers, The Aadhithya Hridhaya in Yudha Kaanda.

When Raama, along with Seetha and Lakshmana visits him, (Aaranya-chapter 12), Agasthya talks about the quality that marks a man of penance "Oh Raama! If a sage does not conduct himself properly, but acts perversely, differently, he will fall down and forced to live upon his own flesh. ***He will be treated with contempt like a False Witness***"

Agasthya, so human and humane, has a word of advice to Raama (Aaranya chapter13) "Oh Raama! Seetha is following you, She is doing a great deed, most difficult for a girl. You must act in such a way, she will be happy here" Even Kowsalya, her mother.in.law did not talk to Seetha like this when she had left Ayodhya. Agasthya talks to Raama as though Seetha is his daughter.

The great lady of mighty penance. Anasooya. (Ayodhya-chapters 117 &118). is the wife of the Saptha Rishi Athri. Valmeeki describes her as one 'who is bathed' in vows! She could bring rain without cloud formations in off season! Such spiritual power she has. She had given up everything for spiritual activity. Yet when Seetha visits her, she becomes a 'woman' like any ordinary woman. She wants Seetha to narrate story of her marriage to Raama! And she wants to see Seetha fully decorated. She had preserved the jewelry she had worn as a girl! "Oh Seetha! wear these. Like Goddess Lakshmi before Vishnu, you will bring lustre to your husband, dressing yourself up and anointing yourself with wonderful unguents! "Vaalmeeki wrote reality. How human can a woman get. Here is Anasooya, the woman of mighty penance, who matches any man of penance in the world, wants to decorate this young Seetha and take a look! Ah!

Yes. Sages and Rishi-s are also human!

19: THE VIMAANA- PUSHPAKA
(Divine Air Carrier)

There is no limit to man's fantasy. But not infrequently fantasy turns out to be reality. We do go to moon and come back safe! Yet, this divine Air craft-Air carrier-Air station-Aerial mansion The Pushpaka Vimaana is beyond comprehension. (In Sundara-chapters 7 to 9) we find the description, which will tax the mind of even a Nobel prize scientist. Gist "It was named Pushpaka. A great space-ship. Glittering with gems, walls decorated with pictures of birds, animals, mountains." When stationary it was a mansion. It becomes a helicopter when it carries you for a short trip over the sky. It becomes a flying mansion when large numbers are to be carried, tt fly at will, does not need aviation fuel. It can fly with the speed of mind.

This was created by the divine architect Vishwakarma for God Brahma Himself. It inflames one's passion when he just takes a look at it. There were mounds made of gold for doing Fire rituals as per Vedhic Rites The steps leading to this was made of Mahaa-neela and Indraja-neela stones. Your writer craves your indulgence as he is unable to give full justice to this divineAicraft. Readers may refer to the original text with translation.

Lord of wealth, Kubhaera, the brother of Raavana obtained this Pushpaka from God Brahma by rigorous penance. His brother could not tolerate this Gem with Kubhaera. In a terrific battle, he seized this from Kubhaera and made it his 'mansion' cum transport! (Sundara-chapter 9-sloka 13)

Raavana protected this Pushpaka, honoured it. It was his symbol of power. He had no problem to travel anywhere in the globe!

During the great war, when the army of monkeys was in disarray and Raama and Lakshmana were down with Brahma asthra, Raavana asks demoness Thrijata, to take

Seetha on this aircraft and fly over the battle ground so that seeing all this Seetha would accept the inevitable and become his wife. Seetha wails on seeing her husband down and his army in chaos. But Thrijata consoles her by saying (Yudha-chapter 48-sloka 25 & 26) "Oh Seetha! If these two, your husband Raama and Lakshmana are really dead, this Pushpaka Vimaana will not carry you there" By this Thrijata gives some 'character' to this divine Aircraft-Pushpaka. Pushpaka will never carry one to cremation ground. It is holy. If Raama is dead, it becomes a warrior's cremation ground. Pushpaka will never get there. So holy it is!

After the war is over, and Vibheeshana becomes the king of Lanka, he offers Pushpaka to Raama to get back to Ayodhya from Lanka. The entire army of monkeys travel in this Air-City- Pushpaka!

Raama is a man of justice. After he reaches Ayodhya along with such a retinue, almost the first act after his coronation is to return Pushpaka to Lord Kubhaera. King Vibheeshana had no say in this matter! Pushpaka goes back to Kubhaera from whom Ravan had seized it by force. (Yudha- chapte 130-sloka 61) "Oh Pushpaka! From now on you carry Lord Kubhaera"

Yes. You will not be stranded at airport or be on waiting list when Pushpaka is around.

20: SHOKA = (Grief)

This is not a profound statement. Grief affects us all. There is no human being who is not afflicted by grief at some stage in his life. This is the reality…

We may write a few lines on 'shoka' as Vaalmeeki sees it. When Raama is sent away on exile, his father Dhasharatha who had really no hand in if but had to submit to this because of the boons he had given to Kaikeyi, long long ago, suffers, and suffers terribly. Grief of separation from his beloved son takes his life away. But Raama's mother Kowsalya bears the grief of separation from Raama, and lives on although she wails (Ayodhya-chapter 20-sloka 51) "My heart is indeed a stone. It has not split up into thousand bits, although it is afflicted by grief and sorrow."

When Bharatha performs the last rites for his father and his mind and heart were not on the rituals because Grief had seized him, Vasishta is rather severe on him (Ayodhya-chapter 76-slokas 1 & 11) Gist: "Oh Bharatha! Enough of grief! You must do the last rites for the king (your father Dhasharatha) at the proper time. (bear in mind) Such of those rites for the king that are to be done, must be done calmly, clearly" Life must go on. Grief should be borne with equanimity and we must carry on with our duty. (Ayodhya-chapter 77 -slokas 22 & 23). He again admonishes Bharatha, but this time with philosophy. "Oh Bharatha! Today is the 13th. day. Why are you delaying in collecting the remains to perform rituals." Vasishta realising that he had been rather severe on the grief stricken Bharatha enlightens him philosophically.

"In all living beings. there exists without discrimination, The Pair = The Duality: The Universal law or truth, namely birth and death; male and female; happiness and grief =

WhenVaali's wife Thaara grieves over her husband in the field, it is Raama who enlightens her philosophically. (Kish-chapter 24) "Oh Thaara! The world is per the decree of God Brahma. Indeed! The World of Scriptures says Happiness and Grief are created by God Brahma, the creator" Thus Raama says that when the Creator Brahma created us, he created happiness and grief also for us with our birth. Raama adds (chapter 25-sloka2) "By merely tormenting ourselves by grief over the dead, he is not bestowed with fortune by our grief!"

Hanumaan goes further. He makes a mockery of those who grieve. He asks "Who is to grieve, for whom?"

Let us hear what Lakshmana has to say about Grief. (Kish-chapter 27-slokas 33 to 40) "Oh Raama! Enough of this!

You should not grieve thus. If one grieves, all efforts are wasted. Uproot your grief from the roots. Take to effort and perseverance" Time and again. Lakshmana who is Raama's mentor, stimulates Raama, telling him that no purpose is served by wasting ourselves by grieving.

Even Kowsalya who wails in utter grief has this to say about Grief (Ayodhya-chapter 57-sloka 30) "Oh Dhasharatha! Arise. Help rarely comes by to one in grief!"

Vaalmeeki says grief and self pity only add to our suffering. She says further (Ayodhya-chapter 62-sloka 15): "Grief destroys courage; Grief destroys understanding; Grief destroys everything. ***In fact there is no enemy greater than grief"***

Yes. We are human. We grieve. But we must bear grief with equanimity submitting ourselves to the will of God Brahma, the creator. Vaalmeeki advises us thus.

21: **PAITHRIYA:** (Heritage)

In the entire epic, Vaalmeeki stresses the importance of observing traditional values, respecting norms, protecting ancestral properties, trees and garden forests, grown through years and years and rivers. In this short write up we shall refer to Raama, which will give an idea of what Heritage is to Vaalmeeki.

Even when a person was taking bath in a fast flowing river, he had to observe norms. Rivers are public property and must always be clean. In Baala kaanda, chapter 2 we find Vaalmeeki taking bath in river Thamsa. He addresses his disciple thus Gist "See this beautiful bathing place with clear waters, ***like the heart of a pure man"*** Vaalmeeki compares the river to a pure man! He says further 'Keep down the water pitcher. Let me have my (bathing costume) of bark material. I am going to take bath "Vaalmeeki does not plunge directly into the river. The language used is suggestive. (sloka 20) ".....after bathing in river ***as per norms = Yathaa- Vidhi***-......" Even bathing in river is as per norms.

When Raama is about to leave with Seetha and Lakshmana on exile, he disposes of all his private wealth and belongings. But he makes a special request to his staff (Ayodhya-chapter 32-sloka 25) "Our separate houses, mine and Lakshmana's palaces, should not become dilapidated: must be maintained till we come back"

Raama's and Lakshmana's, palaces are not private property. They are heritage buildings, the property of Ikshwaakus. So Raama makes this request. Vaalmeeki brings home this point through one such example.

22: PUTHRA-BRAATHA-BHAANDHAVA

(Son, Brother, and Relatives)

There is no world without sons, brothers and relatives.! Vaalmeeki naturally touches upon their qualities. We know how close the brothers Raama, Lakshmana, Bharatha and Shathrugna were. A famous sloka is attributed to Raama. (Yudha-chapter 102-sloka 12) who talks about his relationship with his brother Lakshmana: Gist "In country after country, everywhere, one can find (obtain) wives. In country after country, everywhere, one can find relatives! But I cannot possibly see any country, anywhere in the world, where a ***constant companion is his brother***" Shathrugna was ever with his brother Bharatha. The brothers were good sons of their father. Dharma guided them.

It will not be out of place to mention that in the other great epic, The Mahaa Bharatha which was presented to the world thousands of years later, we find that war resulted between first cousins, sons born to two brothers. It became Adharma versus Dharma! In Raamaayana, these brothers were all endowed with noble qualities. They set an example how brothers should behave in the mundane world.

Interestingly, talking about sons and how sons should behave towards a father, Raama a man of modesty, loses this 'character' in him when he proudly tells Sugreeva (Yudha-chapter 18-sloka15) "Oh dear Sugreeva! All brothers are not like my brother Bharatha. ***All sons are not like me***! And ofcourse all friends are not like you!" Raama unwittingly pays himself a compliment. What Raama says is true. There can never be another son like Raama.

Talking about sons, their relationship with father, we find from Vaalmeeki sons with a totally different character than that of Raama. In Bala-chapter 62 Vishwaamithra's 100 sons are cursed by their father for not obeying his command. (Sloka 9 &10). He tells his sons why a father begets sons at all! "The purpose for which fathers beget sons who are desirous of their parents welfare, is only for the sake of welfare in the upper world. The time for such service is here and now."

Vishwaamithra wants one among his 100 sons to offer himself before Fire, as a substitute to another boy Shunashepa who wants to live on and who had sought Vishwaamithra's refuge and because Vishwaamithra had promised him that he would be alive at any cost. and need not offer himself to Fire. Naturally, the sons of Vishwaamithra are aghast by this 'unnatural' demand. Sacrificing one's own flesh and blood for another totally unrelated to you just to protect your ego. The point is, Vaalmeeki portrays the sons of Vishwaamithra as normal sons. In contrast we have Jamadagni's son Parashu-Raama obeying his angry father without question, strikes down his mother with one stroke of the axe. Raama had said that he 'will even jump into fire' if his father Dhasharatha wanted him to immolate himself. Vaalmeeki offers 'sons' to readers in his great epic! Ah!

We have brothers and brothers. Let us take a look at Raavana's brothers. We have also Vaali and his brother Sugreeva. Vaalmeeki projects brother-brother relationship differently in all these cases.

In the case of Vaali, it was love-hate relationship with his brother. Blood tells, and as they say blood is thicker than water! In Kishkinda kaanda, chapter 16-sloka 7 Vaali tells his wife Thara who does not want his brother killed " Oh Thaara! I am merely going there to fight him, to 'kill' his insolence I will not kill him, rest assured" When Vaali falls down, mortally wounded, he makes peace with his brother and he even removes the golden chain presented to him by his foster father Lord Indra and asks Sugreeva to wear this always when he is crowned king of monkeys. He regrets (Kishkinda-chapter 22) Gist: "Oh Sugreeva! It is not ordained that between us brothers, there can be that brotherly happiness that is associated with brothers which they can enjoy together." Vaali puts the blame on Fate. He grieves that he and Sugreeva could not live happily as brothers! Sugreeva too on seeing his brother Vaali who had tormented him for so long, about to lose his life, wails. He says he has no interest in life, is not interested in even becoming Vaali's successor to the throne of monkey kingdom! Yes. Blood tells!

Vibheeshana and Kumbhakarna are brothers of Raavana. They love him as a brother. Kumbhakarna admonishes his brother Raavana when he had kidnapped Seetha. (Yudha - chapter 12) Gist "Oh Raavana! When one who desires to do tasks that should be done first. later on, but does tasks first which should be done only later, he does not understand what is right and wrong. Oh Raavana!

You have no judgment. Only after taking a decision on the matter judiciously, one must act. You should have discussed all this with us before you undertook the kidnapping of Seetha" Ofcourse Kumbhakarna, like a normal brother who feels he should not let down his brother when he needs him most fights war for Ravana. But Vibheeshana acts differently. He defects to Raama.

Now comes Raavana's tirade against Vibheeshana (Yudha-chapter 16): Sometimes we are indebted to evil men for enlightenment. Here is a case of the 'devil quoting scriptures' as Raavana starts his diatribe, on brothers and on relatives in general. Gist: "Oh Vibeeshana! One can live with an enemy or with a cobra in wrath, but not with a brother like you. I know the behaviour of relatives (brothers) like you. Relatives always rejoice at the suffering of relatives." After 'hitting' out at Vbheeshana, Raavana quotes a parable "When an elephant in forest was caught it was bemoaning thus = it is not man's ropes that caused the loss of my freedom, but one of my own kind, the elephant" Readers know that to capture an elephant men use elephants that are already tamed for such jobs. Raavana goes poetic when he talks about relatives "Like rain drops on Lotus, there is no genuine attachment!"

Jealousy seizes relatives when they see prosperity abiding in their relatives. Ingratitude is normal with relatives. Like a honey bee jumping to another tree to suck more honey, a relative quickly abandons a relative after sucking him dry!

Even Raama makes reference to relatives, but in an oblique way. (Yudha-chapter 83-slokas 33 to 35) Raama expounds a truth Gist "For a man of substance, friends and relatives are many".

By nature human beings are selfsih, jealous, and egoistic. But with relatives these 'qualities' become severe and many of our troubles in family life, may be linked to this.

23: PAAPA-KALMASHA (Sin-Stain)

The concept of sin is historical, geographical and religious. This subject is intriguing! A person having more than as wife is considered a sinner and is charged with bigamy. But in a different world, in a different society, a man can have 4 wives without being called a sinner. Vaalmeeki talks about 'Sin' at various places. Under Character in Part II, we have already talked about 'Sin' as Bharatha sees it. Bharatha has listed quite a few, which he considers as sin. We may now look at 'Sin' as Vaalmeeki sees it through eyes of his other characters in the epic.

Sin is committed by a warrior if he shows his back during battle A warrior never kills a woman an old man or children. In Baala-chapter-5-slokas 21 &22, Vaalmeeki talks about warriors in Ayodhya thus: Gist "Bows are never stretched by experts in archery with dexterous hands, never hit those who are helpless, blind, or have no children...." Yet, Vishwaamithra (in Baala kaanda) admonishes Raama when he hesitates to kill the demoness Thaataka. Killing an evil woman is no sin. Infact it becomes the duty of a warrior.

According to the noble and virtuous lady Seetha, there are atleast three sins which should be avoided (Aaranya-chapter 9) First and foremost is to speak untruth. Second, going after another's wife and another woman. And third, violence. Here we may mention that Raama always followed Truth. He never cast his eye on any woman other than Seetha. He did not kill for killing's sake. He treated women as mother or sister. Vaalmeeki says that when his father fancied a woman and eventually married her, she became his 'mother' (Ayodhya-chapter118-sloka 6).

In law and justice, Vaalmeeki through Sage Agasthya says that the most obnoxious sin is false witness (Aaranya-chapter 12-sloka16).

The King of monkey world, Vaali has his own view on Sin (Kish-chapter 17- slokas35 to 37) The "Killer of a king, killer of cows, an atheist, one who marries before his elders get married, an informer-betrayer, an avaricious man, treacherous friend, defiler of teacher's wife, are all sinners who go to hell".

Raama's mother Kowsalya thinks that she is suffering without Raama because she had sinned in her previous birth. What is her sin? (Ayodhya-chapter 43-sloka 17) "Perhaps, in my previous birth, out of my avarice, the udders of cows, were hidden from their calves, pitilessly, denying milk for the young ones" According to the Indian traditional view, sins committed on earth will chase us in our next birth. Justice may be delayed. But sure enough we will have to bear the consequences of our sins, if not in this birth, surely in our next birth! Even Seetha bemoans thus (Yudha-chapter 32-sloka 30) "Perhaps, in my previous birth, foremost gifts as charity to the poor, was prevented by me. Thus, preventing charity is a sin.

Bharatha has more in his list of sins. Readers may refer to his long list in Part II. In Ayodhya-chapter 72, "I trust Raama has not swindled any poor brahmin of his wealth. I hope no sinless man, poor or rich, was harmed by Raama"

In International politics, killing an ambassador is a great sin. Having sex at improper times is sin, even with one's wife is a sin (Bala-chapter 48-sloka 19)

24: MADHU (Intoxicants)

In Vaalmeeki there is reference to Liquor at a few places. Incidentally there is no evidence that in those days there was smoking. Perhaps because tobacco is of recent origin.

Wines like Sura, Maireya, Aasava were popular. We are not competent enough to classify these, but students interested may do some research on Wines of the Vedhic era.

Even ladies of royalty must have consumed wines. We get an oblique reference to this from queen Kaikeyi. (Ayodhya-chapter 36-sloka 12): When Raama is about to leave Ayodhya, Dhasharatha, orders his treasury & staff. to calculate Raama's 'needs' during his 14 year exile and provide him with all moneys and necessities. He wants a retinue to accompany Raama so that his forest life will be comfortable. But Kaikeyi is terribly angry and she gives vent to her feelings thus. Gist: "My son Bharatha will not accept the kingdom barren after you provide Raama so lavishly from the Royal exchequer" And she adds "It will be like drinking slurry of wine, bereft of taste!" Obviously wines those days were not clarified like Vintage wines of today! But Kaikeyi made her point clear. She uses 'wine' to press home her objection! Nothing should go with Raama from the kingdom, as her son Bharatha is going to be king. Ofcourse Raama would want nothing from the kingdom. His exile is without any condition. He will live like a mendicant all these 14 years. He wants nothing from any one.

Liquor is part of the monkey world. When Sugreeva, after being crowned as king of monkeys, takes to wine, women and song, and forgets his commitment to Raama to search for Seetha, Raama is rather annoyed with him. He puts it to the evil of Drink (Kish-chapter 30-sloka 79) "Oh Lakshmana! Sugreeva is addicted to Drinks, so he is not showing compassion to me". Sugreeva is a noble man, yet this is what 'drink' does to a person.

When angry Lakshmana makes a call on Sugreeva to warn him about his lack of interest in Raama's matter, he finds Thaara in a state of stupor due to liquor. In fact the entire harem of Sugreeva seems to be 'tipsy'. (Kishkinda-chapter 33) Vaalmeeki through Lakshmana states a Truth which is rarely accepted by men addicted to Liquor. (sloka 46) "Drinking and the like is not commended for Dharma and Artha." But what follows is very significant. "All our objectives fail, even Dharma and ***Kaama*** (Passion, sex etc)" A drunken man cannot really enjoy the good things of life. (Even sex with a woman.) Only fringe benefits may appear before a drunken man. A drunkard is blinded by illusion, as he loses his mind.

For Raakshasaas Liquor is their very life. There is the Paana Bhoomi in Raavana's Lanka. In Sundara kaanda, chapters 9 to 11, Hanumaan narrates the state of all the women of the harem of Raavana after an orgy of drinking at midnight. There is no need to give the gist. But it is interesting reading. Vaalmeeki describes the scene,, of Ravana's harem, Banqueting hall and night orgy.

Yes. Liquor was part of society even those days. But liqour was always considered evil as it did not serve any purpose. Neither, Dharma, nor Artha, nor Kaama, nor Moksha.

25: PATHI -VRATHA (Virtuous-devoted wife)

In Vaalmeeki we find references to a few of the most remarkable women who were totally devoted to their husbands. It is Indian tradition that behind a successful man there is always a noble woman as a Saha=Dharmini. Even Gods are backed up by powerful noble women! We have Uma-Parvathy, the consort of God Shiva. Infact she is Ardha-Naari - Shiva's half - half male. We have Vishnu with goddess Lakshmi. We give a short list below. The list is not complete.

1: Suvarchala wife of Lord Sun

2: Sachi wife of Lord Indra

3: Arundhathi wife of sage Vasishta

4: Rohini wife of Lord Moon

5: Sukanya wife of sage Chyavana

6: Lopamudhra wife of sage Agasthya

7: Saavithri wife of king Sathyavaan

8: Shreemathi wife of Saint Kapil

9: Madhavanthi wife of Sowdhaasa

10: Keshini wife of King Sagara

11: Damayanthi wife of Nala

12: Mandodhari wife of Raavana

Seetha is Raama's soul in another body, always, even when Raama is in dire circumstances! In Sundara kaanda when she is threatened by demonesses, she tells them all that like these women in the list she has heart only for one and that one is Raama.

Before we conclude this short note we should mention what a respect Sage Athri had for his wife Anasooya. Athri talks about the power of his wife's penance to Raama. The old Anasooya, although a great woman of penance, behaved like a simple woman. She decorated Seetha and enjoyed the 'sight' at her hermitage.

Sages are human!

26: CHAARA: GOODA-CHAARI: DHOOTHA

(Spy, Secret agent, Ambassador-Emissary)

An old veteran who had half a century of life in international affairs once remarked that an ambassador is not worth half the value if he is not a spy as well. In the great epic, Vaalmeeki refers to spies, emissaries (ambassadors), enemy agents. As war between Raama and Raavana became imminent, there is reference to spies and spying. by Vaalmeeki.

When Bharatha is summoned from his grandfather's capital by Vasishta at Ayodhya, senior ministers are sent to fetch him from Rajgrigha. This is as per protocol. Bharatha is prince of Ayodhya and his maternal grandfather happens to be king of Kekeya kingdom. These emissaries not only carry good wishes from Ayodhya but also carry gifts with them. They are good will ambassadors.as well, although on a delicate mission. In fact seniors are sent, like ministers, Vijaya, Jayantha Sidhaartha (Ayodhya-chapter 68)

When Raavana's cousins, demon chiefs Khara, Dhooshana and Thrishiras, along with 14,000 warriors are annihilated by Raama, it is spy Akampana who carries news from India to Lanka to Raavana, who had the wisdom to be served by spies. (Aaranya-chapter31)

After abducting Seetha and returning to his capital, the first action he takes is to send 8 spies to India and watch the movements of Raama and Lakshmana. (Aaranya-chapter 55)

There is the protocol. War Ultimatum. Raama observes the code. He sends Angadha as his envoy to give an ultimatum to Raavana to avoid war. (Yudha-chapter41-slokas 61 to 75). This is a short but effective ultimatum. Vaalmeeki, gives us an idea what an ultimatum before war should be like. And how it should be presented. You must assign reasons why you are contemplating war with the enemy.

Even at the last minute you should show your sincerity to avoid conflict by stipulating your demands which should not sound unreasonable. Raama's ultimatum is: "If you do not restore Seetha back to me, and surrender, I will make your world free of any demon"

Angadha, the emissary announces himself before Raavana as per protocol "I am ambassador of Raama, the lord of Kosala kingdom. Perhaps, you might have heard about me, as the son of king Vaali"

Raavana rejects the ultimatum, war ensues and the demons are destroyed along with Raavana by Raama. But Raavana commits a grave sin.in not treating Angada, the envoy as per (Geneva!) convention!

When Raavana's brother Vibeeshana defects to Raama, the first reaction of Sugreeva and others is that he is a spy posing as a defector with good intentions. In the World war we have seen this. Ofcourse, on the advice of Hanumaan Raama easily accepts Vibheeshana and events proved that Raama was right in not rejecting Vibheeshana as spy thoughtlessly. (Yudha-chapter 17 there is lively discussion)

A point raised by Sugreeva we may observe, although Raama rejected his advice. "Whether Vibeeshana has come to us with good intentions or not, why bother. He is from the enemy, why risk at all?" Chapters 17 and 18 are interesting reading.

Raama being wise, considered Vibeeshana from two angles. Raama is the one who gives refuge to all. Secondly, he felt Vibeeshana, coming from the enemy's camp would be useful because he knew everything about Lanka its strength and weakness. As events turn out, Vibeeshana came up with an important piece of advice to Raama. in constructing a bridge over the Ocean for the monkey army to invade Lanka. (Yudha-chapter 19)

When Raama and Lakshmana are on the search of Sugreeva to make a treaty of friendship with him for seeking his assistance in the search of Seetha, Sugreeva was ever in fear of his wrathful brother Vaali, suspects these two as agents approaching him, to harm him. From the mountain top, he asks Hanumaan to find out who Raama and Lakshmana really are. Are they agents of Vaali? In Kishkinda-chapter 2, on the woes of Sugreeva, Vaalmeeki indicates the importance of agents and spies.

Gist: "Oh Hanumaan! I suspect that these two are agents, sent by Vaali. You know well that kings have many 'friends' to achieve their objective. They destroy enemies with great prudence, choosing diverse ways," Hanumaan not only sets Sugreeva's mind at rest but ensures that Raama and Sugreeva are enjoined as friends by a treaty of friendship.

On the subject of spies-emissaries, Vaalmeeki leaves us with a lot of imagination. We feel that Vaalmeeki could have indicated the functions and the specific duty of a spy, an agent, an emissary or an ambassador. Sundara Kaanda is the most beautiful piece among the 6 books of his epic. It is Hanumaan's kaanda. It is Hanumaan who finds Seetha in Lanka after flying 1,000 miles over the ocean all by himself.

The 'Brief' given to Hanumaan by Sugreeva was clear. He was to find Seetha and report back within one month. In Sundara Kaanda, we find Hanumaan a spy on search of Seetha, an emissary of Raama before Seetha when he meets her, and an ambaassador when he is presented before Raavana in chains as he gives a sort of ultimatum to him as though issued by Raama.!

Before we take up Hanumaan's activities in Lanka, a thought crosses our mind. Here is Hanumaan, flying 1,000 miles, overcoming all obstacles and finding Seetha in

Lanka that is totally guarded. This is no mean achievement. Hanumaan is not only a dexterous person, but also wise. When Seetha wails and expresses grave concern how a monkey army can cross over Lanka, by way of assuring Seetha, and to build confidence in her, assumes modesty and assures her thus (Sundara-chapter 39-slokas 38 &39)

Gist: "Oh Seetha! In my king Sugreeva's assembly, there are monkeys who are equal to me, nay, even more distinguished than myself. None inferior" This is indeed unjustified modesty serving a purpose. Hanumaan gives reasons why others back home are more distinguished than he. He adds "Oh Seetha! You know very well that only ordinary people are sent as emissaries and messengers! Distinguished persons never are emissaries or messengers. They are commissioned with more responsibility." How modest can you get? And he says further Gist "When an ordinary monkey like me can cross over to Lanka, will it not be child's play for those monkeys with Sugreeva back home!" The point here is Vaalmeeki through lips of Hanumaan says that emissaries need not be brilliant. We may not agree with this reading though!

Let us get back to Hanumaan the 'ambassador'

When 'spy' Hanumaan is captured and dragged in chains and presented before Raavana after he had destroyed many demon chiefs and played some havoc in Lanka, he is questioned by Raavana's chief Prahastha. (Sundara-chapter 50/ 51) Gist: He tells Raavana that as an envoy of Raama he is to give him this warning "Oh Raavana! Enough of this wearing the 'Noose of death' in the form of Seetha. Give up Seetha. May proper steps be taken by you." This is an ultimatum, given only by an envoy. We go back to our introduction to this topic. Here a spy, or an agent of 'enemy' on a search mission in enemy territory, allows himself to be captured so that he can convey a warning or an ultimatum to the enemy. Why did not Hanumaan fly back to India after finding and meeting Seetha.? His brief was clear to find Seetha. Hanumaan gives us a clue for his further activities in Lanka after fulfilling his mission of finding Seetha (Sundara-chapter 41) Gist "The dark eyed Seetha is seen and found by me. There remains some balance of work here for me" Hanumaan talks to himself as he feels that war is imminent and so he must do some preparatory work before he gets back to India and Sugreeva. He takes a rather a dangerous decision "One can do a job satisfactorily only when he completes the preliminary work pertaining to his job. Knowing the relative strength is the key to success. Only with this information, I should go back to my Lord Raama and my king Sugreeva" Hanumaan wants to test the enemy. He plays havoc, that finally leads to his tail being set fire to.

We crave your indulgence when we remark and observe that Vaalmeeki has not been specific about Hanumaan. Perhaps he wanted us to use our imagination, because Hanumaan was a super natural monkey. A spy, an emissary, an envoy all rolled into one.

When war breaks out or when war is imminent, spies have their work 'cut out'. As Raama gets ready for invasion at the southern tip of India along with Sugreeva's huge army of monkeys, Raavana for once is shaken. He sends his ace spy Shaardoola to fly to India and find out about the army. Shaardoola is stunned by the vastness of the army. (Yudha-chapter 20) he reports to Raavana thus: Gist:

"Oh great king Raavana! The reality that this army of invasion is covering an open space in all directions upto 10 yojanas (about 100 miles) must be understood quickly by you" Your emissaries should look into this "It is the duty of a spy to speak the truth, not hiding facts to please his boss. Raavana is taken aback. He sends his emissary Shuka, to meet Sugreeva, the king of monkeys, not on a peace mission with Raama, but to tell Sugreeva that as he has no enmity with Sugreeva, Sugreeva should also not have enmity with him. This is to split Raama and Sugreeva. But Sugreeva is totally devoted to Raama and when his army catches Shuka, he sends this message to Raavana Gist: "Oh you fool. I am not your friend. You are not to my liking. Evil as you are, you are going to be killed like Vaali.. Coming over to Lanka with my army, I am going to reduce Lanka to ashes"

Envoy Shuka's mission fails. Raavana accepts the inevitable, War with Raama and Sugreeva and their army.

Viewing the vast army as it besieges Lanka, Raavana through his spy Saarana takes a good look from his watch tower, This able spy points out the formation of the army of invasion along with their respective chiefs. (Yudha-chapter 26)

There were spies in Vaalmeeki's days. There are spies even today. Spies never die. They are caught and sometimes executed.

27: ARAAJAKA-DHUR-AVASTHAA
(Travails of a Kingless kingdom)

The King is dead. Long live the king. There are not many monarchies in the world today, but a nation cannot be without a 'Head' even for a moment. Vaalmeeki stresses this in his epic.

King Dhasharatha is dead. Raama and Lakshmana are away in deep forest on 14 year exile. Bharatha and Shathrugna are away on holiday at Rajgriha of the Kekeya kingdom. Thus the four sons of the king are away from Ayodhya. The situation is desperate for ministers. And advisers of the realm. (Ayodhya Kaanda chapter 67). Wise men like

Maarkandeya, Moudgalya, Jaabaali express their concern thus:

Gist: "A Kingless kingdom, will perish soon without a head. There will be no daily rituals at home or in temples. No offering of moneys to priests who do prayers for the welfare of the State. Businessmen will not venture out to do business out of fear of robbers and thugs. No law and order. People in cities and towns will not decorate themselves and enjoy their evenings. There will be no assembly in public places. No music, dance or drama. Historians will not expound ancient history as there will be no listeners. Men will take law into their hands, break norms of propriety, as they do not have to fear punishment under a king. There will be no discipline even in the army."

The list is long, the travails of a kingless kingdom. They conclude by saying a King is like a father and mother.

When these noble men expressed their concern thus, Vasishta the priest of Ikshwaakus, took a decision. He commands ministers to rush to Rajgriha, and bring Bharatha and Shathrugna at once to Ayodhya, cutting short their holiday.

The King is dead, Long live the king. Yes. Vaalmeeki knew this adage even before it was 'coined'!

28: MUNI SATHKAARA-AASHRAMA AATHITHYA

(Hospitality - Hermitage style!)

Bhardhwaaja's Hospitality

We had observed that a sage does not cease to be a sage because he treats citizens like any other. A sage may live in isolation in deep forest, observing vows and penance, but at every opportunity, he will show deep concern for fellow beings. The only difference between a sage and a common person is in attachment to mundane things. His goal is

Moksha, salvation. But he knows the values of Dharma (Norms, code), Artha (activity, wealth, substance) and Kaama (Love and pleasures)

Deeply religious folks, 'fundamentalists', and 'die hards', are shocked that such a thing can happen in a hermitage. But Vaalmeeki never wrote 'Untruth'. Brahma had ordained him thus. He presented facts without fear or favour. We have two incidents from Vaalmeeki where a sage offers lavish hospitality, not in keeping with traditional hospitality associated with sages and men of penance. By the power of their penance, they treated their visitors and guests with such a hospitality at their hermitage, that would make a Five star Hotel look like a youth hostel or a resting place for the poor and needy

We know that (Bala Kaanda-chapter 52), when the then king Vishwaamithra visits him, Brahma Rishi Vasishta treats him and his vast army to such a hospitality in his hermitage, that the mighty king Vishwaamithra is seized with jealousy and envy, resulting in his enmity against the great sage. But we shall talk about Bharadhwaaja's hospitality to crown prince Bharatha at his hermitage in Prayaga-Sangam.

Bharatha, after performing the last rites for Dhasharatha at Ayodhya, takes a huge army with him along with ministers, his 'mothers', VIP-s and citizens, to bring back Raama from forest after crowning him there itself as king of Ayodhya kingdom. As Bhardhwaja knows the whereabouts of Raama in forest, he makes a call on the great sage. Out of respect to the sage and observing the sanctity of the hermitage, he stations his army at a few Kroshas-miles, from the hermitage and walks to meet the sage. (Ayodhya-chapter 90) The sage is immensely pleased to receive the prince of the Ikshwaaku clan. After extending the traditional hospitality of hermitage, like Arghya-Paadhya, fruits and tubers, and after inquiring about the purpose of his visit, the sage questions him thus (Sloka 5) " Oh Bharatha! Why did you station your vast army away from hermitage and come here to me alone?" Bharatha replies; Gist: "Oh great sage! Sages who are men of penance, should be zealously kept away and guarded against kings in the matter of their daily rituals and penance. Out of respect for you, I kept the army away. I came alone, because they should not cause harm to your trees and disturb the peace and quiet"

Pleased with his reply, Bharadhwaja tells Bharatha that he wished to extend hospitality further, to him and to his army and retinue. Bharatha is rather surprised. What hospitality this man of forest can extend at all, and to such a vast retinue, he wonders. Bharatha, to save the great sage from hardship, says "In this, your hermitage, I have been favoured with all hospitality at your hands, like Arghy, Paadhya, fruits." Then he adds "This further hospitality that you are planning for us all, pray, what may that be? "Bharadhwaja has a word of praise for this noble prince Bharatha. "Oh Bharatha! I know you well. I know you are already satisfied with my hospitality" with a smile praises him thus "Because, Oh Bharatha, you are pleased and satisfied even with a 'little'!" Bharadhwaja gives reasons why he wants to entertain them all further "Oh Bharatha! I desire to feed your vast army. You should satisfy my desire to fulfill my hospitality to them in the manner I have planned for them" Bharatha is amused to say the least but accepts gracefully.

We are in for a surprise. But 'surprise' is not the word. We are about to witness a miracle. By the power of his penance, Bharadhwaja organises a feast. (Ayodhya-chapter 91) Gist: Entering the hall of ritual fire in his hermitage, Bharadhwaja invoked divine architect, Vishwakarma thus:

"I invoke Vishwakarma! I desire to extend hospitality to (my guest Bharatha) Therefore may preparations be made for me.Likewise, I invoke the protectors of the world, the three deities (Lords of fire, wind and lord varuna). May arrangements be made. All the rivers should flow out to this place to provide ample waters. Let a river flow out Maireya liquors and Sura wines! I invite ladies from Ghandarva clan, Apsara maidens. Particularly Dhrithashee, Vishaashee, Mishrakaashi and Naagadhantha.All these ladies who serve Brahma, must come here for the party at my hermitage. They should come with their numerous attendants. Let the foremost forest of Kubhaera in the region of Kuru over Himaalyas, where the leaves of trees are ornaments and dresses, come and station itself at my hermitage. May the Lord of Moon offer me in plenty, foods, various cereal foods, eats, sweet foods, syrupy foods. Various drinks, meats. May Lord wind blow cool with fragrance."

When the great sage invoked all these, with prayers in his hall of ritual fire, the miracle happened. The hermitage was transformed. Flowers rained constantly from the sky. The entire area was airconditioned. Musical strains reverberated. Gandarvas sang softly. Rivers flowed around the hermitage.

Wines and liquor flowed out through a few rivers while sweet drinks were offered by another river. (Beer on draught! No need. You just take a plunge in the river of scotch. or vintage wines). Suddenly, from nowhere, houses and mansions sprang up, comparable to mansions in capital Ayodhya! After all it is the work of the first architect of India-Vishwakarma.

When Bharatha was offered a mansion as per protocol, he refused it because he felt that only his brother Raama is fit to occupy the royal chambers where a 'Royal Seat" had been provided. Out of respect for his brother Raama,

Bharatha merely took a whisk fan and cooled off the throne, as though Raama was before him! The first musicians of India, Naaradha and Thumbura sang before Bharatha, Celestial dancers like Alambusa Pundarika, Mishrakeshi and Vaaman danced before him. Let us look around and see how Bharatha's army was faring by this hospitality of the sage. "Every man was bathed in river, massaged by herbals by 5 or 6 maidens. When their bodies were dried up, the maidens offered them liquors. The maidens spoke thus to them = You drink as much as you like, eat as much as you like =. The army did not have to worry because, the horses and elephants were fed sweet cakes and sugarcane"

To cut the story short, the army of Bharatha was treated to such great hospitality that they acclaimed "We will not get back to Ayodhya. We will not go to Dhandaka forest (to search for Raama). May there be welfare for Bharatha and Raama always!"

The peaceful and serene hermitage was transformed into a place of merriment and joy. = wine, women-song= As we said 'Hindu' chauvinists will be aghast by all this. But this is not ours but Vaalmeeki's reading! Yes, wine women and song at a hermitage' But let us remember Bharadhwaja has nothing to do with wine, women, song.

29: VIVAAHA: KANYAA DHAANA

(Marriage- Offer of bride in marriage)

In this world, like in ancient times, great importance is given to the institution of marriage. In the foursome journey of our lives, from childhood, studentship, family life and retirement, the Grihastha-ashrama (family life with a woman), is considered as much a Dharma as spiritual enlightenment.

In ancient times, the parents of a girl were always worried about the future of their child. They wanted to marry off their girl to a righteous man. King Janaka was no exception. But he had a problem with his daughter Seetha. Seetha was 'obtained' by him while he was ploughing and levelling up a bit of land for a Yaaga Hall, as he was to perform a great Yaaga. As Seetha was not born to him in a conventional manner and as he considered her birth divine, he decided, like a true Kshathriya warrior, that she must be 'offered' as a bride only to one who is brave and valiant.

The test for valour and bravery was the stringing up of a divine bow- The Shiva bow he had acquired from his forefathers. (Baala-chapter 66).

We know that Raama not only strung up the bow but breaks this with the pressure of his arm. So by his commitment, Janaka offers Seetha to Raama. The marriage of Seetha with Raama is rather unique as it is not covered by various other forms of marriage listed in our Shaasthras-from Manu onwards. Seetha's marriage was not even through Swayamvara (the bride chooses from persons who present themselves). The Kanyaa-dhaana (offer of girl) for Vivaaha- (marriage) by Janaka was through a Test- Neither Janaka nor Seetha had a choice in choosing the bridegroom. But all other formalities are observed. Vaalmeeki writes about the marriage, although the rituals of marriage listed, are not complete. But we write at length on this topic because we wish to get an idea how marriages were performed during Vaalmeeki's days.

When Raama breaks the bow, Janaka happily requests Vishwaamithra with these words (Ayodhya-chapter67) "Oh Vishwaamithra! This- the breaking of the divine bow- is indeed most wonderful, surpasses everything. Raama is indeed a man of 'tested' bravery! Therefore, as a prize for valour, my daughter Seetha must be given to Raama. My resolution is fulfilled"

With the approval of Vishwaamithra, Janaka sends emissaries to Ayodhya to inform Dhasharatha about the happenings in Mithila and about his offer of Seetha in marriage to Raama. And to invite Dhasharatha to Mithila to attend the marriage of his son, if it meets with his approval.

When Janaka's emissaries meet Dhasharatha in Ayodhya, they have some apprehension whether Dhasharatha will approve this alliance (Ayodhya-chapter 68 sloka16). Dhasharatha is only too pleased and he leaves with a large retinue to Mithila to participate in Raama's wedding. Being a democratic ruler he addresses his ministers thus Gist: "Raama has been found by the great soul king Janaka to be truly brave and wishes to offer his daughter Seetha in marriage. If this pleases you all, then we shall leave for Mithila without delay" And all ministers and Rishi-s there said =Baadam= Okay. Then the king ordered journey the next day. Incidentally, there is no evidence that Dhasharatha consulted his wives. There is some doubt whether his wives accompanied him to Mithila.

(Ayodhya-chapter 69): Dhasharatha orders the officer of his treasury to draw out gold, and traditional ornaments as gifts to be given at Mithila. This is rather interesting. In modern marriages, it is the bride's side that spends, rarely the groom's. It was not so in Vaalmeeki's days. A mighty foursome army leaves with Dhasharatha, accompanied by Vasishta, Vaamedeva, Jaabali, Kaashyapa Maarkandeya. It took them almost 4 days to reach Mithila and Janaka receives Dhasharatha and the marriage party. (By slokas 10 to 12) Gist: "Oh emperor Dhasharatha! Your arrival is auspicious. WELCOME! All my troubles are over. It is my good fortune..... that Lord sage Vasishta has come here with you ! My family is honoured by this alliance with you."

Reading Vaalmeeki's description we know that marriage is not merely an affair between boy and girl those days.

Friendship marked an alliance. Formally Dhasharatha accepts the alliance with sloka 15.

"***That the acceptance of gifts, daughters, depends on the will and pleasure of the donor, is known to me for a long time.*** Whatever you say, we shall abide by" Traditionally the bride's father is The donor and the bridegrom's father is The recipient.

Dhasharatha tells Janaka, that in all matters, the chief priest of Ikshwaakus, Vasishta is the 'First'to speak on behalf of Ayodhya kings, he will be requesting Vasishta to describe his lineage. (Bala-chapter70). Then Janaka reveals his lineage. The point to remember is that there is no uncertainty or ambiguity who is marrying whom. Even in modern marriages, in quite a few marriages, a ***short lineage*** of the bride and bride groom is recited. ('A' son, of B, grandson of C and great grandson of D = E, daughter of F, granddaughter of G and great grand daughter of H). This practice, we presume, must be from Vaalmeeki's days!

(By Bala-chapter 72-sloka 9 & 10) when Vishwaamithra had suggested and requested Janaka that simultaneously with the wedding of Raama with Seetha and Lakshmana with the other daughter of Janaka, Oormila, the daughters of the brother of King Janaka should marry the other two sons of Dhasharatha. Vishwaamithra's request becomes command, and Janaka accepts this "Hearing the words of Vishwaamithra with the approval of Vasishta, king Janaka, cupping his hands in Anjali, replied = I consider my family most blessed as the two 'tigers', amongst sages, Vishwaamithra and Vasishta, are ***themselves commending alliances with my family***. May the daughters of my brother marry the other two sons of Dhasharatha" We may note a point here. The marriage of Lakshmana, Bharatha and Shathrugna follows the code of marriages that existed as per shaasthras unlike Seetha-Raama wedding which is rather unique. Great sages 'fix' the marriages here. Even today when elders suggest alliances, it is accepted as command. A lot of changes in the institution of marriage is taking place today, though. It is getting to be just a boy-girl affair unlike in Vaalmeeki's time when marriages are alliances between families.

Both sides perform pre-marriage rituals and ceremonies separately. There is a mention about Shraadha ceremony being performed by Dhasharatha, the day before the marriage. The Shraadha ceremony is a long ritual, performed by one who seeks the blessings of his forefathers. It is wrong to associate Shraadha with 'funereal' service for the dead. Ofcourse rituals may vary.

(Bala-chapter 72-slokas 19 and 21) "Oh Janaka! Swasthi and welfare to you. I am now going to my 'cottage' And I will do all the Shradha ceremonies "Reaching his place Dhasharatha,. Did the shraadha ceremony as per norms" for his forefathers.

Dhasharatha offered gifts in thousands befitting his status cows, gold, other items, as part of Godhaana ceremony.

The ritual of marriage is entrusted with Vasishta. This is interesting because the main marriage rituals are performed by priests of the bride's family. But Janaka himself requests Vasishta thus: (Bala-chapter 73-sloka 20) "Oh Brahma rishi Vasishta! There is nothing that is unknown to you. Therefore you should perform the ceremony"

Some rituals are described in slokas 21 to 25 of Bala-chapter 73., as performed by Vasishta. But if the readers are interested to know about mariage rituals and customs, they should study Gobhila and Paraskara.

When the rituals are over, Janaka 'hands' over the brides to their respective grooms. We may mention how he hands over Seetha to Raama. The sloka 30 and 31 of chapter 73 is considered sacred by the deeply religious because even today, during marriage they recite this. Gist "Oh Raama! This is Seetha, my daughter. She will always be with you in the duty of Dharma. Accept her. Clasp her hand with yours. She is most virtuous. Most illustrious. And she will follow you ever as your shadow"

Vaalmeeki by these two slokas affirms the quality of a wife as per Sanaathana Dharma.

We have written at some length about the wedding. This is to indicate Vaalmeeki's description of wedding between two noble souls. Seetha-Raama: Oormila-Lakshmana: Maandvi-Bharatha: Shruthakeerthi-Shathrugna.

We have to get back to a few observations we made earlier. Marriages those days were not just boy-girl affair. It was to practise Dharma together that two of the opposite sex were enjoined as we could see from Vaalmeeki's rendering of the famous two slokas.

Further, marriage was an alliance of two families. Friendship marked their relationship. Hospitality is a gift of friendship. Today it is a sort of 'demand' on marriage alliance, by the groom's party.

We may conclude with a few slokas from Vaalmeeki. (Bala-chapter 72-sloka16) Janaka is so exhilarated he says "My Mithila, is Dhasharatha's. And his Ayodhya is mine. And you two tigers of rishis (Vasishta-Vishwaamithra)!. May you occupy the throne and command at will. There is no uncertainty about the power that you have in Mithila! You command as you please "

At one point, Janaka is rather vexed when Vasishta announces that the bridegroom's party is ready waiting for permission to enter. (Sloka 15 of chapter 73) "Who is the Gate keeper who is standing between you and me. As this is your kingdom, whose orders are you awaiting? Where is the need to seek permission to enter one's own house".

Vaalmeeki may not have elaborated on the Rituals of a marriage ceremony in his epic. But as a man of Dharma he wrote about the esence of Dharma of marriage between noble souls and between an alliance of two noble men.

30: THEEKSHNA-THEEVRA SAMBAVA

(Some Poignant Scenes)

The most cruel event in Raamaayana is the kidnapping of Seetha by Raavana when she was alone in her hermitage. But this event falls in the category of divine sanction! (Ofcourse every thing in life is ordained!) Without Seetha being kidnapped there was no possibility of Raama going to war with Raavana and destroy all the evil demons and make the world freed from evil forces. Let us take up some poignant and heart rending scenes.

(a) Cruelty of Kaikeyi

Instigated by her mentor and confidante, hunchback Manthara, Kaikeyi drives away Raama to forest on a 14 year exile, exercising her options of the two boons her husband had given her long, long ago. In Ayodhya Kaanda, as Raama takes leave of all to go out on exile, we witness some poignant scenes.

(Ayodhya-chapter 19): Raama tries to console his father through his step mother Kaikeyi who had just ordered him to go to forest on exile to make way for her son Bharatha who is on holiday with his maternal grandfather at Rajgriha. Gist "Oh Kaikeyi! the king, my father, is shedding tears, looking down on earth, with 'detached' eyes. Why should it be so? You please console him. May couriers be sent at once to Rajgriha on fast moving horses to fetch Bharatha to crown him instead" Now comes the poignancy. How cruel can this Kaikeyi get? This is the unkindest cut of them all. Raama was so attached to his brothers that he desired not only to see Bharatha before he left on exile, but wanted to see him crowned. But Kaikeyi would have none of this

"Oh Raama! The couriers will ofcourse go forth with fast moving horses to fetch Bharatha. Be that as it may! I think it is not necessary for you to delay your departure. ***So, leave Ayodhya at once*** "

Certainly Raama obeys his 'mother' unconditionally. He prepares to leave on exile within a couple of hours after Kaikeyi had ordered him to go.

Again we have a terrible scene. Kaikeyi was not just satisfied with sending away Raama with his wife, but humiliate them as well. (Ayodhya-chapter 37) She wants Raama and Seetha to leave Ayodhya at once, wearing the dress of a mendicant, of bark material, discarding his royal robes. Slokas 6 to 16 describe this heart rending scene. Gist: "At that moment, the shameless Kaikeyi, before the multitude, brought the dress of a mendicant and ordered Raama thus = Wear this =. Accepting the dress (with grace) Raama threw away his royal robes and wore the bark dress in the hall. Lakshmana did likewise. Seetha who was dressed in the silken robes as a royal princess, receiving one set from Kaikeyi became embarrassed as she had not known nor worn bark dress in all her life. She stood there bashfully. Raama himself dressed her up with the bark dress"

Seetha, the princess was denied even the privacy of a woman.

Can there be anything more cruel. The entire assembly is aghast at this sight. No wonder.

(b) **Shathaanandh -Vishwaamithra**

Sage Shathaanandh was the son of Sage Gauthama and Ahalya. He was the principal adviser to king Janaka. We know from Bala kaanda-chapters 48 &49, how his mother Ahalya who had been cursed by his father to become a stone for her 'affair' with Indra., was resurrected by Raama when Vishwaamithra took Raama to the scene of curse.

When Vishwaamithra, along with Raama and Lakshmana, reach Mithila, he is honoured by Janaka and there was special attention for him from Shathaanandh. After all Vishwaamithra had taken Raama to the scene of the curse upon Shataanandh's mother Ahalya!

No son wants divorce or estrangement between his parents. Here Shathanaand's mother Ahalya had committed, what in those days was considered a terrible sin- an affair with another man- And his father Gauthama could have condoned her sin and taken her back, but cursed her without mercy to become a stone. Poor Shathaanand although a man of vows and penance, had to bear all this and was awaiting the day when the effect of the curse on his mother would end, and his parents would live together amicably. That day had come with the arrival of Vishwaamithra to Mithila along with Raama. after Raama had resurrected Ahalya on the way. (Bala-chapter.49).

Let us describe the scene how Raama's presence had resurrected Ahalya. Gist: "She, this Ahalya the wife of Gauthama, who had been unseen as she was a stone by the curse of Gauthama, at once (rose up from stone) and came to be seen, as Raama visited the scene of curse upon her. As she came up, Raama and Lakshmana touched her feet in reverence. She extended them hospitality. The most obedient Ahalya was then enjoined with her husband, Gauthama......." Shathaanand was waiting for this, all these years. No wonder after the formalities were over at Mithila, he asks Vishwaamithra, excitedly, with great curiosity. We can understand the suffering of a son when his parents are estranged. Vaalmeeki brings this home clearly through the Ahalya-Gauthama estrangement. We must read this in Vaalmeeki's language! (Bala-chapter 51) Gist: "Oh Vishwaamithra! Oh the 'tiger' amongst Munis! Was my most famous mother Ahalya who had entered into a state of penance for 1,000 years introduced by you to Raama" Here we may make a point. Shathaanandh like a dutiful son, like a man of vows and penance, considered his mother remaining a stone for 1,000 years by curse as penance! Ahalya had remained 'motionless', impervious to anything around her, for 1,000 years because she had become a stone by curse. This was indeed her penance of 1,000 years. Shathaanand asks Vishwaamithra further, with great expectation, joy and curiosity, "Did my famous mother honour Raama who deserves to be honoured." Shathaanand being a man of penance did not want anything to be hidden from Raama. So he asks Vishwaamithra thus. "Was Raama fully told by you about all the happenings (between my parents), due to fate?"

Now comes the poignancy. Shathaanand could not wait to hear from Vishwaamithra about his parents who had been estranged for 1,000 years. This is indeed heart rending when he asks "Oh Kowshik! Oh foremost Muni. Oh Vishwaamithra! From the time of meeting ('seeing') Raama was ***my mother enjoined with my father"***

The poignancy is referred to because, Shathaanand was not merely interested to know whether his mother had shaken off from the shackles of the curse on her. What was of grave concern to this man, was that his father must accept his mother and they should live happily together. Shathaanandh may be a sage, but he was a son as well. This scene is indeed a poignant one as Vishwaamithra sets Shathanand's mind at rest thus, by a very short, crisp statement "Oh Shathanandh! The foremost of Munis! Whatever was to be done, all that was done. Nothing was transgressed, it was done by me......Like Renuka with Bhargava, your mother Ahalya was enjoined with your father Gauthama"

In a fit of temper and wrath, Bhargava(Jamadagni) commands his son Parashu-Raama, to kill his wife Renuka. Obeying his father, with one stroke of his axe, Parashua Raama kills his mother, but being wise, is quick to ask for a boon. His father was pleased and he left the option of the boon with Parshu Raama. The 'son' in Parashu Raama reveals itself when he asks that his mother should be resurrected and come back alive at once. The story goes that Jamadagni was pleased with his son and the parents of Parashu Raama lived happily ever after. Nothing can give greater joy for children than to see their parents live together. ***Vaalmeeki through Parashu-Raama and Shathanandh expounds this***. We should read the Vaalmeeki text to understand the pathos of Shathaanandh when he asks Vishwaamithra about the fate of his parents. Even a man of composure and restraint, Shathanandh, behaves like a son! And he was no mean sage either!

(c) **Seetha-Raama at Lanka**

In the entire Raamaayana, which ever way you look at it, this Seetha-Raama episode at Lanka, soon after war was over, is something unbelievable. We will be brief. Raavana and his demons are destroyed by Raama and Sugreeva's vast army. Raama sends Vibeeshana to fetch Seetha who was prisoner in Raavana's Lanka, and to present her before him. The shame of it is that Seetha does not even have privacy of a long separated wife, but is brought before Raama by Vibheeshana in front of the multitude. When Seetha wants to present herself before Raama in just the way she had been all through the year of her separation from her husband Raama, even this is denied, as Raama had commanded Vibheeshana to present Seetha, only after she had her bath, manicuring and after she had dressed up well with all her ornaments on her body! (Yudh-chapter117) Seetha wanted Raama to see her only in her condition as a prisoner. She wanted Raama to know.what she went through. But Raama has other ideas. Indeed very painful. But more to follow.

When Seetha is being brought before Raama, the vast crowd naturally is curious, wants to have a glimpse of the royal princess. But Vibheeshana's guards are using 'lathi charge' to disperse the crowd. Rama is angry and admonishes Vibheeshana (Yudh-chapter117-slokas 25 to 30) Gist: Raama, who was very angry as though he would burn with his fiery eyes, addressed Vibheeshana thus "Why are these people tormented and driven away from me. Stop this action. These are my people" And he follows this admonishment by talking ethics in such a painful situation. "For a woman, good conduct alone protects her modesty. not veil, nor house, nor dress....." Raama's remark on modesty of a woman is uncalled for; He was angry for an entirely different reason. Hanumaan and Lakshmana who were watching all this were terribly upset by Raama's behaviour. "By Raama's signs and behaviour and gestures. they (Hanumaan and Lakshmana) conjectured that Raama had no affection or regard for Seetha any more!"

As Seetha, led by Vibheeshana, approaches her husband, her body became shrunken out of bashfulness and modesty. What follows, in chapter 118 of Yudhakanda is most painful. It is poignant, more so because one never expected Raama, the most noble man on earth behaving like this towards a noble and most virtuous lady Seetha who had undergone such a torment at Lanka. We wonder why Vaalmeeki had to write in detail about the meeting of Raama and Seetha after Raavana is killed and Lanka is conquered. But Vaalmeeki has his purpose, always!

This is how Raama begins his address to Seetha after meeting her for the first time in a year or more. (Yudh-chapter 118) "Oh Seetha! You have been retrieved by me who conquered the enemy in war. What should be done by a warrior was done by me" This is rather strange. But Raama continues "I have come to the end of my wrath. My dishonour and my enemy have been simultaneously wiped away" No mention about how happy he is to get Seetha back! Now comes the unkindest cut from this most noble man. Gist:

"Oh Seetha! Let this be known to you. The war was not fought for your sake. It was fought to wipe off the stain to my family and the insinuation against me, that I did not exhibit my valour" More cruel thrusts by Raama upon this most virtuous lady Seetha. "Which man born in good family will accept a woman who has enjoyed life with another man in another house? There is absolutely no affection for you. You may go as you please" If Raama had no intention of taking Seetha back he need not have invited her fully dressed up, and presented her before the multitude. This is the poignancy we are talking about. You present this noble lady, dressed up with all jewelry as though she had enjoyed all these with Raavana at Lanka! And then go on a tirade against her, with character assassination. There are about 25 slokas in this chapter. We have given only the gist. For once, Raama's character takes a beating. Later he justifies his action. Even making allowances for his reasons, we have to conclude that Vaalmeeki wrote about Raama this way because he 'wrote without fear or favour'

Seetha ofcourse talks back. To prove her innocence, enters Fire. Fire cannot burn Fire. The lord of Fire tells the world that Seetha is pure. Raama takes her back. All is well that ends well. But this entire episode is most painful because it deals with two most noble persons on earth.

31: RANABHOOMI-DHARMA SABHA-NEETHI VAALI -_RAAMA SAM-MUKHA

(Court at Battle field: Vaali-Raama confrontation: Law and Justice)

Vaalmeeki gives great importance to law and justice. To which we find frequent reference. Laws are man made and justice is also as per whims of society although we may not like to accept this truth.

Vaalmeeki, man of Dharma, wrote at length about the difficulties faced by us in understanding what laws really are and how difficult it is to base justice on man made laws. Scientists have no problem. They base their laws on Nature. They are quick to reject or alter laws if laws are statistically wrong, and if laws don't stand the scrutiny of 'experience'.

Vaalmeeki wrote at length about the episode - Raama-Vaali - confrontation which resulted in a never ending debate. Even after thousands of years, this is debated. Vaalmeeki was aware that the debate will continue for ages, when he described the Vaali-Raama confrontation in detail and left posterity to make its judgment.

"Was Raama justified in killing Vaali?" This is the never ending debate.

We shall write a short note before we take up this question. Raama meets Sugreeva and forms friendship with him. Both of them have vested interests. Raama wants Sugreeva's assistance in finding the whereabouts of his wife Seetha who had been abducted. Sugreeva wants Raama to kill his vengeful brother Vaali and retrieve his wife Ruma and the kingdom of monkeys. This is the scenario.

Sugreeva assures Raama that he will make a search of Seetha once he becomes Lord of monkeys after his brother Vaali is killed.. Raama is quick to promise him that Vaali is as good as killed when he unleashed his arrow upon him from his bow.

What is surprising is, that Raama, man of justice and norms, is quick to assure Sugreeva that he will kill Vaali without hearing Vaali's side of the story. Raama knows the Four Way strategy, the Laws' (Saama-conciliation, talks: Dhaana- settlement through gifts, bribes. Bhedha- threats, division among enemy and finally Dhanda-the stick, war and violence) Only after you exhaust the first three options, you seek remedy and justice by the use of force. (Kishkinda-chapter8-sloka24)

Yet Raama vows at once "Oh Sugreeva! You will see the evil mongering enemy Vaali, a brother to you only in name, killed by my arrow"

But we must give Raama his due. Raama's character asserts itself when he asks Sugreeva (Slokas 42 to 44) "Oh Sugreeva! On what account did the enmity between you two brothers come about? ***I desire to know exactly. After hearing and deliberating upon the strengths and weaknesses, I will take action that will be good for you" Raama 'recovers' from his impetuosity!***

When Raama decides to kill Vaali, he suggests to Sugreeva that he should 'invite' his brother Vaali for a combat. While they were fighting fiercely, Raama, with a single arrow and from behind a tree, unseen by Vaali, discharges a lethal arrow that takes away Vaali's life. Vaali falls in the battlefield, mortally wounded. Some breath is in him and now begins the debate. Vaali treats Raama with contempt and charges Raama with the following offence.

He censures him. (Kishkinda chapter 17) The Gist:

"Oh Raama! When I was engaged in a two some combat with my brother Sugreva, I was hit on my chest by an arrow from you. What merit do you see or obtain by this deed of yours?" Readers know that warriors were men of chivalry those days. When a soldier is fighting with some one, you don't interfere in the combat. Vaali in effect calls Raama a man lacking in qualities of a true warrior. .

"Oh Raama! You are a noble man. You are the son of a great king. Most presentable, brilliant, endowed with qualities. You come from a noble family (of Ikshwaakus). You are a man of Dharma, and you are famous, man of compassion, merciful, devoted to the welfare of citizensl. So they talk about you!" By all this 'praise' on Raama, Vaali says he never thought Raama would stoop so low to intervene in his fight with his brother. "You would not fight me when I was exasperated, fighting with some one else. I had not even seen you as you were not within my sight. I paid no attention to you." Vaali adds "But I did not realise that you have no self respect, that you are a man of Non Dharma, who falsely holds on to the 'banner' of Dharma, that you indulge in sinful activities, and you are like a well covered by 'loose' grass.. I have not committed any aggression on you or on your kingdom. Nor have I treated you with contempt. When that is so, how come you did harm to me as though I have sinned (against you). I am a mere monkey, roaming in forest, sustaining myself in forest products, and was fighting with some one else.and not fighting with you at all." After saying all this Vaali reminds Raama about some Dharma, thus "Oh King Raama! Saama-reconciliation; Dhaana- Act of giving by way of settlement; Kshama-Tolerance; Dharma-Moral code (in this case warrior code); Sathya-Truth; Veera-Valour; Dhrithi-Firmness; Apakaara-Dhanda- Punishment to transgressor; These are the qualities only of kings (of the human world). But we are of the animal world, roaming in forest. Our trait is different from yours. You are a man and I am animal." After telling Raama about his 'world' being different from the 'world' of humans, Vaali talks further. "Oh Raama!

Land, gold and silver are common reasons for quarrel and dispute. We have no such dispute, here in this vast forest. Having killed me who had not transgressed you at all, what are you going to tell your assembly in Ayodhya?. My hide cannot interest you, you cannot be interested in such meat" Vaali hits Raama where it will hit a man sharply. "How is it you were begotten by such a noble man like Dhasharatha?" He taunts Raama, about his lack of effort in finding the abductor of his wife and offer that sinner, punishment "Oh Raama! That bravery (of killing me from behind my back, hiding yourself) you exhibited on me when I was not 'involved' with you, I do not see that, being exhibited before transgressors who have caused harm to you" Vaali boasts "If you were seen by me when you fought me, that would have been your end, you will now be with the Lord of Death, Vaivaswatha" If Raama had to kill him because of pressure from Sugreeva whose help he had sought, Vaali questions Raama's wisdom and judgment "The purpose for which I was killed by you, out of your desire to do good to Sugreeva for his requital, had you directed me in that task, I would have brought your wife Seetha in just under a day" By this Vaali says he was the right man for service to Raama and on this score he need not have killed him to win over Sugreeva's friendship to trace Seetha.

Vaali goes on and on. We shall condense Vaali's charges, his accusation against Raama.

(a) Vaali was in combat with Sugreeva, and Raama, like a true warrior of chivalry should not have intervened.

(b) Vaali had never shown disrespect to Raama, nor had he harmed him in anyway. Nor his kingdom. So Raama had no reason for this killing.

(c) Raama had forgotten the rudiments of valour and bravery. If he wanted to kill him, he should have faced him.

Infact, had he done so Raama would now be lying flat in the battlefield instead.

(d) Raama being of royalty could not have killed him for meat. He is no goat! Monkey's meat is no delicacy!

(e) They had no dispute over land, gold or silver. The forest is vast like an ocean. There could be no dispute!

(f) If Raama killed him because he was a sinner, (of having snatched away his brother's wife) then he had to remind him that as he belongs to animal world man made laws are not applicable to the animal world. No jurisdiction!

(g) If Raama thinks that he is no monkey but a king (of monkeys) and so as a king, Raama had to punish him as he had gone astray, Vaali had to remind him about the four way laws that are to be followed between two kings to settle disputes. Raama was quick to use the stick- arrow. He should have talked to him first. (Saama)

(h) If Raama, because of his friendship with Sugreeva who had promised him help in the retrieval of Seetha, had to kill him to please his newly acquired 'friend' Sugreeva, against norms of Dharma, he has to say this. It would have been child's play for him to bring Seetha before him, if Raama had sought his help instead of seeking Sugreeva.

Concluding his charge against Raama, Vaali who is about to give up life says "Oh Raama! After I die and go to heaven my brother Sugreeva should obtain this kingdom of monkeys. This is proper. But that I was killed by you by Non Dharma. That is not proper"

Raama answers Vaali's charge. This is in Kishkinda chapter 18. This is a long chapter. Almost 40 to 45 slokas adorn this. Raama counters Vaali's charges and justifies his killing. Raama wants Vaali to die in peace. So talks back to him at great length. But Raama is rather severe when he begins thus Gist: "Oh Vaali! Uneducated as you are you are blabbering like this because of fickleness associated with monkeys!. "Raama tells him that as he is of Ikshwaaku clan and as his brother Bharatha is ruling over the land, any 'crime' committed in his land must be identified and the sinner punished "The noble soul man of Dharma, Bharatha, who knows the essence of Dharma is ruling from Ayodhya. We are under his authority and when such a Bharatha is ruling over the land, who can dare to transgress Dharma" Raama comes to the main charge. Vaali's crime. "Oh Vaali! For a man who follows the righteous path and conduct, a father, an elder brother, and a teacher are to be considered as 'father' An younger brother, a son, a disciple, are to be thought of as sons. But you having abandoned Dharma, are living with your younger brother's (Sugreeva's) wife. I can never tolerate this sin committed when Bharatha is a ruler. Punishment for this is death" Raama says further that as Vaali is a monkey and just an animal, and he being of the royal family, he has the right to hunt him down as he chooses, .to offer punishment" Raama tells Vaali he has no sadistic pleasure in killing him "Oh Vaali! Your killing was because of my duty to Dharma. We are not so independent as to do what we like" As for his charge that he killed Vaali only to please Sugreeva so that Sugreeva will help him to find Seetha, Raama says " My friendship with Sugreeva is like my attachment to Lakshmana" By this Raama tells him, that it is Sugreeva alone whom he will look up to for finding his wife. Raama while concluding, expounds law & justice.

Crime and Punishment

Men, even if they have committed sins, go to heaven after they receive punishment for their sins. A criminal ceases to be a criminal once he discharges his debt to society.

A thief is discharged from his sin, after he receives punishment.

But a king who does not punish a thief, takes that sin on himself

Let us summarise Raama's arguments before Vaali.

(a) Raama is king Bharatha's representative and as such he has a duty to punish sinners. So he has jurisdiction.

(b) Vaali had not only kicked out his younger brother Sugreeva but committed the greatest crime of keeping his wife as mistress when he should have treated her like his daughter. Punishment for this is death

(c) Sugreeva had narrated everything and so Raama was convinced that Vaali was the real culprit. This killing was after deliberation and not due to sadism.

(d) For Ikshwaaku kings, justice has nothing to do with their vested interests. Raama would have killed him even if Sugreeva had not promised help to him in finding Seetha.

(e) As for killing him from behind with a single arrow like a 'coward', Raama is of Royalty and has the right to hunt an 'animal'as he chooses.

(f) Raama acted as per norms of Dharma only.

Thus, this battle field becomes a Court of Justice. An unique court! Because there are no lawyers. There is no judge. Posterity is the judge. Both Vaali the 'criminal' and Raama the 'prosecutor' and 'executioner' have had their say. Yet this question = Was Raama Justified In Killing Vaali=is not satisfactorily resolved.

A question will always linger in our minds because we are dealing with a very noble man of Dharma, Raama. He is about the near perfect human being. Raama is known for compassion. He is a conciliator (Read Bala kanda). He is endowed with all virtues. He would offer refuge even to enemies like Raavana if he seeks his refuge. When such is the case, why did not Raama strive to meet Vaali and talk to him and settle this matter without offering him punishment straightway with a single arrow?

Raama, still could have killed Vaali after he goes through the first three of The Four Way (Saama-Dhaana-Bhedha-Dhanda) law. If Vaali had realised his sin and sought pardon and refuge, Raama as King Bharatha's representative had the option of offering pardon to Vaali.

Like the President of India, the king of Ayodhya had the 'Right to Pardon' any one.! (Readers, sorry, it should be the other way, surely)

But surprisingly Vaali accepts Raama's arguments and reconciles himself to the killing and his inevitable death. He tells Raama just before his death "Oh most noble Raama! The 'defects' you pointed out are indeed such! You must enlighten me, nourish me with 'true' knowledge. You delight in doing good to all." Vaali wants to die in peace and wants Raama, his executioner, to guide him to 'heaven' Ah!

Vaali, before he gives up life speaks some words of wisdom to his son Angadha (Kish-chapter 22-slokas 20 to 23) and gives advice to his brother Sugreeva.

But the debate continues. Vaalmeeki wrote two long chapters. In Kishkinda kanda. It is difficult for us to know Vaalmeeki's mind. But as usual he presented both sides. He observed the Dharma of Law and justice. Legal brains are not convinced about jurisdiction in this monkey-man affair. The laws of the monkey world are different and we cannot apply man made laws. In the monkey world, monkeys snatching some other monkey's wife is not a crime. But Raama thinks so. Vaali thinks so. So the matter should rest

But the debate Continues!

32: NAASTHIKA-AASTHIKA: JAABAALI-RAAMA SAM-MUKHA

(Atheism-Theism: Jaabaali vs Raama)

We begin this topic with a short introduction:

India is an enigma. The name India itself is a misnomer. So is the word Hindu! This land used to be called Aarya Vartha where noble men lived. It was called Bhaaratha Varsh. From root = Bru-Bar = to bear, to sustain, we have the name Bharatha Varsh. This land is 'bearer', the land that 'sustains'. A Karma Bhoomi-Work is salvation! It encompasses all thoughts, views, religions.. Quite true, 'Indians' have faith in God, infact ***'Hindoos'*** have many Gods! Indians may be men of Faith like devotees of other Faiths. But with this difference: Philosophers here directed their mind ***beyond the concept of God***. They introduced the concept of thinking before accepting.

That philosopher saint, Aadhi Shankara (700 AD) introduced the expression = Thathvam Chinthaya= Think!

This, inspite of the fact that Shankara wrote =Baja Govindham= (Surrender to God Krishna) and wrote a dissertation on the 1,000 names of God Vishnu. (Vishnu Sahsranaama). There may be apparent contradictions, but the great saint merely gave the masses a dose of faith, through such prayers, to attain Moksha = Salvation.

What then is the religion of 'India'. It is Sanaathana Dharma.= The Eternal Dharma is the religion of India. Dharma as 'seen' in unwritten texts like the Vedhas, the Dharma as seen in epics like Raamaayana and MahaBhaaratha.

If a person tries to practise Dharma as he sees it, and as is 'seen' in Shaasthras, even if he does not believe in Gods, he is a 'Hindoo' if you can call any one a Hindoo at all.

The very old wise Jaabaali was one such noble person.

Jaabaali did not believe in conventional religion.. He tried to follow Dharma as he saw it from a practical view. He had only the welfare of the citizens in mind. No wonder he was a renowned minister-adviser - to Dhasharatha who was 'surrounded' by men of religion, like Vasishta, Suyagnya, and Vaamadeva who treated Jaabaali with great respect and consideration inspite of his Atheistic-agnostic beliefs.

We shall now take up the Jaabaali-Raama confrontation.

Dhasharatha is dead. Raama and Lakshmana are away in the forest on exile by the command of Kaikeyi and Dhasharatha. Bharatha would not want to usurp the throne. He is determined to get his eldest brother Raama, back to Ayodhya, cutting short his exile. As far as he is concerned, it is Raama who is successor to the throne. With a large army, VIP-s, ministers, mothers, and advisers like Jaabaali, he goes to forest to crown Raama there itself with full honours and bring him back to Ayodhya as king.

Bharatha meets Raama who is firm. He will honour his father, although dead, by going through with his exile. He will not return to Ayodhya for 14 years. Bharatha does not want to get back to Ayodhya without Raama. This is the scenario. The situation in Ayodhya is hopeless, disastrous. Ayodhya is without a king!

Jaabaali, who had seen long years with his king Dhasharatha, was worried. The situation is getting out of hand. It is intolerable that while Ayodhya is without a king, these four princes are 'discussing' about a successor to the throne. Jaabaali talks to Raama in forest in the midst of all VIP-s and citizens who have accompanied Bharatha. Raama must take over. He must forget about his exile.

There are two major chapters Ayodhya kaanda. The confrontation between atheist Jaabaali and the theist Raama (Chapters108 and 109)

It is not merely a confrontation between two noble men, but virtually a discussion between Atheism and theism. If Vaalmeeki devotes two chapters it is because he wanted to convey to the world, to posterity, India's liberalism. An Indian, even if he is a strong believer and a man of faith, liberalism is born with him. Jaabaali addresses Raama.

"Oh Raama! It is not proper for a man like you enlightened with the ways of royalty and nobility, and steadfast (in duty) to indulge in purposeless, useless talk." Jaabaali begins his own reading of 'Indian' philosophy "Who is related to whom? Who should obtain what from whom? Life begins alone and departs alone. Therefore when a man clings to father and mother (and talks about duty to them) he is really a fool ! Because no one is any one to him" This is indeed strange to all of us. Father and mother are Gods to every Indian. Yet Jaabaali disowns them. He justifies this with such an example "It is like a man going to a place and after spending the night, leaves the next morning. Father, mother, house, property are all like this. Temporary meeting place like in a hotel where we meet so many and forget about them. Oh Raama! Wise men don't cling to 'relationships"

Jaabaali wants Raama to do his duty first instead of 'clinging' to his father and his command. He must take over the kingdom and forget about his dead father who really is no one to him. Take what comes is Jaabali's philosophy.! Jaabaali adds "Dhashratha is no one to you. You are no one to him either. The so called father is such a 'trifle' For a man or woman, birth is merely connected with his or her mother's monthly seasonal periods, caused by biological factors like Mucus. Nothing more to a relationship" Birth is merely a biological accident!

"Dhasharatha is dead and gone (to heaven) because this is the law of nature. The destiny of mortals. Yet you are grieving for him and thinking about your commitment to him"

Like Omar Khayyam, Jaabaali swears by "eat, drink and be merry" philosophy when an opportunity appears before you. He says "I grieve and pity those, who, who giving up what they have, go and seek the so called Dharma that is not perceivable. I do not grieve for others who are materialistic. These men of Dharma undergo only suffering and ultimately give up life itself" Jaabaali takes a dig at these men of Dharma who follow rituals. "These men observe Ashtaka and Pithru rituals and Pindams, waste of food if you ask me. Will and can your dead (father) eat at all? More sarcasm to come from Jaabaali.. As we all know we offer Pindams (choice of foods) to the dead through the ritual of Shraadha. Inevitably, it is the brahmin priests who eat them all! So Jaabaali takes a dig. His sarcasm is at his best "If what is eaten by one can enter the stomach of another by a ritual, the next time your friend or relative goes out on a long journey, you dont need to send packets of food with him. You eat all you can and to your heart's content comfortably at your home.. And Lo! By the miracle of a ritual, your friend's or relatives's stomache will become full. As he continues his journey"

Like physicists of ancient times who maintained that atoms dont exist because no one has 'seen' them., Jaabaali expounds his materialistic philosophy thus "There is no other 'world'. Hold on to what is before you and what you perceive. Reject those that are not visible"

Jaabaali has such a contempt for religious men and high priests that he 'fumes' thus: "Perform Yaaga. rituals. Give liberally during ceremonies. Give up luxury. Take to abstinence...... all these 'teachings' are conceived by clever priests to make money out of you ***"Jaabaali thus expounded his materialistic philosophy to Raama".***

And even as Jaabaali was speaking Raama is enraged. He could not tolerate to hear such blasphemy from an old, noble wise man who had served his father for long years with distinction. Raama begins thus, Gist: "These words spoken by you, ostensibly to do good to me, cannot be accepted by me because they are really not salutary" He comes to the point thus "Tell me, Jaabaali! If I abide by this conduct of forsaking my promise (my commitment to my father) whose traditional practices will I follow?" By this Raama is firm that he will go by tradition, rather than by Jaabaali's advice. Raama warns Jaabaali of the consequence of not following norms. "Oh Jaabaali! If your advice becomes right, the entire world will be stricken with licentiousness" By this Raama says, that unless we follow laws and norms, the world will be in chaos and go topsy turvy. And Raama adds "As the saying goes, "Like king, so are his subjects = Yathaa Raaja-Thathaa Praja =", I, who am a prince, will not set a bad example or a precedent" Raama had sworn on Truth. He will go on the 14 year exile. He will be a man of Truth So says "Truth is the harmless, royal conduct. The Eternal: The World rests on Truth. A kingdom is indeed sustained by Truth." Thus Raama affirms that he will ever be a man of Truth although his father is dead.

Supporting his vow of Truth, Raama says "Great Rishi-s abide by Truth. Even heaven is sustained on Truth. Truth is God! Everything is rooted in Truth. There is nothing greater than Truth"

(It may not be out of place to mention. Mahatma Gandhi considered Truth, supreme even in political life.)

Jaabaali had been sarcastic about rituals, yaagas, gifts. Raama answers him: "Charity, gifts during ceremonies, Yaagas, all abide in and by Truth."

Having truthfully sworn and committed, how will I and for what purpose will I not follow my father's command. I will not give up my bond with Truth, in ignorance, greed or passion. I see the Dharma of Truth as concerning itself with 'soul'. Only for this reason the burden and suffering of persons doing vows and rituals is hailed"

Raama while appreciating Jaabaali's sincerity in asking him to return to Ayodhya condemns him thus "Considering it as beneficial to me you spoke to me with many suitable words. and asked me to return = Do this which is good for you = But what you said is Un-Aryan- most ignoble!"

"Before my father this vow was taken. My 'mother' Kaikeyi was also pleased. I will live in forest, eating forest fruits, live a life of restraint for 14 years and thus please my forefathers". India is a karma boomi. All are there to serve, to do duty. Raama tells Jaabaali "Even celestials like lords of fire, wind, moon, are enjoying the fruits of their service.. Even Indra is lord of the celestial world only after performing and taking the burden of 100 Yaagas on himself" By this Raama says that vows, yagas, rituals are not physical exercises but for salvation and for enjoying the 'fruits' of heaven. Not just for mortification of the body.

As he speaks on and on, denouncing materialism, Raama gets so 'worked' up that he is angry with his father for having had Jaabaali as his adviser for so long!

"I despise the action of my father, in having accepted you (as his adviser), accepted one who is an atheist, who, in this manner, with an evil mind, has strayed from the path of Dharma." Raama condemns people who put on the garb of Budhdha the wise! "The Budhdha, the clever man, the agnostic who chisels logic, is just like a clever thief, who pretends to be clean"

As Raama was speaking like this against the old noble and wise man, Jaabaali, Vasishta who was standing near them all and who was watching this tirade against Jaabaali from Raama, was rather upset Among persons of religion, rituals, and Yaagas, Vaalmeeki portrays Vasishta as supreme. Vasishta is the Chief Priest of the Ikshwaakus. So he curbs Raama thus "Remember!. Jaabaali knows the origin of the world!" Thus in one line he admonishes Raama for speaking so harshly. Jaabaali may not be a man of religion, but he is a wise and noble man. He must be treated with honour and respect even• if you don't care for his materialstic philosophy.

Jaabaali justifies himself thus before Raama. "Oh Raama! I did not preach atheism to you. I am not an avowed atheist. There is nothing that is for me, that 'belongs' to me. Taking note of circumstances I will be an Aasthika, a man of religion, if need be. I spoke all this because I wanted to get you back to Ayodhya. To suit this occasion, for the welfare of all, I spoke atheism".

Vaalmeeki wishes to convey to posterity how liberal they were those days. Vasishta a man of religion, and of utter faith, an authority on rituals, speaks on behalf of Jaabaali, the agnostic!. Infact he defends him. In one line Vaalmeeki conveys that it is not the monopoly of a religious man to be be noble and wise. Jaabaali was as much concerned about the welfare of the kingdom and its subjects as Vasishta. Vaalmeeki would not waste two chapters. So this Jaabaali-Raama confrontation.

33: ARTHA-KAARYA NIRVAAHA: (Management)

Although this chapter particularly refers to management of royal affairs, this study is profitable to every one. Whether a common man or a businessman, every citizen has to manage his affairs with prudence. For a prosperous life, good management is an essential requisite.

When Bharatha meets Raama in forest, Raama's first concern is the welfare of his kingdom. After inquiring about his father, ministers and others, Raama asks Bharatha about his administration of Ayodhya. Raama, ofcourse is unaware that his father is dead and Bharatha had refused to take over as king. Infact Bharatha had come to forest to take back Raama as king of Ayodhya.

In Ayodhya-chapter 100, Vaalmeeki through lips of Raama, enlightens us about management. His concern is affairs of the state. But, if we read between lines, it is enlightenment for us. Even mundane activity calls for good management.

Gist: "Oh lad, Oh Bharatha! I hope you do not let our eternal kingdom of Ayodhya 'slip' away from your hands"

We must be vigilant and matters must always be under control, never be allowed to slip away. This is the advice that every a man of business remember with profit. The businessman can never rest content.

"I hope you have appointed ministers, who are unequalled in bravery, who have knowledge, who are men of composure, who come from noble families, and who can understand other's feelings even by their gestures"

What is applicable to affairs of state, is applicable to affairs of business. The staff must be from noble families (honest), they must have knowledge and they must be clever enough to understand others even when they don't express themselves.

"The advice given under oath of secrecy by ministers who are expert counsellors, well versed in shaasthras, is the foundation for success for kings"

Here again, we can draw some enlightenment. A businessman or a top official of Government, should seek advice from experts who are men of experience, who have knowledge of their subjects (Shaasthras) and they should have confidence in you when they tender advice in secrecy.

"I hope you do not go to 'sleep' and resort to slumber! I hope you are awake at the proper time. At midnight do you contemplate about your actions (Artha-Naipuna)"

What applies to the king applies to leading men of profession. While sleep is integral part of life, we must be 'awake' always and not resort to the easy way of taking to bed to avoid facing problems. We should contemplate calmly and what better time can there be than midnight when you won't be disturbed!.

"I hope you take counsel all by yourself. I hope you seek counsel along with others as well. I hope the decision arrived at is not allowed to spread across. Having decided upon an action, you should act quickly. Never procrastinate"

A top man must talk to his advisers separately, individually. He must discuss in meetings. Once a decision is taken only action must result. Others should know only the fruits of your decision. You should not procrastinate.

"Oh Bharatha! All discussions and decisions taken with the advice of able ministers either by enquiry or out of expediency, which are not acted upon, should not be known to others" Comment is unnecessary!

"Oh Bharatha! I trust you prefer one man who is wise rather than have a contingent of 100 fools." Again comment is not called for!

"Oh lad! I hope you have entrusted men of great wisdom and knowledge with the most difficult jobs, average men with average tasks and inferior ones with menial jobs." It is the duty of a top executive or chief administrator, to divide the work of an organisation, apportioning the tasks. If a person in an organisation does not do his job properly, the reason is that he is not properly 'placed'. The top man himself should know 'Man power management'. The secret of success of Japan lies in this. In Japan, most of the staff in an organisation are content because they are well 'placed'

Raama gives advice to Bharatha about the rule of kingdom through, ministers, spies and ambassadors, and commander-in-chief. "Have you appointed a Commander-in-chief, who is brave, intelligent, resolute, dexterous, pure, born in a noble family, a totally devoted to the state and who ***bristles with joy***"

The Commander of the army must always be cheerful.

"Oh Bharatha! Your army officers, are they well versed in the science of war? Are they strong and ever 'seek' victory. Do they learn by experience?"

As war is a tricky business, officers must always 'learn' through mistakes, theirs and enemy's.

Raama gives a bit of advice to Bharatha, You may delay payments but never in case of salaries of army men.

"Oh Bharatha! Have you appointed as ambassadors, men who are our citizen learned and clever, 'scholarly', quick witted, and can communicate fast?

Hanumaan was a perfect ambassador as he had all these qualities.

Raama describes how one must keep an eye on various departments. "Oh Bharatha! With three, that is with three of your own trusted 'spies', on every one of the 18 administrators of other States and on every one of the 15 administrators of your own kingdom, do you keep a watch at all times"

We may list some of these departments office of the army Chief, City Protection, Prisons, Treasury both for civil and military, Publicity, Civil Justice, Central bureau of Investigation, Criminal Justice, Defence, Public works, Protocol, Ecology, Rivers, Taxes, Property.

Raama warns Bharatha about enemies who are driven away "I hope you keep a check at all times about the enemy and his movements. Enemies driven away return. You should not be indifferent" Raama emphasises an enemy is an enemy, more so if he wants revenge.

Although money and finance have high priority, Raama advises Bharatha that he should not honour clever Brahmin (advisers) who may be knowledgeable but are totally materialistic.

Raama has a lot to say about protection of heritage buildings and temples, halls etc. Festivities are an integral part of life of the citizens of the Ikshwaaku kingdom. Canals, rivulets around the city must be well maintained. Water supply continuous without depending on the mercy of 'Water' Gods like Varuna.!.

Raama has a special word for businessmen "Oh Bharatha! I hope members of the business community are all happy and prosperous." He has concern for agriculture.

"I hope farmers and cowherds cherish you always."

Raama warns Bharatha against excessive taxes on citizens. "Citizens must always be protected by the state at all times. Do you nourish and support them. Do you burden them with heavy taxes"

But Raama cautions Bharatha about Treasury. "Is your income always above expenditure? I hope Treasury has not fallen into wrong hands!"

This is of universal appeal. Finance management. Finance must never fall into wrong hands!

In the matter of justice, Raama cautions Bharatha. "I hope you do not punish the sinless and an honest man who may be falsely accused by persons out of passion or greed. I hope you always seek the counsel of experts in law and investigate" And he warns Bharatha further. "I hope when a thief is apprehended and after proper investigation is done, you do not let him off for pecuniary considerations" Readers know that is what is happening in India today!

Raama speaks some words of Dharma. There should be no discrimination between rich and poor. "I hope your learned ministers who are interested in your welfare do not discriminate between rich and poor when calamity strikes the kingdom." The Dharma of a king is to protect all, particularly when drought or earthquake hits!

We have words of wisdom from Raama "Oh Bharatha! I hope you do not destroy Dharma with Dharma.. Wealth by wealth (money power) Nor these two by passion due to gratification and greed."

The laws of Dharma should be judiciously used to foster Dharma. Wealth must be put to good use. Wealth is capital. Money power should not corrupt us. Greed and self gratification are not the purposes of Dharma or wealth. We refrain from elaborating on Raama's words of wisdom because it will be a long write up.

Raama even advises that one should not be a glutton devouring good food all by himself. He gets great pleasure only when he shares. Even a poor man must enjoy with his friends and folks..

And here is another advice from Raama which is for us all, not merely for 'King' Bharatha! "You must know the proper time and place for all activities. Oh Bharatha! Do you 'divide' your time for pursuit of Dharma, Artha and Kaama? "Dharma covers duty and administration. Artha covers procurement of wealth and substance. Kaama is mundane pleasures. No one's life is complete if he does not judiciously use his time and daily routine.

This is a long chapter. Vaalmeeki through the words of Raama enlightens us all. We have given only the gist of chapter 100 of Ayodhya kaanda.

34: **POOJA-PRAARTHANA** (Prayer)

Vaalmeeki Raamaayana: a Book of Prayer

It is befitting that we conclude Part III -Panorama - This Guide, with Prayer. We may remember what the great English poet Tennyson had said = More Things Are Wrought By Prayer Than This World Dreams of =

Deeply religious people consider Vaalmeeki Raamaayana a book of Prayer. The names of the Lord, Vishnu is found in the book. Most of the 1,000 names =Sahasra-Naama = of Vishnu are found in Vaalmeeki among chants, the Vishnu Sahasra Naama is the foremost. As Raama is the 'Avathar' of Vishnu, in Vaalmeeki Raamaayana, is seen an abridged version of Vishnu Sahasra Naama.

The Gaayathri japa =Prayer, is a mystic prayer of the devoted. The Prayer- Japa is "Thath Savithu Va Rennyam, Bhargo Dhevasya Dhee Mahi, Dhee-yo Yo Naha Pra Cho Dha yaath = Vaalmeeki being ordained by Brahma to write this epic as a Vedha, could not but remember Gaayathri Japa. And he introduced this Japa, The Gaayathri, in a concealed way in his eternal book, befitting the mystic nature of The Prayer- Hymn -Gaayathri itself.

The first letter of the first sloka of Vaalmeeki begins with Th (Thapas -Swaadhyaaya -Niratham- Thapaswi -Vaag vidhaam Varam Naaradham Pari Paprachcha Vaalmeeki Muni Pungavam). Thus Vaalmeeki at intervals of about 1,000 slokas, used the first letter-sound of Gaayathri in his slokas.

Thus The Gaayathri =Japa=Hymns which carry 24 syllables are incorporated at intervals by Vaalmeeki in his 22,000 slokas, the first syllable, sound carrying Gayathri.

Gaayathri		**Kaanda/chapter/sloka(Vaalmeeki)**
Syllable/sound		Sloka begins with Gaayathri Syllable
1:	Th/thath	Baala - Chapter 01- sloka 01
2:	Sa	Baala - Chapter 30- sloka 23

3:	Vi	Baala - Chapter 67- sloka 12
4:	Thu	Ayodh - Chapter 15- sloka 20
5:	Va	Ayodh Chapter 40 sloka 16
6:	R-Ray	Ayodh Chapter 67 sloka 34
7:	N-Nn	Ayodh Chapter 99 sloka 25
8:	Ya-(for NYA)	Aaranya Chapter 11 sloka 44
9:	Bhar	Aaranya Chapter 43 sloka 17
10:	Ga/go	Aaranya Chapter 72 sloka 21
11:	Dh/Dhey	Kishkind Chapter 22 sloka 20
12:	V/ Va	Kishkind Chapter 43 sloka 34
13:	S/Sya	Sundara Chapter 04 sloka 01
14:	Dh/Dhee	Sundara Chapter 26 sloka 41
15:	M/Ma	Sundara Chapter 53 sloka 26
16:	H/Hi	
17:	Dh/Dhee	Yudh Chapter 41 sloka 69
18:	Ya/Yo	Yudh Chapter 59 sloka 150
19:	N/Na	Yudha Chapter 94 sloka 26
20:	Pr/Pra	Yudh Chapter 119 sloka 24
21:	Ch/Cho	Uttara Chapter 16 sloka 25
22:	Dh/Dha	Uttar Chapter 33 sloka 41
23:	Y/Yaa	Ayodhya Chapter sloka 01
24:	Th	

Thath ends with Thath. Gaayathri is encompassed with THATH. This Syllable, sound, is highly philosophical.

"THATHVAM ASI" = That thou art= Realise who you are! Realise the Soul Supreme in you.

Vaalmeeki Raamaayana is a prayer book highly spiritual in content as well. In the entire epic, we will find prayer being offered. Even the great Hanumaan, when he takes off on flight over the ocean to Lanka in search of Seetha offers prayer (Sundara-chapter 1) "After offering prayer to the Lords of Sun, Wind, and to God Brahma, Indra, and The Bhootha-s he directed his mind on the task. He offered prayer to his father, facing east, cupping his hands in Anjali. He does obeissance to Raama and Lakshmana.

He prays to the lord of rivers, The Ocean. He hugged his folks and went round elders in circumbambulation in reverence"

Prayer is an integral part of all the characters in Raamaayana. Even the demon chief, Indrajith, does not venture to go out on a major campaign without offering prayers to his favourite temple in Lanka. Nikumbila. (Yudha-chapter 89). Infact Vibheeshana warns Raama, that Indrajith becomes invincible after he receives blessings at temple Nikumbila.

We shall restrict this topic to Kowsalya and Agasthya.

Kowsalya is one of those ladies who was ever doing prayer at her palace. When Raama visits her to inform her about his decision to obey the command of his father and go on exile, he finds his mother (Ayodhya-chapter 20-slokas 14 to 19) Gist: "Always seeking the welfare of her son, queen Kowsalya, ever steadfast in meditation, praying during the whole night, offering prayer to Vishnu in the morning, performing rituals in Fire with chants, praying to various deities ...."

We may observe that those days even a woman was doing Fire Rituals. When finally, she reconciles herself to Raama's departure she offers blessings to Raama and this forms part of prayer in this topic.

Koswalya's prayer: (Benediction-Ayodhya-chapter25)

"May those whom you worship in temples, bless you. May divine weapons offered by Vishwaamithra protect you. By the service rendered to your father, by the services rendered to your 'mothers', may you live long." Serving mother and father is a daily prayer for a son. Mother and father are considered 'gods'. "May sacred ritual materials like Dharbha grass ......protect you" The twigs and grass are not mere botanical species! They are sacred! May "celestials The Saadhyas, Vishwa-dhevas, Maruths, Dhaatha and

Vidhaatha, Poosha, Bhaga, Aaryama offer blessings to you. May The Lokpaals -protectors of earth- offer you protection. May The Rithu-s -the cycle of seasons- protect you. May the deities of month, the days, the year protect you. May Lord of Moon, the lord night protect you. May God Skandha, Brihaspathi, Lord Indra, The Saptha-rishis, Sage Naaradha protect you. May the Lord of Mountains, rivers protect you. "And Kowsalya adds "Oh Son Raama ! Those whom I worship daily, the Sidhdhas and the 'tribes', ever protect you" May Lord Varuna, Lord Kubhaera, Lords of day and night, The aadhityhas, the Dhithyas all protect you. May constellation of stars, like Venus, Jupiter, protect you. May Lord Sun and Lord of earth, Yama, protect you".

The list is long. But we have listed most of the deities. It is **interesting to observe that one Deity who is most worshipped in India today does not find a place in Vaalmeeki is Lord Vigneswara- Ganapathi!**

But the prayer of prayers, The Aadhithya Hridhaya Sthothra-chants and hymns by sage Agasthya when he enlightened Raama just before Raama was going to have the final battle with Raavana is ***The Prayer in Vaalmeeki Raamaayana.***

Agasthya's AADITHYA HRIDHAYA : Prayer & Chants (Yudha-chapter 107)

Agasthya enlightens Raama thus "Oh Raama! You listen to this, by which you will conquer all. This is Secret. This is Eternal. Very Holy. The Aadhithya Hridhaya you must recite daily. Most auspicious. Imperishable Truth. Will destroy sins. will destroy enemies. Will destroy worry and disease." And we now have the gist of the chants.

"***You Must Worship Vivaswaan,*** who is The Lord Sun. and lord of earth. He is Light, the creator of light. He is ever saluted by dhevas as He rises. He is brilliant. He is the 'mother' of all souls. He manifests by diverse rays. He serves, dhevas, asuras, mankind, worlds. He is Brahma! He is Vishnu. He is Shiva. He is Skandha. He is Prajaapathi. He is Indra He is Kubhaera. He is Time. He is Yama. He is Soma-moon.He is Varuna, lord of waters. He is The Pithrus, Vaasavas, the Saadhyas, the Ashwinis, The Maruths, The Manu, the Lord Wind, The Fire, The Rituals, The Rythm-the seasons, He is Rithu. He is Life to all. He is The Aadhithya-son of Adthithi. He is Savitha-the instigator-creator of activity. As Soorya he roams in sky. He is The Nourisher. The Creator of day, the very creator of Sperm of life (He rides) the greenish yellow horse. His horse is Saptha. With 1,000 sparks of flame, he illuminates. The worlds. Destroyer of darkness-ignorance. He is Shamba the benevolent. He is Thwashta-instigator.

He is Maarthaanda- (creates out of destruction). He is Amshumaan-one who enlightens. He is Hiranya Garbha-golden foetus. He is Shishira- one who cools the heart of the good. He is Thapana- one who torments, the bad. He is Bhaaskara, who illuminates with right knowledge. He is Ravi. He is Agni garbha (ever pregnant with fire). He is Shanka. He destroys cold (fright). He is lord of sky. He 'Splits' Thamas (removes ignorance by his own logic).

He is Rig,Yajur, Sama and Atharvan vedhas. He is a friend of the Waters. He 'follows' the course of Vindhyas. He 'floats' over sky. Creator of heat. He presents Himself in a circular form. He is Golden. He is the 'burner' of all. He is Kavi-most enlightened. He is Vishwas-all pervasive. Most brilliant. Prime source of all activity. Sustainer of the world. Lord of all stars and constellation. He 'pervades' as Twelve. (Lord of Kubhaera, Indra, Baka, Poosha, Mithra, Varuna, Aaryamaan, Archis, Vivaswaan, Dhwashta, Savitha, Vishnu-He is lord of 12 months of the year).

"Oh Raama! May you offer salutations to Him. To Aadhithya. May you worship Him as he rises in the eastern mountain and sets in the western mountain of Astha-giri. Salutations to you, the lord of the day. Salutations to you, who is Rudhra-the terrible."

We conclude this Part III of our Guide The Revelation with ***Salutations and Salutations to AADHITYHA***

VAALMEEKI RAAMAAYANA

A REVELATION

PART IV

ADDENDUM

PART IV

CONTENTS

(Addenda-Miscellaneous)

A: GUNA-SUGUNA -VISHESHA

(Good qualities, Attributes)

In Vaalmeeki which is also a book on character, we find a list of qualities and attributes that go with noble men. Ofcourse opposite qualities are attributed to bad persons! Raama is portrayed as the most noble amongst them all. Yet Raama himself, we doubt, can qualify to all the qualities listed by Vaalmeeki at various places in his epic.

We shall list most of these good qualities and attributes, with special reference to Raama himself, a man of Dharma

1:	Guna vaan	=	Man of good qualities
2:	Veerya vaan	=	Brave man
3:	Dharma gnya	=	Man knowing Dharma
4:	Kritha gnya	=	Man of gratitude
5:	Sathya vaak	=	Man who keeps his word, who speaks truth
6:	Dhrida vratha	=	Firm in vows (Rituals)
7:	Chaarithriya	=	Man of good conduct
8:	Hitha Kaamya	=	Salutary, desires to do good to all
9:	Vidhwaan	=	Most learned
10:	Aathma vaan	=	Man of composure, self reliant
11:	Jitha Krodha	=	Conquered anger and wrath
12:	Eka	=	Unique
13:	Priya dharshan	=	Handsome, casts pleasing eye
14:	Samartha	=	Most capable, competent
15:	Dhyuthi maan	=	Bright, majestic, brilliant
16:	Un asooyaka	=	Free from jealousy
17:	Niya thaathmaa	=	Resolute with self control

18:	Maha Veerya	=	Immensely brave, (no fear at all)
19:	Dhrithi maan	=	Firm
20:	Vashi	=	One who makes people accept him People willingly submit to him
21:	Budhi maan	=	A man with 'brain', wise man.
22:	Neethi maan	=	Man of Justice
23:	Vaagmee	=	Has command over speech, eloquent
24:	Shreemaan	=	Resplendent, endowed with riches & grace
25:	Shathrugna	=	Destroyer of enemies (external)
	Nithya Shathrugna	=	Destroyer of enemies within, like anger, passion, greed etc
26:	Dhaathaa	=	Bestower
27:	Smrithi maan	=	Man of immaculate memory
28:	Ripu Nishoodana	=	Wipe off enemies
29:	Prathi Bhaana vaan	=	Brilliant, clarity of thought ever 'crosses' mind
30:	Aarya	=	Most noble
31:	Su vikrama	=	Nice gait, strides
32:	Yashaswee	=	Famous
33:	Gnyana Sampanna	=	Endowed with wisdom
34:	Sathya Sandha	=	Truth ever encompasses him
35:	Prathaapa vaan	=	Radiating brilliancy, Energy
36:	Shuchi	=	Pure
37:	Karuna	=	Compassion
38:	Bheebhatsa	=	Revulsion
39:	Bayaanaka	=	Causes fear, Fear
40:	Roudhra	=	Terrible wrath
41:	Haasya	=	Laughter

42:	Shringaara	=	Romance, Passion, endearment
43:	Kshama	=	Forbearance
44:	Thyaaga	=	The 'giving' up
45:	Samaadhi maan	=	A great conciliator (and also) one who 'collects' his thoughts
46:	Thathva gnya	=	Knower of 'real' truth, knows essence of life, knows about 'soul'
47:	Desha Kaala gnya	=	One who knows right time and place for action
48:	**Rakshaka**	=	Protector of ecology, life
	Jeeva Lokasya		
	Dharmasya	=	Protector of Dharma
	Swa Janasya	=	Protector of his own folks
	Swasya Dharmasya	=	Protector of his own Dharma, His commitment to his vocation
49:	Sarva Loka Priya	=	Loved by all – The beloved
50:	Saadhu	=	A good man
51:	Vichakshana	=	Far sighted
52:	A-Dheena aathma	=	Strong in spirit, never despondent
53:	Sarva sama	=	Treats all equal, considerate to all
54:	Eka Priya Dharshan	=	Casts pleasing eye on one & all
55:	Gaambeerya	=	Generosity
56:	Paapa gna	=	Destroyer of Sin
57:	Pavithra	=	Pure, purification through worship
58:	Punnya	=	Merit, Sacred
59:	Prashaantha aathma	=	Tranquil mind

60:	Mridhu Poorva baashi=	Tender and soft spoken
61:	Madhura baashi =	Speaks endearingly, sweetly
62:	Poorva Baashi =	First amongst speakers, Initiates discussion, polite
63:	Na Anrutha Katha =	Never indulged in falsehood in talks, no flippancy
64:	Sa-Anukrosha =	Ever compassionate
65:	Pra Graha vaan =	Takes on responsibilities
66:	Uthara-Uthara-= Yuktha Vakthaa	(A superb conversationalist) who supports arguments with proper rejoinders
67:	A- Roga =	Free from disease, healthy
68:	Purusha-saara gnya =	Could perceive the 'mind' of men (by their appearance)
69:	Guna vath thara =	Foremost amongst men with good qualities
70:	Para-Puram jaya =	Destroyer of enemy fortress,cities
71:	Sthira Chiththa =	Of 'steady' mind, firm
72:	Kshaantha =	Very indulgent, patient
73:	Bhavya =	Gracious, Righteous
74:	Athula =	Incomparable
75:	Nipuna =	Skillful, Dexterous
78:	Lakshmi vaan =	Man of splendour, auspicious
	Lakshmi vardhana =	One who increases prosperity
79:	Vridha say vee =	One who serves elders
80:	Smitha Poorva Baashi =	Speaks with a smile, ever
81:	Shreshtaa =	Most Distinquished
82:	Dheera /Dhairya =	Courageous
83:	Mahesh vaasa =	A great warrior, wielder of Bow
84:	Jithendra =	Conqueror of five 'senses'
85:	Archish maan =	Most luminous
86:	Architha =	Most honoured, worshipped

87:	Sthitha	=	Unshaken
88:	Vineetha	=	Man of modesty
89:	Maryaadhin	=	One who observes norms, and has sense of propriety

Vaalmeeki enumerates above qualities. Almost all these are found in Raama But the above list is not exhaustive.

Vaalmeeki describes some physical features of Raama. For detailed write up on Raama's physical attributes, we have already referred to these in Sundara kaanda chapter 35 where Hanumaan describes Raama's physical features. We may add to the above, as found in Baala kaanda-chapter 1

"Broad shoulders, Neck Conch shaped, Robust cheeks, Broad chest, Long hands reaching up to knees, collar bones well concealed, Nice head, lovely forehead, good height, magnetic-attractive complexion, lovely eyes, with tinge of red, beautiful eye brows"

B KAALA, VIDHOORA, GANA-SAMKYA-AKSHOWHINI

(Time, Distance, Numbers, Regiment)

One of the reasons why we shy away from ancient books, epic like Raamaayana is because we are not able to swallow mythological numbers. In Vaalmeeki we find that gifts of 1,000 elephants are made. To manage one elephant itself is tough. Here Vaalmeeki speaks in terms of thousands and millions. Be that as it may, we will write a few words about, measurement of time, distance and numbers.

Muhoortha: They did not have clocks those days but they measured time by day's cycle. A Muhoortha is a short period of time. We find reference to Muhoortha in Vaalmeeki. But we may say that a Muhoortha is Thirty-th part of a day's time.We dont need to be a Ramanajum to figure out in minutes. A Muhoortha is 48 minutes...

Vidhoora: Yojana; Krosha: Distance is also very tricky subject. When the great Hanumaan takes off from southern tip of India to fly over the huge ocean to island of Lanka, he had to cover 100 Yojanas. Now what may be a Yojana? Now Hanumaan is Maaruthi, He has the speed of Wind. From experience, even tornado is not expected to hit us by a speed of more that 200 Km per hour. Hanumaan had started early morning and was flying more than 10 hours with breaks for obstacles while flying over Ocean (Sundara - kaanda-chapter 1). Thus we may work out the distance- Yojana- to be around 9 to 10 miles. There is some difference of opinion. Some maintain it is less than 6. We will not enter into a debate. A Krosha thus becomes 4 miles, some say it is only 3 miles or less.

Gana Samkya: Before we enter into this subject, an observation cannot be overlooked. In India today we have any number of scientists and scholars, but very few are interested in study of all these ancient terms on a scientific basis. Ancient subjects are more exciting for research and study because mythology encompasses them. Vaalmeeki at many places talks about 'Elements' being found in Himaalyan range. He talks about life saving drugs-plants in upper regions and remote areas of Himaalayas. Yet, there is no sustained Geological survey in these difficult terrain. Nor study of herbals by Pharmacy men. Even in Geometry, as for instance in a simple theorem like area of a right angle triangle attributed to Greek mathematician Pythagoras, it is even simpler at the hands of mathematicians in India of ancient times. Western mathematicians are stunned by the proofs offered by Vedhic scholars!

In India, it is generally believed that numbers were based on 12. A dozen was the unit of trade and commerce.Even our old Rupee was 192 damdies (12 by 16) But metric system prevailed in Vaalmeeki's time. 10 was the unit. When

Raavana wanted to know the size of the monkey army of Raama-Sugreeva that had besieged his island, we find the number and size being indicated through metric system. (Yudhdha -chapter 28)

We have 10 to the power of zero	=	Eka	1
We have 10 to the power of one,	=	Dhasha	10
We have 10 to the power of two	=	Shatha	100
We have 10 to the power of three	=	Sahsra	1,000

A lac is 10 to the power of 5 and crore is to power of 7
What about huge numbers? We shall see presently

Name:	**Multiples of 10**	**Power of 10**
Crore	Hundred of hundred thousand	10^{7}
Shanga	Hundred of thousand crores	10^{12}
Mahaa Shanga	Hundred of thousand shangas	10^{17}
Brindha	Hundred of thousand Maha shangas	10^{22}
Maha Brindha	Hundred of thousand Brindhas	10^{27}
Padma	Hundred of thousand Mahabrindhas	10^{32}
MahaPadhma	Hundred of thousand Padmas	10^{37}
Kharva	Hundred of thousand Mahapadmas	10^{42}
Mahakharva	Hundred of thousand Kharvas	10^{47}
Samudra	Hundred of thousand Mahakharva	10^{52}
Ogha	Hundred of thousand Samudras	10^{57}
Maha Ogha	Hundred of thousand Oghas	10^{62}

These astronomical numbering becomes mythological. But the point is that even during Vaalmeeki's time, they adopted metric system

AKSHOWHINI

Like in modern days where army is divided into divisions, formations and services like Army, Navy and Air force etc, in Vaalmeeki's time they had also divisions of army. There was ofcourse no Navy those days. They did not need Airforce as quite a few of the soldiers-monkey chiefs could also fly 'solo' They had a 'select' Air force men! Ah!

The Akshowhini is a term found in Valmeeki. It comprises: A foursome Army of:

1:	21,870	Elephants
2:	21,870	Chariots
3:	65,000	Horses
4:	109,350	Infantry

It is interesting to note that those days elephants were an integral part of an army. It must have cost hell of a lot of money to maintain this army. Feeding one elephant is king's ransom. Here we talk of elephants in thousands. By present value of Rupee, an annual budget of Rs.800 crores is needed just to maintain Akashowhini. Ofcourse other wings of army is also there.

(Note: How staggering is numbers, we cannot but fail to appreciate Number 'Maha Ogha' is 10 to the power of 62.

To comprehend this, let us look at this, this way. Light which is the fastest in the Universe, travels at ***186,000 miles per second***. In one year, if light travels unchecked, it would cover a distance of around 10 to the power of 13 miles! This figure is the astronomical figure. We express distances in terms of "light" years, that is light travelling at 186,000 miles per second taking a year to reach us! But in Vaalmeeki we find numbers so staggering that we have 10 to the power of 62!)

C: PAADHYA, ARGHYA, AASANA

(Feet, Water, Seat)

We have already referred to hospitality that we must extend to a guest. One of the commandments is that a Guest must be well received and honoured.

When a guest arrives, invariably after a long walk, it is his feet that would be tiring most. Thus Paadhya, a traditional method of service to a guest as he enters your abode gets the first priority. A Guest's feet must be washed with good water and massaged.

And ofcourse the next on the list is Arghya. Arghya is general term but Water is the first to be offered to quench the thirst of a tired guest. In Rajasthan, a desert land, even today, when you visit a house hold, even without a request you will be received with a tumbler of water and cool drinks. Sanskrit word = Argh=is a general term, meaning worth, value etc. And ofcourse for a thirsty man the first is drinks. Then you offer eats, and in forests, fruits and nuts.

Aasana offer of a comfortable seat is next on the list. Naturally your tired guest must first relax.

It is interesting to note that in Baala kaanda, chapter 2 when God Brahma Himself condescends to come down to earth to visit Vaalmeeki, the sage naturally is excited but he does not fail to honour God Brahma with Paadhya, Arghya and Aasana. Not that the Lord needs cleaning up, nor was the lord ever thirsty!

D: VASANTHA, GREESHMA, VRISHTI, SHARAD, HEMANTHA Kaala

(Seasons- Spring, Summer, Rainy, Autumn, Winter etc.)

Vaalmeeki describes in his unique poetic style various seasons in his epic. Scholars and Indologists maintain that none can match the literary genius of the 6 th.Century poet,

Kaalidhaasa. Vaalmeeki lived in post Vedhic period while Kaalidhaasa was a 'modern' poet. We need not entertain a debate, but we can affirm that Kaalidhaasa like another poet-philosopher Bharthruhari, must have drawn lot of inspiration from Vaalmeeki, who is the first amongst poets in India. Vaalmeeki had a constraint. He could not be carried away by poetry because he had to stick to Truth and write without fear or favour. Yet he forgets himself as a story teller and takes liberty as a poet, now and then! In describing seasons, his poetry 'flows'!

We are in the Northern hemisphere, north of equator. Our seasons may be broadly classified as (1) Vasantha (spring- between March-April) (2) Greeshma (summer between May-June) (3) Vrishti (Rainy season between July August September) (4) Sharad (Autumn between October November) (5) Hemantha (Winter between December-February)

Before we proceed to give a gist about Vaalmeki's description of seasons, we cannot but fail to observe a remark made by Raama himself as he was pining away in grief over the abduction of his beloved wife Seetha. In Kishkinda kaanda- chapter 1- slokas 49 & 50 Raama grieves over Seetha thus "Where my beloved is, if there is spring there also, then like me Seetha will be pining away in grief during this beautiful season, like me, as she is without me". Yes! Raavana's Lanka is quite far in Southern hemisphere, Seasons are different there.

Yes! They had knowledge of geography.

MAADHAVA Season:

Spring season (Ref Kishkinda-chapter1) Raama bemoans!

"This lovely Maadhava-spring season torments me as I am without Bharatha and Seetha is abducted away. This month of Surabhi season, brings in pleasant winds. It is time for abundant ***Love Making*** for lovers, with smell of beautiful flowers all around." Poet Vaalmeeki goes 'poetic' "It appears as though Lord of Wind, is 'playing' with flowers, that are either clinging to tree or are blown off to rest on the slopes of mountain. The Lord of wind is 'sung' to by the humming bees, as they shake up the branches of the trees and shift places. And as the Lord of wind makes his way through caves of mountain, it appears as if he is sung to by the cooing peacocks, even as the Lord of wind shakes the trees, making them appear as though they are dancing before him. In this Maadhava season, the Karnikara trees in blossom appear like men dressed up in Peethaambara (silken) robes." And Vaalmeeki describes Raama's grief of separation from Seetha, unable to enjoy the season as he is without her.

"With flame, that is the cluster of flowers of Ashoka tree, the red sparks that are the buds that open up, the burning sound of 'flame' that is the humming of bees hovering over the tree, this Fire That Is Spring Season, is Burning me". And Raama is almost certain that Spring will burn him up as his grief is increasing by its diverse beauty.- the beauty he cannot enjoy as he is without Seetha. By this ***Vaalmeeki brings home a truth we all know***. We cant enjoy unless our close ones are happy and are with us to share. "It appears to me as though Fire of Grief caused by pangs of 'love' (of separation from Seetha), inflamed by the beauty of Spring, will soon burn me up!"

Raama wails "Ah! In this Spring, the season of flowers, this life of separation is unbearable. The captivating wind of the season that comes through gaps of mountain carrying pollen of lovely flowers, is like breath of Seetha"

VRISHTY -Rainy Season (Gist of a few slokas)

Vaalmeeki, as he describes the Rainy Season through lips of Raama, begins by talking about cycle of seasons.

"Having drunk the vapours of the Ocean, with the help of

Sun (during summer season), the sky is shedding the 'Foetus' that is Rain, that it had 'borne' for 9 months"

How poetic can you get.! Nature's cycle. Comment not necessary.! The clouds are heavy. Some times low as well. Vaalmeeki again goes poetic. "It is possible for one to 'climb' steps of layers of clouds, on to sky, carrying a 'Pitcher' of flowers to garland Sun!" Yes. Indians know monsoons, and the heavy dark and white, low clouds. "Inflamed by the twilight of the evening, with patches of red over fringes of clouds which are white, the sky appears like a body whose wounds are covered with dressing of cloth." (Blood stains of wound, dressed by dressing of surgical cotton cloth). As Lightning strikes intermittently during monsoon, Vaalmeeki describes this beautifully.

"Beaten by lightning that are like golden bridles, the sky, with thunder of clouds, appears as though it is 'groaning' (stricken) with pain." Thunder follows lightning. What monsoon does to citizens is described. "Dust has settled down. Wind is cool, inconvenience of summer gone. Journey undertaken by monarchs (for war etc) has also stopped. Men who are abroad, are rushing back." And Vaalmeeki talks about floods "Sleep reaches but slowly, but rivers rush towards ocean" And Vaalmeeki excels himself. Talks about 'Music concert' and 'Dance recitals"! "It appears as if there is a music concert going on in ('Hall' of) Forest, with sweet strains from humming bees that are the stringed musical instruments, with vocal music from the vocal chatter of monkeys, and Laya-Rythm- provided by thunder of clouds that are the Mridungas"

Vaalmeeki follows this with another comparison; Dance

"It appears as if there is a dance recital going on here by the exhilarated peacocks who are the dancers, whose 'tails' are hanging down like ornaments of dancers, with cooings heard that are the music accompaniment and with birds and monkeys on tree tops, who are the "audience" As torrential rain pours, wind also starts blowing with great sound, (making the sounds from both, deafening)

"The star studded sky is covered by clouds. Sun is rarely visible. Earth is being fully satisfied by new 'flood' of waters.All directions become invisible" Even time of sunset is not clearly known. "Sun, comes to be known as having reached Astha (mountain for sunset) only by the birds seeking repose in their nests and by the closure of loutus leaves and by the bursting of jasmine pods" As roads will be muddy, there will be no easy movement. "The journey of king and army has stopped. Army is in barracks. War, Enmity, and the Roads have been treated the same, by Rain!" And Vaalmeeki compares rain water falling on leaves, floor etc thus "Like pearls, cut off from chains of beautiful Apsara damsels, rain spills are all over"

We have listed only some slokas of Vaalmeeki as this is only a Guide. Vaalmeeki's artistry is revealed again and again as he describes Rainy season.

Sharadh- Autumn season

The Sky is clear. Without clouds, without thunder and lightning, without resonant notes of cooing birds. Lord Indra, having satisfied the earth with waters, having made grains come out, has fulfilled his task! Vaalmeeki poetically describes river banks in autumn "Like maidens running away bashfully on seeing the new lovers, showing their (lovely) backs, rivers during autumn, are showing white sand banks, gently, softly."

"Without clouds, the sky has the lustre of polished sword. Waters of the river are reduced. Wind blows softly but cool. All directions are bright. By rays of bright sun on earth, earth is free of clay. The mud of earth is 'solid', rigid." Kings can now venture out to settle their score. There is no noise of rivers flowing fast, nor noise from clouds; the fierce wind of monsoons has stopped. Waterfalls of mountain flow out without sound.. Vaalmeeki goes poetic when he describes the gentle flow of rivers. "Like frolicking movement of amorous women in early morning after an amorous night and enjoyment with lovers, the movement of the rivers which are like those of women, whose fishes are the Mekala ornaments of women, is very leisurely, casual"

"Having satisfied the world with good rain, having filled up rivers, ponds etc, having made earth sprout out grains, the bearers of waters, the clouds, have 'abandoned' the sky, disappeared!"

"Like a maiden whose body is covered by white upper silken cloth, the night is covered by the whiteness of the moon. Face, the pretty rising moon, the twinkling of stars, the eyes."

"With stars appearing joyous by the 'touch' of rays of rising moon, the evening which is of red colour, is giving up the sky, voluntarily"

"The autumn season starts with its 'distribution' (contribution) of its glory by manifestation of branches in the Seen Leaf trees, by the twinkling of stars, by rising moon and brightness of the sun, making animals like elephants, bulls exhilarated"

We have given only a gist of Vaalmeeki's description of seasons. We know, translation of slokas cannot bring out Vaalmeeki's artistry. We should learn Sanskrit at least to enjoy Vaalmeeki.!

E: VRIKSHA-VANASPATHI-ANGKURA
(Trees and plants)

In ancient times, ecology was foremost. Vaalmeeki refers to various rivers, ponds, trees, plants throughout his epic. We shall list names of a few trees. The list is not exhaustive.

We have given botanical names to a few.

ASHOKA	Jonesia
ANGKOLA	Alanguin hexapetala
AAMRA	Mango, Mangefra Indica
AMALA	Embellica officianalus gaertin
AMALAKA	Embellica rotung
ARISHTA	Azedirachea Indica
ASANA	Terminolia tormentosa
ARJUNA	
ASHWAKARNI	
BHILVA	
BHEEJAKA	Fig tree
BHADARYA	Eyezephus jujora
BHAVYA	Dilinea Indica
CHOOTHA	
CHIRIBILBA	
CHAMPAKA	
CHANDANA	
DHAVA	Grislea tormentosa
DHANVANA	Altagi maurorum
DHADHIMANA	
GANDAPOORNA	
JAMBU	Eugenia Jambalona / bamboo type
KURAVA	
KADAMBA	
KAKUBA	
KUSHTA	Smelling Punnaga type
KETHAKI	
KHARJOORA	Dates
KIMSUKA	
KOVIDHARA	Bauhenia variegata
KAPIMUKHA	
KARNIKARA	

KARAVEERA	
KUNDUGULMA	
KURUVAKA	Dye making plant (Marudaani)
LOUDHRA	Symplocus reacemos
MAALATHI	
MALLIKA	
MAADHAVA	
MADHOOKA	Jonesia asoka
MUCHALINDA	Pierospermum suberifoliocum
NIYAGRODHA	Banyan
NEEPA	Ixorabanduca-Nauclea cadamba
NAAGA VRIKSH	
NEELA	
NAKTHAMALA	
NAARIKELA	Coconut
NIVAARA	
PADHMA	Term for lotus
PADMAKA	
PAATAALA	
POORNAKA	
PRIYALA	Bean creepers
PANASA	Artocarpus Integrifolia
PRIYA	Buchanalia latifolia
PRIYANGO	Synapis ramosa
PUNNYAGANDA	Mrichelia-champaka (plant)
PUNNAGA	
SINDHUVARA	
SPANDHANA	
SHIMSHUPA	
SAALA	Pinus Longifolia
SAPTHAPARNA	Seven leaves plant

SAPTHACHADRA	Alatonia scholaris
SANTHAANAKA	
SPANDANA	
THILAKA	
THINISA	Debergia ujjainesia
THAALA	(coconut-palmyra type)Borassus fabilliformia
THAMAALA	
UTHPHALA	Type of lotus
UDHAALAKA	
VANJULA	
VAASANTHI	
VARANAA	
VAKULA	
VARUNA	Graetaevia roxburg
VETHRA	Calamus rotung -
VITAPI	(For logs and masts)

As we said, list is not exhaustive. In the Himaalyan range, we have any number of Herbals and life saving plants. We may mention that Vaalmeeki specifically mentions a few, like VISHAALA KARNI, SUVARNA KARNI, SANDHANA KARNI. Some 'bold' botanists claim that these species of herbal trees belong to Coccus cardifolius, Creton polyandrums, Methonica superba, Menipermum cordifolius.!

While leaving this topic, we may go back to what we had said earlier. Himaalayas is supposed to be respository of Elements, Herbal plants and so on. Yet no serious exploration-study has been conducted so far.

F: SANGEETHA, VAADHYA - Music and Musical Instruments)

From time immemorial, Music has been an integral part of life in our Bhaarath. Infact, as we have mentioned before,

Vaalmeeki's epic was first introduced to the public as a musical. It is therefore appropriate that we should write a few lines on the subject of music and musical instruments. According to Vaalmeeki, the Ghandharvas like Sage Naaradha, Thumburu, Gopa were the first amongst singers. In dancing we have Alambusa, Mishrakeshi, Pundarika and Vaamana. Incidentally, these celestials performed at Bhardhwaja's hermitage when Bharatha and his army was entertained to a lavish hospitality (Ayodhya-chapter 91)

Laya = Rythm has always been the base of Indian music. No wonder, we have any number of percussion instruments mentioned in Vaalmeeki. ***Mridunga,__Dhundhubhi, Thoorya, Panava, Moorja. Aadambara. Vipangi Murasa, Madduka, Murava, Pataka, Tunduma, Valluka***

And amongst stringed instruments, the pride of place goes to Veena. It is Veena that is frequently mentioned in the epic. The celestial singers carried a form of Veena, called Thumbura, perhaps named after Thumburu. This is without frets as in the case of Veena. We have already mentioned about Veena under 'Panoraama' We may observe a few points about Veena. It is 7 stringed instrument, but possibly in Vaalmeeki's times, it was a 7 plus 3 stringed instrument. The 3 strings at the base without frets constituting the Laya of the Veena, the 7 strings on top over frets, the main strings.

It is rather surprising that Venu = Flute is not listed in Vaalmeeki. (the favourite of Lord Krishna).But then lord Krishna came much later.

How did they manage to produce high tensile steel wire of fine gauge?

G: JYOTHISHA- NAKSHATHRA - THITHI etc

(Astrology, stars and constellations)

In this Bhaaratha Varsh, from Vaalmeeki's days, every one believed in stars and Astrology. When a child is born, the namng ceremony is done after casting its horoscope, When Raama, Lakshmana, Bharatha and Shathrugna were born, family priest Vasishta names these boys as per their characteristic features.

This book is not a dissertation on science of astrology but we give a short note on this. The days of the week are Sunday (presiding deity Lord of Sun), Monday (Moon), Tuesday (Mars) Wednesday (Mercury) Thursday (Jupiter) Friday (Venus), Saturday (Saturn). There are two ethereal planets Raahu and Kethu, thus the horoscope is based on the position of these in a person's astrological chart of 12 houses based on Lagna (birth, time and place). The 12 houses are Mesha, Rishabha, Mithuna, Kataka, Simha, Kanya, Thula, Dhanus, Vrichika, Makara, Kumbha, Meena The Nine 'stars' occupy the 12 houses in a person's horoscope. The position of these in the 12 houses is fixed at the time of birth and is unchanged. ***This is fate***! A study of the chart on the basis of movement of heavenly bodies from time to time, will indicate the person's 'fortunes' at that time!

And we have 28 Nakshathras of the month, that revolves every 28 days throughout the year of 365 days. These are, Ashwini, Bharani, Krithika, Rohini, Mrigasheersha, Aardra, Punarvasu, Pushya, Ashlesha, Magha, Poorva Phalguni, Uttara phalguni, Hastha, Chithra, Swaati, Vishaaka, Anuradha, Jyeshta, Moola, Poorva shaada, Uttara shaada, Abhijith, Sravana-Dhanishta, Satabishaj, Poorva bhadrapaada, Uttara badrapaada, Revathi.

H: KOSHA Glossary.

AYODHYA:	Capital/kingdom of Ikshwaakus. As name suggests, (A-Yudh) kings dare not fight against this renowned kingdom
AARYA	General term. Noble. India used to be called Aarya vartha, where noble men lived
ABHIJITH	A Homa-Fire Ritual
AASANA	Traditional hospitality, offer of seat
ARGHYA	Traditional Hospitality, offer of water, drinks
ARTHA	See Dharma
ADHWARYU	Priests: during sacrifical ceremony. mark out holy mounds for rituals
APSARA:	Celestial maidens of beauty. Unmarried
AAYUSH-HOMA	A Ritual for long life
AMARAVATHY	Celestial capital of Indra
ASHWAMEDHA	Great ceremony.Horse Sacrifice Only mighty kings perform this
AAPTHORYOMA	A Ritual - Homa
ANGA	A Kingdom in Eastern India
ATHIRAATHRA	A Ritual performed at night
ATHIBHALA	See Bhala
AKSHOWHINI	Army formation
ANJALI	Reverential salutation by cupping hands
AGNISHTOMA	A Fire Ritual
ANASOOYA	A great spiritual lady, free from jealousy Wife of sage Athri, daughter of Daksha
ASURA	Celestials, children of Dhithy-Kashyapa

AGASTHYA	Great Rishi. Living in South. Supposed to have quelled fury of Ocean He humbled Vindhyas when it started 'growing'. By his power destroyed demon Vaathaapi. Gave the prayer of prayers AADITHYAHRIDHAYA to world through Raama
ARTHASAADHAKA	Minister in Dhasharatha's Cabinet
ADHOORTH-RAJAS	Son of King Kusha. Vishwaamithra's ancestor
ASAMANJA	Son of King Sagara who was exiled
AMSHUMAAN	Son of Asamanja, who took over Ayodhya after Sagara passed away
AMBAREESHA	A King of Ayodhya
ASTHRA	General term for weapons, both conventional and divine
ADHITHI	Wife of Kaashyapa.She 'bears' Vaamana the incarnation of God Vishnu
ASHTAPAADHA	Ayodhya was artistically constructed in this syle of architecture
AHALYA	Wife of Gauthama who was cursed by him for her affair with Indra. Her son Shathaanand is minister to Janaka. Raama resurrects her
AHEENDRA	A King of birds, a celestial
AMRUTHA	Nectar. Lords churned the milky ocean for this.
ABHEERS	Evil mongers residing under ocean
AVIDHWA	Elder statesman who advises Raavana
ARJUNA	An ordinary Kshathriya chief who killed Brahmin Jamadagni.

	Jamadagni's son Parashu Raama took revenge on the entire race of Kshathriyas
ALAMBUSA	Capital of Vishaala
ASHWINS	Celestials, considered physicians to them
AAYURVEDHA	Science of Medicine and Surgery. Father of this is Dhanvantari who came up when milky ocean was churned by lords
ASTHA	Mythological mountain in west. Sun is supposed to set there!
ASHOKA	A minister in Dhasharatha's cabinet. Also name of a tree. A forest garden in Lanka
ANANGA	Formless.Name of Lord of love, Manmatha who was reduced to this by fury of Shiva
APARNA	Most powerful Goddess, consort of Shiva who did penance without even food of a leaf
ASHWAPATHY	King of Kekeya kingdom, father of Kaikeyi
AMSHUMATHY	Yamuna River, also known as Kaalindhi
ALARKA	A royal sage who plucked his eyes for giving sight to a Bird
AARYAMA	A Deity
APARTHALA	A hill range in upper NE India
ADHIKAALA	A town between Ayodhya and Rajgriha Towns in between are Ailadhaana, Aparapatna, Amshudaana, Amboorprastha
ATHRI	A Saptha rishi, a great sage

ASHMAKUTTA-s	A class of sages
ASCHAYYA-s	Sages who do penance witout rest
ABRA - AVAKAASAKA	Sages who do penance in open sky braving the elements
ANANTHA	Celesial king of reptiles
ARUNDHATHI	Famed wife of sage Vasishta
ANGEERASA	From Prajaapathi, an old sage
ARISHTANEMI	From Prajaapathi, an old sage
ANALA	Daughter of Dhaksha, who married Kaashyapa. Created trees, plants etc
ARUNA	Son of Vinatha. His son is king of birds, Jataayu and Sampaathi
ASHWAGRIVA	Son of Dhanu
AGRAAYANA	Foremost prayers to forefathers
ARDHACHANDRA	A mystic weapon used by Raama to destroy demons
ASHTAVARKA	This great man freed his father from sin
AKAMPANA	Demon chief who rushes to Raavana from Jansthana in India
ASURI	Maya, the master of magic created her.
AYOMUKI	A demoness who tried to entice Lakshmana, who cuts her nose
ASIPATHRA	Trees in hell, its tips are blades!
ANGADHA	Son of Vaali, king of monkeys
ANUHLAADA	Demon who stole Sachi, wife of Lord Indra who retrieves her later
ANGKOLA	A tree
ATHIMUKTHA	A tree
ARBUDHA- AYUTHA	A Numerical term indicating large Astronomical numbers
AKSHA	A son of Raavana
ATHIKAAYA	Demon chief of Raavana

AKAMPANA	Demon Chief
ARISHTA	A Mountain in Lanka
AJAMUKI	Demoness guarding Lanka
BRAHMA	07 The Trinity of Gods: Vishnu, Shiva The Creator, The Pthaamaha.
BRAMMAM	Ultimate Realisation. Spirituality
BHARATHA	Son of Dhasharatha and Kaikeyi As his name suggest, he is the one who 'bears' with equanimity.
BAARGAVA	Jamadagni, Parashuraama are from this renowned sage. The Baargavas of Bhrigu
BALA-ATHIBALA	Vishwamithra initiated these two chants to Raama/Lakshmana. This will free one from hunger, thirst etc. drive away weariness, tiresomeness
BRAHMA-RAAKSHASA	A class of scholars and critics who always find faults, loopholes during a great yaaga or ritual ceremony
BRAHMIN	The First of the four castes
BRIHASPATHI	Sage of great wisdom.
BRIGHU	One of The Seven sages = A saptha rishi
BHARADWAAJA	A great sage, living near Prayag
BARADWAJ	A disciple of Vaalmeeki
BALI	Asura king. Known for his charity son of Virochana. Haughty of his munificence, Vishnu as Vaamana humbles him
BRAHMADATTA	Son of Somada. He marries the 100 daughters of King Kushanaabha
BAGEERATHA	Of Ikshwaaku lineage. Brings down Ganges to earth and underworld to

	resurrect his forefathers, the sons of Sagara who were cursed by Kapila and reduced to ashes
BAAGEERATHI	Another name of Ganges
BHADRA	A Mystic elephant, which supports earth, as per mythology!
BHINDUSARAS	God Shiva first discharged Gange from His HairLocks to this region before its descent to earth and underworld, at the bequest of Bageeratha
BRIGU-	Where King Sagara did penance
PRASRAVANA	A peak in Himaalayan range
BRAAMMANAS	Rules and codes in teaching Shasthra from Vedhas etc Each Vedha has distinct codes- Braammanas
BRIGAATUNDA	Territory where King Ambareesha met Rishi Richika, to give him his son
BRISHASWAS	Celestial weapons. Sons of this 'deity'. Vishwaamithra teaches Raama these weapons
BAGA	Celestial 'dispenser' Gods are Baga-vaans. They dispense.He is Savithru
BAHLEEKA	A territory between Ayodhya-Kekeya
BHOOTHAS	Celestial priests
BADAVA	Mystique - Mystical mare in south pole
BOGAVATHY	A Lord of Reptiles
BRAHMA-	During studentship, one is celibate
CHAARYA	He is called a brammachaari.
BAARUNDA	A forest region in north east

BAHUPUTHRA	A 'prajapathi' was born after Vishrutha, Kardaman, Sheesha, and Samshraya
BADRAMADA	Daughter of Krodhavasha, begat Eyeraavathy
BHUDHDHA	A clever man but an agnostic
BHUDA	Planet mercury
BRAMMAKOSHA	Hermitages in higher Himaalayas
BRAMMASHIRAS	
BRAMMA ASTHRA	The weapon of weapons. Once arrow is fixed, must be discharged
CHANDALA	Untouchable. Has no caste
CHITHRAKOOT	Raama lived here during exile (Near Bundelkand in east.UP)
CHAITHYRATHA	Kubaera's garden
CHAARANA-s	These, the celestial vedhic scholars
CHOODAAMANI	The head ornament Seetha hands over to Hanumaan as token of her remembrance of Raama
DHASHARATHA	King of Ayodhya, an Ikshwaaki
DHARMA	Very difficult to find equivalent Dharma, Artha, Kaama, Moksha Dharma- Duty, justice, moral code Artha - Wealth and substance Kaama- Pleasures Moksha- Ultimate salvation
DHRISHTI	A minister of Dhasharatha
DHEEKSHA	Total vow of silence,abstinence Meditation, surrender to Supreme
DHAKSHA	One of the prajaapathis.Mythology says he is father of 24 divine girls Enemy of Rudhra-Shiva. but he happens to be his father.in.law!

DHARMAARANYA	Capital city established by king Adhoortharajas
DHILEEPA	Father of Bageeratha
DHANVANTHARI	First Doctor of India! Created by churning of milky ocean
DHOOMRASHWAS	King of Vishaala territory
DHRIDANETRA	A son of Vishwaamithra
DHEVAVRATHA	A renowned king. Divine bow was first entrusted by Shiva with him
DHUNDHUBI	A large 'kettle' drum, musical instrument
DHITHY	A wife of Kaashyapa
DHEVI	A 'Goddess' who came out during churning of milky ocean
DHIK GAJA	Mythology states that the entire Universe
DHIK PAALA	is supported by mystical elephants and guarded by celestial men.
DHEVAS	Celestials. Lord Indra is their boss.
DHAANAVAS	Class of asuras- ever against dhevas
DVIVIDHA & MAINDHA	Monkeys created by Ashwinis to help Raama in war with Raavana
DHYUMATH-SENA	A lord whose son was Sathyavaan, a man of Truth.
DHARMA-VARDHAN	A town en route to Rajgriha from Ayodhya
DHRITHASHI	Celestial ladies invoked by Bharadwaja during his hospitality to Bharatha
DHRITHI	Bharatha's adviser
DHURDHARA	A mountain in NE
DHANDAKA	An Ikshwaaku king

DHANDAKA-ARANYA	A forest, named after the king.But later came under control of demons Region, south of Vindhya range
DHANDO LAKAS	Great men of rigorous penance
DHARMABRITH	Great Muni
DHRITHA-RAASHTRI	Daughter of Thamra who begat birds like Hamsa, Chakravaka,
DHOOSHANA	Raavana's demon chief in Janasthana in India. Raama destroys him
DHRITHAACHI	A damsel who enticed Vishwaamithra
DHANU	DHITHI's son by curse became demon Kabandha
DHOOMRA/ DHURMUKH	Monkey chiefs
DHAAKSHAYANI	Queen of reptiles
DHOOSHANA	Raavana's demon chief: Rama kills him
DHANYAMALINI	Raavana's mistress who restrains him from killing Seetha
DHAMAYANTHI	Virtuous wife of king Nala
DHEVANTHAKA	A son of Raavana
DVIJIHVA & DHURMUKH & DHOOMRAKSHA	Demon chiefs of Raavana
DHOOMRA	A mighty bear, brother of Jaambavan
DHADIMUKH	Monkey chief,foster son of Moon
DHANADHA	Lord of wealth Kubhaera, brother of Raavana, and son ofVishrawas
EYERAAWATHA	Celestial elephant that 'rose' from Milky ocean. Indra's elephant
DAMBHA	Monkey chief
EKASAALA	A village between Ayodhya-Rajgriha

EKJATA	Demoness guard who threatens Seetha
GAVA, GOMUKA	Monkey chiefs of Sugreeva's army
GANDAMADHANA	
GAVAKSHA	
GADGADHA	Father of Jaambavaan
GARUDA	Big Bird, son of Vinatha
GOLANGKULA	A species of monkeys
GARUTMAN	Lord of birds
GOPUCHAS	A species: of animal-monkey
GOLABHA	A Gandarva warrior whom Vaali fought for days and killed him
GARGARA	Music drums.
GANGA	Ganges. Daughter of Himavaan
GODAVARI	A mighty river flowing to S.East
GAATHRA-SHAYYAS	Men of mighty penance who rest at night with head on their hands
GANDARVI	Daughter of Surabhi, she begat horses
GAANDARVA	Mystic weapon Raama uses
GANDHARVAS	Class of celestials, famous for fine arts like Naaradha, Gopa, Thumburu
GOMATHI	A river in NE India
GARGYA	Said to be king of Gandarvas
GIRIVRAJA	City near Rajgriha
GUHA	Tribal chief and warrior. Raama's friend
GAYA	Holy city. named after this holy man who pronounced a 'doctrine'. Even now Indians perform Rites for forefathers
GAUTHAMA	Sage, father of Shathanandh, husband of Ahalya
GAADHI	Father of Vishwaamithra

GOKARNA	A holy town in SW India
GODHANA	A pre-purefication ceremony
HEMAVATHY	A tribuary of Ganges
HLADINI	A tributary of Ganges
HALAHALA	Poison it was that came out first when Milky ocean was churned. Shiva drinks this to quell its effect (Neelakanta)
HRISHIKESHA	God Vishnu
HEMCHANDRA	A king of Vishaala territory
HAVISHYANDAN	A son of Vishwaamithra
HOTHAS	High ranking priests in Yaaga
HARITHAS	Class of priests, expert in norms
HARI	God Vishnu
HIMAVAAN	Lord of all mountains. Uma-Parvathy and Ganga are his daughters. Father in. law of Lord Shiva, the Rudhra
HANUMAAN	The Great! Foster son of Lord Wind
HASTHINAPURA	A town not far from Ayodhya
HEMA-HIMA	Celestial ladies of beauty
HAVIS	Oblation in Yaga
HIMAVATSALA	A Mountain / a peak
HIRANYA-NAABHA	Golden mountain that can rise from ocean bed. This Mainaka obstructs Hanumaan's flight to Lanka
HASTHIMUK	Raavana's demon chiefs
HASWAKARMA	
HIRANYA - KASHAPU	An asura who put fear even on Indra
HEMAKOOTA	Monkey warriors
HAILOMA	
INDRA	Lord of celestial world,
INDRAJITH	Son of Raavana who humbles Indra
INDRAJIHVA	Demon chief

IKSHWAAKU	The lineage of great kings of Ayodhya
INDRAJAANU	A monkey warrior
ILVALA	A sadist. A demon brother of Vaathapi Agasthya destroys him
IKSHUMATHI	A river
JAAMBAVAAN	King of Bears, Created by God Brahma
JAMADAGNI	Of Brighu lineage Father of terrible Parashuraama
JANAKA	King of Mithila, father of Seetha
JARJHA	A yaksha, whose son Sunda marries demoness Thaataka
JYESHTA	The first handsome lady who came out of Milky ocean
JAMBUDVIPA	India is part of this. Meru mountain supports the continent
JAABAALI	A renowned wise, old man, atheist. Adviser to Dhasharatha
JAATHAROOPA	Gold that shines like fire.Gold that was 'created' when Skandha was born
JYOTHISHTA-HOMA	An elaborate Ritual (kalpa soothra)
JAYANTHA	A minister of Dhasharatha
JAYA	Father of demon Viradha
JAYA	Dhaksha's daughters Their 500 'sons'
SUPRABHA	are celestials weapons
JAHANU	Sage drinks up Ganges to quell its fury
JAHNAVI	Ganges:
JAMUNA	Mighty river that joins Ganges
JANAARDANA	God Vishnu

JANASTHANA	Place in central India. Raavana's chiefs ravish the place.
JAATHAVEDAS	Holy Ritual Fire
JHRUMBA	A divine Ant that can communicate
JATAAYU	Big Bird that loses life fighting Raavana
JAMBUMALI	Son of Prahastha. This demon was killed by Hanumaan at Lanka
JYOTHIRMUK	A monkey warrior
JATI	Killed by Raavana
KINNARA-s	Species of monkeys; resemble humans
KESARI	Father of Hanumaan. Monkey chief
KUMUDHA KETHUMALI & KRODHA & KAATHNA & KUSHAPARVA	Monkey warriors and chiefs
KUMBHA	Son of Kumbakarna
KUBHAERA	Lord of Wealth. Son of Vishrawas, Brother of Raavana who was his enemy.
KUMBAKARNA	Brother of Raavana. Lived with him
KAMPANA	A Demon chief
KAARTHIVEERA	Renowned son of Dharmanethra
KEYURA	An ornament worn in forearm
KALMAASHI	Divine cow- Kaamadhenu
KHARA	Raavana's chief in India. Raama kills him
KARALA/ KUMBA	Raavana's demon warriors
KUSHAPARSWA	An eminent monkey warrior

KIMKARA-s	Most obedient demon warriors under Raavana
KOWSHIKI	Wife of Usathya - river
KAAKUTHSA	Of Ikshwaaku lineage. A King
KESHINI	Wife of king Sagara
KAANDU	A sage who curses territory when he loses his only son. South of Vindhyas
KISHKINDA	Kingdom of monkeys. Vaali rules.
KAARTHIK	Lord Subrahmanya. Month of Kaarthik
KARTHIKEYA	Lord who is born by divine conception of Shiva. Ganga bears him. Most worshipped deity. Fostered by Krithikas
KSHEERODA	Milky Ocean. Was churned for Nectar
KAIKEYI	Queen of Dhasharatha. Bharatha's mother
KOWSALYA	Eldest queen. Raama's mother
KAASHYAPA	Amongst the oldest of 'creation' Married Dhaksha's daughters - Adhithi, Dhithi Kaalika, Anala, Krodasa
KARDAMA	First of Prajapathi's.Last is Kaashyapa
KRATHU	Amongst Prajapathi-s
KAALIKA	Wife of Kashyapa who begat Naraka
KRADHRU	Daughter of Krodhavas who begat 1,000 serpents, Aadhi sesha
KRODAVASA	Daughter of Dhaksha who begat 10 daughters. Mrigi, Mrigumanda, Hari Badramanda, Surabhi, Maathangi, Shardooli, Shwetha, Surasa, Kadruka
KEERTHI	Sachi, wife of lord Indra

KABANDHA	Son of Dhanu. By curse became demon Raama buries him. He goes to heaven
KROSHA	A measure of distance. about 4 miles
KAANDU	A Rishi who killed a cow! Sin indeed!
KAPAALSHIRAS	God Shiva
KAATHYAAYANA	A Minister/adviser to Dhasharatha A great seer.
KULAPATI	A sage who advises Raama when in exile
KULINGA/ KUTIKOSAKA	Towns
KAASHI	Kingdom, region in eastern India, UP
KURI	Kubhaera's region beyond Himalayas
KOSALA	Kingdom of Ikshwaakus
KAPEEVATHI/ & KUTIKA	Rivers
KAILASH	Region over Himaalyan peaks
KARUSHA	Karusha & Maladha were once very prosperous territories. Ṭhaataka ravishes this favourite place of Indra
KAAMA	Hermitage where God Shiva used to do penance. Shiva burns Lord of love Manmatha when he disturbs penance
KAAMPILYA	City of king Brammadatha
KUSHA	Son of Bramma. Vishwamithra's forefather
KUSHA	Son of Raama - Lava's twin brother
KAAVYA	Her mother who was Brighu's wife was killed by Vishnu due to her arrogance
KUSHANABA & KUSHAMBA	Sons of Kusha

KRITHASHI	Wife of Kushanabha
KUSHASHWA	King of Videha territory
KUSHADWAJA	Brother of Janaka: King of Sankasa
KOWSTHUBA	A Gem that came up from Milky ocean
KAAMBOJA	A territory in east, possibly Cambodia
KIRAATAKA	A fiery tribesmen
KSHATHRIYA	The second of the 4 castes: Warrior caste
KOWTHU-MANGALA	Auspicious ritual ceremony
KALPASOOTHRA	Code, norms for ceremonies, yaagas
KAAPAKSHA	Hermit's Hair style
KUSHAPLAVA	Territory where Dhithi does penance
LAVA	Lava-Kusha, sons of Raama-Seetha
LANKA	Capital, island kingdom of Raavana
LAKSHMANA	Son of Dhasharatha and Sumithra
LOKAS	Worlds; many worlds in Universe
LOKPAALS	As per mythology! They protect Universe
MANU	The first. 'father'of man, the Prajapathi. Great grand son of God Bramma
MAARGA	A Format in style of singing-Music
MANTHRAPAL	Minister to King Dhasharatha
MAAGADHAS	Who sing hymns. Extol kings
MANAS	Mythologically, God Bramma created a huge lake, in upper Himaalayas
MANMATHA	Lord of love
MAREECHI	Prajapathi. First creation. of Bramma
MAAREECHA	Demon: Raavana uses him to kidnap Seetha, using his magical prowess
MAADHAVA	God Vishnu

MADHU - SOODANA	God Vishnu, destroyer of Madhu
MAARKANDEYA	Very old renowned sage-seer, who wrote Puranas. Adviser to Dhasharatha
MADHUSHYANDA & MAHAARATHA	Sons of Vishwaamithra
MAHESHWARA	Usually refers to Shiva
MAHODAYA	Son of Vasishta
MARUTH-s	There are 7 of them. Sons of Dhithi: Eternal, live in ethereal regions
MAIREYA	A Brand of Liquor
MANDARA	Mountain that was the churning rod
MANTHARA	The hunchback who poisoned mind of Kaikeyi to drive away Raama on exile
MANDARA	Virochana's daughter who was killed by Indra
MAATHULA	A Lord of Reptiles
MAHAPADMA	A mystique, which 'supports' world
MAANDVI	Wife of Bharatha
MITHILA	Capital city of king Janaka
MERU	The grand mountain in north, the 'shield' Meru's daughter Menaka is Himavaan's wife
MAHENDRA	Mountain peak where Parashuraama normally lived.
MENAKA	Lovely Apsara lady.who entices Vishwaamithra
MENAKA	Mother of Ganga
MUHOORTHA	Measure of time. About 48 minutes.
MLECHAS	A tribe, like Paplavas, Harrethas, Shakas
MAALYAVATHI & MANDAKINI	Rivers

MOUDGALYA	Renowned sage, adviser to Dhasharatha
MAITHILI	Seetha
MAITHRA	Early part of day
MISHRAKASHI	Celestial maidens of beauty
MAAREECHAPA	A Group of celestials
MANDUKARNI	A great Muni who created lake Pancha parna after doing penance for 100,000 years.
MATHANGA	A Hermitage
MAATHANGI	Daughter of Krodavasa. She begat celestial elephants
MAASHA-s	Great men of penance, south of Vindhyas
MRIGU-	Daughters of Krodavasa. Animals, bears
MRIGA	Deers were created by them
MANDA	
MAATHALI	Lord Indra's charioteer.
MANASSILA	'Mineral Mountain" Rare elements there Denotes elements like Arsenic
MAHODHAYA	The Mighty Ocean South of India
MAYA	Asura Maya master of magic. Indra kills him over a girl Hema
MAYA	Asura.whose daughter Mandodhari is queen of Raavana
MAHA ARUNA	A mountain
MALAY	Mountain in Lanka
MANDODHARI	Wife of Raavana. His queen!
MAHENDRA	Group of mountains in SW India
MAINIKA	Mytholgical winged mountain in ocean
MAALYAVAN	Foremost mountain

MADHUYANTHI	Wife of Sowdhasa
MANIBADRA	Commander of Kubaera's army
MAKARAAKSHA	Son of demon chief Khara
MAHODARA & MAHAPARSWA& MAHANAADA & MRITHAGNYA	Demon chiefs of Raavana
MARUKANTHARA	A place in under world, under the ocean. Raama discharges his asthra
NOOPURA	Lady's foot ornament
NIKUMBHA	Demon chief,son of Kumbakarna
NALA	Monkey chief who was architect in construction of bridge over ocean
NANDANA	Celestial garden of Indra
NABHA	Monkey warrior
NAYANA	A holy hermitage in upper Himaalayas
NEELA	Monkey chief, chief of medical core!
NIKUMBILA	A Temple in Lanka where Indrajith worships before a major fight
NAAGA-s	Celestial tribe
NAAKARAJA	One of the 'heavens'
NIKUMBA &/ NARANTHAKA	Great demon warriors under Raavana
NAAREECHA NAARAACHA	Very powerful weapons
NISHAACHARA	A sage who offers boon to Sampaathi
NARAKA	Place of Hell (for sinners)
NARAVAHANA	Kubhaera
NEELAKANTA	God Shiva when He drank poison Halahala
NATHA	Daughter of Shuki.Her daughter. Vinatha
NAMUCHI	A demon who was killed by 'froth'

NANDHI	The Bull. God Shiva's guard!
NAHUSHA	Raama's forefather. Great king
NANDHAN	A minister
NANDIGRAM	Temporary capital of Bharatha.
NAGADANTHA	Lovely mountain where lovely celestial ladies sport
NALINI	Indra's capital
NAAGA-KANYA-s	Celestial ladies who created warriors for Raama's army
OMKAARA	Symbolically represents The Supreme: A-U-M Represents vital breath of life
OORMILA	Wife of Lakshmana
OORMILA	Her daughter Somadha served rishi Chooli
OORVASI	A celestial lady,Apsara,of immense beauty
OSHADHI	A Herbal mountain in Himaalayan range
PUNJI - KASTHALA	A lady whom Raavana rapes. God Brahma curses him
PRAHASTHA	Raavana's commander.in.chief
PANASA & PRAMATHI & PAAVAAKSHA	Monkey warriors
PAATHAALA	Underworlds
PRAGHASA	Demon chief under Raavana
PAARTHAPANA RASHMIKETHU	Demon warriors under Raavana
PUSHPAKA	Divine Aircraft. Raavana snatched this from his brother Kubhaera
PATAKA	A musical instrument
PRAJAAPATHI	First of God Brahma's creations(Six)
PRASRAVANA	A mountain

PANNAGA-s	A tribe of reptile origin
PANASA	Monkey warrior
PAKA	A demon killed by Indra
PUNNYA	Merit. We obtain merit by our duty. Dharma. Rituals etc
PULOMA	Her daughter Sachi is Indra's wife
PULASTHYA	Pulastha is God Brahma's creation Lineage of demons
PISHAACHA	Cannibals. class of demons
PAARYATHRA	Mountain range in Vindhyas
PAANDU	A mountain
PEETHAMBARA	Gorgeous Silken fabric
PLAKSHA & PRABHASA	Ministers to Sugreeva who had access to him at all times
PROSHTA	Month between September & October
PAMPA	Sacred river in S.W India
PRALAYA	Deluge. End of a millennium
PADMATHALA	Forest. Large congregation of monkeys
PUROORAVAS	The sage who curses Oorvasi when she rejects him!
PRATHYA KASTHALI	Holy place with holy fire mound , Shabari exhibits this to Raama
PINAKAPANI	God Shiva- Rudhra
PRALAMBA	A mountain
PRAAGVAT	A town
PRAYAGA	Holy place at confluence of Ganges-Yamuna Bhardwaja resides near here
PADHMA	Lotus-Goddess. consort of Vishnu
PUSHYARATHA	Raama's royal chariot
PAANCHAALA	A territory
PREETHI	Wife of Manmatha. the lord of love
PAADHUKA	Refers here to Raama's royal sandals

PARASHURAAMA	Terrible brahmin, who wages a caste war on Kshatriyas: Raama humbles him
PAARIJATHA	Tree that came up from milky ocean
PAAVANI	Tributary of Ganges
PAPLAVA-s	A terrible class of warriors created by holy cow Kamadhenu
PASHUPATHI	God Shiva, lord of cows
PADMANABHA	God Vishnu
PRAVARGYA	These are various rituals
PRAATHAS	
SAVANA	
PITHRUDEVA-s	Deities, class of celestial beings
PAVITHRA	A 'raksha' manthra-chant -with tying of thread, for purification
PUSHKARA	Holy place in W.India
RAAMA	Son of Dhasharatha,The principal character in Raamaayana. As name suggests, he is The Delighter
RAAVANA	Son of sage Vishrawas. Demon king As name suggests, he makes every one cry in fear of him.
RAGHU	Raama's ancestor
RAAKSHASA	General term. for demons, evil men
RAAGA	Indian Music system based on this
RISHI	Men of penance. We have Raja rishi, Rishi, Maharishi, Dheva rishi and Brahma rishi
RITHVIK-s	High Priests
RISHYASHRINGA	Son of Vibandaka, a great seer-sage who performs yaaga for Dhasharatha's progeny
ROMAPAADA	King of Anga whose daughter Shantha marries Rishyashringa

RICHEEKA	A Bramma rishi. Of Brighu family
RAJASOOYA	A great sacrificial ceremony. Next only to Ashwamedha yaaga
RENUKA	Wife of Jamadagni, mother of Parashuraama
RAMBA	Apsara sent by Indra to entice Viswaamithra
ROHINI	Wife of Lord Moon
RITHU-s	Time cycle - seasons etc-verily life's cycle
RUDHRA-s	Terrible! At least 11 Rudhras are listed God Shiva appears as Rudhra
RAJGRIHA	Capital of Kekeya kingdom
RATHI	A very lovely celestial damsel
RISHYAMUK	A mountain region. Sugreeva's abode
RIKSHIRAJA	Vaali-Sugreeva's (natural) father
RAMBA-RUMAVAAN	Monkey chiefs (name not to be confused with damsel)
RUMA	Wife of Sugreeva
RAJATHA	Mountain in South
RIKSHIBALA	A lovely cave 'city' in south Care taker Swayamprabha treats Hanumaan and his search army with hospitality
SAARVABOWMAN	Mystic elephant of the Bhoothas
SUGREEVA	King of monkeys. faster son of Lord Sun
SUNETHRA	
SOORYAPAKSHA	
SHARABA	
SUDHURDHARA	
SANNADHANA	
SANNUPRASTHA	

SUMUK, SUBAHU, SHATHABALI SHWETHA, SUKANAASA SHATA	Some monkey warriors
SHONITHAKSHA SOORYASHATHRU SAMHRADI SUPTHAGNA	Some demon warriors
SHUKA, SHARDOOL	A Spies of Raavana
SARAMA	A good demoness, friend of Seetha
SANGKOCHA	Hillock around Gomathi river
SAALVEYA	A mountain
SAHYA	Mountain in south India
SUVELA	Mountain in Lanka
SOORYAPRABA SHANKARA KARMUK	Mountain ranges in Himaalayas
SANJEEVAKARNI VISHALYA	Herbals, life saving plants in Himalayas
SHAMBARA & VRITHRA	Demons killed by Indra
SAVITHRI	Dutiful wife of Sathyavaan
SHAMBASADANA	Demon killed by monkey Kesari
SHREEMATHI	Wife of sage Kapila
SAGARA	King of Ayodhya, Raama's forefather
SAMPAATHI	King of birds, brother of Jataayu, son of Aruna. Directs

	Hanumaan to fly over ocean and search for Seetha at Lanka
SWAAHA	Celestial lady of 'Fire' In all Fire rituals 'she' is invoked with chant 'Swaahaa'
SUKANYA	Wife of sage Chyavana
SEETHA	Daughter of Janaka, wife of Raama
SUVARCHALA	Wife of Lord Sun
SIDDHA-s	Sages who obtain total salvation
SUSHENA	Monkey chief
SURASA	Mother of reptiles
SWASTHI	Blessings, benediction
SIMHIKA	Demoness who could drag people by their shadow!
SAPTHAJANA	Holy hermitage of 7 sages who did penance for years on. Indra used to come down to visit them
SUMITHRA	Second queen of Dhasharatha. Mother of Lakshmana and Shathrugna
SOOPAARSWA	Son of Sampathi
SACHI	Wife of Indra
SWAYAMPRABA	Lady who is care taker of Cave city belonging to Apsara lady Hema
SHATHAHRIDH	Mother of demon Viradha
SHARABANGA	A very great sage Raama meets
SUTHEEKSHANA	Another great sage Raama meets

SAMPRAKSHALA-s	Celestial 'sages'
STHOOLASHIRAS	A sage who curses Kabandha
SHOORPANAKA	Cousin of Raavana. Lakshmana cuts off her nose. Beginning of enmity.
SURABHI	
SRUMARA	
SHARDOOLI	
SURASA, SYENI,	
STHANU, SHESHA,	
SHWETHA,	
SHOOOLA	Origin of all these species
SAMSHRAYA	described in detail
SHUKRA	Priest of Asura-s. Bali's adviser.
SHATHRUGNA	Son of Sumithra, and Dhasharatha Noble man who had conquered enemies like passion, greed, wrath etc
SAADHYA-s	Group of celestials
SUDHAAMA	Celestial abode
SYANDIKA	River Raama crosses
SARAYU	River around Ayodhya
SUYAGNYA	A Great sage-seer at Ayodhya
SRINGABAERA PURA	A town in SE UP in India
SUDHANVA	Teacher, who teaches weaponry to royalty at Ayodhya
SWASTHIKA	Name of boat that carries Bharatha & his army across Ganges.

SHATHRUNJAYA	Celestial elephant Raama's Carrier
SHIBI	A munificent king who gave his flesh to feed a falcon
SHRUTHI & SMRITHY	Prime knowledge. Unwritten Text Acquired through hearing from elders
SAPTHA RISHI	The Seven Rishis: Athri, Brigu, Kutsa Vasishta, Gauthama, Kashyapa and Angeerasa. Renowned Bramma rishis
SHYAAMA	Holy Banyan tree. Raama/Seetha offer prayers for completing 14 years exile
SHATADRI SHARADANDA SHILAVANA STHANUMATHI	A few rivers
SATHYOPACHANA	Holy tree near Kulinga town
SARASWATHI	Mystic river, that confluence with Ganges & Jamuna- Unseen river
SAVATHEERTHA	A town
SANGKAASA	City ruled by Kushadwaja
SIDHDHAARTHA	A renowned minister at Ayodhya
SALYAKEERTHI	A territory
SUMANTHRA	Friend, minister and charioteer to King Dhasharatha

SANDHYA-S	The three times of the day. Early morning, noon and before sunset
SANAATHANA-DHARMA	Eternal Dharma, the religion of India
SANATHKUMARA	The very old ruler, who was a great 'Seer' who could 'perceive' He lived in Krithi yuga
SEEKSHA	A style of recitation, intonation
SHIVA	God Shiva, the Sthooli, the Shankara the Shithi kanta
SHAASTHRA	General term. Compendium of rituals Source of Knowledge
SHATHAGNI	A fierce fire ritual. Doer of this yaga must face heat of '100 fires'
SUKETHU	A Yaksha who prayed for a son but got demoness Thaataka
SUDHAAMAN	A minister of Janaka
SUNDA	Son of Jarjha.Married Thaataka. Terrible demon Maareecha was their son
SUCHAKSHU	
SEETHA	
SINDHU	Tributaries of Ganges flowing west
SATHYAVATHY	Sister of Vishwaamithra who took form of river Kowishki for doing good
SURABI -SHABALA	Holy cow Kaamadhenu

SWARGA	Heavenly world of Bliss. Many worlds Indra's world, Brahma world etc
SOOTHA-s	Royal poets, well versed in recitation
SHOODRA	One of the four caste-s
SHANTHA	Wife of Rishyschringa
SOMADHA	Gandarvi lady.Her son was Brammadatta
SUBAAHU	Terrible demon, who was killed by Raama
SOWMAANASA	A mystic supporter of universe
SUMATHI	Ikshwaaku king of Vishala territory Sumathi Along with Keshini, wife of Sagara
SUPARNA	Celestial bird. in human form. Its sister was Sumathi
SKANDHA	Most worshipped deity. Son of Shiva through Agni. Ganges bears the child
STHAANU	God Shiva
SHRUTHIKEERTHI	Wife of Shathrugna
SHATHAANAND	Son of Gauthama- Ahalya. Minister to king Janaka
SUCHANDRA	
SRINJAYA	
SAHADEVA	King Vishaala's successors
SHUNASHEPA	Son of Richika who offered him as sacrifice for Ambareesha's yaga
SOWRASHTRA	
SINDHU	
SOWVEERA	Regions in India

SUSHENA	
SHARABHA	
SOORYANAN	Great monkey warriors.
SLOKA	A Format of poetry, Vaalmeeki uses this
SEETHA	Wife of Raama daughter of Janaka
SHONA	A River
THRIPADAGA	River Ganges that flows in'Three' ways
THRISHANKU	Raama's forefather who wanted to go to heaven in his own mortal body!
THRIVISHTAPA	Region full of Lingas. Possibly Tibet Nepal areas
THRYAMBAK	God Shiva
THRIPURA	Celestial city built by Asuras.with copper, silver, gold!
THATAKA	A Yakshi who was killed by Raama
THAPAS	General term for penance
THAMASA	River around Vaalmeeki's hermitage
THIMIDWAJA	Demon who used to live in Dandaka
THAITHREYA	A part of Upanishad.
THRIJATA	Of Gargya lineage.Poor but very spritual
THOMARA	A Village
THILAKA	Ladies sport this on forehead -Red mark

THUMBURU	A Gandharva. Artistic.
THUMBURU	Who was cursed to become demon Viradha
THRISHIRAS	Raavana's demon chief Raama kills him
THRETHA AGNI	'Three fires' for rigorous rituals
THAARA	Wife of Vaali, mother of Angadha
THAARA	A monkey chief
THRIKOOTA	Three peak mountain in Lanka
TRIJATA	A good demoness .Friend of Seetha. She conveys a good dream to Seetha
THAKSHA	Mighty reptile in Upper Ganges!
MATHA UDHONMATHA	Cousins of Raavana
VISHRAWAS	Great Rishi. Brahama's great grandson. Kubaera, Raavana, Kumbakarna and Vibheeshana are his sons
VEDHAVATHI	Celestial lady who cursed Raavana
VAJRADAMSHTRA VAJRAHAANU VIROOPAKSHA VIDHYUNMALA THAPANA	Mighty demon warriors under Raavana
VITAPAVATHY	Celestial city of Gandharvas

VIDHYUJIHVA	A demon: Master of sorcery, magic
VIHAGA	Monkey chief who surveyed Lanka's defence
VIBEESHANA	Brother of Raavana. But had no qualities of a demon.
USANA	Adviser to asuras-Shukracharya
USHASHRAWAS	Indra's celestial horse.
VAJRALAYA	Mountain peak in Himaalyas
VRANAKOOPA	Cleavage under ocean bed, underworld
VEGADARSHI	
VINATHA	
VIDHYUDHAMSHTRA	
VEERABAAHU	
SUBAAHU	
THARA	Monkey chiefs under Sugreeva
VIROCHANA	
VIROOPAKSHA	
YOUPAKSHA	
YAMASHATRU	
YAGNYAKOPA	Demon chiefs under Raavana
VISHWAKARMA & USANAS THOMA	The First Architect of India! Father of architecture, engineering Maya learnt this by boon from Brahma, the Usanasthoma. Maya is Vishwakarma
YAKSHA-s	A tribe
YAMA	Lord of Time and Death
YAATHU	

DHAANA-s	Terrible demons defending Lanka
YAAGA-	Exacting ritual cremony, spread over days Like Pundareeka, Vaajapayee, Rajasooya Ashwamedha
VARUNA	Celestial lord,like Indra, Agni,Vaayu,Mitra.
VAIVASWATHA & VIVASWAAN	The Lord Sun
VARDHAMAAN	A type of architecture
VINDHYAS	Mountain range divides North/South
VASU-s	Deities, it is said there are 8.
VIRADHA	Demon whom Raama killed
VISHNU	Of the Trinity of Gods
VAACHASPATHI	Lord of Speech
VAAMANA	Vishnu appears as midget to humble Bali
VIROOPAKSHA	Hanumaan kills this demon chief
YOJANA	Measure of distance about 10 miles
YUGA	Millennium; There are four yugas. Kritha, Thretha, Dwaapara, and Kali We are now in Kali yuga (total 4.32 million years)
VAIDHEHI	Seetha is a Vaidhehi
VAITHARNI	Mythologically river in hell; blood flows
VAIKANAASA-s	Mythologically, born out of fingers of God Bramma.

YUVANA-s	Celestials who are ever under teens
VIDHAATHA	Deities
VINATHA	Daughter of Natha. Her sons are Aruna and Garuda
VINATHA	Wife of Kaashyapa
VIKARNEE	A special weapon Raama uses
VAIDOORYA	A Gem of an ornament, with rare 'stones'
VAJRA	Lord Indra's thunderbolt
VAASAVA	Lord Indra
UPAADHYAYA	General term for teachers.
VARNA	General term. Means Caste also
YAYAATHI	Forefather of Raama, son of Nahusha
YUDHAJITH	Brother of Kaikeyi.
VIJAYA	A minister of Dhasharata
VANGA	Eastern territory, possibly modern Bengal
VASTHU	Ritual ceremony, like house warming
VAIJAYANTHA	A territory in Dhandaka frest
VAAMADEVA	Renowned rishi, adviser to Dhasharatha
VAAJAPEYA	An exacting Yaaga
VIROOPAKSHA	A Mystic that 'supports' universe!
VASHATKAARA	Important chants drawn from Texts
VAIKANAASA	Class of Rishi-s. (thanthrik knowledge)
VIBANDAKA	Father of Rishyashringa.

VIDHARBA	Territory in Central India
VIROCHANA	Her daughter Mandara was killed by Indra
YOGA	General term for meditation, restraint
VASUMATHI	A territory in NE.India
VAISHRAWANA	A path in the ethereal sky
VISHWAAMITHRA	The mighty king who became mighty man of penance. None equal to this Bramma Rishi
VAALMEEKI	Author of the epic. Raamaayana
VEDHA-s	Prime knowledge. No author, but they came to us through experience and wisdom of sages, rishi-s and noble men Basically 4 Vedha-s. Rig, Yajur, Saama Atharvana. Any number of Vedhas like Saanga, Gandarva and so on, Auxillary Vedhas. You may deny Gods, but you cannot deny Vedhas. Because Vedhas constitute Sanaathana Dharma which is. The Religion of India.

In this great epic, there are names and names. In this book we have covered most of the names but list is not exhaustive.

Vaalmeeki, The First amongst pets

By Smt. SHANTA SRINIVASAN

In our country आर्य वर्त Aryavartha (the ancient name of India that is Bharath) the four Vedhas constitute the most ancient collection of Hymns which are handed down to us and are carefully 'preserved' even today. Vedhas have a fruitful purpose, and to achieve and enjoy fruits, they have to be understood properly. They should be recited, pronounced clearly without changing Udatta Anudatta, Swaritha Swaras. For this purpose, the ancient sages have given us six aids or Vedha-Angas. They are:

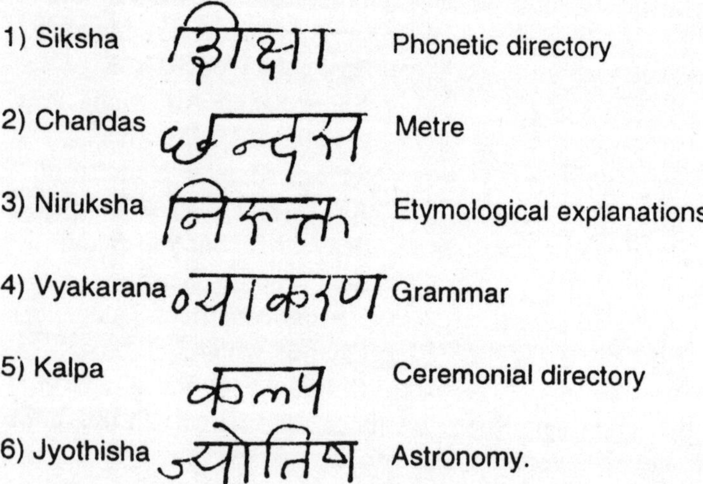

1) Siksha शिक्षा Phonetic directory
2) Chandas छन्दस Metre
3) Niruksha निरुक्त Etymological explanations
4) Vyakarana व्याकरण Grammar
5) Kalpa कल्प Ceremonial directory
6) Jyothisha ज्योतिष Astronomy.

These Angas are directly related to swara or sense aspect of Vedhas. The Brahmanas and Upanishads came next to Vedhas, followed by Smritis and Epics. The epics represent the Vedic Dharma.

And the first Epic, Srimad Ramayana represents the 'Spirit' of Vedhic age. No doubt, the Vedhas have inspired the mode of poetry among the poets. Maharishi Vaalmeeki has written the epic Ramayana, the life story of a perfect man who set an example for observance of Dharma, Truth & Justice धर्म-सत्य-नीति Bhagavan Vaalmeeki visualised the story of Raama with blessings of God Brahma, but his first sloka-stanza, was the outcome of the painful scene when he witnessed the pathetic scene and heard the cry of a Krauncha bird. The painful cry of the Krauncha bird was due due to the killing of its mate by the hunter when both the birds were absorbed in conjugal happiness. The cry disturbed and awakened the poetic mind of Aadhi Kavi Sage Vaalmeeki आदि कवि

The poet spoke with great agony and anguish. And this turned out to be शोकपूर्ण श्लोक Poetry.

To his utter dismay, it was in अनुष्टुप् छन्दस

Anushtup Chandas Metre (in 32 letters-)

The Sage's agony शोक changed and emerged in poetic form, श्लोक रूपेण परिणत coming out as a curse on the hunter, thus.....

"Oh Hunter! When the Krauncha bird was making love and was stupefied by passion, you killed this one. Therefore you will not live long (dwell many seasons in the world)

मा निषाद प्रतिष्ठां त्वं
अगमः शाश्वतीः समाः यत्-
क्रौञ्च मिथुनात् एकं अवधीः
काम मोहितम्-

Mass Nishaada Prathishtaam Thwam Agama Shaashwatheehi Samaaha Yath Krauncha Mithunaath Ekam Avadheehi Kaama Mohitham

But in as much as God Brahma's Grace was upon Vaalmeeki, this very first Sloka also became a Praise, extolling God Vishnu. Thus joining Maa and Nishaada (मा निषाद) and taking note of the fact that a demon goes also by name of Krauncha, Vaalmeeki's first sloka of curse upon the hunter turns out to be a prayer sloka of the lord thus

"Oh Narayana! your glorious Name will be remembered ever as you have slain the wicked Krauncha (demon Raavana) separating him from the virtuous mate (Mandodhari)"

Vaalmeeki is The First And The Foremost amongst poets.

Thus The Vedha, Srimad Raamayana is The First in the form of काव्यम - Kaavyam.

RAMA RAJYA

Sri Rama was Rajadhiraja whose main concern was welfare of the people. Rama was Dharma incarnate, saint and truthful. He was embodiment of Dharma; He always stood by Dharma under any circumstances. Sri Rama ruled the country for a long time to come; and the reign like that the world had never seen; and will never see again. Peace and plenty were found everywhere; and all Rama's subjects were happier than ever; and they all also lived for a long time. The seasons never failed; the land yielded crops in abundance. Trade flourished; and people had everything in plenty. There were no thefts anywhere; and there was no sign of internal troubles at all. Everyone was happy and contented -all these because of the righteous reign of Sri Ramachandra; and for the Ayodhyavasis, it seemed that heaven was on earth (Bhuloka Vaikuntham) because of Rama's reign.

The Rule of Rama has been quoted as a righteous model of administration and has been close to the heart of all Indian thinkers including the father of Indian Nation, Mahatma Gandhi. The full fledged concept of republic was known to India where a monarch had a respectable niche of his own. The Indian king was not an autocrat. In ancient Indian political system, the regal power was circumscribed by his ministers and counsellors. The king was guided by the advice of the senior citizens and the scholars (spiritual sages) and he constantly sought the sagacious directions from his preceptor (the Rajaguru). The political policy of Sri Rama was based on the above Vedic and smritic injunctions. It was based on religion and moral values. It was oriented towards lofty thoughts and good deeds of public welfare where precepts were unhesitatingly translated into practice. It was based on righteous and good conduct.

The modern concept of secularism has been alien to Indian thought as religion has been assigned a pivotal role in one's personal actions and social interactions.

Religion has deep permeability in the Indian social fabric. It is a repository of all human virtues, hence irreligiousness is abhorrent to Indian mind. Religion has been the fountainhead of Indian culture and so it cannot be divorced from any Indian social concept. Selfless renunciation, the spirit of sacrifice and true humanism can be cultivated only through religion which is of paramount importance not only for India but for the welfare of the whole world. Mahatma Gandhi and Vinoba Bhave believed in assigning to politics an important role for religion. The west oriented secularism is eating into the vitals of Indian politics and is at the root of all the prevailing nefarious political conditions and socio- political chaos.

THE SOCIAL PHILOSOPHY OF SRI RAMA

Sri Rama wanted his subjects to be virtuous, religious-minded, God-fearing, truthful, of unimpeachable conduct and of noble character.

Rama was an apostle of human virtues (Maryada Purushottama) and he wanted his subjects to follow suit. He wanted his people to act according to religious edicts and to follow the path of virtue Satya (truth). His advice to Nisadaraja was unequivocal when he said -"Follow religion by thought and deed. Rama was convinced that social-welfare could only be achieved when people led a religious life. The purity of life was believed to percolate downwards. If people in authority (the ministers, the high-ups and the king himself) were honest and pure, the people were bound to follow their example. It has been said "where in a meeting irreligious prevail over religious and untruth rules over truth, where vice has an upper hand on virtue and violence has a sway on non-violence, there is surely to be absolute lawlessness and the people in such a gathering are spiritually dead". Rama was of the firm opinion that religion is one's true friend who accompanies him after his death also. So a person should never act against the religious precepts and his conscience.

Rama's sense of detachment from power made Him an ideal king. Rama as a king never suffered from internal conflicts nor had he any mental reservations. Rama had many remarkable virtues like politeness, fitness, fortitude and equanimity of mind. He was a dutiful king who attached great value to the opinion of the subjects. Rama was a great king who ruled gloriously and redressed the grievances of His people.

DEMOCRATIC KING WAS RAMA

The Government was in spirit a republic where Vasistha's advice was an order, where ministers' counsel was fully heeded and where public opinion was absolutely unsuppressed and completely free. Rama was a popular king who was a beloved benefactor of his subjects. His sole aim of life was to keep his people happy and contented and the worst curse for him was to fail in this paramount duty of kingship. Subjects were free to express their opinion.

Rama did declare in a public assembly

I speak to you not sheltering under any commanding
Authority or unjust order. Please listen to me,
but do as you like; should I indulge in any loose
talk, please check me without fear .

This is the height of king's humbleness, politeness, simpleness and sublime behaviour. There was absolute freedom of thought and action in Rama Rajya. Liberty, equality and fraternity had full play in his system of Government, which pursued an unobtrusive policy dedicated to public welfare and people's service. It was a government pledged to the "public good" and it acted with full vigour for the "public benefit."

In Rama Rajya, there was only one caste -caste of humanity .All sections of people were treated alike irrespective of their profession.

The special features of Rama Raja were:

They were all happy and contented in the pursuit of their own Dharmas for the good of society as a whole. Complete honesty and Dharma formed the basis for all their actions. All were healthy, long lived and free from disease. No one was in want. Monsoon was on time and in the required quantums. Floods, Cyclones etc., were unknown. Thieves and robbers were non-existent. Wind was always blowing pleasant. Trees and vegetation blossomed with abundance of flowers, fruits and vegetables. The elderly people never had to perform the funeral rites of the younger.

It was truly a people's government run for the people by a beloved king. Raama Rajya, was a true welfare state.

Thoughts compiled and presented by:
SANJEEVI ARJUNA RAJA
Director, Ramco Industries Ltd.

The Glory of RAMA NAMA

Mahamantra Rama is the most powerful Mantra in this universe. The Mantra is more powerful than Lord Rama, Himself. Lord Rama was present in Treta Yuga and helped the people whoever approached Him. But the Maha Mantra has helped innumerable people before and after incarnation of Rama. Today you cannot find Rama, but the Name is there and people are solving their problems with the help of the Name.

Mahatma Gandhi is quoted to have said that he was surprised to know how people do without **RAMA NAMA.** It was not possible for him to do without it even for a single day. All great saints like Tulasidasa, Kabira, Nanaka, Dadu have realized the importance and power of the name and written about it at many places.

RAMA NAMA is derived from the Astaksara Mantra ('Ra' from "Om Namo Narayanaya") and the Pancaksari ('Ma' from "Om Namah Sivaya"). Hence **RAMA** established the identity of Vishnu and Siva.

Just 3 times repetition of "RAMA" (Sri Rama Rama Rama) has potency equal to the Vishnu Sahasranama as advised by Lord Siva to Sri Parvati. It is the same Lord Siva who propagates the glory of Rama Nama most to the world and by delivering Rama Nama into the ears of all persons giving up their bodies at Kashi (Banaras) confers on them the qualification for Moksha - liberation.

According to the numerology called \'Katapayadi. each letter of the Sanskrit alphabet has a specific numerical values. 'Ra' has the value of 2 and \Ma' the value of 5. So, saying once **RAMA** means saying it 2 x 5 = 10 times. *So* when we say the name thrice, it becomes 10 x 10 x 10- 1000 fold in potency. Such is the mystery about the Name "RAMA".

The two lettered name **RAMA** is most supreme and is most worthy of Japa by one and all.

RAMA is the Siddha Mantra worshipped by Brahma, Yogis and Munis. It destroys poverty, sorrow, all diseases including the Bhavaroga (Transmigration).

The name **RAMA** is the abode of all welfare; it can destroy the sins of the Kaliyuga. It is the holy of the holiest; it is the good that one can take with him on his onward march to liberation. It is the sole resting place for the words of all great poets. It is the very life of the virtuous. It is the seed for the tree of Dharma.

With 'Ra' the mouth opens and all sins get out; with 'Ma', the lips close (mouth gets shut) preventing their re-entry.

Saint Thyagaraja who was a great Ramabhakta, explains the secret power of this Name in one of his immortal songs thus -
"Sivamantramunaku Ma -Jivamu;
Madhava -mantramunaku Ra -Jivamu"

("Ma" is the very life of the Pancaksari Mantra, dear to the heart of Lord Siva. *"RQII* is the very life of the Astaksari Mantra, dear to the Lord Madhava (i.e Vishnu).

In other words, if we remove the letter 'Ma' from the Pancaksari, it becomes lifeless; it then reads thus -Na-Sivaya -(meaning there is no welfare). If we

take away the 'Ra' from the Astaksari, it also becomes lifeless, reading thus - Om Mamo Na-yanaya (meaning there is no way to go).

Seeing the potency of these two Bijaksaras (Seed letters) the great sage Vasistha joined them thus 'Ra + 'Ma' and gave it as the name to the first son of Dasaratha. So according to Saint Thyagaraja, Rama contains within Himself, the powers of both Lord Vishnu and Lord Shiva.

Now we come thus to another dimension of the import of the word "Rama". It not only means one who is himself cheerful and makes other also cheerful (by his wonderful sweet Name) but also one who is extremely handsome.

Rama Manthra is to be uttered while eating, drinking, sleeping, walking and sitting. By doing SO, one gets rid of all troubles - physical and mental. When every hope is gone, when friends fail and comforts flee, one finds solace in God's Name. With the help of Rama Sabda, Kundalini Sakti is awakened. If we want to end the cycle of birth and death, we should take refuge in **RAMA.**

Only **RAMA** Nama can save us. Let us pledge to chant **RAMA** Nama and request others to do so. In this way we can usher in an era of peace and prosperity.

Thoughts compiled and presented by:
SANJEEVI ARJUNA RAJA
Director, Ramco Industries Ltd.